Sensational Devotion

Evangelical Performance in Twenty-First-Century America

JILL STEVENSON

The University of Michigan Press
Ann Arbor

First paperback edition 2015

Published in the United States of America by
The University of Michigan Press
Manufactured in the United States of America
♾ Printed on acid-free paper

2018 2017 2016 2015 6 5 4 3

A CIP catalog record for this book is available from the British Library.

Library of Congress Cataloging-in-Publication Data

Stevenson, Jill.
Sensational devotion : evangelical performance in twenty-first century America / Jill Stevenson.
pages cm
Includes bibliographical references and index.
ISBN 978-0-472-11873-1 (cloth : alk. paper) — ISBN 978-0-472-02909-9 (e-book)
1. Theater—Religious aspects. 2. Theater—United States—History—21st century. 3. Performance art. 4. Evangelicalism in literature. 5. Evangelicalism—United States—History—21st century. I. Title.
PN2049.S665 2013
792.0973—dc23 2012044694

ISBN 978-0-472-03651-6 (pbk. : alk.paper)

Sensational Devotion examines contemporary Passion plays, biblical theme parks, Holy Land recreations, creationist museums, and megachurches in order to understand how they serve their evangelical believer-users while also shaping larger cultural and national dialogues. The book examines how performative media support specific theologies and core beliefs by creating sensual, live experiences for those who use them. Because they often appear in accessible, familiar forms (such as theme parks) and employ pop culture motifs, a wide range of people—including those hostile toward Christianity or religion generally—are often willing to "try out" these genres, even if only for curiosity's sake. This familiarity not only helps these genres achieve their goals, but it also enables them to contribute to public dialogue about the role of religious faith in America. The book demonstrates the unique ways in which these genres, which certainly reflect religious belief, also simultaneously *make* religious belief.

Jill Stevenson explores evangelical performance across a range of media and sites, including film, television, theater, tourist attractions, museums, and places of worship. Using historical research coupled with firsthand experiences at the evangelical venues, Stevenson not only critically examines these spaces and events within their specific religious, cultural, and national contexts, but also places them within a longer devotional tradition in order to suggest how they cultivate religious belief by generating vivid, sensual, affectively oriented, and individualized experiences.

Stevenson shows how the genres analyzed function through a distinctive dramaturgy that assumes certain interpretations of representation, realism, enactment, spectatorship, and presence, in order to achieve particular aesthetic, ideological, and experiential effects. The performances don't simply represent theological concepts and depict biblical stories, but confront users with vivid, sensual, and rhythmic experiences designed to foster embodied beliefs that will respond to specific devotional needs and desires. Employing cognitive theory and theories of affect, the author demonstrates how these performative forms effectively foster the personal and experiential aspects of American evangelicalism, thereby reinforcing core theological tenets by means of the believer-user's body.

For Kelly

Acknowledgments

I am very grateful to many individuals and institutions for helping me to make this book a reality. First, I wish to thank the peer readers and editorial staff at the University of Michigan Press, especially LeAnn Fields and Alexa Ducsay. They have been incredibly supportive and helpful from the moment I contacted them about this project. I also wish to thank Ann Pellegrini for her encouraging remarks and useful suggestions about the manuscript. I wish to thank Palgrave for allowing me to reproduce sections of the Coda from my book *Performance, Cognitive Theory, and Devotional Culture* (2010). I'm also very grateful for the editorial advice I received from Richard Schechner and Mariellen Sandford; an earlier version of Chapter Five appears in the Spring 2012 issue of *TDR*.

Thanks to two institutions for providing support for this project. First, the American Society for Theatre Research for awarding me a 2010 Research Fellowship. That generous award made this project possible. I would also like to thank my institution, Marymount Manhattan College, for granting me a Sokol Award to help cover travel costs, as well as a Junior Fellowship, which allowed me to devote a full semester to writing. Thanks to the faculty members on the Leaves and Fellowships Committee for selecting me for those awards, as well as to Dean David Podell and President Judson Shaver. I am surrounded by many hardworking, intelligent colleagues at MMC. In addition to thanking this community as a whole, I am especially grateful to David Mold and Mary Fleischer for their professional and personal support.

A number of other professional colleagues have provided guidance or informal encouragement during this project, among them Heather Hendershot, Pamela King, Gail Gibson McMurray, Margaret Rogerson, Richard Emmerson, and Judy Milhous. I am especially grateful to the generosity and collegiality of John Fletcher. Pamela Sheingorn continues to be an incredible mentor and friend. She is a professional model for me, as she is for so many others, and I cannot express how much I appreciate her trusted advice and feedback.

It's not really surprising that this topic interested my friends to the incredible extent that it did. However, their curiosity resulted in many forms of concrete support—sending me articles, referring me to performance pieces, and—at times—accompanying me on trips. Special thanks to David Baumann and Kent Rutter, who joined me on both visits to Lakewood Church, as well as on my trip to see the Hell House at Trinity Church in Cedar Hill, Dallas. Thanks for their insightful thoughts about both venues. (Sorry gentlemen, Hell Houses didn't make the cut.) I am also greatly indebted to David for his help with the Praise Song analysis in Chapter Six. Jen-Scott Mobley deserves a great deal of thanks for being a trusted friend; she stands by me even when I'm spinning on my axis. Sincere thanks to Kim Edwards, Mark Ransom, Erin Canning, Jen Brown, Jeff Nemanick, Denise Schneider, Barbara Rockenbach, Amy Hughes, Thomas Meacham, Christopher Swift, Ken Nielsen, and Elina Gertsman. Special thanks to my family: Sarah, Liam, and Vera; Candy; and my parents, who are always so enthusiastic and supportive that it leaves me a bit stunned. And, finally, to Kelly, my faithful and insightful companion on this journey with Jesus. To think . . . it all came together on a cocktail napkin in Orlando.

Contents

Introduction
Evangelical Performative Culture

Mel Gibson's 2004 blockbuster film *The Passion of The Christ* not only created a media storm, but the popularity of this film among Christians, and particularly evangelical Christians, took many people by surprise. In the months before and immediately following its premiere, articles about the film dominated the mainstream press.[1] This discourse engaged many important issues, chief among them the anti-Semitic legacy of Passion playing. Yet, despite this intensive scrutiny, and even as church congregations across the nation reserved blocks of seats in movie theaters and youth groups held pre- and post-viewing prayer sessions in cinema parking lots,[2] few critics assessed or critically discussed how the film might function as an effective and legitimate devotional device for its target audience—Christian believers. Although certain writers acknowledged that Gibson was employing the "dolorous" visionary texts of the German nun Anne Catherine Emmerich (1774–1824), which contain Passion imagery that builds upon the "Man of Sorrows" representations of Christ that first emerged during the later Middle Ages,[3] the film's extreme violence seemed to hinder those critics from reconciling this iconographic tradition with an ability to provide genuine spiritual value to contemporary spectators. Without such assessment the film did not cultivate the informed dialogue that some hoped it would,[4] but instead, as Marcia Kupfer writes, it "polarized the nation, demarcating the faithful from nonbelievers, insiders from outsiders."[5] In fact, as Mark C. Taylor notes, the very elements in the film that many reviewers believed would make it a failure with U.S. audiences—such as the extreme violence, lack of any major stars, and Latin and Aramaic dialogue with English subtitles—ultimately helped it achieve unprecedented success.[6]

This discursive gap occurred largely because *The Passion of The Christ* functioned differently than had previous films or plays characterized as Christian that had entered the mainstream market. In Margaret Miles's work on religion in film she differentiates between movies that raise religious issues and those that act religiously.[7] Writing about the late 1980s and early 1990s, she argued that the Passion films of that period—such as *Jesus of Montreal* and *The Last Temptation of Christ*—raised religious issues but did not act to intensify the viewer's devotion.[8] In contrast, I would assert that Gibson's film does exactly that—it acts religiously—a function that most critics of the film were not prepared to engage. In this respect, I believe *The Passion of The Christ* exposed a difficulty that many critics have in analyzing the very real spiritual power that contemporary Christian media possess for believers, especially those forms that circulate through popular culture.

In the years immediately following *The Passion*'s release, a variety of special journal issues and essay collections explored the film from a range of critical perspectives.[9] Yet, in many respects, this intense scholarly interest was a striking anomaly; as John Fletcher contends, contemporary Christian performances are all too often dismissed by theater scholars as merely forms of proselytism.[10] And, indeed, even some notable scholars struggled to assess how Gibson's film might function as a devotional medium. For example, in her 2006 article on *The Passion of The Christ,* Miles contends that "we are trained by our many viewing experiences to expect and respond to a number of film conventions," and she identifies "detachment" as one of the foremost conventions. Arguing that "movies are entertainment, and entertainment places the viewer in a position of distance and passivity," she implies that it is extremely difficult for spectators to resist this conditioning and employ an alternative spectatorial mode.[11] Therefore, in response to reports that Gibson's *Passion* provided stimulus toward increased Christian commitment, she writes, "On the one hand, viewers' reports of their own experience are to be respected. On the other hand, there are reasons to doubt that the movie ultimately enhances understanding of, and empathy with, Christianity's founder."[12]

I agree that many viewers not already familiar with the biblical account were likely confused by the lack of a coherent, linear plot and left the film without a clear understanding of the Passion narrative; as Beal writes, "The movie gives [non-Christians] no way to interpret the violence, no way into its symbolic world. As a result, they come away alienated, feeling like outsiders."[13] However, the film's popularity among two particular groups of religious viewers—traditional Catholics and evangelical Protestants—suggests that it did effectively operate for certain believers as a devotional device.[14] In order to understand that function, we must critically analyze the film's formal characteristics and features, as well as the live, variable, moment-to-moment encounters that users have with it. This kind of analysis requires that we, as Donnalee Dox suggests, "take the spiritual dimension of religious belief seriously as a formative component of the mode of performance."[15] Religious belief does not passively stand beside this film, but instead it infuses the work, as well as the viewer/user's approach to, and live encounter with, that work. In this case, Gibson is a member of a traditionalist Catholic church, and the film clearly reflects certain aspects of Catholic theology; however, as I will discuss in a later chapter, many of Gibson's directorial choices also resonate strongly with core evangelical tenets.[16] Consequently, specific Catholic and evangelical Protestant beliefs shaped this film's mode of performance.

Many elements of belief, including formal theology, devotional practices, and the framing provided by religious leaders, texts, and institutions, contribute to how each spectator will uniquely experience a religious mode of performance. Accordingly, although *The Passion of The Christ* was especially popular among both traditional Catholics and many evangelical Protestants, these groups likely perceived the film quite differently precisely because of variations in theology and religious practice; the film could act religiously, but in distinct ways.[17] In this book, I propose various ways that religious belief shapes how evangelical Christians engage performative genres, in this case, genres constructed specifically for evangelical believers. By *engage,* I mean the ways that believers approach, respond to, interact with, understand, and generate meaning from these genres, as well as how they conceive, design, market, and deploy them.

Deidre Sklar contends that because the aesthetic patterns of performances shift how we "configure aesthetic information" in new and unique ways that "can jostle the whole epistemological structure," ultimately "performance becomes a kind of insight meditation."[18] In the following chapters, I analyze the strategies that evangelical performative media employ to reconfigure aesthetic information in ways that will support certain evangelical Christian epistemologies. Admittedly, many denominations and nondenominational groups fall under the evangelical Christian rubric; as is the case with all religions, it is critical to recognize not only that there is variety within and between denominational categories but also that differences exist among believers within a single denomination. Therefore, although I use *evangelical* as an umbrella term throughout this book, I am careful to recognize that while certain evangelical denominations or groups of believers may embrace a performative genre, others may reject or simply ignore it. Accordingly, my analysis situates each example I study within its own social, cultural, and evangelical context. However, as Randall Balmer explains, despite the variety "it is still possible to identify some generic characteristics" of American evangelicalism: "an embrace of the Holy Bible as inspired and God's revelation to humanity, a belief in the centrality of the conversion or 'born again' experience, and the impulse to evangelize or bring others to the faith."[19] Consequently, throughout this book I will assert ways that different performative genres respond to these central tenets, even as I simultaneously acknowledge that—as is the case with all audiences—each spectator/user's desires and beliefs are unique. For this reason, I also see this project as revealing the diversity found within evangelical religious expression.[20]

The forms I study—contemporary Passion plays, biblical theme parks, Holy Land recreations, creationist museums, and megachurches—are not simply filling existing generic structures with core theology. Instead, I argue that these genres function through a distinctive dramaturgy that I call *evangelical dramaturgy*. Like all dramaturgical systems, evangelical dramaturgy assumes certain interpretations of representation, realism, enactment, spectatorship, and presence, in order to achieve particular aesthetic, ideological, and experiential effects. Moreover, I contend that evangelical genres that utilize this dramaturgy do not merely represent theological concepts and depict biblical stories; rather, they confront users with vivid, sensual, and rhythmic experiences designed to foster embodied beliefs that respond to specific devotional needs and priorities. There is a dynamic and, perhaps, necessary tension between the media forms I examine and the construction of belief.[21] These genres often constitute a worldview even as they reinforce it; belief may be necessary for the form's efficacy, but in another way that efficacy also generates belief.

I also interpret this (seeming) circularity as related to a specific way of reading scripture that many evangelicals employ. In his study of biblical literalism, Vincent Crapanzano explains that for many evangelicals, especially Fundamentalist evangelicals, "Interpretation, reading, is always cyclical: it is at once progressive and retrogressive, though never repetitive in the usual sense of the world, for it is always uncovering new relationships, new pre- and postfigurements."[22] Such an encounter with scripture is meant to affirm and generate belief simultaneously and connectively; evangelicals certainly bring a system of beliefs to the Bible that shapes how they interpret scripture, but their mode of reading is also very creative and dynamic since it aims to construct new, previously unrecognized, networks of relevant meaning and, ultimately, embodied belief. As the anthropologist Susan Harding argues, for such reader-believers "their bible is alive, its narrative shape enacts reality, infills it with form and meaning. It is, we might say, miraculous, this discourse which effects the world it speaks by constituting subjects who bring it about."[23] This way of reading not only challenges notions of linearity, something that many of the genres I examine also accomplish, but it also reminds us to question any straightforward causal relationship between practice and belief within the evangelical tradition. Moreover, as I will suggest in my Coda, practices that emerge directly out of one particular set of religious beliefs may nurture another belief system if there is enough affinity between the two, thereby creating a kind of "resonance machine" that opens "new circuits of contagion."[24]

Before outlining the dramaturgical system I see operating within evangelical performative culture, I will first provide a brief overview of evangelicalism in the United States in order to situate the genres I examine within their specific historical, cultural, and devotional traditions. I will also explain the theoretical approach I use to engage this religious tradition and to explore its performative dimensions. Finally, I will conclude by introducing evangelical dramaturgy itself.

Christianity and Popular Culture

If performance scholars hope to remain relevant participants within our national conversations about religion's impact on culture and society, then we cannot ignore religious pop culture. Far from tangential phenomena, genres like creationist museums and biblical theme parks are significant and influential cultural products that utilize sophisticated performative tactics to reach large audiences comprised of firm believers, extreme skeptics, and those in between. Moreover, precisely because they often appear in accessible, familiar forms (such as theme parks) and employ pop culture motifs, a wide range of people—including those hostile toward Christianity or religion generally—are often willing to "try out" these genres, even if only for curiosity's sake. This familiarity, a quality that Linda Kintz would argue resonates through the body, not only helps these genres achieve their goals, but, I assert, may also give them the power to engender constructive and responsible dialogue about the role of religious faith in America.[25]

As Stewart Hoover explains, until recently

> the whole literature of media and religion has been typified by a sort of dualist instrumentalism which sees the question solely in terms of cause and effect, as though "media" (or commodity culture, or popular culture) and "religion" are more or less equivalent and autonomous historical categories and it is possible to understand them only as competing with and contesting one another.[26]

This perspective severely limited scholars' ability to understand contemporary culture, since "evidence suggests that media and religion occupy some of the same turf in modern life."[27] In addition, the prevalence of various sociocultural binaries within Western culture—namely, body/mind, reason/emotion, and matter/spirit—has for centuries impacted how scholars discuss and analyze the role of physical, emotional, and material practices within the Judeo-Christian tradition.[28]

Yet, in the last two decades, a number of scholars have published studies that seriously examine the use and function of popular Christian media.[29] This work challenges long-held assumptions regarding the relationship between popular culture and religion. For instance, although some scholars still view material media as undermining spirituality,[30] this recent work validates the idea that Christianity and popular media work symbiotically. As Heather Hendershot notes, "rather than critiquing religious commodities as evidence of how commercialism dilutes faith," most scholars now take popular genres seriously in order to demonstrate the sophisticated ways in which believers generate and sustain belief through material objects and spaces.[31] This is especially the case with evangelical Christianity, which has always had a complex, multidirectional relationship with popular media; as D. G. Hart writes, evangelicalism has "been one of the most modern and innovative forms of Christianity in using the cultural vernacular to restate the claims of an ancient faith in a modern tongue."[32] However, evangelical Christians employ popular media not simply to reflect or communicate theology but, more important, to increase religious accessibility in ways that give lay believers agency over their faith. This is especially true of evangelical Christianity in the United States and is a characteristic evident from the movement's very beginning.

Laypeople powered the vernacularization and particularization of American evangelicalism, in many cases using popular culture as part of their efforts.[33] In fact, Nathan Hatch suggests that evangelicalism's success in the United States had "less to do with the specifics of polity and governance and more with the incarnation of the church into popular culture."[34] Whether it was evangelical publicists in the 1820s mass-producing religious tracts or members of twentieth-century evangelical movements like Fundamentalism and Pentecostalism broadcasting radio programs, the narrative of American evangelical Christianity—and perhaps even of American religion generally—is a story about religious popular culture.[35] This is also a unique story. Hatch writes,

> The United States contains more citizens who value religion than other Western industrial societies. This odd combination of modernity and religion defies conventional wisdom . . . [and] raises interesting questions about the nature of popular religious movements in the United States and about the contrast between American popular culture and that of other Western industrial nations.[36]

As scholars like Heather Hendershot, Linda Kintz, Timothy Beal, and David Morgan have demonstrated, understanding the distinctive characteristics of this "odd combination" requires us to move beyond these simplistic distinctions of secular and sacred, tradition and innovation, public and personal, and church and state.

Most work on evangelical popular culture has focused on film, video, and print media, with far less attention paid to live performances; live Christian performances and performative genres, in particular those aimed at evangelicals, remain largely unstudied.[37] For example, there are no major theater or performance studies of the "Great Passion Play," which since 1968 has been staged annually from May through October, five nights a week, in Eureka Springs, Arkansas.[38] The same is true of Holy Land Experience (HLE), a Bible-based theme park in Orlando, Florida. Studies of HLE published since its opening in 2001 consider it primarily in the context of contemporary pilgrimage and Holy Land recreations.[39] I am aware of no critical analysis of HLE by theater scholars, even though the park experience largely consists of attending live performances and theatrical presentations, and the main event at HLE is an outdoor Passion play presented once—and sometimes twice—daily.

Moreover, in most cases, Christian performances staged by and for believers have also been excluded from more general studies of twentieth- and twenty-first-century popular theater and performance, an omission that not only obscures the important role that theatricality continues to play within U.S. Christianity, but one that also excises significant examples of religious performance from histories of popular American theater, thereby perpetuating the conventional narrative of Protestantism's inherent antitheatricality. In this book, I examine a variety of evangelical performances and performative genres in order to understand how they work for believer-users, while also recognizing them as contributing to U.S. popular culture more generally.

Evangelicalism and American Identity

Evangelical Christianity's history is tightly linked to American history, and evangelicals remain the largest religious denomination in the United States. The Pew Forum's U.S. Religious Landscape Survey provides some of the most comprehensive statistics available on religious affiliation. The report is based upon data drawn primarily from a 2007 nationwide survey of more than 35,000 adults.[40] According to this survey, 51 percent of Americans are Protestants, with 26.3 percent of the overall adult population self-identifying as evangelical Protestants, 18.1 percent as mainline Protestants, and 6.9 percent as historically black Protestants. Significantly, bracketing black Protestants in this way distorts the figures somewhat since the breakdown of historically black Protestants indicates that the majority of the respondents are affiliated with evangelical churches.[41] Of the remainder, Catholics accounted for 23.9 percent, Mormons and Jews each constituted 1.7 percent, and 16.1 percent of respondents identified themselves as unaffiliated.[42]

The term *evangelical* is deployed in a variety of ways, as I have already noted. The Institute for the Study of American Evangelicals at Wheaton College acknowledges the expansive history of the term, while also situating it historically. As their website explains, while *evangelical* "is a wide-reaching definitional 'canopy' that covers a diverse number of Protestant groups," within the English-speaking world "the modern usage usually connotes the religious movements and denominations which sprung forth from a series of revivals that swept the North Atlantic Anglo-American world in the eighteenth and early nineteenth centuries."[43] The Institute thus acknowledges the term's political, social, and historical associations within U.S. culture, and the "Defining Evangelicalism" section of the Institute's website includes pages devoted to Fundamentalism, Pentecostalism, Politics, the Media, and End Times or Apocalyptic theology, which, as the website explains, has become "a highly-visible aspect of the evangelical subculture."[44]

Regarding specific theological tenets, both the Institute at Wheaton College and the National Association of Evangelicals (NAE) cite historian David Bebbington, who identified four primary characteristics of evangelicalism:

> Conversionism: the belief that lives need to be transformed through a "born-again" experience and a lifelong process of following Jesus. Activism: the expression and demonstration of the gospel in missionary and social reform efforts. Biblicism: a high regard for and obedience to the Bible as the ultimate authority. Crucicentrism: a stress on the sacrifice of Jesus Christ on the cross as making possible the redemption of humanity.[45]

These categories are quite similar to those that Randall Balmer delineates.[46] As the NAE explains,

> Evangelicals take the Bible seriously and believe in Jesus Christ as Savior and Lord. The term "evangelical" comes from the Greek word euangelion, meaning "the good news" or the "gospel." Thus, the evangelical faith focuses on the "good news" of salvation brought to sinners by Jesus Christ. We are a vibrant and diverse group, including believers found in many churches, denominations and nations. Our community brings together Reformed, Holiness, Anabaptist, Pentecostal, Charismatic and other traditions. Our core theological convictions provide unity in the midst of our diversity.[47]

Ultimately, all of these definitions underscore the personal and experiential nature of American evangelicalism. Born-again evangelicals have experienced God directly and personally through conversion, and sustain that relationship thereafter through activities such as daily Bible study and prayer, and by witnessing to others, often through one-on-one encounters.

In addition, most evangelicals consider the Bible a text that all people have the ability to understand, regardless of education or training. As Crapanzano explains,

> the Bible is said to be perspicuous; its meaning is open to all. . . . Interpretive authority may be enhanced by scholarship (though in some evangelical churches scholarship is treated with suspicion) or by force of personality, but, ultimately, having no secure institutional support, it rests on the perceived moral and spiritual condition of the interpreter.[48]

Therefore, while the Bible itself is considered infallible, the threat of human error lingers over the practice of Bible reading. Consequently, according to biblical literalists, what might appear to be inconsistencies or contradictions are actually the results of human fallibility; "if sin is the chief obstacle to our relationship with God . . . then sin is going to hinder any interpretation."[49] Evangelicals therefore recognize the necessity of rigorous, continual study that will help them to understand the Word as God intended.[50] Although such study might be pursued in small Bible study groups and during sermons, true understanding ultimately results from each person's own individual effort, determination, and spiritual state.

Evangelicalism is therefore a democratizing religious force, with, as Hatch writes, American evangelicalism in particular shaped not by "central ecclesiastical institutions and high culture" but instead "by a democratic populist orientation" that produced a distinctive form of democratic Christianity.[51] Other Christian and non-Christian traditions certainly reflect similar impulses toward religious populism, such as Reform Judaism, a religious and social movement that developed in the United States and Europe during the nineteenth century and sought, among other things, to modernize aspects of Jewish tradition.[52] Yet, arguably, evangelical Christianity has been the religious movement in the United States most dramatically shaped by the common people. Empowering laypeople to take control over their own spirituality was a theological goal for even the earliest, pre-Revolution evangelical leaders. For example, in his study of the eighteenth-century preacher George Whitefield (1714–70), Harry Stout contends that Whitefield's mass preaching "helped to introduce a new concept of religious experience that grew throughout the nineteenth century into a recognizably 'evangelical' movement," an emphasis that shifted piety from a local and corporate spirituality "to a more individualistic and subjective sense of piety that found its quintessential expression in the internal, highly personal experience of the 'New Birth.'"[53] Although Whitefield's religious revivalism also had a major impact on Christianity in Scotland and England, Stout writes,

> In colonial America his significance had an added dimension. There he became not only the prototype for future mass evangelists but the prototypical culture hero as well. . . . the first in a long line of public figures whose claims to influence would rest on celebrity and popularity rather than birth, breeding, or institutional fiat.[54]

Whitefield illustrates the notable consonance between evangelical theology and certain foundational U.S. principles that were only just emerging in Whitefield's era. This relationship intensified as the nation developed. According to Hatch, the American Revolution situated issues of freedom, equality, and representation as key to the common person's experience and central to the definition of "American," and these very issues ultimately "left an indelible imprint on the structure of American Christianity."[55] This was especially true of the evangelical movement; evangelical leaders of the late eighteenth and early nineteenth centuries who were "intent on bringing evangelical conversion to the mass of ordinary Americans . . . could rarely divorce that message from contagious new democratic vocabularies and impulses that surged through American popular culture."[56] In this respect, evangelicalism in the United States became, and is still perceived by some to be, an expression of American values and ideals.[57]

A Cognitive Approach to Evangelical Entrepreneurialism

Throughout the late eighteenth and nineteenth centuries, American Christianity was an enterprise of the masses, with many new denominations developing rapidly, and evangelically oriented insurgent groups, often led by young, self-conscious outsiders, attracting the most followers.[58] These leaders, like their predecessor Whitefield, were successful largely because they devised new popular modes of religiosity that gave each lay believer personal, unmediated access to God and, in consequence, a great deal of agency over his or her individual religious experience.

As I have noted, scholars of American evangelicalism emphasize believers' skepticism regarding hierarchical religious institutions. This uncertainty is grounded in evangelical theology itself. Most evangelicals do not consider personal belief and experience as subordinate to institutional teaching and formal doctrine; on the contrary, they regard personal knowledge acquisition and experience as privileged sources of faith. As Wade Clark Roof explains, many contemporary evangelicals are inclined to regard "the truths found through self-discovery as having greater relevance to them than those handed down by way of creed or custom. Direct experience is always more trustworthy."[59] Christian Smith's study of contemporary American evangelicalism confirms this fact:

> Evangelicals appeal primarily to the Bible and secondarily to their personal relationship with God as their sources of spiritual and life-direction. While not a strict measure of Christian orthodoxy, per se . . . these results at least indicate an aversion among evangelicals to humanly and institutionally grounded sources of authority in favor of more spiritually grounded ones.[60]

This inclination has significantly impacted notions of church development and leadership within evangelicalism, resulting in a largely entrepreneurial religious movement.[61]

Certain aspects of U.S. culture may, in fact, reinforce this entrepreneurial urge. William Connolly makes a compelling case for the "affinities of sensibility" between the U.S. evangelical movement and "the right edge" of corporate capitalism, arguing that one connection "is the conviction by many evangelists that entrepreneurial activity is the one worldly activity endowed with divine providence."[62] As Bethany Moreton demonstrates, business programs at Protestant colleges have helped to reinforce this notion. For example, at "Regent University's School of Business in Virginia, the Christian Broadcasting Network's Pat Robertson promoted 'Entrepreneurial Tentmaking.'"[63] By promoting this image of the entrepreneur as a kind of "mythical figure" who is "the presumed lineal descendent of the independent small businessman," these Christian colleges and universities encourage evangelicals to see "entrepreneurs as public benefactors who [bring] the blessing of goods and services to an ever-wider public."[64]

Crucially, this image of entrepreneurship is also linked to free-market economics. Crapanzano identifies a "popular chain of associations between the creative power of God, His mundane expression in entrepreneurial life, and the automatic justice of the unregulated market."[65] Such a network is not surprising given the American cultural imagination. For instance, Crapanzano contends that in the United States "the conception of the 'market' has deep theological roots and that our attitude toward it, our faith in it really, verges on the religious."[66] Moreover, he notes how evangelical personal conversion accounts are oftentimes "success stories in miniature—the American dream cast in spiritual terms (that are not altogether resistant to material claims)."[67] The American and evangelical cultural paradigms therefore both present the (spiritually) driven entrepreneur as a heroic ideal. This confluence promotes the idea that building a personal, unmediated relationship with God is not only God's will but also an individual's right.[68] Such an entrepreneurial spirit helped to shape U.S. evangelicalism from its very beginning.

The theological emphasis on the believer's unmediated access to God meant that leaders of new evangelical movements that emerged in the eighteenth and nineteenth centuries could not simply borrow or recycle existing institutional structures. Instead, in order to gain traction in this populist religious climate, many leaders drew upon their personal skills and resources, often using performative popular media to translate theology into experience. This was true as early as Whitefield, a preacher who "transformed the traditional sermon into something different: a dramatic event capable of competing for public attention outside the arena of the churches—in fact, in the marketplace."[69] In doing so, Whitefield not only reshaped his sermons into readily available, consumable products but also revealed the value of emotional production to evangelical religious consumption.[70] Whitefield illustrates how, since the eighteenth century, American evangelicalism has been an entrepreneurial venture in which believers utilize popular media in innovative ways in order to commodify personal, affective religious experiences, a strategy that evangelicalism's democratizing theology intrinsically validates.[71] As I will demonstrate throughout these chapters, this practice continues today.

Providing believers with direct, live religious encounters that are not only dynamic and flexible but easy to personalize also serves to disavow any distinction between the secular and the sacred, another important facet of evangelical belief. According to Smith, a common theme among evangelicals is their "critique of compartmentalized 'Sunday-morning' faith." As one Presbyterian man in Smith's study said, "Evangelicals try to maintain a biblical worldview that follows the Scriptures and encompasses our ideas on things from education to our stewardship of the earth. Just a whole realm of things, in essence saying our relationship to God affects our everyday living."[72] An effective way to promote that message is through bodily practices, since believers continue to inhabit their bodies after they leave church and travel through everyday life. Therefore, evangelicals use spaces, events, and objects to instantiate belief in the body.

For example, daily Bible study and devotions are an important part of many evangelical Christians' lives.[73] Physically participating in these devotional rhythms provokes people to understand and experience everyday life through a spiritual lens. Linda Kintz discusses how "daily prayer sessions and study gives believers a world always already biblically written, as the Bible becomes the Book of the World. The Bible in this sense provides the frame, or the Symbolic order, that grounds belief *and* the body" (my emphasis).[74] This kind of activity is also entrepreneurial in nature, since it allows believers to remake their worldview and everyday experiences through a self-directed, personal ritual;[75] although they may follow a devotional guide, each person ultimately chooses when, how, where, and even why to practice. Moreover, Kintz recognizes this kind of bodily activity as giving the believer's personal relationship with Christ an aesthetic dimension: "There is also a comforting physical, tactile sense to all of this, as well-thumbed Bibles become the reservoir of sensual memories, most often linked to family and church and to periods of mourning and of loss, as well as of joy and birth."[76] However, rather than grounding belief *and* the body, as Kintz suggests, I would argue that a performative devotional activity such as this also generates embodied belief.

Recent research in cognitive science validates an embodied model of perception and, alongside work in phenomenology, has helped scholars recognize that we construct meaning through our bodies. Such work has significantly influenced conceptualizations of embodiment and perception. Drawing upon this data, cognitive theory aims to better understand how humans perceive and, more precisely, how our material, biological bodies contribute to perceptual experience. As Naomi Rokotnitz explains, according to cognitive scientists,

> human minds do not, strictly speaking, produce meaning but, rather, process relationships between brain and world. These relationships are not simple cause-and-effect connections or on/off functions but systems of implications . . . [that] differ from individual brain to brain because they are formed by active, creative—and thus personal—participation.[77]

Cognitive theory allows us to investigate the way our individualized physical interactions with and in the world impact our knowledge of that world, and, as such, this theoretical approach has helped scholars move beyond the Cartesian mind/body binary that has dominated much of Western scholarship since the Renaissance.[78] Cognitive theories of embodied perception therefore provide an especially productive framework for this project because they resonate with evangelical theology's emphasis on personal experience as a basis for "making" theological belief.

Not only does cognitive theory help us investigate how religious belief manifests in and through physical interactions with evangelical media, but an embodied mind approach to emotion also supplies ways to theorize affective piety, another important element of evangelical Christianity. Hart explains,

> One of the striking aspects of evangelical cultural expressions is how personal their plots and subject matter tend to be. . . . This tendency in evangelical popular culture is natural, given the importance of conversion. Born-again Protestantism is primarily a religion of the heart, and it stresses the subjective experience of the convert and his or her spiritual struggles.[79]

For many evangelicals, emotion—even extreme emotion—is not an overwhelming force that impedes a relationship with God, but one that can instead offer direct access to, and even a clearer understanding of, God. Some scholars argue that misunderstandings about this relationship between feeling and knowledge have hindered the study of evangelically oriented denominations.[80] Models of embodied perception, like those proposed by cognitive theory, therefore give us ways to analyze this kind of religious discourse constructively and to recognize how emotion and reason together promote affective piety. This piety aims to support the evangelical believer's spiritual journey—a journey over which the devotee exerts incredible control and agency, and that I therefore recognize as a kind of entrepreneurial event.

In the chapters that follow I use performance and cognitive theories to argue that performative genres like creationist museums, Holy Land recreations, and megachurches generate vivid, sensual, affectively oriented, and individualized experiences that will reinforce and clarify the believer's faith, thereby sustaining the devotee's personal relationship with Christ. They accomplish these goals by means of performative strategies that link dramaturgy to evangelical theology in ways that expand the aesthetic possibilities of devotion, while simultaneously expressing and reinforcing certain social and cultural ideologies. Consequently, as I asserted with respect to *The Passion of The Christ,* understanding how these media function devotionally for believers does not mean ignoring that they impact larger social, cultural, and political trends.[81] But it does entail approaching them on their own terms and recognizing that, while these genres may mystify or repel some groups, their popularity is not simply due to their position within the current "culture wars,"[82] but is also evidence that they do legitimately address the spiritual needs and urges of a specific audience.

Cognitive theory also helps me to examine how these performative genres influence what "matters" to people. Using David Grossberg's theory of the national popular, Kintz explains that *matter* refers to both "the very nature of materiality in general and the body in particular," as well as "the way things come to matter, the way emotions are learned and taught."[83] "Mattering" therefore provides not only mental stability but also stability through the heart and body, since, as Kintz reminds us, "The intensity of mattering, while ideologically constructed, is nevertheless 'always beyond ideological challenge because it is called into existence affectively.'"[84] Consequently, studying how a genre activates "maps of mattering" requires us to consider the genre's affective potential, as well as the ways it works on and through the believer's body. Cognitive theory offers useful ways to engage these very elements.

Medieval to Modern: A Devotional Continuum

Although acknowledging American evangelicalism's historical trajectory and placing the examples I study within their contemporary milieux are both critical to my analysis, these contexts do not necessarily offer us sufficient insight into the affective side of evangelical devotional practice. These genres certainly express American values and contemporary concerns, but they also simultaneously operate within a longer Christian tradition of affective, material piety that extends at least as far back as the medieval period. Affective piety in the Middle Ages often revolved around meditation on images of Christ's Passion—mental, visual, textual, and verbal images. This piety emerged in the late eleventh and twelfth centuries as part of a larger devotional trend that included an iconographic shift toward Passion imagery that focused more directly and vividly on Jesus' suffering and humanity. As Kupfer writes, the medieval transition to "pictorial description of physical suffering was by no means a foregone conclusion. It required a shift in theological perspective and a radical reschooling of religious emotion."[85] As I will discuss at greater length in Chapter One, medieval affective piety helped devotees establish and maintain certain spiritual identities. Affectively oriented media supplied what Sarah McNamer calls "'intimate scripts' . . . quite literally scripts for the performance of feeling—scripts that often explicitly aspire to performative efficacy."[86] In some cases, these scripts aimed to cultivate compassion that would then serve as evidence to God of the user's spiritual worthiness.[87] Consequently, the emotional production that affective piety triggered fulfilled very real and quite serious devotional goals.

The pre-Reformation Christianity of the Middle Ages might initially seem diametrically opposed to contemporary U.S. evangelical Protestantism, an American movement that in many respects emerged out of and helped to sustain anti-Catholic, anti-European biases. In fact, American evangelical Christianity embraces many devotional proclivities with roots in the Middle Ages, specifically the centrality of material, affective piety within lay devotion. For example, various scholars have noted the relationship between Mel Gibson's *The Passion of The Christ* and medieval piety; David Morgan explains how Gibson's film "returns to a premodern iconography of Catholic art once used to visualize the passion of Jesus."[88] While this connection might elucidate the film's popularity among certain Catholics, as Mark C. Taylor asserts, "the tradition of *theologia crucis,* or theology of the cross, which dates back to Martin Luther, makes the resonance of the film among certain Protestant groups less surprising" than we might think.[89]

My own interest in contemporary Christian media emerged as I was studying the popular devotional culture of the later Middle Ages, and I have proposed elsewhere that many evangelical phenomena popular today function through modes of sensual piety similar to those operating within medieval culture.[90] I interpret this similarity as due, at least in part, to the fact that medieval devotional culture and evangelical devotional culture both resist the categorizations supplied by the traditional Western mind/body and reason/emotion binaries.[91] Moreover, as I will argue in Chapter One, the contemporary genres I examine here also supply evangelical believers with intimate scripts that, like the medieval texts McNamer analyzes, help to prove that the user's faith is genuine. Accordingly, I recognize related tactics and goals of affective piety across these two historical contexts.

By highlighting similarities between the medieval and modern, I do not wish to underestimate the differences between these periods and traditions, and my references to the Middle Ages in subsequent chapters are sparing. However, I am suggesting that acknowledging similarities between these systems of Christian piety may encourage those who study contemporary evangelicalism to consider the large body of evidence related to medieval popular piety as relevant to their work. For example, during the Middle Ages, and especially by the fifteenth century, it was increasingly the norm for lay Christians to use mass-produced media to promote and sustain their personal faith, with many of these forms designed specifically to support affective piety. Scholars have produced a large body of work that analyzes how medieval laypeople employed the popular media of their own time—inexpensive sculptures and images, printed books, pilgrimage badges, and civic performances—to cultivate personal piety.[92] This scholarship has challenged a number of generalizations about lay piety, such as the assumption that medieval laypeople were passive believers easily manipulated by religious rhetoric, doctrine, and media. I recognize such work as pertinent to the study of contemporary evangelicalism, especially since similar arguments about lay passivity often arise in discussions of evangelical believers. As Amy Johnson Frykholm notes, explanations about the reception of popular evangelical media usually "stem from understanding mass culture as the realm of domination and manipulation by those with cultural, financial, and religious power over those who are inactive and passive consumers." Such interpretations presume "the easy compliance of the audience that 'unwittingly' accepts both the political and religious assumptions" of popular media, and are often "based on a largely unidirectional model of reception that is concerned about the audience . . . but dismissive of it at the same time."[93] As a result, Frykholm contends that users of evangelical media are typically "assumed rather than investigated."[94]

In fact, as I have suggested, studies of religious media reveal a multidirectional, ongoing, and dynamic process of meaning-making in which users are not always in agreement and regularly express resistance, conclusions that medieval scholars have repeatedly asserted in their work on lay piety. Even within the ostensibly undemocratic, prescriptive religious environment of the European Middle Ages, the medieval laity revised, recreated, and transformed devotional media to fulfill their own needs. For example, laypeople sewed images into their devotional books, commissioned architectural elements such as stained-glass windows and sculptures for their churches, dressed statues of saints in their own clothes and jewelry, and staged religious plays in the streets and inns of their towns.[95] While there were also other "unorthodox" ways in which laypeople used devotional media, the practices I have listed here were, for the most part, among those that religious authorities deemed acceptable, despite the fact that they allowed the laity to operate outside of, or at least parallel to, institutional religious structures.

Scholarship therefore demonstrates that laypeople in the Middle Ages did not passively accept a single, dominant, institutionalized system of religious beliefs, but instead they constructed a relevant network of religious meaning, continually testing and revising it based upon new inputs, needs, and experiences, oftentimes using popular media to do so. The same could be said of evangelical piety. For example, in her study of the popular apocalyptic-themed *Left Behind* book series, Frykholm suggests that, for many believers, reading these books serves "as an act of social connection" that "is perhaps as close to ancient practices of 'oral, social, and collective' reading as it is to the modern notion of individual and private reading."[96] Moreover, she notes that "for the most part, readers engage with *Left Behind* for two primary and intertwined purposes—entertainment and edification."[97] Therefore, like medieval devotees, evangelicals today engage popular media through practices that merge secular with sacred, material with spiritual, and public with private.[98] For this reason, scholars studying evangelicalism may find research on the Middle Ages, which exposes the agency and performativity of lay devotion, valuable to their own work.

In both the medieval and modern contexts, lay piety does not merely reiterate or refute doctrine, but instead it remakes doctrine into material products that effectively address laypeople's desires, concerns, and needs. And while the same could be said of other contexts, I would argue that it is important to reference the Middle Ages within this study because that is when this system of affective Christian piety, and the desires, urges, and predilections it inspired, first emerged. Moreover, medieval Christian piety produced various iconographic, spatial, aesthetic, and performative tactics in response to those devotional trends. I identify many of those same tactics operating within evangelical performative culture today.

Correspondences between the medieval and modern may also suggest that certain devotional tactics employed within popular piety are not wholly dependent upon—nor entirely reflective of—social, political, or ecclesiastical circumstance, but may serve religious desires that transcend such local contexts. To some degree, then, I analyze evangelical media as a "living history" of medieval affective piety.[99] This is another reason I find cognitive theory valuable—it not only "offers a concrete reminder of powerful aspects of human existence that historians cannot directly see," as Anne Clark writes, but "with the cognitivists' claim that the mind they observe is the same mind that inhabited the world so recently past as the Middle Ages, cognitive theory may indeed offer a bridge to the past."[100] By bridging past and present, cognitive theory helps us to identify similarities between how people conceptualize and exert agency over their lived experience, even between contexts that initially appear vastly different.

Finally, I am inspired by scholars who have recognized how the "relational aspects of affect" can help us to build bridges across periods.[101] As Rebecca Schneider explains, many scholars "argue for the value of crossing disparate and multiple historical moments to explore the ways that past, present, and future occur and recur *out of sequence* in a complex crosshatch not only of reference but of affective assemblage and investment."[102] One particularly relevant example is Carolyn Dinshaw's work, which uses concepts like "affective writing" in order to find points of contact—moments of touch—between medieval and postmodern phenomena.[103] Therefore, while connections between medieval and U.S. evangelical devotion may be conceptual, the bodiedness of affective piety—and especially the way in which these practices are archived in bodies—may suggest that certain instances of cross-temporal touch also have a material dimension.[104] Furthermore, as I will argue, many of the evangelical genres I examine employ anachronism in order to generate exactly this kind of contact across time. My use of the Middle Ages to examine contemporary evangelicalism might represent a similar kind of generative "anachronistic" encounter.[105]

Evangelical Dramaturgy

Most evangelical traditions see the world as fundamentally fallen and recognize Christ as the only hope for salvation. Until Christ's second coming, the evangelical's mission is to spread this message of damnation and salvation—to witness.[106] Indeed, popular, recognizable artistic genres, some of which I study in this project, have proved useful for such proselytism. However, as

Hendershot explains, although evangelicals have always embraced modern "secular" media as a way to spread the Gospel, typically the main consumers of these genres "are assumed to already be saved," and, consequently, these media are more often designed to "reflect and construct evangelical understandings of the sacred and the profane, of the saved individual and his or her place in the wider world."[107] What ultimately makes these genres valuable to believers is their unique ability to clarify, secure, and reinforce faith. By situating popular evangelical media within specific historical, cultural, and devotional traditions, and using cognitive and performance theories to analyze how they cultivate physical faith experiences that endorse and fortify those traditions, I will suggest various ways in which religious belief plays a role in the evangelical user's gestalt experience of these performative media.

In some respect, then, this project is a response to Donnalee Dox's assertion that the "complexity of linking religious belief to modes of performance suggests the need for analytical theories that can accommodate religion and spirituality as conceptual foundations for some performance practices."[108] In Chapter One I propose such a theoretical lens for examining contemporary evangelical performative media, what I call "evangelical dramaturgy." Combining scholarship that explores evangelical theology and notions of religious re-representation with recent work on embodied knowledge, in this first chapter I introduce evangelical dramaturgy and identify its key strategies.

In the remaining chapters I focus on different performative forms that illustrate evangelical dramaturgy's various functions and applications. In Chapter Two I analyze acting and suggest that evangelical dramaturgy assumes a kind of energetic exchange between spectators and actors similar to what Phillip Zarrilli proposes in his theory of psychophysical acting.[109] Chapters Three and Four consider how contemporary Passion performances deploy acting; Chapter Three focuses on "Behold the Lamb," the Passion play staged daily at Holy Land Experience, while Chapter Four examines the "Great Passion Play" in Eureka Springs. Here I use theories of intermediality alongside cognitive theory to explore the different ideological purposes these Passion performances serve. In Chapter Four I also introduce the cognitive theory of conceptual blending to analyze Holy Land recreations, the performative context of both "Behold the Lamb" and the "Great Passion Play." In Chapter Five I continue to apply conceptual blending, this time to the 70,000-square-foot Creation Museum in Petersburg, Kentucky.

Evangelical dramaturgy assumes an energetic exchange between performers and spectators, but here I propose that this exchange is not limited to interpersonal encounters and can also occur between space/place/objects and visitors. The Creation Museum also illustrates how modern culture, rather than undermining evangelical dramaturgy, actually fosters the very desires and needs that this dramaturgy aims to satisfy. I consider this issue in greater detail in Chapter Six, where I explore megachurches.

Megachurches provide the ideal genre with which to conclude this study. These high-tech venues offer worshippers performance-like services oftentimes led by dynamic, charismatic, and entrepreneurial leaders. These spaces are sometimes repurposed, such as the central campus of Lakewood Church in Houston, Texas, a nondenominational church with 43,500 members that is led by the influential evangelical minister Joel Osteen. Lakewood's main house of worship is the Compaq Center, which formerly served as a sports arena for various teams including the NBA's Houston Rockets. Megachurches also regularly house facilities like coffee shops, cafeterias, and recreation centers, and therefore members come to these churches not just for Sunday services but also for many other weekly or daily activities. In these and other ways, megachurches supply congregants with a religious experience that blends the sacred and extraordinary with the everyday and secular. Moreover, megachurches allow me to address the issue of religious consumerism and branding in greater detail. Finally, although megachurches are large, technologically sophisticated spaces, and therefore may initially look and feel markedly different from the small parish churches of the Middle Ages, I conclude Chapter Six by proposing that, in fact, these two religious spaces share many characteristics and that megachurches may represent a nostalgic attempt to recreate the medieval parish community model. Megachurches therefore knit together many of the key ideas that surface across these chapters, while simultaneously complicating conclusions about the relationships between religious belief, authenticity, and modernity.

The cultural forms I analyze in the next six chapters do not merely reflect belief, they *make* belief. I visited, attended, and actively participated in all of the venues and events I discuss. In each case, I tried to enter into a relationship with the form in a way that allowed me to stay open to its possibilities, while also remaining aware of its spatial, temporal, rhythmic, and visual vocabularies and of the other spectators/visitors around me. Although I maintained a critical stance, I agree with Rachel Fulton's assessment that it is nearly impossible to use certain religious artifacts—especially those specifically designed to cultivate religious feeling—"without experiencing something of their intended effect."[110] Therefore, although I did not approach or engage these media as a devotee, and at moments (as I will admit) I could not prevent my own personal aesthetic or moral objections from distorting my critical frame, this does not mean I was ever entirely immune to the devotional force of these encounters.

In his study of roadside religious attractions in the United States, Timothy Beal describes the study of religion as

> encountering religious ideas, practices, traditions, and institutions that initially appear to us as "other," disturbingly foreign, and coming to a point where we can understand how they can make sense given a certain set of circumstances. Such work requires not only critical rigor and tenacity . . . it also requires imagination in order to put oneself in another's situation.[111]

However, Beal also reminds us that despite our best efforts "to bridge otherness" by finding our way "into the other's story," we can never understand that story completely: "I can never become the other I wish to understand. To presume I can is dangerous, because then I risk reducing the other, incommensurably rich in particularity, complexity, and wonderful strangeness, to myself."[112] I use evangelical dramaturgy to outline an analytical framework that I believe respects the "particularity, complexity, and wonderful strangeness" of these evangelical media even as it explores them through a rigorous critical lens.

1
Embodied Belief, Affective Piety, and Evangelical Dramaturgy

The performative genres I study in this book both reflect and engender religious belief. I argue that they accomplish this, in great measure, through what I call *evangelical dramaturgy,* a system of performative tactics designed to manipulate the physical, rhythmic encounter between user and medium. As Simon Shepherd contends, because performances are

> gatherings of bodies as much as minds. . . . Effects are produced in the spectator simply as a result of materially sharing the space with the performance. Many of these effects, bypassing the intellect, are felt in the body and work powerfully to shape a spectator's sense of the performance.[1]

Rhythm is a fundamental way that performances produce these effects, with the actor's body generating particularly powerful rhythms; "a play's rhythm works on an audience. It does so through the agency of the performer body rhythm which stimulates response in audience bodies."[2]

However, a variety of other performative elements also produce rhythms: the stage space and environment surrounding the spectators, material props, costumes and set pieces, lighting and soundscape, staging and textual choices, and the spectators' own bodies. All of these components enter the performance frame rhythmically, impacting the aesthetic texture of the performance experience and, thus, the meaning spectators derive from that experience. Consequently, Shepherd argues that when a spectator arrives at a performance, his or her body arrives "in a more or less heightened state of openness to rhythmic possibility. And in this state of openness it is confronted by the play's own rhythms."[3] Moreover, spectators have their own bodily rhythms, which may be "confirmed or drawn into a new rhythm by the play." In this respect, as Shepherd asserts, rhythm constitutes "the agency whereby a play may negotiate with its audience an affirmation of or deviation from the rhythmic experience of their everyday lives."[4] Evangelical dramaturgy's overarching goal is to shape this rhythmic point of contact between performative event and believer-user so that it supports certain ideologies and cultivates particular religious beliefs.

Evangelical dramaturgy is therefore founded upon the principle that live performances are rhythmic experiences and that this rhythmic dimension helps performances function as powerful religious tools. Yet, this dramaturgical system also recognizes that many genres generate rhythms and, therefore, users may also approach these other performative forms as they do live performances—with bodies prepared for and expecting rhythmic engagement.

I have suggested elsewhere that late medieval devotional culture acknowledged this characteristic of religious media, with certain extant examples still revealing the creator's attention to rhythm.[5] For example, in order to make their ideas more accessible to lay readers, some medieval writers employed rhythmic devices to integrate "secular" elements into devotional texts. We find this in Robert Mannyng of Brunne's *Handlyng Synne,* an early fourteenth-century penitential manual written for laypeople that tackles complicated theological issues, in particular those concerning the nature of the Eucharist. As Jennifer Garrison explains, although this text urges lay readers "to contemplate the paradoxical inaccessibility of Christ," Mannyng chooses to deliver this message through a highly accessible vernacular narrative form.[6] Not only did writing the manual in English affirm the importance of lay salvation and of the vital role that theological education played in that salvation, but Garrison argues that this choice also suggests that Mannyng recognized English as the "language of narrative" and wanted to use this specific association to his pedagogical advantage.[7]

As Garrison explains, *Handlyng Synne* begins with a prologue in which Mannyng "laments that the laity are unknowingly falling into sin for two distinct reasons: doctrinal texts are not widely available in the vernacular, and laypeople prefer entertaining tales to sermons."[8] He aims to remedy this situation, not only "by interspersing penitential doctrine with entertaining exempla" but also by using "rymys" (rhymes) like those employed in narrative.[9] Therefore, rather than requiring the laity to "renounce their old habits, such as storytelling," the narrative form of *Handlyng Synne* instead encourages them "to integrate greater piety into the practices in which they already engage." In this way, Mannyng hopes to "compete with popular forms of entertainment."[10]

Garrison's analysis of this manual focuses primarily on the appropriation of entertaining exempla, but I am interested in Mannyng's use of "rymys," a device that implies he was not focused exclusively on generic content and structure. By using rhymes, Mannyng borrows a kinaesthetic element from vernacular narrative; in the service of devotional efficacy, he invigorates sacred content by appropriating a familiar, secular, and popular rhythmic program. That program is composed of not only the text's sounded rhymes but also the actual encounter between those uttered sounds and the listener/reader, a rhythmic encounter that produces certain kinaesthetic effects. I propose that such borrowing acknowledges that a genre generates valuable meaning through the user's felt experience of its rhythmic features. As Shepherd writes, "the mobilization of bodily value is ideologically more successful because it produces responses that are felt rather than discussed."[11] Mannyng uses "rymys" to embed his religious ideology into the lay reader/listener's body.

Like *Handlyng Synne,* the contemporary evangelical genres I analyze in this book also communicate important meaning through their rhythmic dimensions. Evangelical dramaturgy is therefore a system of strategies aimed at situating users/readers/spectators within kinaesthetically constructed encounters that will promote specific embodied beliefs. By beginning my analysis with a medieval example, I wish to demonstrate that evangelical dramaturgy's attention to the sensual, rhythmic contact between user and devotional medium has roots in an affective religious tradition that worked, and oftentimes worked very well, for many people. Religious objects, spaces, events, and performances in the Middle Ages functioned effectively not only because they communicated doctrine in accessible ways and gave the laity greater agency over their piety, although both of these functions were certainly important, but also because they supplied believers with devotional encounters that fulfilled their needs, and in doing so, as I will argue, helped resolve their problems. By making things happen for the devotee, these genres, in turn, made belief. The same is true of evangelical performative media today.

Naturalized Phenomenology and Embodied Belief

Dramaturgy is a slippery term, but I am inspired by Cathy Turner and Synne K. Behrndt's multivalent definition that suggests dramaturgy not only is brought to a play and thus has an end point, but that dramaturgy continues to emerge and develop as the play changes with each performance encounter.

> It would seem that dramaturgy may not be inherent in the play text, but may be produced and shaped through the work of a particular company, reflecting the process and production conditions that impinge on it. It will also be shaped by the audience, by its responses and what it brings to the work. Dramaturgy is therefore produced through a dialogue between the play and a particular community of people in a particular time and place.[12]

This definition is especially relevant to my examination of evangelical media because it reminds us to consider not just the philosophy (or theology) that undergirds a form's creation and design, but also the principles that spectators bring to the artwork, as well as the ways that each live encounter between audience member and performance impacts the work. This definition encompasses the horizon of expectations that impinge upon a work during its creation, production, and ongoing reception.[13] Understood in this way, dramaturgy helps us recognize the many different elements that contribute to a religious mode of performance.

Moreover, Turner and Behrndt encourage us to expand the applications of this term beyond drama and theater:

> If "dramaturgy" is a word we use when we discuss structural, compositional and contextual principles of a work, and the ideas and narratives that drive these principles, it may have applications beyond drama or indeed, the theatre. . . . Dramaturgy can, in fact, be considered as a term for many kinds of "cultural assemblage."[14]

In this project I use the term *evangelical dramaturgy* to interrogate all kinds of genres, not strictly theater. Across these various evangelical cultural assemblages, I identify recurrent material, aesthetic, compositional, and experiential principles and ideologies, similarities that, I argue, reflect a shared dramaturgy.

The term dramaturgy also reminds us that the relationships between text/performance/audience are inherently unstable; evangelical dramaturgy's performative strategies are only attempts to orient the dynamics of that relationship in certain directions, but the results are never guaranteed. Consequently, while exploring how, where, when, and why each genre deploys evangelical dramaturgical strategies, and identifying certain consistencies across these examples, I will also note the productive tension between the doctrine or ideology each genre aims to promote and the individual's live experience of the form itself. Cognitive theory offers us valuable ways to examine this tension and, thus, to critically analyze how religious belief might shape each spectator's unique experience of a mode of performance.

As I noted in the Introduction, cognitive theory draws upon empirical evidence of bodily response to investigate perception and processes of meaning-making. Because cognitive theory and phenomenology share certain guiding concepts and foundational principles, scholars like Shaun Gallagher, Dan Zahavi, and Evan Thompson have integrated these two theoretical approaches in productive ways. Such work, sometimes called "naturalized phenomenology" or "neurophenomenology," proposes "that biology and phenomenology can stand in a mutually enlightening, explanatory relation."[15] These approaches maintain that "phenomenology needs to be able to understand and interpret its investigations in relation to those of biology and mind science."[16] Rather than universalizing claims about perception or meaning formation, naturalized phenomenology integrates empirical evidence from cognitive science into a phenomenological framework that acknowledges the body's unique role in forming conceptual knowledge.

Mark Johnson, in particular, has argued for a redefined aesthetics that blends cognitive science with traditional phenomenology "in order to provide an enriched view of human meaning-making."[17] Johnson's work is founded on the principle that "we are born into the world as creatures of the flesh, and it is through our bodily perceptions, movements, emotions, and feelings that meaning becomes possible and takes the form it does . . . What and how anything is meaningful to us is shaped by our specific form of incarnation."[18] In order to move away from a purely linguistic model of meaning construction, Johnson uses the term *embodied schema* to analyze "embodied patterns of meaningfully organized experience (such as structures of bodily movements and perceptual interactions)." Embodied schemata are unconscious maps that emerge as part of our meaningful interactions with things outside of us.[19] They are "that portion of the entire perceptual cycle which is internal to the perceiver, modifiable by experience, and somehow specific to what is being perceived."[20] As Johnson notes, embodied schemata "are not just templates for conceptualizing past experience" and constructing meaning from that experience, but they also constitute "*plans* for interacting with objects and persons. They give expectations and anticipations that influence our interactions with our environment" (original emphasis).[21] In short, an embodied schema is an internal, physical memory that may influence future activity and meaning creation. Concepts like this one allow us to investigate understanding as each individual's unique way of "being in a world."[22]

Naturalized phenomenology therefore provides us with tools for critically analyzing how we make meaning out of our individualized rhythmic encounters with events, objects, spaces, and other phenomena. As Tobin Nellhaus reminds us, communication practices have cognitive effects because they generate embodied schemata that establish epistemological and ontological assumptions.[23] Consequently, the embodied practices that are most closely connected to how we obtain knowledge of the world also impact how we subsequently develop knowledge.[24] Like all social groups, evangelical Christians use and deploy modes of communication that will serve their unique needs and priorities.[25] Each of the genres I study in this book represents a communication practice that utilizes a combination of "the visual, the body, objects, experience, and rituals," resources that, Stewart Hoover argues, "have long been repressed in the American (particularly the Protestant) context" but that have grown increasingly popular among today's evangelical Christians.[26] Consequently, the genres I analyze are not only reactions against a long-standing repression of the somatic and material within mainline U.S. Protestant devotion, but, as modes of knowledge acquisition, they also instantiate and reinforce a certain epistemology within users' bodies. I contend that evangelicals may seek out communication practices that engage the entire spectrum of their senses not only because, as Hoover notes, they "address hungers and needs not met by conventional religious practice,"[27] but also because these practices affirm evangelical beliefs about the legitimacy and efficacy of certain modes of knowledge acquisition. In particular, these genres reinforce the evangelical emphasis on immediate, personal experience as a trustworthy, even superior, source of religious knowledge.[28] A concept like "embodied schema" can help us analyze how evangelical dramaturgy's strategies work on and through the user's body to accomplish this goal.

Evangelical Dramaturgy: Popular Media, Resonance, and Commodification

I will spend the remainder of this chapter outlining the key methods and goals of evangelical dramaturgy. The first tactic is one that I have touched upon already: reappropriating "secular," familiar, and often popular cultural forms—such as paperback thrillers, museums, theme parks, and sports stadiums—for sacred purposes. As I noted in the Introduction, rather than shunning new media, evangelicals, and especially those in the United States, have repeatedly embraced such innovations as opportunities to create novel devotional vehicles. This strategy lowers the barriers to entry for new users by packaging theology in a nonthreatening, accessible form.

For example, in some respects the *Left Behind* book series is a modern-day equivalent of Mannyng's *Handlyng Synne*—a complicated theological system delivered to lay readers through a familiar, highly accessible, rhythmic program. This twelve-book series, written by Jerry B. Jenkins and Tim LaHaye, is based upon the End Times account described in the New Testament book of Revelation. The authors published the first volume in 1995, and the series has since sold over sixty-three million copies, a number that includes the *Left Behind* "Kids Series."[29] Each of the last six books in the adult series reached number one on the *New York Times* bestseller list.[30] In 2000 and 2002, Cloud Ten Pictures released film versions of the first two books, both starring Kirk Cameron. A third installation, coproduced with Sony Entertainment, appeared in 2005 and starred Cameron and Louis Gossett Jr. According to an October 2010 press release, Cloud Ten was planning a fourth installment to begin production in late 2011.[31] However, that film is currently on hold because "Cloud Ten has agreed to allow Dr. LaHaye the opportunity to make a *Left Behind* film. . . . If Dr. LaHaye does not go forward with his plans to produce a *Left Behind* movie, then Cloud Ten will resume development of the next *Left Behind* film."[32]

Before coauthoring the series, Jenkins was already an established writer with many Christian-themed books to his credit. In addition, he helped Reverend Billy Graham write his autobiography, *Just as I Am,* and he also owns the Christian Writers Guild, an organization that "aims to train tomorrow's professional Christian writers."[33] Although LaHaye has also written several books, publicity materials usually describe him as the theologian behind the *Left Behind* series. LaHaye is the founder and president of Tim LaHaye Ministries and the founder of the PreTrib Research Center.[34] The biblical interpretation offered by the *Left Behind* books is founded in pre-tribulation End Times theology. The series has even spawned "The Left Behind Prophecy Club," described online as "a website and newsletter to help you understand how current events may actually relate to End Times prophecy."[35]

Although not all evangelical Christians subscribe to a particular End Times narrative,[36] among those who do the theology typically falls into three main categories: pre-tribulationist, post-tribulationist, and pre-wrath.[37] All three represent complicated exegetical systems based upon biblical passages that include, but are not limited to, those in Revelation; as Timothy Beal notes, "each is armed with an arsenal of biblical proof texts and each accuses the other of twisting holy scriptures to serve their own wishful thinking."[38] A key difference between the three groups is when they believe the Rapture will occur in relation to the Tribulation. The Rapture is "the moment when all believers will rise to meet Christ in the air."[39] These true believers are taken up bodily to meet Christ, leaving behind all of their earthly possessions (clothes, jewelry, contact lenses, etc.). According to pre-tribulation theology, the Rapture will take place before the seven years of great tribulation. The Tribulation is a period when God's wrathful judgment is brought down upon those who remain on Earth. It is a time of false prophets, including the Antichrist, and of great calamity that is followed by Christ's Second Coming to Earth.[40] The *Left Behind* series begins at the Rapture and proceeds through the seven years of tribulation that follow. By borrowing familiar generic and material rhythms, the books communicate pre-trib theology in a way that is accessible to a wide readership. In this respect, the series provides a useful example of evangelical dramaturgy.

The books follow a group of people who are thrown together when they are "left behind" after the Rapture. The core group in the first book includes an airline pilot named Rayford, his daughter Chloe, a reporter named Buck, who was on Rayford's flight when the Rapture occurred, and Bruce, a pastor who was only "born again" in Christ after the Rapture. The first book slowly unpacks pre-trib theology as each of these survivors tries to make sense of what has happened. One by one, these characters also convert, with each given his or her own "born-again" scene. In every case, the decision to accept Christ as a personal Savior involves a great deal of personal reflection; rather than instantaneous conversions, these are thoughtful and emotional experiences involving individual choice and rigorous internal debate. Characters who have not yet converted resist believers' persuasive efforts, while those who have already accepted Christ struggle not to urge them too insistently, as Rayford's thoughts about Chloe illustrate:

> He wanted to tell Bruce to keep praying, that [Chloe] must still be thinking about things. Maybe the invasion of the house had made her feel vulnerable. Maybe she was getting the point that the world was much more dangerous now, that there were no guarantees, that her own time could be short. But Rayford also knew he could offend her, insult her, push her away if he used this situation to sic Bruce on her. She had enough information; he just had to let God work on her.[41]

Although the *Left Behind* series has a global scale, with the Antichrist figure gaining more and more international political control, the books communicate this larger End Times narrative by means of different personal journeys. The books repeatedly remind readers that what matters most during this worldwide crisis is each individual's eternal soul. Therefore, although believers know that conversion necessitates a personal and wholehearted decision, they also recognize that the stakes are high, which gives their circumstances a degree of conflict and urgency:

> The chaos would make peacemakers and smooth talkers only more attractive. And to people who didn't want to admit that God had been behind the disappearances, any other explanation would salve their consciences. There was no more time for polite conversation, for gentle persuasion. Rayford had to direct people to the Bible, to the prophetic portions.[42]

While many large-scale disasters occur throughout the books, ultimately the series builds a sense of urgency around every believer's fundamental obligation to bring others into the faith before it's too late.

The *Left Behind* books are successful at making the complicated pretribulation theology memorable and understandable for a number of reasons, many of them related to performative rhythms. The vernacular of the books is easy to follow, with a great deal of dialogue, short paragraphs, and simple sentence structures. There is also very little subtext; characters either say exactly how they feel or readers are given direct access to their inner monologues. For example, Chapter Eleven of Book One begins:

> Rayford was glad he could take Chloe out for a drive Saturday after having been cooped up with their grief. He was glad she had agreed to accompany him to the church.
>
> Chloe had been sleepy and quiet all day. She had mentioned the idea of dropping out of the university for a semester and taking some classes locally. Rayford liked it. He was thinking of her. Then he realized she was thinking of him, and he was touched.[43]

In addition, the books employ familiar tropes from the international espionage thriller genre, a choice that radically increases their accessibility. Car chases, plane crashes, spying, and various international locations are combined with cliff-hangers and a tremendous amount of foreshadowing. Moreover, the episodic structure and focus on several central characters, rather than on just one or two, keep the story moving quickly; most chapters change locale multiple times. In short, the books are page-turners, largely because these well-worn devices invite readers into a familiar rhythmic encounter they can immediately and easily engage. Once readers are attuned to these stylistic and structural rhythms, their bodies may absorb the authors' complicated theological messages more willingly.

The rhythmic quality also pertains to the books' material aesthetic. The physical experience readers have with the *Left Behind* books contributes to "affective literacy," what Mark Amsler defines as the "ways we develop emotional, somatic, activity-based relationships with texts as part of our reading experiences."[44] Affective literacy helps us recognize how the material page itself "is assimilated into the reading situation, the 'hinge of reading' linking reader and text," thereby displacing "literate ideology in performative practice, through the construction of interactive textualities, textuality beyond the page."[45] The books I read were paperback copies of approximately 5½ by 8¼ inches in size and published as higher-quality trade paperback editions, rather than as mass-market paperbacks. The cover designs are attractive and somewhat abstract without any overt religious iconography.

Moreover, in 2011 Tyndale House Publishers repackaged the books with a new look that even more strongly evokes the espionage thriller genre. As a March 2011 press release from Tyndale House explains:

> The fresh covers have a feeling of immediacy, as if the action of the plot is happening alongside today's headline news. With powerful graphics and

> bright orange spines, they are big, bold, and dramatic—both to reflect the urgency of the news and to stand out among today's best-selling suspense thrillers. "The new designs for the *Left Behind Series* imagine how TV networks would cover the end times as the sequence of events takes place," adds [senior marketing manager Cheryl] Kerwin. "We approached the imagery and composition with an eye for photojournalism rather than pure fictional drama. The result is a collection of covers as arresting as a breaking news bulletin."[46]

Affective literacy reminds us that such visual and material characteristics also generate rhythms that reverberate through the body, thereby impacting the performative reading experience and the embodied schema it produces. The sensual encounter between book and reader is a space in which meaning develops out of materiality.[47]

The recognizable narrative and generic devices that Jenkins and LaHaye employ certainly make the complex End Times theology intelligible for readers, but appropriating a familiar and accessible rhythmic experience may also encourage readers to engage the books with bodies open to that theology, thereby prompting the series' ideological messages to resonate within the user's body in comfortable and comforting ways. As Linda Kintz explains, because "children are raised to feel and experience their own sensuality, their own bodies, in very particular ways, and to look for and find others whose feelings, values, and identities are intimately familiar to them," familiarization often resonates through the body.[48] Resonance is, therefore, an intensification of passion that uses familiarization to link people together through feelings.[49] This is usually experienced so deeply that it is not only inarticulable, but also "readily available for displacement" onto other issues or ideas.[50] Presenting evangelical theology by means of a familiar rhythmic experience might provoke such displacement. The familiar international espionage thriller tropes produce a resonant emotional charge that readers might then displace onto the End Times narrative, thereby imbuing pre-trib theology with meaningfulness.

Left Behind illustrates how the resonance afforded by popular media supplies evangelical dramaturgy with an effective means of encouraging new usership, as it simultaneously fosters or strengthens religious feeling. In addition, some evangelical genres that borrow popular art forms also contain elements like vivid imagery, stunning lighting effects, or catchy, recognizable songs, embellishments that make the user's encounter with the familiar genre even more memorable by enhancing it sensually. Moreover, by cultivating a direct, physical, felt experience of God that reverberates through the user's body, such enhancements also help to generate embodied schemata that will reinforce evangelical epistemology.

Finally, appropriating popular media also allows evangelical dramaturgy to commodify these resonant devotional experiences. The *Left Behind* books, for instance, package theological experience into an accessible, transportable, and material form that consumers can easily purchase for themselves or others at relatively low cost through mainstream venues like Wal-Mart, Amazon.com, or Barnes and Noble. But the original books have also been repackaged into various (arguably, even more accessible) forms, including a children's book series, audio books, and films. All of these iterations serve as gateways to other materials on End Times themes, such as the products available for sale at the official *Left Behind* series website,[51] as well as to a larger community of readers who participate in chat rooms and reading groups devoted to the books.[52] Therefore, appropriating the popular international espionage thriller genre not only reconstitutes the book of Revelation's End Times theology into a democratic commodity that offers readers a user-friendly experience and understandable biblical exegesis, but, as a form of cultural capital, the series also gives readers access to other commodities and to meaningful conversations about current issues that are related—but are not exclusively confined—to *Left Behind.* The familiar genre is intended to serve as a point of access to other experiences so that, eventually, the *Left Behind* exegesis will resonate through many parts of the reader's everyday life and, thus, begin to "matter."[53]

Evangelical dramaturgy's commitment to commodification, while certainly mercenary to some degree, also reflects a sincere attempt to help believers (physically) carry devotional experiences into their daily lives. Although the kinaesthetic experiences offered by evangelical media trace themselves into the believer's embodied schema, merchandise like T-shirts, DVDs, and bumper stickers remind believers of that original live encounter, thereby stoking embodied belief and religious resolve in the days, weeks, and years thereafter.

"Religiously Real" Re-representations

The *Left Behind* books are compelling, in part, because they take the book of Revelation's End Times account, which is written in largely abstract, figurative, and allegorical language, and reshape it into a realistic story set in a modern-day context. As I argue above, readers can easily relate to the dense theological material because it is communicated through familiar tropes, modes, and sensualities, in particular, a straightforward realistic style. Realism is the artistic mode that evangelical dramaturgy most often employs. Yet, as I hope to demonstrate, the function and goal of realism here are different in significant ways from traditional European and U.S. realism. Rather than realistic representation, evangelical dramaturgy instead aims for realistic re-representations.

The re-representational realism that evangelical dramaturgy uses is grounded in incarnational theology. Incarnational theology, which developed in the later Middle Ages, is often associated with a devotional shift toward affective piety. As Sarah Beckwith explains, incarnational theology accomplished a number of things, among them sanctifying the human body, sanctioning material images, and endorsing certain forms of affective devotion:

> Christ's willingness to be incarnated, his embodiment, is crucial because it is only this condescension to the flesh which will allow other images to signify. . . . The material world becomes a text which may be interpreted, scrutinized, allegorized and investigated for the way it pointed to its exemplar and author: God. In this extraordinary renegotiation . . . there are new possibilities for the body as text and instrumental medium. . . . Part and parcel of this renegotiation of the role of the body in worship, was a new appreciation and re-evaluation of the role of experience, affectivity and emotion.[54]

Medieval genres that put the fleshy human body on display, like liturgical drama, were dependent upon, and simultaneously reinforced, incarnational theology's emphasis on the material world and the body's place within it. Consequently, such genres assumed a mode of performance that, as Donnalee Dox explains, hinged "on a notion of 'the real' that presumes the material world (including the human body) to be infused with spiritual meaning."[55] In such performances, the body does not merely signify; rather, because "belief in the Incarnation of God is inextricable to a mode of performance" for the believer-spectator, "performance allows the historical event to be re-experienced as a spiritual event through the bodies of the performers and spectators."[56] Theology does not merely inform the performance but actually creates theatrical theory and shapes dramaturgy.

The *Bordesholm Lament of the Virgin* (ca. 1476), a large-scale liturgical drama that is usually categorized as a medieval Passion play, illuminates this tradition. The text begins:

> Here begins the deeply devotional lament of the most Blessed Virgin Mary, with a very pitiful and devout music. The Blessed Virgin Mary delivers this lament together with four pious performers very devotedly on Good Friday before dinner, in the church in front of the choir on a slightly elevated place, or, when the weather is fine, outside the church. *This lament is not a play nor an entertainment, but the lamentation, wailing, and religious compassion of the glorious Virgin Mary.* Whenever it is done by good and pious people, it very much moves the people standing around to pious weeping and to compassion, both collectively and individually, in the same way as does a pious sermon on the suffering of our Lord Jesus Christ on Good Friday. (my emphasis)[57]

This opening rubric complicates the issue of representation. As Nils Holger Petersen argues, the phrase "The Blessed Virgin Mary delivers this lament," alongside the rejection of this event as performance (*ludus*),

> may be read to indicate that the ceremony is thought to bring the "original" lament of the Virgin Mary to the bystanders. This must, of course, necessarily happen in a spiritual way. What is established in such a way is seemingly thought of as more "real" than the "acting" which, clearly, cannot be denied to have to be done at some level.[58]

The rubric implies a knitting together of time and place, between the biblical/historical event and what the medieval spectators witness. Consequently, Petersen concludes that this performance aimed to bring "the congregation *in direct contact* with the lament of the Virgin Mary, a voice and an action needed for the salvation of the faithful" (my emphasis).[59] The material, physical presentation does not merely give spectators an idea, or even just a *feeling*, of what it might have been like to attend the original event. Instead, it puts them in direct physical contact with the original event in a way that transcends traditional notions of realism.

Dox recognizes a similar dynamic operating in Living Nativity tableaux, a genre that first emerged in the later Middle Ages and that continues into the present day: "The Nativity tableau both testifies to and for some believers *is* that reality. For a believer, performance can articulate a sense of the ineffable in material forms without displacing or deferring" (original emphasis).[60] The spectator's re-experience of this "authentic realism" is vital to the performance's religious meaning and efficacy; as Dox writes, "The immediacy of re-representing the presumed authenticity of traditional imagery generates emotive and spiritual responses, which function as testimony to the reality of the Nativity as a historical event and to the truth of the Incarnation of God in human form."[61] The event's dramaturgy can only be fully realized by means of the spectator's religious beliefs.

Evangelicalism's emphasis on the born-again experience, coupled with its crucicentric theology, ground it in many of the same ideas inherent to medieval incarnational theology.[62] It is therefore no surprise that evangelical performative media function through a theology of realness very similar to what Dox identifies within medieval liturgical dramas and Living Nativities. Like those genres, the evangelical forms I analyze oblige us to reconsider relationships between mind and body, secular and sacred, sign and signifier, spirit and matter, as well as past, present, and future; as Dox cautions, "What might appear to be theatrical realism, realistic representation, or mimesis is more complicated."[63] Contemporary Passion plays or Holy Land recreations challenge us to, as Timothy Beal says, understand "'real' in a sense very different from what we mean by empirically or objectively real. Real, rather, in the sense of being religiously real, an experience of ultimate reality. Real in the sense that one feels as though one has become a part of it. As though one has lost oneself in it."[64] One of evangelical dramaturgy's main goals is to generate this kind of "religiously real" re-representational encounter.

Evangelical dramaturgy accomplishes this is by using devices that urge spectators to oscillate between "presence" and "representation." Erika Fischer-Lichte argues that rather than being oppositional concepts, presence and representation are, in fact, processes of embodiment that differ as a result of perception. Dramaturgical systems usually encourage spectators to employ one mode of perception over another in order to emphasize either presence or representation; however, evangelical dramaturgy's goals require spectators to perceive (and experience) presence and representation simultaneously. Religiously real re-experiences aim to give incarnational theology an accessible, tangible material form, while also providing believers with the experience of ultimate reality that Beal describes.[65] Re-representational performances must, therefore, keep spectators in a state of perceptual flux or, as Fischer-Lichte describes it, "suspended between two orders of perception, caught in a state of 'betwixt and between.'"[66] By accentuating the sensual and material aspects of the performative encounter, evangelical dramaturgy seeks to prompt this kind of "perceptual multistability" in order to generate re-representations.[67]

For a re-representation to function effectively, the materiality of the sign cannot disappear but must remain present in the user's frame. Hoover's analysis of the cross at Willow Creek Community Church, a megachurch outside of Chicago that I discuss at length in Chapter Six, illustrates this point. According to Hoover, the cross does not "disappear by referring to some external idea of atonement," but instead it materially represents "atonement as a physical object in space and time. . . . The physical manipulation of the cross, its availability for use in a very concrete sense and moment, makes manifest a transcendent meaning."[68] Likewise, evangelical dramaturgy also aspires to keep the sign within the frame as a concrete material presence; by focusing on the rhythmic elements of a genre, evangelical dramaturgy tries to situate the physical encounter between object/event/space and believer as central to religious meaning-making. In doing so, the re-representation reinforces evangelical theology, in particular the notion of direct access to an incarnate divine presence.

Manipulating time and space can also trigger perceptual multistability. Although many of the forms I analyze reflect (or at least espouse) a meticulous attention to historically accurate details, historical accuracy is not, in fact, their primary goal. Instead, anachronism is a prevailing strategy within evangelical dramaturgy. In this respect, the genres I study are related to the theatrical reenactments, specifically Civil War reenactments, that Rebecca Schneider analyzes. Schneider identifies "the syncopated time of reenactment, where *then* and *now* punctuate each other," as offering participants—both re-enactors and observer-bystanders—the possibility to "*touch the actual past*" (original emphasis).[69] Anachronism, which Schneider argues "is at least a two-way street, with possibly more counter-directions than two," is therefore inherent within such reenactment events.[70] Yet while she identifies the "tangled temporalities and crisscrossed geographies" of reenactments as generative sites for meaning-making, she also contends that they have the "capacity to flummox those faith-keepers who hold that the present is fleeting and entirely self-identical, or who hold that the movement from the present to the future is never by way of the past, or who believe firmly in absolute disappearance and loss of the past as well as the impossibility of its recurrence."[71] Significantly, this kind of belief in a fixed, linear notion of time is not consonant with the worldview held by many evangelicals.

As Vincent Crapanzano's work demonstrates, an approach to time that is "at once progressive and retrogressive, though never repetitive in the usual sense of the word," in which time "cycles in backward movement forward to its own end," is familiar to (and resonates with) many evangelical Christians.[72] Consequently, as I will demonstrate, rather than hindering evangelical dramaturgy's goals, anachronistic reenactment is an important strategy; many evangelical media aim to collapse time and space in order to generate re-representational encounters that will allow users to get in (physical, material) touch with a past, present, and future simultaneously. Here again, dramaturgy explicitly reinforces evangelical epistemology by privileging direct personal lived experience, over a standard, prescribed narrative, as a reliable source of religious knowledge.

Holy Land Experience (HLE) in Orlando, Florida, illustrates this dramaturgical strategy particularly well. Visitors to HLE see a variety of live shows, attend historical presentations, and visit exhibitions, all of which are situated within a fifteen-acre park designed to replicate Jerusalem from approximately 1450 BCE to 66 CE. HLE allows each guest to construct his or her own spatial journey and experience during a visit. As Beal explains, "there is no guided tour through a biblical narrative space. In fact, there is no single, coherent narrative space. The place reads like a collection of biblical passages or scenes, presented in no particular sequential order, so that each can be experienced independently of the others."[73] Upon entering HLE, visitors receive an 8½ by 14 inch paper that displays a map of the park at the top and a color-coded schedule of shows and presentations at the bottom. A few key events happen only once a day, but most of the presentations and performances occur several times daily. Therefore a visitor might choose to see Jesus crucified in the "Behold the Lamb" Passion drama before venturing into the "Last Supper Communion" performance, then head over to the Celebrate America musical performance, stop for a hot dog and soda at Simeon's Corner, follow this with a trip to the Empty Tomb at Calvary and the fifty-five-minute tour of the Scriptorium, before ending at the Wilderness Tabernacle. The theme park is a visitor-curated collage of encounters that fuse the biblical past, twenty-first-century present, and apocalyptic future into a concrete, lived, and highly personalized experience for each visitor.

Many of the performances at the park also support this goal. As I will discuss in the next chapter, during HLE's "Last Supper Communion" performance a single dramaturgical choice—an actor playing Jesus enters the room—suddenly transforms the event into the kind of religiously real re-experience I have described. Moreover, this performance takes place in a reconstruction of the Upper Room where the biblical Last Supper is believed to have taken place. Yet, rather than appearing as it might have in first-century Jerusalem, signs posted outside the room explain that it was designed to replicate "the Gothic structure which was built by the European Crusaders in the early 14th century and still stands today." Therefore, while spectators stand in a Gothic-styled space, complete with pillars, arches, and stained-glass windows, "Jesus" speaks to them as if they were present at the original, first-century biblical event. In addition, visitors receive bread and grape juice to consume when Jesus speaks the words of institution, and, after this ritual, Jesus walks around the room laying his hands on each spectator as the audience sings a popular hymn. These sensual elements, which reinforce the visitor's moment-to-moment physical presence at the event, suspend spectators between presence and representation in order to prompt a re-representational re-experience.

Notably, "Last Supper Communion" reflects more than typical theme park anachronism, and, ultimately, its devotional efficacy is dependent upon a particular religious mode of performance. As Beal explains, "The retellings and reenactments performed at the Holy Land Experience are forms of apocalyptic expectation. Here one is meant to experience the past in order to anticipate the future."[74] In subsequent chapters I explore how venues like HLE and other Holy Land recreations use sensual devices to keep visitors looking forward and backward, even as they simultaneously remain grounded physically in the present moment.

Affective Forces and Intimate Scripts

Spectators' responses during "Last Supper Communion"—crying, shouting "Halleluiah," responding to the actor's touch by saying "Thank you, Jesus"—reveal the potential affective power of a re-representational encounter. Recent theoretical work has defined affect in ways that put it into productive dialogue with both cognitive theories of embodied knowledge and with Simon Shepherd's theory of performance rhythms. Melissa Gregg and Gregory J. Seigworth argue that "affect is in many ways synonymous with *force* or *forces of encounter*" and should be understood "as a gradient of bodily capacity . . . that rises and falls not only along various rhythms and modalities of encounter but also through the troughs and sieves of sensation and sensibility" (original emphasis).[75] Evangelical dramaturgy manipulates performative rhythms in order to manage affect, to, in effect, direct "those intensities that pass body to body . . . those resonances that circulate about, between, and sometimes stick to bodies and worlds."[76] In other words, the strategies evangelical dramaturgy employs serve as forces designed to direct people toward/into certain emotional responses and ideologies. For example, as I have suggested, this dramaturgical system recognizes anachronism not simply as a narrative or structural device in the conventional sense but as an affective force that moves a spectator toward or away from certain religious beliefs.[77] I would therefore argue that, like Gregg and Seigworth, those who employ evangelical dramaturgy understand affect as something that can be strategically deployed to "drive us toward movement, toward thought and extension, that can likewise suspend us (as if in neutral) across a barely registering accretion of force-relations, or that can even leave us overwhelmed by the world's apparent intractability."[78]

It is important to mention that many theorists currently writing on affect distinguish between affect and emotion. However, as Ruth Leys discusses in her excellent critique of the "turn to affect, particularly the turn to the neurosciences of emotion," much of this work proposes "that affect is independent of signification and meaning."[79] Leys cautions us against this model for a number of reasons, one of which is that it effectively reinforces certain binaries, including the mind/body dichotomy.[80] I agree with Leys and, thus, will employ a neurophenomenological approach to affect that, I believe, allows for a distinction between affect and emotion that does not empty the former of meaning. I see this as especially important when studying affective piety, a devotional system in which affective forces carry ideological content.

I am therefore compelled by Sianne Ngai's work, which Leys also cites. According to Ngai,

> the difference between affect and emotion is taken as a modal difference of intensity or degree, rather than a formal difference of quality or kind. My assumption is that affects are *less* formed and structured than emotions, but not lacking form or structure altogether; *less* "sociolinguistically fixed," but by no means code-free or meaningless; *less* "organized in response to our interpretations of situations," but by no means entirely devoid of organization

> or diagnostic powers. . . . What the switch from formal to modal difference enables is an analysis of the *transitions* from one pole to the other: the passages whereby affects acquire the semantic density and narrative complexity of emotions, and emotions conversely denature into affects. (original emphasis)[81]

She also writes, "Rather than also trying to dissolve this subjective/objective problematic by creating two distinct categories of feeling," her work "aims to preserve it for its aesthetic productivity."[82] Ngai captures the elasticity of affect; it is not without meaning, but the meaning it carries is—as she says—less "fixed" and, therefore, perhaps more potential than certain. Therefore, it can be manipulated in different ways and for different purposes than emotion. Consequently, although I will continue to describe affect as a force or intensity, I am not suggesting that it is unstructured or meaningless.

Genres like Holy Land Experience actually give users the freedom to curate the order of events and, thus, to personalize their rhythmic encounter. Ultimately, such forms allow visitors to generate their own "affective scripts." Anna Gibbs explains that the "process of translation between different sensory modalities is what initially enables experience to be ordered into familiar patterns, including the formation of affective scripts."[83] Although these scripts "operate largely outside of awareness," they "form an experiential matrix for ongoing affective responses to and constructions of the world."[84] Gibbs's notion of scripts presses embodied schemata into the affective realm, a productive shift that returns us to the late medieval "intimate scripts" that Sarah McNamer believes reveal "a performative model of affect."[85] I contend that evangelical dramaturgy functions through a similar model.

McNamer proposes that the compassion cultivated by medieval texts on the Passion "could exert forms of cognitive pressure, provoking new ways of thinking."[86] Significantly, some of these texts utilize rhythmic strategies to engender affective meditation. For instance, McNamer suggests that one mid-thirteenth-century text "harnesses the power of the native alliterative style to build a driving rhythm that has profound somatic effects. . . . This stirring up of passion would have facilitated an immediacy of experience that was fully of the body as well as of the heart and mind."[87] As Gregg and Seigworth might say, such devices function as affective forces intended to drive the reader toward compassion.

However, McNamer is concerned not only with how these affective texts generate compassion but also with what problems this emotional production was meant to resolve—in other words, she examines the cultural work of affective piety. She argues that some of the earliest affective texts on the Passion were designed for religious women and that the compassion they generated was intended to help these women verify their status as true brides of Christ, both to themselves and to "the ultimate authority, the one whose judgment really mattered: Christ himself."[88] Because the rewards of a spiritual marriage with Christ were material—"eluding designing kin and zealous suitors and obtaining a degree of power over their earthly existence"—as well as eternal, it was important to distinguish between "true" and "false" brides.[89] McNamer interprets these affective texts on the Passion as offering one solution to this issue of proof.

By engendering compassionate devotion, these affective texts helped medieval women verify their commitment to God, with the women's "willingness to participate affectively in Christ's sufferings" serving as "proof of their worthiness to be accepted as a true bride."[90] McNamer proposes that, in this model, "feeling" earns "the reader the name of spouse" with affective prayer becoming a practice that enables "an ostensible spouse to become a true one."[91] Furthermore, because the promises of heavenly reward required constant striving and continual commitment, and consummation of spiritual marriage could only occur upon death, the performative iteration that these texts offered became important tools within the woman's "lifelong process of marriage-making."[92] The devotional text therefore provided these medieval women with an intimate script—an affective force that pushed the devotee toward and into a compassionate meditative experience that could verify her eternal salvic state, not simply through her external performance of the text but, more significantly, through its ability to generate intense internal emotion.

I see valuable connections between these tactics and goals of medieval affective devotion and the devotional practices and concerns of today's evangelical Christians. The state of being saved is critical to evangelicalism; salvation is what separates believers and nonbelievers both in earthly life and for all eternity. However, as Amy Johnson Frykholm notes, salvation

> has no necessary tangible form. Salvation, in the evangelical imagination, often "happens" at a particular moment in time. It involves an act of going forward at a church service to "accept Christ" or the recitation of a formulaic prayer, often called the "sinner's prayer." At this moment, many evangelicals believe, an invisible transformation takes place. The "sinner" is "born again"

> to new life in Christ and her salvation is assured. On the one hand, this moment is so crucial in evangelical belief that nothing can ever transform it. . . . On the other hand, this moment must be maintained through prayer, Bible study, and interaction with other believers.[93]

Therefore, although there is usually an act that marks this spiritual transformation—as was also true of medieval nuns who participated in rites of consecration that looked very similar to contemporary wedding ceremonies—after this initial ritual activity, the evangelical's internal state of salvation, like the spiritual state of the true bride, remains elusive.[94] Moreover, Frykholm explains that as believers get further from this original moment of conversion, "doubts about salvation creep in."[95]

Apocalyptic theology, especially as it is presented in media like the *Left Behind* books, fuels this salvation anxiety. For example, in the *Left Behind* series, Pastor Bruce is not raptured; this religious leader's public displays of faith, which fooled his congregation, family, and, to some degree, even himself, were not, in fact, evidence of a "true" belief in Christ. Pastor Bruce explains his story to Rayford and Chloe at great length. This is an excerpt from his cautionary tale:

> I was raised in the church. My parents and brothers and sisters were all Christians. I loved church. It was my life, my culture. I thought I believed everything there was to believe in the Bible. The Bible says that if you believe in Christ you have eternal life, so I assumed I was covered. I especially liked the parts about God being forgiving. I was a sinner, and I never changed. . . . I thought I had a great life. I even went to Bible college. In church and at school, I said the right things and prayed in public and even encouraged people in their Christian lives. . . . Down deep, way down deep, I knew better. I knew it was too good to be true. I knew that true Christians were known by what their lives produced and that I was producing nothing. But I comforted myself that there were worse people around who called themselves Christians. . . . I see now, of course, that God *is* a sin-forgiving God, because we're human and we need that. But we are to receive his gift, abide in Christ, and allow him to live through us.[96]

Pastor Bruce was raised in the church, attended a Bible college, and became a pastor. He appeared to be a model Christian, reading the Bible with his congregants, visiting people in the hospital, and helping to lead people to faith in Christ; the grand majority of his congregants were, in fact, raptured. However, these external actions did not accurately reflect his internal salvic state. It is only after God's final judgment begins, and he is left behind, that Pastor Bruce truly recognizes his lack of sincere faith in Christ and is "born again."

Although actions like leading a moral life or witnessing to others are important to evangelicals, they are not decisive evidence of salvation; as Frykholm explains, "'Being saved' is a state of grace that cannot be confirmed by action; the most inauthentic person can pretend to be a Christian, and one might never know. Likewise, one's own authenticity can be in doubt."[97] Self-verification therefore requires something more intense than external deeds and actions. Accordingly, many evangelicals search for ways to rededicate their lives to God over and over again in order "to keep that spiritual fervor alive. Because the uncertainty of salvation can only be known 'down deep, way down deep.'"[98] As a religion of the heart, it is no surprise that evangelicals would turn to affective devotional practices as part of these efforts.

I contend that, like medieval religious women, many evangelical believers today are seeking ways to verify and demonstrate the true sincerity of their faith to God and to themselves. This is not an incidental need, but one upon which the believer's eternal soul depends, and evangelical dramaturgy supplies intimate scripts that will fulfill it. As with the texts that McNamer studies, the evangelical genres I analyze are designed to cultivate powerful feelings that will resonate through the believer's body and thus serve as "felt" verification of the devotee's true inner faith. As Andy Lavender writes, "The functionality of staged elements lies in the way they impact upon a spectator. This impact is likely to be in relation to meaning-effects—but it may also have a *felt* charge that structures our experience of the event."[99] Through the tactics I have described—borrowing familiar and accessible media forms, supplying a physical commodity that can extend the experience beyond the original encounter, employing anachronism in order to construct live re-representations—evangelical dramaturgy generates religiously real re-experiences that will trace felt patterns of personal salvation into the believer's embodied schema.

Evangelical Dramaturgy as Engaged Orthodoxy

The popularity of the performative genres I study suggests that evangelical dramaturgy's strategies effectively respond to the devotional longings of many contemporary evangelical Christians, longings that are, in part, a result of the modern condition. Christian Smith's work has productively complicated assumptions about the relationship between modernity and religion, especially with respect to American evangelicalism. He maintains "that religion not only survives modernity, but that in important ways modernity itself actually *promotes* strong religion . . . [and] the formation of strong religious subcultures" (original emphasis).[100] Smith's sociological study of American evangelicalism proposes many reasons for this. Among these is the fact that although

> modernity maximizes material abundance and individual autonomy . . . it affords insufficient insight into the rightful purpose and meaning of material things and provides little direction regarding what people should actually do with their freedom. The modern public realm, the system-world . . . simply lacks the force of normative direction that human beings appear to need and want.[101]

As a result, modernity creates "social conditions which intensify the kinds of felt needs and desires that religion is especially well-positioned to satisfy."[102] I would argue that religious leaders, organizations, institutions, and individuals use evangelical dramaturgy to satisfy these same felt needs and desires; this dramaturgical system aims to create resonant, religiously real re-experiences that will supply believers with a felt sense of direction and certainty, but without eliminating the personal freedom and individuality that are essential components of evangelicalism. This is precisely why these genres "matter" to believers, because, as I noted in the Introduction, "mattering" not only provides mental stability, but also stability through the heart and body.

By using tactics that work on and through the spectator/visitor/user's physical body, this dramaturgy, in theory, reinforces evangelical theology's emphasis on individual experience as a privileged source of knowledge. Moreover, some evangelical forms even market personal choice as an ideological principle. As I will discuss in Chapter Five, the first section of the Creation Museum's "Museum Experience Walk" is structured around the idea that creationists and Darwinists both begin with the same evidence, but simply interpret it differently. This difference is determined by what "starting point" a person chooses—human reason or God's Word. Moreover, the museum depicts creationists as open-minded and inquisitive critical thinkers, as opposed to evolutionary Darwinists, who rashly and blindly follow a theory. In Chapter Five, I demonstrate how sensual features of the Creation Museum exhibits (such as sounds, lighting, colors, textures, and shapes) incorporate this ideology into the pattern of experience—the embodied schema—that the museum journey maps within the visitor. In this case, the Creation Museum uses evangelical dramaturgy in order to help visitors resolve any tension between personal freedom and biblical infallibility. The museum trip matters to the creationist visitor, in part, because it generates an intimate, affective script that supplies a felt solution.

The emphasis on personal choice not only complements the evangelical tenet of conversionism, since the "born-again" experience necessitates an independently motivated and wholehearted personal acceptance of Christ as the only means of salvation, but it also bolsters a certain image of modern American identity.[103] As Smith writes,

> For moderns—perhaps especially modern Americans—the ultimate criteria of identity and lifestyle validity is individual choice. It is by choosing a product, a mate, a lifestyle, or an identity that one makes it one's very own, personal, special, and meaningful—not "merely" something one inherits or assumes. In the value-epistemology of modern American culture, to believe, to want, or to do something simply because that is what one's parents believe, or what one's friends want, or what everybody else does is considered inferior and unauthentic. . . . And even if (as is often the case) one chooses what one was already inheriting or assuming, it is only through the observance of individual choice—whether actual or ritualized—that it becomes "real" and personally meaningful.[104]

Evangelical dramaturgy appreciates the rhythmic point of contact between user and medium as a productive space for realizing religious choices and, thereby, making them meaningful. In this way, the embodied schemata generated by evangelical genres establish epistemological assumptions that support both theology, as well as a specific interpretation of American identity. Moreover, in some cases, the religiously real re-experience purposefully conflates the two by situating a "true" evangelical Christian faith as essential to a bona fide American identity. As I will demonstrate in Chapter Four, this is especially the case with the Sacred Projects in Eureka Springs. Constructing an embodied, felt blend of evangelical faith and national identity is therefore an important way that some of these media address the social conditions and uncertainties of modern American life.

Finally, even as evangelical dramaturgy works to confirm and bolster the faith of existing believers, it also appropriates the resonant rhythms of popular culture in order to invite new users into an otherwise unfamiliar belief system. Borrowing familiar genres therefore helps dissolve the already porous boundaries between secular and sacred, or church and state. Moreover, these genres also give evangelical Christianity a presence within the public arena that challenges binaries like private/public and faith/politics. In my brief Coda, I expand upon this point as I suggest how certain tactics of evangelical dramaturgy are employed in explicitly political contexts. Accordingly, I interpret evangelical dramaturgy as representing the kind of outwardly directed engaged orthodoxy that has been an important principle within many evangelical denominations since the 1940s.[105]

In the next five chapters, I analyze different performances, events, and venues in order to demonstrate more specifically how evangelical dramaturgy embeds feelings of direction, stability, and reassurance within the believer-user's body and, as a result, fosters specific embodied beliefs. Phillip Zarrilli argues that "an actor's performance score is a structure that is available to the actor as a certain range of possibilities based on the aesthetic logic of a particular dramaturgy."[106] Therefore, I will begin by examining the "Last Supper Communion" performance at HLE in order to consider how the goals of evangelical dramaturgy might translate into an acting theory.

2
Energetic Enactments of Jesus

As with all dramaturgical systems, evangelical dramaturgy's tactics promote certain ways of seeing or experiencing the world. In the previous chapter, I argued that evangelical dramaturgy shapes the rhythmic points of contact between medium and user in order to create resonant and commodifiable experiences. Those experiences orient the believer-user's religious self-discovery through certain conceptualizations of representation and religious experience, affective piety, and engaged orthodoxy. In this chapter I focus on the specific point of contact between actor and spectator. Borrowing concepts from Phillip Zarrilli's psychophysical acting theory,[1] I will suggest that actors in certain evangelical performances use dramaturgical strategies designed to cultivate an "energetic" performer-audience dynamic that will foster "religiously real" re-experiences for spectators. To demonstrate this, I analyze "Last Supper Communion," the performance event at Holy Land Experience (HLE) that I described briefly at the end of Chapter One.

Holy Land Re-Experience

Holy Land Experience promises visitors an inspiring, educational, theatrical, and historical multisensory encounter "that takes you 7000 miles away and 2000 years back in time to the land of the Bible." The park's website claims, "Its combination of sights, sounds, and tastes will stimulate your senses and blend together to create a spectacular new experience."[2] ITEC, the theme park design company that worked on HLE, "thoroughly researched every detail of biblical Jerusalem and its environs" as part of their "commitment to accuracy."[3] Yet, as the ITEC project description explains, because of the vast time span that the park tries to represent, the designers had to make very specific choices about what to include in order to make HLE understandable for guests:

> Every ITEC project begins with the crafting of a story that forms the heart of the guest experience and guides the designers in the creative development process. With The Holy Land Experience, where the "story" is the entire Bible, ITEC's designers carefully selected personalities, places and events that best represent key biblical ideas identified by the client. The larger story was thus broken down into separate museum-quality experiences, each able to stand alone. Collectively, however, they provide guests with a deeper, more thorough understanding of the Bible as a whole.[4]

This approach alone suggests compatibility between the theme park genre and evangelical dramaturgy. Both use material, spatial, and performative means to engage visitors in lived experiences that will engender meaningful knowledge.

The Christian missionary organization Zion's Hope opened HLE in February 2001. The motivating force behind the $16 million project was Marv Rosenthal, founding president and executive director of Zion's Hope. Rosenthal was raised in a conservative Jewish household but converted to Christianity as a teenager and later became an ordained Baptist minister. Conversion, particularly of Jews, is the central mission of Zion's Hope:

> The Purpose of Zion's Hope is a simple one, yet also bold, direct, and far-reaching. Zion's Hope seeks to graciously proclaim to the Jewish people their need for personal salvation through Jesus the Messiah and to proclaim the gospel of the Lord Jesus Christ to all men regardless of race, religion, gender, education, or national origin. Accordingly, Zion's Hope seeks to educate the Bible-believing Church concerning the place of Israel in both history and prophecy and assist it in fulfilling its God-given obligation to rightfully include the Jewish people in its program for world evangelism.

Zion's Hope is also committed to using the latest resources and media forms to achieve these goals:

> Our call is to communicate the unchanging message of saving grace through faith in Christ alone. But while our message is fixed, our methods of communicating that message are flexible. We continually strive to employ new and innovative ways of sharing the truth of God's Word with a world that is desperately searching for real answers.[5]

In many respects, Holy Land Experience represents the perfect manifestation of that philosophy.

Almost 30,000 people visited HLE in its first year of operation. However, in subsequent years dwindling numbers led to financial problems until, in 2005, HLE and Zion's Hope parted ways.[6] Tom Powell was named president of the park, and in 2007 he brokered a merger between HLE and Trinity Broadcasting Network (TBN), the largest religious broadcasting network in the world.[7] A 2007 TBN press release asserted that the network viewed this acquisition as bringing "unprecedented synergy," since "both ministries are about changing and effecting people's lives."[8] TBN made certain immediate improvements to the park, such as upgrading the shows and facilities, and these changes helped HLE return to profitability; in 2008, the park was hosting between 1,500 and 2,500 visitors daily.[9]

Significantly, after TBN took complete control over HLE they modified the park's evangelizing goals. In particular, as Joan Branham reports, TBN "softened the language that once targeted Jews."[10] Currently, the park's lengthy mission statement begins:

> The Mission and Purpose of the Holy Land Experience is to demonstrate the "greatest commandments" of our Lord Jesus Christ as set forth in Matthew 22:37–39, "To love the Lord your God with all your heart and with all your soul and with all your mind" and "To love your neighbor as yourself" and to fulfill the Great Commission of Jesus Christ as set forth in Matthew 28: 19, "Therefore go and make disciples of all nations, baptizing them in the name of the Father and the Son and the Holy Spirit, and teaching them to obey everything I have commanded you." HLE accomplishes its mission and purpose in the following manner:
>
> HLE is a house of worship. As a Christian Church, HLE is a gathering place for believers to experience and share in worship, ministry, preaching and teaching in a non-denominational setting. All are welcome, regardless of who they are, where they come from or how they believe.[11]

Other changes within the park itself also reinforced this shift. For instance, the half-scale replica of the first-century Jewish Temple, which serves as the park's visual and material centerpiece, was previously called the Temple of the Great King; it is now simply the Great Temple.[12] Jewish history remains a critical component of Holy Land Experience, but rather than pointedly using it to convert Jews to Christ, this element now helps to furnish Christian believers with a particular kind of religiously real re-experience.

HLE markets itself as offering visitors sensual encounters with biblical history. The park's publicity materials and website repeatedly describe Holy Land Experience as a "living" museum where visitors are "immersed in ancient Jerusalem." On the "About the Experience" web page, a section entitled "It's Inspirational" reads,

> Imagine entering an exact replica of the Garden Tomb where the body of the Lord Jesus Christ was buried. In reverence, you approach the tomb where He emerged victorious over death. Then at the grand entrance to the Temple Plaza, walk under a massive archway and behold the gleaming white stone plaza surrounding you with its thirty Roman columns crowned with gold capitals. All this grandeur majestically frames the imposing Great Temple, the place held in highest reverence among the Jewish people. It is a truly breathtaking representation of the Temple that once stood on hallowed Mount Moriah in 1st century Jerusalem.[13]

Marketing language such as this—which begins with the verb *imagine,* but then shifts to verbs like *approach* and *walk*—promises Christian visitors a physical pilgrimage more ideal and satisfying than they would experience if they traveled to the actual Holy Land as it exists today.

In this respect, as Ronald Lukens-Bull and Mark Fafard note, HLE functions as a substitutional pilgrimage site akin to those that first became popular in the Middle Ages when Muslims controlled Jerusalem, such as the "Road to Jerusalem" labyrinth walk in Chartres Cathedral that was built circa 1200. In effect, HLE "represents an ancient Jerusalem that not only acts as an alternative to visiting Israel, but also symbolizes a Jerusalem in a pure, true form."[14] This is exactly the kind of re-representation that Donnalee Dox describes and that evangelical dramaturgy seeks to create. However, for certain visitors, this representation not only looks backward, but also forward. For instance, unlike pilgrims in the real Holy Land, visitors to HLE see the Holy Jewish Temple occupying the Temple Mount, not the Dome of the Rock Muslim shrine that actually stands there today. As Timothy Beal explains, for those visitors who subscribe to pre-wrath or pre-trib theology, the restoration of the Jewish Temple is considered "the necessary precursor to and sure sign of the immanent Second Coming" and it therefore plays a significant role in "the fulfillment of God's salvation history."[15] Consequently, while the Temple does point backward to biblical times, it may situate certain evangelical visitors in the past, present, and future simultaneously, generating the kind of re-experience at the heart of evangelical dramaturgy.[16]

Park employees also reinforce this re-experience. As is typical of most theme parks, staff dressed in period costumes roam around HLE and interact with visitors as if "in character." Male Israelite characters have real beards and greet visitors with "Shalom," while glaring Roman centurions appear unapproachable and stern. As with actors on stage, the words, gestures, and costumes of these characters generate rhythms that support the park's overall re-representational goals. Again, this is true of theme parks generally. Yet, the one-on-one interactions between characters and visitors at HLE reveal strategies and goals specific to evangelical dramaturgy. For instance, I saw an actor, who was still "in character" as one of the disciples, asking a group of preteen visitors if they each had their own copy of the Bible and, specifically, a copy they could "read and actually understand." After talking with them about the Bible for a few minutes, he encouraged them to read it daily and then directed the group to one of the bookstores in the park where they could purchase a young adult Bible.

I identify many elements of evangelical dramaturgy shaping this exchange: past and present converging as this disciple, whom most visitors have just seen performing in HLE's Passion play, remains in character but talks about the Christian Bible (Old and New Testaments); the actor's performance as a biblical character, which makes the encounter between the actor/character and spectator into a re-experience that "matters"; the commitment to engaged orthodoxy that guides this meaningful and (what I interpreted as) sincere conversation about the importance of owning a Bible written in comprehensible language and reading it daily; and the opportunity (and encouragement) to commodify this encounter by purchasing a Bible in the "Holy Land" that will subsequently remind the owner of this visit and perhaps also of this very conversation. This exchange, like many actor-spectator interactions at HLE, constitutes a complicated performative encounter that aims to suspend visitors perceptually between presence and representation. The efficacy of this point of contact therefore relies upon an acting style that can facilitate this perceptual suspension and thus invite visitors into resonant and meaningful religiously real re-experiences.

Attendance before God

In his work on the performance sensorium, Stephen di Benedetto maintains,

> We do not only attend the event, we are also attendant to the event and participate in it. We become actors responding within the constraints of an artistically mediated structure designed to trigger behavior or sensorial memory. . . . Artists who harness more than our eyes and ears encourage us to wake up, to be alert to the world around us, and to interact actively with the objects and creatures around us. It is an invitation to live, to feel, and to be a part of a larger community.[17]

HLE is ultimately a kinaesthetic ministry, and therefore *attendant* is a particularly accurate word to use when describing park visitors. Many people who visit—or attend—Holy Land Experience are evangelical Protestant Christians who select this destination for its specific religious message. According to Beal, the majority of visitors are conservative Protestants, and the park provides "a popular alternative to the theme parks operated by Disney, which the Southern Baptists, Assemblies of God, and other conservative Christian groups have boycotted on account of its support of 'Gay Day' and its progressive partner benefits for gay employees."[18] A number of church groups were visiting the park on the weekend of my trip, and many of them wore matching T-shirts that indicated their denominational affiliation; Baptist and Assemblies of God groups comprised the vast majority of those I noticed. On the days I visited, I would estimate that close to half of park visitors were African Americans, with Caucasians representing the next largest racial demographic. Latinos/Latinas were a close third.[19]

Assemblies of God currently constitutes the largest Pentecostal denomination in North America.[20] As Randall Balmer explains, Pentecostalism "coalesced as a movement" in the early twentieth century, and "Pentecostal worship today is characterized by ecstasy and the familiar posture of upraised arms, a gesture of openness to the Holy Spirit. Pentecostals generally believe in the gifts of the Holy Spirit, including divine healing, in addition to speaking in tongues."[21] As I will suggest later, those particular religious beliefs and practices may prepare these visitors to be more open to the specific kind of actor-audience interaction that HLE constructs.

Testimonials on the park's website suggest that for some visitors a trip to HLE not only "wakes up" their faith but also provides them with an evangelizing tool that they can use to help others deepen their own beliefs:

> In January, myself and thirty-three women from our church drove about an hour to your facility. We want to take this opportunity to tell you what a magnificent experience we had. The presence of the Lord dwells there and it can be felt enormously. All the exhibits were done so tastefully and carefully researched to bring the audience the best that you can bring. . . . Continue to glorify the Lord with all that you are doing! Shalom!
>
> A blessing that everything points to Christ. We loved it! Many people from our church in Indiana told us to come here. . . . We are glad we put this BEFORE Disney World this year and we will encourage others to do the same. God bless you!
>
> Keep up the good work. It's wonderful to know there is someplace like Holy Land Experience that is glorifying our God in a way that brings families together for fun and education! I know we'll be back for another visit someday, and I am telling all my friends and family to visit![22]

These visitors took their experiences at the park back into the world by spreading the "gospel of HLE" to those around them. They arrived at the park with a purpose and left with a tool for discussing their faith in the public arena.

Notably, many of these testimonials use language that implies a very interactive park experience—both physically and spiritually. This is also the case with many of the HLE reviews posted on TripAdvisor.com, where the park ranks seventieth out of 162 attractions in Orlando and has an average ranking of 3.5 out of 5.[23] Although these reviews must be considered cautiously, trends among them offer insight into how visitors conceive of the park experience. There were 220 reviews total as of mid-April 2012; 99 of these gave the park an overall "excellent" grade, and 38 rated it as "very good" on the whole. Most of the reviews appear to be written by Christian believers; this is also true of the negative reviews, most of which criticize HLE for not sincerely glorifying God or not doing "justice to stories of the Bible or the life and death of Jesus."[24]

The majority of the reviews posted on TripAdvisor.com are well over five lines long and quite detailed. Many contain visceral or experiential language that recalls Beal's definition of religiously real experience. For instance, a review dated 8 May 2011 reads: "Watched passion twice. . . . second time was so anointed couldn't stop the tears. so many things opened up to me concerning Jesus . . . it is like i became part of it." Another review posted on 19 March 2011 begins:

> My husband and I thoroughly enjoyed every inch of the park. We felt the Holy Spirit stirring in us even before we purchased the extremely reasonable tickets. All I could say is to all the actors and everyone involved, "Well done, good and faithful servants." I was on a spiritual high for weeks after spending the wonderful day there.

Likewise, a review dated 22 February 2011 reads:

> We just come home from seeing The Holy Land. I thought it would an interesting a day trip. But actually see "Jesus" and what he did for us, brought out feelings of thankfulness from my heart. . . . I had a lovely moment to speak with "Jesus" (the actor that played Jesus) after the Last Supper. I felt the Holy Spirit in that moment, and will never forget it.

According to these writers, the park makes a physical impact—they feel the Holy Spirit; they become a part of the events they see; they experience a stirring that lingers within them for weeks thereafter. Reviewers also acknowledge a kind of engaged evangelism at work, with some—like this last writer—hinting at the slippery relationship between presence and representation, between real and reconstructed, that is a hallmark of religiously real re-experience.

Notably, a reviewer who posted on 1 February 2011 appears to acknowledge that religious faith largely determines how someone will experience HLE:

> Before making the decision to visit the Holy Land Experience, I read the Reviews on tripadvisor. I was somewhat baffled because they seemed to be so

> opposite in contrast—either people hated it or they loved it. It was then that I decided that the beauty was in the eyes and heart of the beholder.

Another review, this one dated 17 April 2010, implies something similar with respect to the park's spiritual benefits. Referring to one of HLE's dramatic presentations, this reviewer writes, "It is both emotional and spiritual, But you must have a heart open to receive it." These reviews and others suggest that although HLE creates opportunities for having meaningful religious experiences, the visitor's own physical and spiritual openness to these encounters will largely determine their devotional efficacy.

I propose that evangelical dramaturgy's ability to achieve its goals rests, in great part, on similar degrees of openness. More specifically, re-experience necessitates a user/attendant who is willing to enter into a particular kind of sustained, intensive, and energetic relationship with the medium itself. In the case of HLE, certain exhibits in the park, such as the empty tomb at Calvary that visitors can enter, clearly supply momentary interactive encounters between visitor and venue. However, maintaining an interactive dynamic during more traditional theatrical performances requires that both actors and spectators understand acting not as a unidirectional mode of communication but as a way of cultivating attendance at an event. I propose that Phillip Zarrilli's psychophysical acting theory presents one such model. Significantly, Zarrilli draws heavily from Eastern performance forms—such as kathakali and noh—traditions that most Western theater scholars readily accept as having an inherent (even indispensable) spiritual dimension; in some respect, religious belief is inextricable from these modes of performance. This is one reason I believe Zarrilli's theory can offer us insight into the actor-spectator encounter at a venue like HLE.

Before introducing Zarrilli's theory, I wish to clarify that I do not believe psychophysical acting is exactly what takes place at HLE or at the other venues I analyze in later chapters. Rather, I believe Zarrilli's work supplies a language and theory of acting that can help us to examine critically the actor-audience relationship that evangelical dramaturgy fosters. In addition, I see my analysis of acting as related to Rebecca Schneider's work on reenactment. Like the events that Schneider studies, I interpret evangelical performative media as resituating the "knowing of history as body-to-body transmission."[25] Yet, while Schneider encourages us to "approach performance not as that which disappears," her alternative is to engage performance "as both the *act* of remaining and a means of re-appearance and 'reparticipation' (though not a metaphysic of presence)."[26] This parenthetical qualifier highlights an important distinction between the reenactments that Schneider examines (as well as many other kinds of theatrical reenactments) and the evangelical genres that I analyze. Evangelical dramaturgy is, in fact, fundamentally concerned with reappearance and reparticipation in a metaphysical sense.[27] I recognize Zarrilli's theory as offering us a way to consider how an acting style might encourage spectators into a perceptual mode that will cultivate this kind of performance re-experience.

Zarrilli describes psychophysical acting this way,

> Optimally, the actor's constant flow of *prana/qi/ki* or energy enlivens and qualitatively vibrates or resonates each action as it extends to and is shared with the other actors as well as the audience. The entire performance space is (ideally) suffused with/by the actor's individual and collective energy-in-action. The actor senses and experiences both *the feel* and *the subtle movement* of this energy within *as it is shaped* by the dramaturgy and aesthetic form in the moment of performance. As each action in an actor's performance score extends outward taking shape in kinesthetic and/or verbal form reaching, touching, or vibrating other performers and the audience that action simultaneously *moves within the actor herself.* Inner feeling and outer (physical) form are two sides of the same coin. The actor simultaneously senses the inner feeling of the kinesthetic/verbal form-in-action as it is performed. (original emphasis)[28]

To achieve this kind of acting, performers must develop "a certain type of awareness, attentiveness." Zarrilli claims that this kind of self-presencing "works against the normative disappearance of the body" and, thus, that it lies outside of most people's everyday conscious experience.[29]

Yet, as I noted in the Introduction, many evangelical Christians set aside time each day to read the Bible and to pray, a purposeful self-presencing ritual through which they enter into a heightened, open relationship with God that has both mental and physical components; in part, this is a kinaesthetic endeavor. This daily activity allows believers to practice cultivating awareness and attentiveness, and therefore it may prepare them to engage other religious media with bodies primed for an energetic devotional encounter. In the case of live performance, both actors and spectators might enter the space with bodies open to engaging a performance score that takes shape kinaesthetically. I therefore interpret Zarrilli's psychophysical acting theory as relevant to a performance like "Last Supper Communion."

"Partake of the Last Supper Communion"

The daily program reads, "NEW! Partake of the LAST SUPPER COMMUNION WITH JESUS and disciples, 20 min, Qumran Caves." Ten show times are listed, the earliest at 10:30 a.m. and the last at 4:00 p.m.[30] As I explained in Chapter One, this performance takes place in a space designed to replicate the Upper Room in Jerusalem as it has looked since European Crusaders reconstructed it in the early fourteenth century. The room helps visitors leave the "Orlando theme park" world behind. Its stone walls and Gothic architectural features, complete with artificially lit stained glass windows, create a visual and material aesthetic markedly different from anything else in the park.

Upon entering the room, each visitor receives a piece of bread and a 1½ inch tall wooden communion cup filled with grape juice. (Visitors are encouraged to keep these cups, which are apparently made of olive wood from Jerusalem.) A long table marks the front of the room, and during both of my visits the first people who entered sat down at the twelve stools surrounding the table. The rest of us stood around the space, some leaning against the walls or sitting on stone benches at the back. Spectators packed the room at both performances I attended. Yet in neither case did the room feel uncomfortably full; instead, it felt calmer than the rest of the park. One reason was the air-conditioning, which provided a welcome respite from the hot Memorial Day weekend weather. However, the sudden intimacy of this room also prompted a tonal shift. As visitors filed in, their voices dropped. The energy in the room grew still, but not flat, and a sense of focused expectation seemed to fill the space.

The performance began with the disciple John entering the room and recounting the biblical story of the Last Supper from his personal perspective as a follower of Jesus. Like nearly all of the actors in HLE, he wore a headset microphone; however, his melodious, serene voice sounded natural and not overly produced. John prepared the audience to receive Holy Communion, even saying, "Some of you might be healed today." As he spoke, some spectators shouted "Halleluiah" or "Amen," which caused the energy in the room to intensify palpably; John's own zeal matched it. A few times John directly prompted, "Can I get a Halleluiah?" or "Can I get an Amen?" and each time he did. At the first performance I attended, John said that a woman sitting up front was "testifying," and this comment was greeted with a number of loud "Amens" from the crowd. Many people's hands were raised in the air, palms up, ready to receive the Holy Spirit. And then suddenly Jesus entered.

There were many audible gasps when Jesus appeared. John's verb tenses—although far from consistent—had led me to believe that he was describing a Last Supper that had already taken place. Despite the title of the performance, I—and seemingly many people around me—did not expect "Jesus" himself to actually show up. Or, if they did, they were still stirred by his entrance. (Notably, John also appeared surprised when Jesus walked in.) However, this slight dislocation did not last long. Soon, Jesus was lifting the bread and wine, speaking the biblical words of institution, and the audience was suddenly, seamlessly in the past with Jesus and John at the original event. Visitors ate and drank in a physical present with Jesus as had the original disciples in the biblical past. Yet, most audience members already knew the words that Jesus first spoke in that biblical past, and many now recited them aloud with the actor. In these moments, firm distinctions between past, present, and future disappeared.

After Jesus completed the communion ritual, John began leading spectators in a hymn that was familiar to many people in the room but also easy to pick up quickly for those who did not already know it. As the audience sang, Jesus walked around the room and briefly, but resolutely, placed his hands upon each individual attendant to bless them. Many people were sobbing and swaying as this occurred, more arms were raised in the air, and many more "Halleluiahs" and "Amens" uttered. From what I witnessed around me in that small space, it appeared that many people were responding to this man as if he were Jesus himself—they looked into his eyes and said things like "Thank you, Jesus" and "I love you, Jesus." These attendants were physically present with Jesus, the actor's touch grounding this encounter into a concrete religiously real re-experience, as they also stood in a reconstructed fourteenth-century room during a reenactment of a biblical event in a twenty-first-century Orlando theme park. Furthermore, some spectators may have simultaneously been living in a future encounter with their Savior, an event that many evangelicals actively anticipate.

Nothing about this performance is simple—re-representation, re-experience, time, space, and affect all become slippery as they serve the unique needs and desires of each individual attendant. In this respect, "Last Supper Communion" recalls medieval liturgical performance. Bruce Holsinger asserts that we must understand medieval liturgy not only as a "ritual fusion of religious belief and religious practice, but also and simultaneously as the *space between professed belief and material practice*" (original emphasis). In this space, theology becomes radically "particularized, decentralized, and miniaturized," and thus "functions as a constant incentive to more localized creative gestures."[31] This is a useful way to think about "Last Supper Communion"—as a space between belief and practice that each spectator radically particularizes.

Consequently, not only does the actor who plays Jesus supply some of the most dominant performance rhythms, but his tangible physical presence also actualizes core theology; just as Donnalee Dox argues with respect to the participants in Living Nativities, here too the actor portraying Jesus "literally demonstrates how the theology works, how God (spirit) infuses the human (material) world."[32] During the performance, belief and practice converge—but never entirely meet—as visitors gain direct, unmediated spiritual access to their Savior through this actor's physical presence. The rhythmic point of contact between attendant/spectator and the actor playing Jesus is therefore one of the most complicated, as well as theologically and epistemologically generative, spaces that evangelical dramaturgy shapes.

Evangelical Enactment

Zarrilli's notion of energetic enactment provides ways to theorize the kind of actor-spectator dynamic that governs a performance like "Last Supper Communion." Zarrilli proposes that while "meaning and representation may present themselves to the viewer . . . they are the result of the actor's immediate energetic engagement in the act of performance and the spectator's experience of that performance."[33] Consequently, rather than looking at acting from the outside, at what it presents or represents to spectators, his "enactive" theory reconceives acting as a psychophysiological process that involves embodying and shaping "energy."[34]

For Zarrilli, ideally when enacting "one does not 'think about' the form/structure or draw upon some mental 'representation' of it; rather, one *enters a certain relationship* with the form/structure through one's cultivated perceptual/sensory awareness" (original emphasis).[35] Building on Alva Noë's assertion that "qualities are available in experience as possibilities, as potentialities, but not as givens,"[36] Zarrilli argues that when the performer "continues to repeat a particular form or structure over time, a larger 'field' of experience accumulates as an expanding 'field' of possibilities."[37] In this way, "a (theatrical) world is made available at the moment of its appearance/experience for both the actors and audience."[38] Such a performance does not try to depict one precise meaning; instead it gives spectators access to an experience that is full of possibilities for creating personalized meaning. With regard to "Last Supper Communion," the actors' performances allow spectators to enter into a new enactive relationship with a recognizable resonant form composed of the familiar biblical words and physical ritual of Holy Communion. This relationship prompts new meaning and possibilities to accumulate on and around the familiar form, thereby allowing attendants to perceive the Last Supper afresh. In this way, the energetic encounter makes a meaningful, religiously real world available.

One particularly potent moment when this expansion of possibilities occurs is when Jesus enters. While this sudden collision of past, present, and future could be confusing, for those spectators who arrive at the performance expecting a religiously real re-experience, this moment only intensifies and multiplies the devotional possibilities. By resisting a clear demarcation between presence and representation, Jesus' entrance shifts the perceptual event from reenactment to (decentralized and particularized) re-experience. Moreover, the kinaesthetic nature of this re-experience supplies the visitor with an intimate affective script. Traced into the spectator's embodied schema, this script may continue to influence the visitor's future experiences and interpretations of Holy Communion. Furthermore, the small wooden communion cup condenses the event into an object that visitors can take with them and that may trigger memories of that re-experience in the weeks or years after the visit.

Zarrilli's psychophysical theory proposes a mode of acting that is not fundamentally about producing finite meaning or representations, but is instead a means of activating and shaping forces. As Zarrilli employs the term *psychophysical, psycho* does not refer to "psychology per se, but rather the actor's complete engagement of her energy, sensory awareness, and perception-in-action in the moment."[39] I interpret "Last Supper Communion" as effective, in great part, because the actors actively develop a sensory and energetic awareness similar to what Zarrilli describes. This complete engagement is not aimed at presenting a representation of the Last Supper event but is instead intended to foster a re-representational re-experience of the Last Supper through which spectators can receive the Holy Spirit and, thus, gain direct access to God.

The affective power of this acting style therefore does not emerge from a particular visual style but rather from the actor's own inner convictions. As Zarrilli explains, actualizing the psychophysical acting paradigm does not demand overt representations of emotions or actions because "behind the apparent inaction is the blazing flame of an active, inner, vibratory perceptivity. An inner necessity informs this psychophysical task."[40] In "Last Supper Communion," that inner necessity is a religious, evangelical one, a claim that comments by Holy Land Experience staff members help substantiate.

Many staff members envision their work at HLE as part of a ministry. Ronald Lukens-Bull and Mark Fafard undertook intensive on-site research at HLE from January to May 2004, with follow-up visits and ongoing communication continuing through August 2005.[41] As part of this work they conducted interviews with a number of HLE employees. They write that, in nearly all of their interviews, "the staff express that a benefit of working at the Holy Land Experience is the opportunity to share their Christian faith. For example, one respondent said, 'I'm being used as God's servant to minister here.'"[42] Moreover, being "in character" does not preclude HLE actors from discussing their own personal faith with visitors and may even enable a more meaningful exchange, as I suggested with respect to the conversation between the "disciple" and the preteen group.[43] As Lukens-Bull and Fafard note, "The opportunity for the pilgrim to interact with the staff, most of whom wear costumes depicting Old and New Testament characters, provides the chance to learn and share pious beliefs on a personal level rather than through observation and lectures."[44] It also seems that staff members assume that visitors desire such encounters. As one employee remarked,

> I am able to share my faith to everyone around me because everyone has the general beliefs. . . . The sharing can act as a serious relationship towards God while allowing guests to become more motivated in their faith. . . . I work here for a purpose, not [just] a paycheck. I feel it is God's plan for me.[45]

I would argue that such religious convictions not only impact the actors' personal exchanges with visitors but also inform the way they approach their performances in the HLE shows.

Using a technique akin to Zarrilli's psychophysical acting theory—but one that builds upon a perceptual and sensory awareness that they may cultivate through daily activities like Bible study and prayer, and that is motivated by an inner conviction to evangelize—the performers at HLE generate re-experiences that give visitors direct access to divine presence.[46] As a result, a performance like "Last Supper Communion" aims to produce an intimate affective script that will satisfy visitors' religious needs and solve their spiritual problems. This approach to acting therefore supports the overarching goals of evangelical dramaturgy—it fosters re-representational re-experience, uses anachronism to suspend spectators perceptually between presence and representation, constructs devotionally valuable affective intimate scripts, and, finally, serves as a form of engaged orthodoxy. I therefore call this acting technique *evangelical enactment*.

"A Place of Miracles"

Many of the audience members standing around me at the "Last Supper Communion" performances interacted with "Jesus" as if he were Jesus. I do not suspect that any of them actually mistook the actor for Jesus himself; instead, the actor's live body served as a means of religious enquiry into the real Jesus and thus, as I suggest above, it infused the familiar biblical event with new and meaningful devotional possibilities.[47] Evangelical enactment, therefore, challenges traditional definitions of mimesis and, for this reason, relates to Anna Gibbs's work on mimesis. Gibbs asserts that mimesis "is not a property of either subject or object, but a trajectory in which both are swept up."[48] This definition is quite relevant to evangelical enactment; I interpret re-representational mimesis as sweeping both the actor and spectator/attendant into a re-experience. However, the devotional effectiveness of that trajectory depends upon (as it simultaneously reinforces) a specific philosophy of religious knowledge acquisition. Consequently, evangelical enactment's mimetic goals are grounded in evangelical epistemology.

The use of touch within "Last Supper Communion" illustrates this point. As Erika Fischer-Lichte explains,

> various examples have shown that the fundamental opposition between seeing and touching in performance is connected to a number of other interrelated oppositional pairs: public vs. private, distance vs. proximity, fiction vs.

reality. They are all based on the seemingly insurmountable, fixed opposition between seeing and touching.[49]

For this reason, integrating physical contact into a performance can effectively "destabilize the binary relationship between reality and fiction, public and intimate" and thus encourage spectators "to move beyond established spheres of communication and into new experiential realms."[50] I would argue that this is precisely what Jesus' haptic journey through the audience at "Last Supper Communion" accomplishes; his touch not only situates each spectator in the present embodied moment but also encourages religious meaning to develop from that individual, direct encounter.[51] The touch punctuates the spectator's affective intimate script in a compelling fashion by concentrating the entire performance into a single energetic moment that not only challenges traditional binaries and boundaries, but also validates the notion that direct, personal experience is a legitimate, even necessary, source of religious truth. In this way, touch not only radically expands the spectator's possibilities for meaning making, but as a communication practice it also produces an embodied schema that establishes (or reinforces) particular epistemological assumptions.

Yet, I also interpret Jesus' touch as vital to how this performance creates an intimate script that will solve the spectator-user's problems. There is a marked break in the dramatic structure of "Last Supper Communion" following the re-representation of the Holy Communion ritual. That structural shift necessitates a perceptual shift as well, and touch facilitates this. Jennifer Fisher contends that, because touch forces spectators into an awareness of their bodies, these gestures "are acts of connecting that, in the moment of contact, make it difficult to sustain an analytical frame of mind."[52] The moment of physical contact in "Last Supper Communion," underscored by the group singing that becomes louder and more passionate as the moments pass, as well as by the sounds of crying and shouts of "Halleluiah," directs spectators toward the emotional production characteristic of affective piety.

More specifically, Fisher argues that in a performance, touch can carry "a politics of tactile consolation" that will "shift habitual defenses" and thus contribute to "a climate of recovery."[53] I am suggesting that Jesus' touch may also function in this way. As I noted above, many people in the room were crying as Jesus walked around and offered his blessing. For some of these spectators, the brief moment of physical contact did, indeed, seem to create a climate in which they could purge emotion and then recover. It was perhaps a moment like this that prompted one HLE visitor to remark, "This is more than a park, it is a place of miracles."[54]

I propose that certain evangelical believer-spectators, particularly those who belong to more charismatic denominations or congregations like Assemblies of God, will be even more open and receptive to such an experience. For these visitors, the epistemological assumptions that this performance ultimately establishes within spectators are already a fundamental part of their piety. Moreover, Pentecostalism contends that Christians must have a Second baptism in the Holy Spirit, a doctrine primarily based upon passages in the New Testament book of Acts.[55] Believers actively seek this Second baptism through frequent and disciplined devotion.[56] In some respects, then, the worship and devotional experiences of Pentecostals are related to the psychophysical actor's training process that Zarrilli describes—both involve preparation of the bodymind in order to awaken an inner energy. Moreover, in both cases continuous training is meant to result in "attunement and sensitization of awareness" that will open the individual's "ability to sense and feel deeply."[57] Certain evangelical spectators may, therefore, enter a performance like "Last Supper Communion" in the same state as the actors—physically prepared for evangelical enactment's energetic dynamic. This may be why the audience responses at the performances I attended were remarkably intense.

The intimate script that "Last Supper Communion" produces also resolves problems by offering spectators comforting feelings of stability and belonging that will help to sustain their faith after they leave HLE. At the end of "Last Supper Communion," after Jesus has exited, John asks spectators to look around the room and then says, "This is your family." At both performances I attended, John told the audience that those people standing around them were part of their eternal family, the people who would be with them in heaven. This assertion not only suggests something about TBN's assumptions regarding the park's visitor demographic but also exposes a goal that will reappear throughout the different performative genres I analyze in this book—these genres remind evangelical believer-users that, although their religious faith and beliefs may at times place them at odds with the modern world and the people around them, they are, in fact, part of a community that will extend beyond this world and into eternity. By affording the felt sense of a true, everlasting community, "Last Supper Communion" tries to resolve those stresses of the modern condition that I discussed in Chapter One—autonomy and a lack of clear direction—while it also reassures visitors of their own righteous salvic status.

Ultimately, a performance like "Last Supper Communion" functions as a dynamic space strategically designed for a specific target audience in order to encourage their spiritual transformation, rehabilitation, and self-discovery. As Bruce McConachie maintains, "Certain kinds of plays fashion certain groups of spectators and vice versa."[58] Although Holy Land Experience does try to convert new believers, staff comments imply that a large part of the park's work concerns reinvigorating and strengthening the faith of existing believers. Lukens-Bull and Fafard note,

> According to park staff, the first message is simply the Christian Gospel. However, given that most of the visitors are already Christian, significant effort is directed to the related goal of reinforcing and intensifying the visitor's commitment to Evangelical beliefs.[59]

Therefore, understanding the "religiously real" devotional potential of a performance like "Last Supper Communion" requires us to acknowledge the kinds of actors and spectators for whom it is intended and then to consider the religious beliefs and specific enculturated ways that these groups have learned to make religious meaning from the world.[60] I propose evangelical dramaturgy and evangelical enactment as theoretical lenses that can help us to accomplish this goal.

On my second day at Holy Land Experience, I was detained at another exhibit and therefore arrived too late to get a seat for the "Behold the Lamb" Passion play. Since I could not even get close enough to find an unobstructed place to stand, I ended up watching the play from the other side of the park and, thus, from behind the set. I could hear most of the music and dialogue, since both are piped over loudspeakers, but I couldn't see very much of the play's action; I could watch the backs of those actors who were standing on top of the Calvary Garden Tomb rock for scenes like the crucifixion, but that was about all I saw. However, when the performance ended, I noticed the actors playing Jesus and the Centurion leaving the stage together. They walked behind the Tomb rock and knelt down together to pray—or to do what appeared like praying. This post-performance act occurred out of the view of those spectators who had just watched the play from unobstructed positions. And I suspect others like myself who could not get a good view for the performance had already moved on to other things by this point and were not watching the two actors, especially since it was lightly raining and the area of the park from which the actors were visible was mostly uncovered. I even scanned the crowd, and no other visitors around me appeared to be watching. Therefore, I suspect this (ritual) moment was intended for the actors themselves and not specifically designed to be seen by park visitors.

I obviously can't say whether or not this is true. Nor do I know if this moment of prayer (if indeed it was prayer) is a daily ritual or if it was simply a random event. But this act of self-presencing, of cultivating awareness, may suggest a connection between acting and prayer that supports my claims about an enactive approach to enactment at HLE.

I am aware that throughout this analysis of "Last Supper Communion" and evangelical enactment I have used my own felt bodily experiences of performances and spaces as evidence. Stephen di Benedetto argues,

> [Because] artists make conscious use of triggering our sensations, analysts must be bold and break from passive modes of critical inquiry. If we embrace the subjective personal sensations generated by an event and tie them to the form of the artwork, then we can make tangible the sensorial experience of the arts.[61]

Naturalized phenomenology helps me to activate my inquiry along these lines in a responsible fashion, since it offers a theoretical approach to bodily experience supplemented by empirical evidence. Moreover, Zarrilli acknowledges that his enactive approach to acting is informed by, among other things, recent research from phenomenology and cognitive science that analyzes how people make meaning from their synaesthetic bodily experiences at/in a performance.[62] Therefore, in the next chapter I will use evidence from cognitive science to develop my concept of evangelical enactment further and to apply it to HLE's "Behold the Lamb" Passion drama.

3

"Behold the Lamb"

Passion Playing, Intermediality, and the Gibson Affect

Claire Sponsler's work on Passion playing reveals the vexed history of this performance tradition in the United States. Publicly marketed, commercial Passion plays staged in the United States during the nineteenth and twentieth centuries often faced resistance. For example, Sponsler describes how an 1879 performance of Salmi Morse's *The Passion: A Miracle Play in Ten Acts,* which starred James O'Neill (Eugene O'Neill's father) as Jesus, "fell victim to attacks by a loose alliance of Protestant preachers, politicians, and the press." While many clergy members believed "a stage play in which a mere mortal represented the deity" was blasphemous, others attacked the play for "its supposedly pernicious influence on the lower classes, whose religious passions they feared it would inflame."[1] As a result, many producers who wished to stage Passion plays thereafter developed strategies for mitigating these same concerns.

The Black Hills Passion Play, performed annually in Spearfish, South Dakota, from 1939 until 2008, provides one example. This production allayed anxiety by, in Sponsler's words, "cannily invoking the play's medieval origins." By referencing a medieval tradition, the play claimed "historical stability for itself while, not coincidentally, also removing itself from history and especially from that part of modern history that enfolds current controversies over the role of religion in public life."[2] Furthermore, this kind of medievalism also served as an interpretive strategy designed to differentiate acting in the Black Hills Passion from acting in a traditional theatrical piece.[3]

Associating the Black Hills play with medieval religious performances ultimately framed it as a "traditional ritual of devout amateurs," a fundamentally antitheatrical appraisal that the producers emphasized in a variety of ways.[4] For instance, Sponsler explains how the 1939 brochure for the play suggested a kind of "subjugation of the performer to the role and to the tradition," with each actor presented "as inseparable from the role and as fulfilling a sacred trust, a relationship that is signaled in each actor's pledge to conduct him- or herself onstage and off 'as a worthy member of the Passion Players.'"[5] Years later, the brochure used in the 1950s took the additional step of leaving the actors unnamed, a decision designed "to draw attention away from the act of impersonation and to emphasize instead the religiosity of these representations."[6] Moreover, the Black Hills production also tried to expand this pious frame to include the audience; the 1939 brochure asked spectators not to applaud, while the 1950s brochure contained a Prologue that ended in a prayer. Sponsler concludes that these elements were intended "to position the passion play as devotional practice rather than theater."[7]

Sponsler identifies two main sources of anxiety with respect to U.S. Passion playing: "the immediacy of the experience (and its attendant emotional impact, as witnessed in the spectators who fell to their knees during O'Neill's performance as Jesus) and impersonation of divine figures (with its suggestion of blasphemy)."[8] I would argue that these concerns stem, at least in part, from a belief that popular commercial entertainment cannot also provide spectators with a meaningful devotional experience. When the plays do evoke pious responses, these are either deemed too emotionally extreme to be legitimately valuable or they are labeled idolatrous. Passion playing therefore provides a kind of case study for investigating the relationship between U.S. popular culture and Christian devotional experience.

I have demonstrated in the previous chapters that many forms of evangelical media purposefully use elements of popular culture to cultivate valuable religious experiences, thereby challenging any entertainment/devotion binary. In the next two chapters I will analyze the ways in which certain large-scale contemporary Passion performances utilize popular entertainment devices in order to provide evangelical believers with meaning-full religiously real re-experiences. In addition, I will argue that rather than trying to neutralize immediacy and divine impersonation, these Passion plays actively promote those very concepts. This dramaturgical choice successfully expands the devotional possibilities for re-experience precisely because these plays are designed to serve an audience of believers who enter the entertainment space for the specific purpose of having an immediate visceral re-experience and who understand the actors not as impersonating or representing divine figures but instead as providing direct access to divine presence through re-representation.

While "Last Supper Communion" blurs the lines between liturgy, ritual, and theater, "Behold the Lamb," which is performed daily at Holy Land Experience, is a full-scale, technologically enhanced dramatic production; it is undoubtedly a piece of theater. After introducing Holy Land Experience's "Behold the Lamb" Passion drama, I will explore the performer-spectator relationship during this play by considering the physiological processes behind this energetic encounter. In particular, I will use research on mirror neuron responses and rhythmic entrainment to suggest how evangelical enactment promotes certain embodied beliefs. In the second half of this chapter, I analyze this play alongside Mel Gibson's film *The Passion of The Christ*. Not only do I see evidence of that film's influence throughout "Behold the Lamb," a dramaturgical strategy that I call the Gibson affect, but *The Passion of The Christ* supplies a useful example of intermediality and will help me begin to examine how evangelical dramaturgy uses intermediality to enhance the attendant's re-experience.

"Behold the Lamb" at Calvary's Garden Tomb

The "Behold the Lamb" Passion drama was staged at noon on both days I visited Holy Land Experience. Most of the other HLE performances take place in spaces that create a more traditional and circumscribed actor-audience physical relationship. For instance, the "Woman at the Well" play is performed on a raised outdoor stage in the "Judean Village," with spectators sitting on fixed stools arranged like typical auditorium seating. Various shows and lectures are presented on the steps of the Great Temple, and the audience sits on benches facing the performers/presenters. HLE also has two indoor theater spaces—the Shofar Auditorium and the Theatre of Life—and a variety of events occur in each. Even with "Last Supper Communion," which is performed in a small, indoor room, the table and stools help to establish an audience zone that is distinct from the acting area. Although actors may move through the audience at times during some of these events, in every case the spectators sit or stand in a designated audience space that is clearly distinct from the acting or performance space.

HLE stages its Passion play quite differently. The daily schedule indicates that "Behold the Lamb" is performed at Calvary's Garden Tomb, and a good deal of the play does take place around, in, and on top of the large Tomb structure. But a considerable proportion of the play occurs along park pathways around the Tomb or at nearby sites, such as outside the Qumran Caves. The play's action moves through the park space, creating a *via dolorosa* in HLE's reconstructed Jerusalem.[9]

On the days I visited, spectators began staking out viewing spots more than forty-five minutes before the Passion drama was scheduled to begin. The prime seats are the stools at the Judean Village stage; spectators simply turn the opposite direction of that stage to face Calvary's Garden Tomb. However, since there are nowhere near enough stools to accommodate every visitor, at least on the weekend I attended, a large percentage of spectators must stand wherever they can find a space that has a good view of the Tomb and surrounding area. Although ropes separate some of these "standing room" areas from the acting space, this is not always the case, and spectators are quite close to the actors during long stretches of the play, particularly during Jesus' scourging and his walk to Calvary. This intimate physical relationship between actors and audience supports evangelical dramaturgy's re-experiential goal.[10]

Thirty minutes prior to the play, a park employee delivered "The Empty Tomb," a presentation that historicizes the Garden Tomb for visitors, while also keeping them occupied before the show begins. As Timothy Beal explains,

> There are two tombs in Jerusalem that claim to have been the site of Jesus's burial, the one at the Church of the Holy Sepulchre and the Garden Tomb. Scholars disagree as to which, if either, is the right one. The Holy Land Experience opted for the latter, based in part on Jesus's post-Resurrection visit with Mary in the Gospel of John, in which she initially mistakes him for a gardener.[11]

The pre-performance "Empty Tomb" presentation explains the reasoning behind HLE's choice, and, thus, for some visitors, it may add a sense of authenticity to the re-experience the Passion drama affords.

A musical interlude helps to shift the audience from this presentation to the play itself. Music is prevalent throughout HLE and underscores most of the visitor experience. Songs are piped over the amplification system, and music is used throughout many of the presentations, performances, and exhibits. In this case, some of the Passion play actors came out to lead the audience through a few singable, hummable Praise Songs. Many audience members were already familiar with these songs, but, as with the hymn in "Last Supper Communion," the songs were also catchy and easy to learn. Although these actors wore headset microphones, they also used handheld microphones during this warm-up musical set. As I will discuss at length in Chapter Six, Praise Music is a major component of evangelical worship, especially at megachurches. Most services begin with a lengthy musical set during which worship leaders, who are usually holding microphones, lead the congregation in Praise Songs.[12] Therefore, including a musical introduction that replicates this format, down to the presence of handheld microphones, may frame the play as a worship event for many spectators. After the songs, the actors leave the stage area, and a shift in musical tone signals the formal start of the Passion drama; the upbeat Praise Songs are replaced by a more cinematic-sounding score, and Jesus enters with his disciples.

In a mere thirty minutes, "Behold the Lamb" depicts the story of Christ's Passion, death, and resurrection. The play begins with Jesus praying in the Garden of Gethsemane. Audiences then witness Judas' betrayal of Jesus to Caiaphas, a Jewish high priest, followed by Jesus' arrest and trial before Pilate. When Pilate decrees that Jesus be flogged, the Roman soldiers take him to a whipping post set outside the Qumran Caves. As Jesus is scourged, his body grows bloodier; for the rest of the day, the blood-covered whipping post will stand as a reminder to guests of Christ's sacrifice. After this scourging, the soldiers toss a very bloody Jesus to the ground and Caiaphas kneels down to taunt him. The head Centurion also mocks Jesus, and various Roman soldiers punch and kick him before placing the crown of thorns on his head, a purple cloak around his shoulders, and the cross upon his back. They then drive Jesus past the audience on his walk to Calvary; during this segment the actors are usually just feet from audience members. Along this *via dolorosa,* Jesus falls three times and meets the apocryphal figure Veronica. Once he can no longer carry the cross himself, the soldiers instruct Simon of Cyrene to carry it for him. As shown in Figure 1, at one point the head Centurion pushes Jesus into the audience where he kneels, inches from the front row. A female actress playing one of the weeping daughters of Jerusalem stands among the seated spectators. Jesus reaches out to her—and, thus, into the audience.

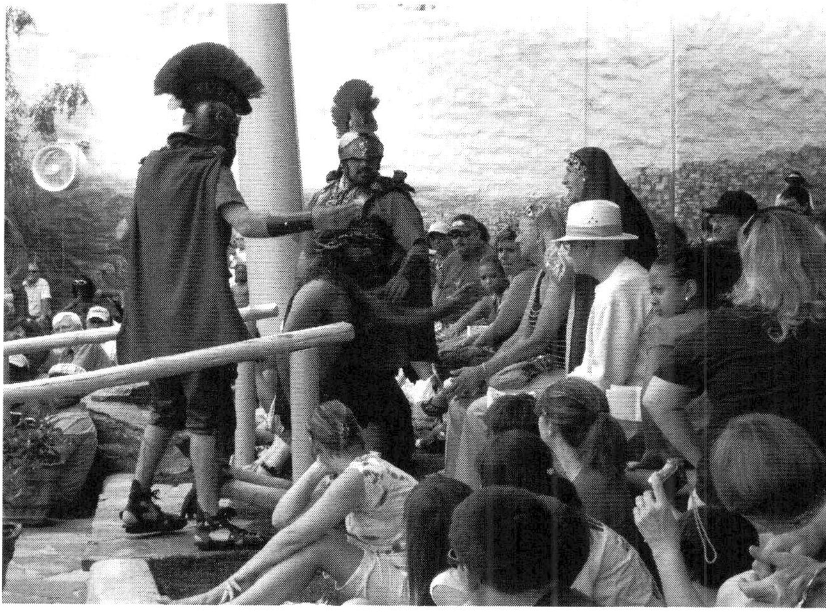

Figure 1. Actor playing Jesus reaching into audience during "Behold the Lamb" Passion Drama, Holy Land Experience, Orlando, Florida. May 2010. Photo by author.

Eventually, the soldiers lead Jesus behind the Garden Tomb where the actors ascend stairs and appear on top of this giant rock structure. Here they enact the crucifixion. The location high on top of the tomb, along with the use of broad gestures, amplified voices, and musical underscoring, helped focus the audience on each moment of this biblical event. For instance, as the soldiers pounded the nails into Jesus' hands, the disciples, who were scattered around the playing area, convulsed violently with each blow; many spectators around me shuddered. The play's director also takes advantage of the set's many different levels; Roman soldiers, the Virgin Mary, and the disciple John stand on top of the Tomb, circling the base of the cross, while other disciples, the female followers of Jesus, and Caiaphas remain on the ground. Some of these actors stand on rock formations near the Tomb, while others stand farther back and, thus, closer to the audience. During the crucifixion, dialogue is exchanged among these characters. Therefore, although the play's visual focus is Jesus hanging on the cross, the dialogue, music, and staging choices prevent the dramatic energy from remaining too tightly concentrated around this crucifixion image. Instead, these devices draw the energy out toward the large audience, thereby fostering an energetic encounter.

After Jesus dies, the soldiers remove his body from the cross, wrap it in a white burial cloth, and cover it with a Jewish prayer shawl or *tallit*. Rather than descending stage right, a more expedient route to the tomb, the soldiers depart stage left. This direction allows them to process past most of the audience as they carry the body to the tomb trailed by the disciple John and the Virgin Mary. From my front row seat I noticed the bloodied "holes" in Jesus' feet as the soldiers passed by me. After placing the body in the tomb, the soldiers roll the stone to cover the entrance and the weeping disciples depart. Two Roman soldiers remain to guard the tomb and the scene grows quiet.

A loud crash breaks this silence. The soldiers run away as smoke erupts from the tomb and the stone rolls away of its own volition. Two female characters approach and, finding the tomb empty, they run to get the other disciples who enter the tomb and bring out the prayer shawl as evidence of Jesus' disappearance. They pass the cloth among themselves, lamenting that someone has stolen the body and praying for its return. The head Centurion, who became a believer at Christ's crucifixion, also enters. Taking the prayer shawl from a disciple, the Centurion delivers a lengthy monologue about his own journey to faith in Jesus. He walks into the seated audience and, at times, thrusts the cloth toward spectators to punctuate his distress over coming to true belief too late. He confesses that he was wrong to demand physical proof of Christ's divinity; sincere belief should not require such signs. The verb choices and direct address in this monologue collapse the time and space between this new believer in ancient Jerusalem and the believer-spectators in the Orlando audience.

In another haze of smoke, Jesus suddenly appears on top of the Tomb. He stands victorious, smiling and no longer bloodied, wearing a flowing white robe with long feathered hair framing his face. Jesus explains how his death and resurrection have won humankind victory over death's bondage, at one point lifting up a giant set of keys that are perhaps two feet long in order to make his point clear. After he concludes, lively music begins to play over the sound system as the disciples, jubilant over Jesus' return, laugh, dance, and sing off the stage. The play ends with applause from the crowd.

Passion Entrainments

Although both "Last Supper Communion" and "Behold the Lamb" aim to generate an energetic encounter between spectators and actors that will cultivate re-experience, the two plays occur in markedly different settings. Unlike "Last Supper Communion," "Behold the Lamb" is staged outside and is therefore more directly tied to the theme park environment. That environment expands the performance frame in ways that may make it harder to generate evangelical enactment's energetic dynamic. However, evidence from cognitive science suggests how specific devices within the play may help it to overcome this obstacle.

In her discussion of mimicry, Anna Gibbs suggests that communication is not merely the "transmission of information" but is instead "action on bodies . . . as, for example, when reading fiction produces new affect states in us, which change not only our body chemistry, but also—and as a result—our attitudes and ideas."

> This sharing of form comprises information in the pre-cybernetic sense: it represents the organization or communication of relationships (which might be spatial, temporal, tonal, energetic, logical, causal, and so on) through temporary captures of form by way of mimesis.[13]

As Gibbs herself notes, this model of mimetic communication implies a degree of shared physicality that research into the mirror neuron system corroborates.[14]

Mirror neurons are a class of visuomotor neurons that scientists originally discovered in the brains of monkeys. For many years, research into a human mirror neuron system (MNS) was based, in great part, on indirect evidence.[15] However, more recent experiments provide relatively conclusive data supporting the existence of a MNS in humans. As Christian Keysers and Valeria Gazzola explained in a 2010 article, "Following a period in which it had become fashionable to claim that there is actually no evidence for mirror neurons in humans" new work "brings us two leaps further in our understanding of this system: we now know that humans have mirror neurons."[16] Subsequent studies have substantiated such evidence.[17]

Mirror neurons are cells in the brain that fire when we observe an action, execute that same action, or even simply imagine that action. This neural simulation also occurs in response to sounds; if we hear another person performing an action that makes a distinctive sound, such as cracking open a nut or hammering a nail, our own bodies simulate that same action neurally. Evidence about the MNS suggests that, on at least one level, we understand another person's actions because our sensorimotor system reconstructs these as if *we* were also executing those same actions. Vittorio Gallese argues that this "as if" response "enables the observer to use her/his own resources to penetrate the world of the other by means of a direct, automatic, and unconscious process of motor simulation."[18] Although some researchers suggest that mirror neurons may also respond to emotion and, thus, play a role in emotion understanding, the current evidence remains inconclusive.[19] Therefore, while the relationship between the MNS and higher cognitive functioning remains highly speculative, as scholars like Jean Decety note, research appears to "strongly support the role of the MNS in motor resonance."[20]

Mirror neuron research does, then, supply evidence for a kind of "form sharing" between spectator and actor. Accordingly, a specific type of mimetic communication is, in fact, "action on bodies,"[21] since the actor's actions are, at a certain neural level, reenacted within and by the spectator. Furthermore, in some respect this research substantiates evangelical dramaturgy's premise that actors in plays like "Behold the Lamb" or "Last Supper Communion" are not merely representing forms but are providing spectators with direct access to a shared experience. MNS research may therefore help us to identify how dramaturgical devices that prompt simulation can enhance the energetic relationship between actor and spectator in order to shape the intimate script that the play produces.

Such devices may be particularly valuable for a performance like "Behold the Lamb," a spoken drama staged outside within a large, synaesthetically rich, potentially distracting theme park environment that does not appear to promote the awareness, attentiveness, and self-presencing that evangelical enactment necessitates. Musical underscoring, which is used liberally throughout "Behold the Lamb," is one device that may help to counter that environmental obstacle. Music not only focuses the spectator's attention on certain actions but also can induce emotions, adding a "felt" tactile trace to the performance itself and, perhaps, even to the motor resonance the performance triggers. Interdisciplinary research has tried to assess how music communicates and, particularly, how it communicates emotion. Patrik Juslin explains that musical expression is "a set of perceptual qualities (e.g. structural, emotional, motional) that reflect psycho-physical relationships between 'objective' properties of the music, and 'subjective'—or rather, objective but partly person-dependent—impressions of the listener."[22] Musical expression resides in, and is therefore dependent upon, music's acoustic properties, as well as the listener's mind. But, as Juslin explains, musical communication also requires "both a composer's (or performer's) *intention* to express a specific concept and *recognition* of the same concept by a listener" (original emphasis).[23] In other words, musical communication demands a degree of consistency between creator and listener.

According to Juslin, studies of how music communicates emotion indicate that "there is usually high agreement among listeners about the *broad* emotional category expressed by the music, but less agreement concerning the nuances *within* this category" (original emphasis).[24] This may be one reason that film scores seem to operate through a handful of tropes; aiming for broad emotional categories might guarantee accurate communication. But Juslin also sites research that examines how music induces emotion, and these studies reveal that the emotions typically *expressed* by music, according to respondents, are somewhat different from the most typical emotions *induced* by music, since the latter "are more determined by the nature of the appraisal of the musical event and the specific reasons for engaging with the music in a particular situation."[25] This research implies that how spectators will understand and respond to music in a play is, in part, dependent upon their expectations of, and experiences at, the event itself. The religious beliefs an audience member brings to "Behold the Lamb" will certainly influence what emotions its musical elements induce in that person. But other elements, like the appearance of handheld microphones in the opening musical set or the play's placement immediately after a historical presentation, may also impact how spectators appraise and engage the event itself, and thus may direct them toward certain emotional responses.

Moreover, music does not simply induce emotions, it also entrains the body. Experiments that examine finger-tapping to a randomly changing tempo indicate that "auditory rhythm communicates stable and precise interval-based temporal templates to the brain, to which the motor system has 'privileged' access even below levels of conscious awareness."[26] A similar kind of rhythmic entrainment is visible within human conversation; in one study, a frame-by-frame analysis of videotaped conversations revealed that "speaker and hearer look like puppets moved by the same set of strings."[27] Studies of infants as early as twenty minutes after birth reveal rhythmic mirroring, strongly suggesting that we are "born with an ability to engage in rhythmically coordinated interpersonal interaction."[28] When this response is prompted by musical rhythms that also induce emotions, listeners may be physically entrained by an emotionally dense soundscape.

The prevalence of song and musical underscoring before and during "Behold the Lamb" may reflect an attempt to overcome the theme park setting by entraining spectators into the physical and emotional life of the play. For example, looking at my photographs of the bloodied actor playing Jesus carrying the cross, what strikes me now are the twenty-first-century tourists surrounding the scene, standing in their shorts and T-shirts, wearing baseball hats, carrying canvas totes and shopping bags, and holding video cameras. The close proximity between these contemporary tourist-spectators and the actors in their "biblical" clothes—with both groups set against an obviously fabricated first-century background—is almost laughable; in a photograph like Figure 2, the juxtaposition seems to dissolve the possibility for dramatic energy or emotional intensity.

And yet, that is not what the faces of people in the crowd register, nor is that how I remember the scene—physically and mentally. One reason may be that Jesus' walk is choreographed to a swelling cinematic score, which might focus spectators' attention and induce emotions during the dramatic action. At various key moments the music also punctuates physical actions, such as each time Jesus falls to the ground while carrying the cross, and thus it may help to entrain spectators into the actor's rhythms. Moreover, the music may prompt those spectators with obstructed views to imagine (and thus simulate) the actions it marks. In these respects, music powerfully shapes the intimate scripts that spectators form during "Behold the Lamb."

I therefore interpret the musical occurrences in "Behold the Lamb" as forms that are shared physically between performers and spectators. Music's ability to entrain spectators into a performance's temporal and tonal rhythms makes it an especially valuable tool for encouraging spectators into energetic relationships that will foster religiously real re-experiences. Furthermore, although it is not clear if mirror neurons themselves play a role in emotion understanding per se, musical underscoring can align an actor's gestures and expressions with musical tropes that are likely to induce certain emotions in the majority of spectators; in other words, music might trigger a kind of emotionally thick motor resonance. Therefore, musical shifts and underscoring in "Behold the Lamb" may add an emotional dimension to the motor resonance the play prompts. This is one way in which music contributes felt texture to the spectator's intimate script.

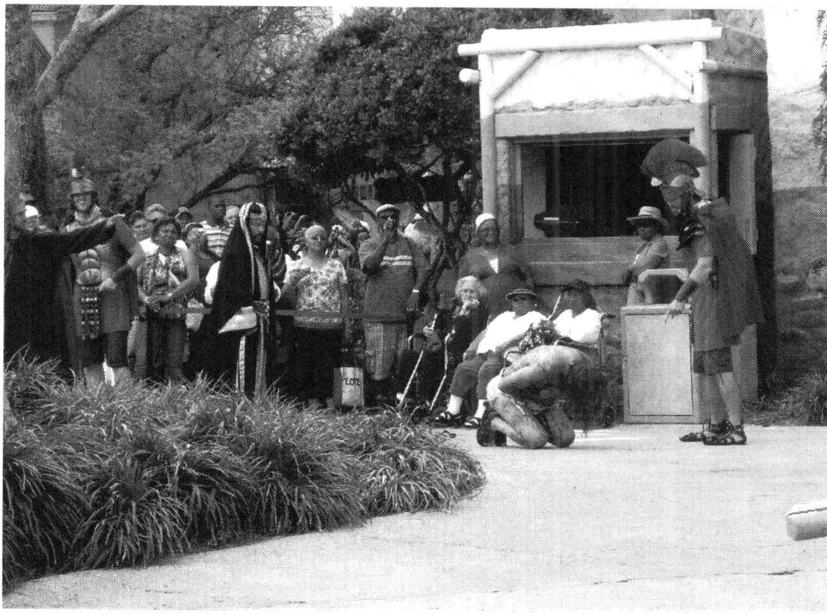

Figure 2. Scene from "Behold the Lamb" Passion Drama, Holy Land Experience, Orlando, Florida. May 2010. Photo by author.

Music not only enhances the emotional and mnemonic potential of "Behold the Lamb," but it also helps to generate and sustain an active energetic exchange between a large, diversely configured audience and the actors who re-represent Christ's Passion in only thirty minutes at a Disneyland-like Jerusalem. Another dramaturgical device also aims to achieve this goal—intermediality. Drawing on the Greek word *aisthestai,* meaning "to perceive," Peter M. Boenisch defines intermediality as "an effect on the perception of the observers. . . . an *aisthetic act* located at the very intersection of theatricality and mediality" (original emphasis).[29] Accordingly, integrating other media into a live theater performance expands or contracts the spectator's experience by impacting the very act of perception itself.

Boenisch suggests that intermediality is particularly powerful when used during live theater because of a doubleness that lies at the heart of theatrical spectatorship. Unlike other genres, theater is largely transparent with respect to how it incorporates other media:

> Imagine, for example, the same actor appearing in a movie and on stage: on stage, he remains the physical actor and is never transformed into a projection of light on a screen. A photograph might be displayed as part of a stage set, and liking it, I might scan it and use it as a screen saver; yet that photo on stage still remains the photograph, but not so as my new screen saver.[30]

Boenisch asserts that although "theatre leaves the thing itself intact," at the same time the actor and picture "are *theatrically reproduced* into something beyond their mere (even less: *pure*) original presence" (original emphasis). Consequently, "theatrical mediation is produced in the observers' perception alone."[31] This ability to present and represent simultaneously, and thus to provoke a kind of generative double-vision in spectators, makes theater an especially effective artistic medium for Christianity, a religion in which presence and re-presence must often coexist.

Live theater's innate intermediality is especially valuable to evangelical dramaturgy because it constitutes a re-representational advantage with respect to cultivating uniquely powerful religiously real re-experiences.[32] In addition, Boenisch concludes that intermediality "is very literally located inter-media, inhibiting, blending and blurring traditional borders between genres, media, sign-systems, and messages."[33] Intermediality therefore represents an ideal strategy for activating the perceptual multistability that evangelical dramaturgy desires.[34]

I recognize a specific form of intermediality operating within "Behold the Lamb," which—like music—is used strategically to encourage spectators into an energetic relationship with the performance event. Although footage from Mel Gibson's film *The Passion of The Christ* does not actually appear as part of "Behold the Lamb," I contend that the play directly references the film in various ways and that these moments generate the kind of perceptual effect that Boenisch describes. By pointedly replicating or recalling the film, the play seeks to activate a heightened, deeply engaged awareness within spectators that will foster a religiously real re-experience. I call this intermedial strategy the Gibson affect.

Sensual Passions

The Passion of The Christ begins in the Garden of Gethsemane and follows the major events of the Passion through Jesus' crucifixion, death on the cross, and deposition, which ends in a striking pietà image. Throughout the film there are flashbacks to key events in Jesus' life and ministry, most of them biblical in origin. These flashbacks are rarely complete scenes; instead, they provide only brief, fragmented glimpses of past moments. As many writers have noted, a moviegoer who is unfamiliar with the biblical source material would likely struggle to understand how these short, interpolated scenes relate to the brutal Passion events that constitute almost the entirety of the film.[35]

Arguably, the most memorable aspect of *The Passion of The Christ* is the film's violence, which is startling, in great part, because of Gibson's detailed attention to (even fetishizing of) realism. A. O. Scott captures this aesthetic in his *New York Times* review:

> The final hour of the "The Passion of the Christ" essentially consists of a man being beaten, tortured and killed in graphic and lingering detail. Once he is taken into custody, Jesus (Jim Caviezel) is cuffed and kicked and then, much more systematically, flogged, first with stiff canes and then with leather whips tipped with sharp stones and glass shards. By the time the crown of thorns is pounded onto his head and the cross loaded onto his shoulders, he is all but unrecognizable, a mass of flayed and bloody flesh, barely able to stand, moaning and howling in pain.[36]

For viewers not already familiar with the biblical Passion narrative, the physical violence provides a foothold of sorts; as William G. Little suggests, "in the absence of personal narrative, the viewer's attention is drawn to the presence of the flesh," particularly "the sheer weight of [Christ's] body" and its "surfaces and extremities,"[37] all of which the camera explores in excruciating detail. Moreover, Gibson uses cinematic techniques, such as shot-reverse shots, to situate moviegoers in viewing positions that replicate those of live witnesses.[38]

Many of Gibson's directorial choices, including the realistic violence, supply spectators with felt experiences. I have argued elsewhere that it is not merely *The Passion of The Christ*'s violence, but instead the accentuated materiality of that violence, which is so remarkable.[39] For example, although the two-dimensional medium of film has the potential to eliminate any awareness of the bodied similarity between actors and audience, Gibson regularly uses close-ups and slow motion sequences to draw attention to the fleshy (often mutilated) body of Christ. Yet, watching the film now, it is not the extreme violence that strikes me, but instead the way in which the film pulls viewers into the felt texture of a physical world. The brief resurrection scene that ends the film exemplifies this sensual language. From inside the dark tomb we hear the rough sound of a stone slowly shifting. The camera follows a shaft of light as it moves across the coarse wall. A burial cloth softly settles, as if deflating, and the profile of Jesus' unbloodied, calm face enters and fills the frame. He looks up to heaven, closes his eyes, and rises. The camera does not follow, but holds fast so that viewers see the side of Jesus' naked leg and his hand; a nail hole, which pierces clean through his palm, appears in the center of the frame. Jesus steps forward toward the light and the film ends in a blackout. Gibson's attention to texture, sound, and lighting results in a highly tactile final scene.

This is the case throughout the film, as the camera explores the materiality of objects, bodies, and environments. For instance, at several moments Gibson focuses viewers on the *Arma Christi*—the hammer, nails, crown of thorns, and other instruments of the Passion. We see close-ups of the nails as they are hammered into Christ's hands and feet, actions that are sometimes presented in slow motion. We watch a soldier making the crown of thorns and then pressing it down firmly onto Jesus' head, blood oozing from the wounds it creates. During a slow motion sequence, we hear the creak of the wood and watch the soldiers strain as they lift the heavy cross onto which Jesus is nailed, until we finally see the base of the cross fall into a hole in the stony ground. Gibson also includes two close-up shots of the instruments lying in the dust at the foot of the cross. Devotion to the instruments of the Passion is part of a long-standing visual tradition, but Gibson's film tries to expand the devotional possibilities of that tradition by giving viewers access to the specific material contours of each item.

This attention to materiality extends to many objects—the smooth sides of wooden bowls, water running over the hands of the disciples, and the soft loaves of unleavened bread at the Last Supper; a bright red smear of blood on the Virgin Mary's dirt-streaked cheek after she kisses Christ's feet while he hangs on the cross; the metallic clink of bridles, the crunch of hoofs on stony ground, and the sharp crack of cloaks flapping in the wind as the Roman soldiers enter on horseback; the soft, thin, white linen sheets that Pilate's wife hands the Virgin Mary so that she can wipe up Jesus' blood after the scourging; the sound, sight, and even "feel" as Christ draws a line in the sand with his finger and dust rises around him; and even the heat, which gains a material presence in the film as sweat and dirt collect on the actors' bodies. The camera guides viewers into the sensual texture of Gibson's first-century Jerusalem, accentuating tactility in ways that, I would argue, pull the spectator into the film synaesthetically. This tactic has a powerful impact on the intimate affective script that the film produces.

Gibson is therefore not simply creating a realistic replication of the Passion; but, instead, his attention to material, sensual details urges spectators into a perceptual relationship with the film that moves beyond that of passive witness. Thomas J. J. Altizer suggests that the "immediacy" of the film's violence is meant to provoke an "ecstatic response" in audience members.[40] However, I would argue that this violence is consistent with the film's overall sensual vocabulary and is therefore only one of many elements in the film designed to recreate an immediate material world for viewers that will provoke this ecstatic response. For instance, Gibson chose to use "original" languages in the film—characters speak in Latin, Aramaic, or Hebrew, and are subtitled. Although this choice adds a patina of authenticity to the film, more importantly it functions as synaesthetic currency. The unfamiliar language compels viewers to forge visual, auditory, and rhythmic, rather than verbal, connections with the dramatized action. Moreover, in general there is very little spoken language in the film and so relatively few extended periods that viewers must spend reading the subtitles. Consequently, I would argue that Gibson's film primarily communicates sensually through images, sounds, and felt textures. *The Passion of The Christ* is therefore similar to a live performance in that it engages viewers kinaesthetically.

However, I would also assert that the devotional value of this kinaesthetic mode of communication is contingent upon viewers bringing a particular set of religious beliefs and biblical knowledge to the film. Beal raises a related point with respect to the use of subtitles. He notes, "Given that so much of the dialogue is drawn from gospel texts, these captions are relatively easy to follow for the biblically literate, for whom a few words call whole lines to mind."[41] On the other hand, for spectators without that literacy, the subtitles could become a frustrating distraction that keeps them mired in the realistic details rather than helping them gain access to the religiously real.

Other scholars have also recognized the connection between theology, belief, and religious spectatorship in their analyses of *The Passion of The Christ*. For instance, as Vincent Miller writes:

> Evangelical Christians were enormously influential in the success of the film. To it they brought their own devotional and imaginative resources. . . .

> It is precisely the biblical literalism of evangelical Christianity that is relevant to the film. The film's hyperrealism can be understood as the visual equivalent of biblical literalism.[42]

Other scholars discussed how religious belief influenced interpretations of the film's violence in particular. George Smiga asserts:

> Because they brought to the movie a faith conviction that Jesus was divine and that he chose to suffer for their sakes, they "jumped" from a cruel human crucifixion to an experience of divine love. The concrete and common experience of human suffering became for many the vehicle through which they might touch, if only in part, the immensity of God's love. The movement was instinctual to most, unreflective.[43]

Similarly, Beal writes that one of his students cried during the film "not because she was overwhelmed by the violence, but because she felt it provided a 'visible reality' of what she already knew about Christ's sacrifice on her behalf."[44]

However, I contend that such responses not only rely upon a particular interpretive theological context but also depend upon a certain physical expectation and openness to the film encounter itself. I am claiming that many evangelical believers approached the film in bodies prepared to engage it as re-representational realism. Accounts of church groups praying in parking lots and ticket lines before the film or of youth ministers instructing spectators not to buy popcorn and soda not only support this claim, but these measures also promote the awareness and attentiveness that I discussed in Chapter Two and that evangelical enactment requires.[45] These spectators did not jump over or transcend the material, but instead their bodies arrived ready to engage the film as a religiously real re-representation that could give them direct access to the divine. The film's emphasis on materiality may have provided those viewers with a deeply felt re-experience of the Passion.

As I discussed at the beginning of this book, *The Passion of The Christ* was, and still is, embedded within a particular cultural dialogue. I contend that this dialogue also encouraged evangelical believers to approach the film in bodies prepared for a religious encounter.[46] Criticism of the film in the press helped fuel the film's popularity among evangelicals by serving as an opposing force. As Christian Smith argues, American evangelicalism "is strong not because it is shielded against, but because it is—or at least perceives itself to be—embattled with forces that seem to oppose or threaten it. Indeed, evangelicalism . . . *thrives* on distinction, engagement, tension, conflict, and threat" (original emphasis).[47] The debates surrounding the film may have prompted evangelicals to enter the movie theater in bodies open to, and expecting, a religiously real re-experience of Christ's Passion, one whose power could serve as evidence of the film's veracity, as well as of their own true faith. Consequently, the larger public discourse enabled *The Passion of The Christ* to provide evangelical believers with a useful affective intimate script that validated their Christian identity and bolstered feelings of religious certainty.

The Gibson Affect

The Passion of The Christ was released on Ash Wednesday, 25 February 2004. Although it only played on 4,000 screens in 3,043 theaters, it earned \$117.5 million in ticket sales in the first five days. After twenty-two weeks in theaters, the film's U.S. box office total reached \$370,782,930; it grossed \$611,899,420 worldwide. As of mid-April 2012, the film's U.S. home DVD sales totaled \$2,828,439.[48] It is obviously not possible to claim with certainty that every visitor to Holy Land Experience has seen Gibson's film.[49] Yet, as I have mentioned, box office figures, post-screening surveys, and marketing strategies indicate that evangelical Christian communities and congregations were, and remain, a significant and, for the most part, enthusiastic proportion of the film's core audience.[50] Therefore it is no surprise that references to the film might circulate within evangelical performative culture. Moreover, as I have argued, for those spectators who approached the film as a religious event, and thus in bodies ready for a religiously real encounter, the film likely created a powerful affective intimate script. The intermedial strategy I call the Gibson affect endeavors to trigger that same script in order to appropriate its devotional value and apply it to other venues.

The performance of "Behold the Lamb" that I attended recalled Gibson's film in a variety of small ways. Most simply, unlike the four other Jesuses I saw during my two-day visit to HLE, the actor who played Jesus in "Behold the Lamb" looked remarkably like James Caviezel, the actor who played Jesus in Gibson's film. The flogging scene also reminded me of the film; not only was it lengthy and quite bloody, but, as in Gibson's film, just when I thought the scourging was finished, the soldiers turned Jesus over and whipped the front of his body too. Moreover, like the film, HLE's play included the apocryphal Veronica scene.

Yet, these features are all close enough to being Passion tropes that they may not be, or register as, direct references to Gibson's film. I would suggest however that two characters in the play—a black-cloaked figure and the Jewish high priest Caiaphas—are evidence of the Gibson affect. Moreover, based upon other reviews of "Behold the Lamb" that I have read, all of which were published either before or just as TBN took control over the park, I suspect that the Passion play I saw at HLE in May 2010 differed markedly from the version staged at the park during its first years of operation. In particular, these two characters are either not mentioned (the black-cloaked figure) or described in very different ways (Caiaphas). Although I cannot demonstrate with certainty that these characters were added or changed in direct response to Gibson's film, I suspect that, at the very least, they evoke memories of *The Passion of The Christ* for many HLE visitors.

In May 2010, "Behold the Lamb" contained two symbolic characters who first appeared during the opening Gethsemane scene. As Jesus knelt and prayed to God for strength, a white-cloaked figure stood behind him with his hand resting reassuringly on Jesus' shoulder. Meanwhile, on the other end of the playing space, a black-cloaked figure roamed the stage menacingly. Figure 3 shows this second figure a bit later in the play's action. While the white-cloaked actor remained largely passive and disappeared for most of the play, the other figure was a central character throughout, and he repeatedly exerted a kind of negative force over other characters. For instance, as Jesus continued praying silently in Gethsemane, the scene depicting Judas' betrayal occurred simultaneously. During this episode, the black-cloaked figure extended his hand out toward Judas and seemed to compel him to betray Jesus to Caiaphas. Likewise, on the left edge of Figure 2, this figure is seen compelling the Centurion to mock Jesus. This character served as a symbolic presence at particularly poignant moments, such as when he stood at the foot of the cross during the crucifixion. He also mimicked the actions of certain characters, such as when the soldiers punched or kicked Jesus. This figure mimed these same gestures simultaneously, thereby coding them with additional negative meaning and multiplying the possibilities for motor resonance.

As I note above, I have found no reviews of the play that mention either this character or the white-cloaked character. The black-cloaked figure is reminiscent of the androgynous, black-hooded figure in Gibson's film who

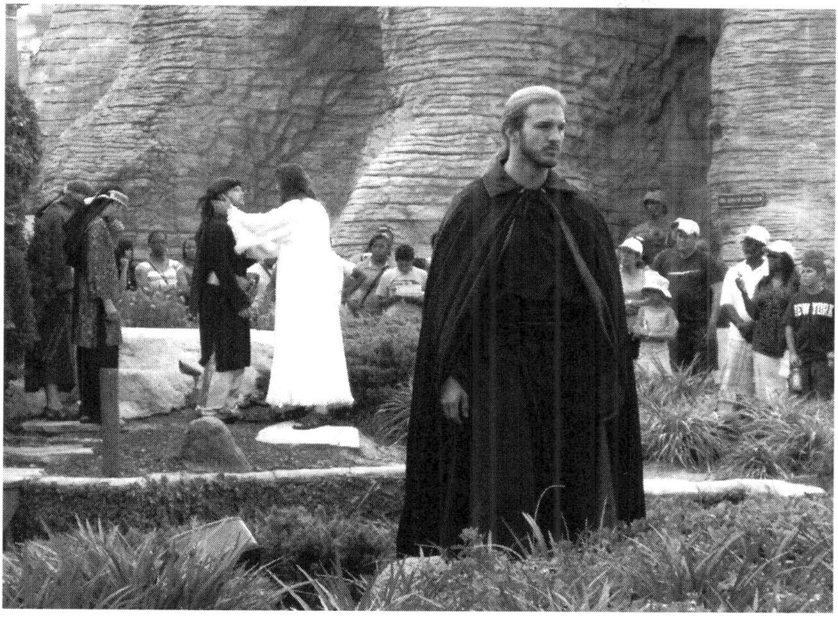

Figure 3. Black-cloaked figure in "Behold the Lamb" Passion Drama, Holy Land Experience, Orlando, Florida. May 2010. Photo by author.

appears to haunt and mock Jesus at his weakest moments. While in the HLE play characters, including Jesus, do not seem to actually see this figure, in Gibson's film Jesus does acknowledge the character, suggesting that it is Satan in the flesh. The figure therefore functions differently in the two Passions, but in both cases it gives evil a tangible, embodied presence. Moreover, for HLE visitors familiar with Gibson's film, the figure in "Behold the Lamb" could serve a unique intermedial function: it may prompt the spectator to perceive the play by means of the film experience and, thus, trigger the intimate affective script that *The Passion of The Christ* originally traced within that spectator's body. That script becomes a potent force within that person's re-experience, shaping how he or she will actually perceive and make meaning from "Behold the Lamb." Moreover, given the sensuousness of Gibson's film, this intermedial intervention may add felt texture to "Behold the Lamb," a tactility that the large, fabricated theme park space might otherwise hinder. Consequently, I would argue that the black-cloaked figure harnesses the rhythmic, synaesthetic power of Gibson's film in order to enrich the religiously real re-experience that "Behold the Lamb" cultivates.

The appearance of this cloaked figure is therefore an aisthetic act that pulls the past experience of watching Gibson's film into the performance frame so that spectators may draw upon its affective power during their re-experiences at "Behold the Lamb." (Likewise, subsequent viewings of the film on DVD may draw upon the intimate affective script formed during the spectator's live re-experience at "Behold the Lamb." Gibson's film is available for purchase in HLE's gift shops.) As with all performances, what spectators actually re-experience while watching the Passion drama at HLE is uncertain, but for many believer-spectators this interplay between the two Passions likely forms a new, unique, "religiously real" script that expands the possibilities for creating personal devotional meaning.

Another key difference between the play I saw and earlier versions presented at HLE concerns the depiction of Jewish characters. The May 2010 play strongly implicated Jews in Jesus' death through the character Caiaphas. Once Jesus was in custody, Caiaphas brought him before Pilate. As opposed to Caiaphas, who is a central character throughout the play, the audience sees Pilate only briefly—that is, if they can see him at all. I watched the play from a coveted spot in the first row of stools in the main seating area. Yet, when I heard Pilate's voice over the amplification system, I could not initially locate him; I noticed many other spectators who, like me, were scanning the playing area and looking a bit confused. After craning my neck around and looking up, I finally saw Pilate and his wife high above the action, perched on the top of a classically designed "Roman" building stage right of the tomb. Although very tall, the structure is situated on the periphery of the park grounds and seems to serve as part of the exterior façade rather than as part of the interior "Jerusalem"; in fact, I had not even noticed the building until that moment although I had been wandering around the park for two hours by that point. In addition, I suspect many of the audience members who were behind me, sitting on stools shaded by an overhead covering, could not see Pilate at all.

Placing Pilate literally high above the action reduces his dramatic presence and implies that he is not deeply invested in, nor accountable for, what takes place. (Although I may be mistaken, I do not recall him speaking again after the scourging.) In contrast, Caiaphas, who represents the Jewish High Council, was on the ground, level with the rest of the characters, and playing a significant role in the action throughout the entire play. Caiaphas made demands and seemed to control the narrative at many key points. For example, there were no trial scenes with Pilate; although Pilate condemned Jesus to be scourged, he then immediately washed his hands of the entire matter, even before the flogging occurred. On the other hand, Caiaphas stood nearby to watch the scourging and then remained part of the action until Jesus' burial was complete. Moreover, the menacing black-cloaked figure lingered beside Caiaphas for much of the play's first half, often mouthing Caiaphas' accusations against Jesus as the actor playing Caiaphas spoke them aloud. Finally and perhaps most surprising, Caiaphas proclaimed the controversial blood libel curse from Matthew 27:25: "His blood be on us and on our children." Although the play acknowledged that Jesus was Jewish—he was buried with a tallit—and, as I have noted, the black-cloaked figure influenced other characters besides Caiaphas, such as Judas and the Roman soldiers, Caiaphas' prominent visual and vocal presence situated him as the mastermind behind the crucifixion. This Passion did not take place under Roman law, but in a Jerusalem controlled by Jews.

In this respect, the 2010 play I saw was markedly different from what Beal describes seeing on his 2002 visit to Holy Land Experience. He writes, "Interestingly, and commendably, in this Passion play, Jewish leaders and crowds don't play the negative role of Jesus' conspiring accusers and antagonists, as they so often do in other renditions (Mel Gibson's *The Passion of the Christ* being the most recent example)."[51] Beal is very knowledgeable about the Passion play tradition and its anti-Semitic legacy, and has written articles and coedited a collection specifically about Gibson's film; he therefore almost certainly saw a very different Passion drama in 2002 than the one I watched. Ronald Lukens-Bull and Mark Fafard's 2004 research at the park also suggests a significant change with respect to the Jewish presence in the play. They specifically note:

> One telling element of the Holy Land Experience passion play is the complete absence of the role of Jewish leaders in the crucifixion. This is in marked contrast to Mel Gibson's *The Passion of The Christ*. . . . The conspicuous absence of characters representing Jewish leaders in the passion play also contrasts with other dramas in the park. Moreover, priestly characters wander the site interacting with guests between dramas, but they deliberately withdraw for the passion play. The Jewish leaders' absence from the play can be seen as a deliberate attempt to edit them out of the crucifixion story.[52]

By contrast, the 2010 play placed a Jewish high priest at the center of the dramatic action. Thus, the very same elements whose absence previously provided evidence for why HLE's Passion play was, laudably, different from Gibson's film, are now, in fact, present. I propose that the depiction of Caiaphas in HLE's play fulfills the same goal as did the cloaked figure—to trigger the intimate affective script associated with *The Passion of The Christ*. However, in this case, I would argue that the intermedial intervention also constitutes a concerted effort to revive and appropriate the passionate feelings of religious conviction that the original film event produced in many believers.

Caiaphas' central dramatic role in "Behold the Lamb," as well as his visual resemblance to the film Caiaphas, were striking. Compare the Caiaphas in Figures 2 and 4 with Figure 5, an image from *The Passion of The Christ* that shows Caiaphas, Annas, and other members of the Jewish council. The inclusion of the blood libel curse was also notable, especially since that line became a pivotal point of debate with respect to Gibson's film and, incidentally, remains in the movie, if unsubtitled. Therefore, in many respects this depiction of Caiaphas dramatically reversed the tone and sentiment that Beal, Lukens-Bull, and Fafard describe. Although many factors likely contributed to this representational change, I posit that, to some extent, this characterization represents a strident response to the debates about anti-Semitism in Passion plays that Gibson's film reignited within popular discourse, in particular, the arguments pertaining to who has "ownership" over the Passion story and its representation. HLE may purposefully reference Gibson's film in order to revive within spectators the sense of embattlement they felt in the wake of this discourse and, in doing so, to trigger the feelings of "distinction, engagement, tension, conflict, and threat" that, according to Christian Smith, ultimately strengthen evangelical identity. In other words, by recalling the film Caiaphas so overtly, "Behold the Lamb" may reactivate the felt sense of meaning and mission that the larger cultural event of *The Passion of The Christ* initially instantiated within many evangelical believers. In doing so, the play produces a new, richly layered intimate script that confirms the spectator's commitment to and belief in the "true" Passion account.

A final, but even more explicit reference to *The Passion of The Christ* occurred at the end of the play. As the disciples rushed to the empty tomb, "Resurrection," a song by composer and instrumentalist John Debney, began to play over the sound system. It continued for many minutes as the

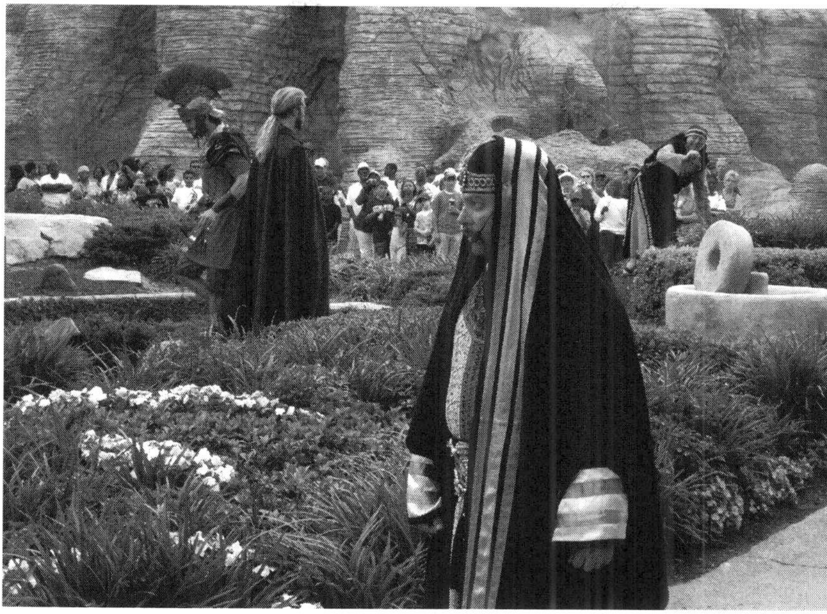

Figure 4. Actor playing Caiaphas in "Behold the Lamb" Passion Drama, Holy Land Experience, Orlando, Florida. May 2010. Photo by author.

disciples frantically searched the tomb and discussed the disappearance of Christ's body. The score changed during the Centurion's monologue, but "Resurrection" resumed when Jesus appeared, and it played during his final resurrection speech. Debney's "Resurrection" is the song that immediately follows the resurrection scene in *The Passion of The Christ,* playing through the film's closing credits.[53] In some sense, it serves as the film's recessional hymn. Choosing to underscore the resurrection scene in "Behold the Lamb" with this song fulfills two main goals. First, if spectators were not already connecting the play to Gibson's film, this music would likely prompt those familiar with the film to do so. But, more important, the music adds gravity and emotional dimension to a moment that is essentially a vocally amplified, broadly acted scene with smoke effects. This function is critical because while the crucifixion is important, it is not Christ's death, but his resurrection that yields salvation. Yet, unlike the Passion events, with their physicality and violence, Jesus' resurrection has no material texture; it lacks

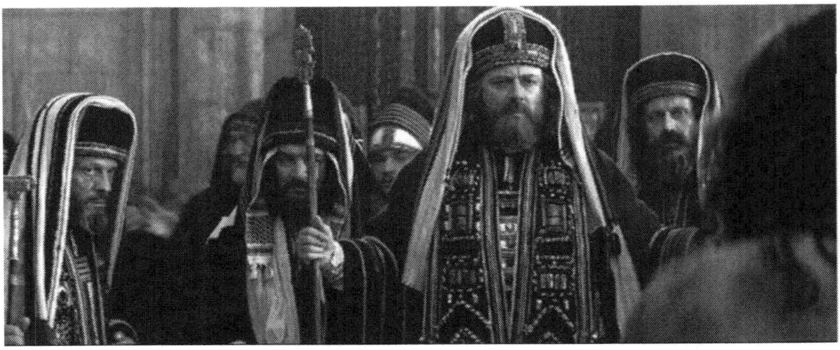

Figure 5. Jewish priests including Caiphas, played by Mattia Sbragia (center), and Annas, played by Toni Bertorelli (far left). From *The Passion of The Christ*, 2004, directed by Mel Gibson.

tangibility. Perhaps this is why Gibson offers his viewers a sensually oriented resurrection scene that intimately explores the texture of space and bodies. But "Behold the Lamb" cannot provide visual close-ups, and therefore it employs music to give the resurrection scene a felt texture and to direct emotional production. Once again, Gibson's film intervenes in order to intensify the spectator's re-experience.

These examples of intermedial intervention are related to the use of medievalism that Sponsler identifies in nineteenth- and early twentieth-century U.S. Passion playing. By referencing the medieval Passion play tradition, an American production could gain legitimacy and value. Allusions to Gibson's film may likewise imbue "Behold the Lamb" with a sense of authority and ongoing significance. Consequently, the value of these references lies in their ability to serve as forces that will direct the spectator's experience in productive directions. In this case, the Gibson affect may aim to cultivate the same kind of perceptual awareness and attentiveness in spectators that Gibson's film encourages. By doing so, the Gibson affect fosters an energetic relationship between spectator and performer within a theme park environment that might otherwise thwart the engagement that evangelical enactment requires.

Sponsler also explains that invoking the Middle Ages helped certain U.S. Passion plays avoid the controversy that often surrounds the role of religion in the public sphere. In this respect, the Gibson affect operates quite differently. Rather than removing the play from current religious controversies, recalling Gibson's film directly and purposefully inserts "Behold the Lamb" into those debates. By working on and through the spectator's body, the Gibson affect seeks to appropriate the affective power of *The Passion of The Christ* in order to revive strong feelings of devotional certainty and evangelical commitment, and thus to prompt the park visitor to take sides in those contemporary debates. In this respect, "Behold the Lamb" uses the Gibson affect to promote engaged orthodoxy.

A Screen-Sized Passion

Unlike many live performance venues, HLE allows visitors to videotape most of its productions. I would estimate that about a third of the spectators around me watched much of "Behold the Lamb" through video cameras, with many more (myself included) frequently taking pictures during the play. This form of self-imposed intermediality may initially seem to work against evangelical enactment's energetic goals. Yet, Bruce Barton's work, which examines "the possibilities of intimacy in intermedial theatrical performance," suggests otherwise.[54] While Barton acknowledges that theatrical intermediality often evokes a degree of anxiety, like Peter Boenisch he believes this anxiety is usually productive: "Rather than an ancillary impediment or distraction, by heightening vulnerability, immersion, interactivity, and investment—of performers as well as spectators—intermedial anxiety can be seen to both pinpoint and activate vital possibilities of/for/in theatrical intimacy."[55] Therefore, viewing "Behold the Lamb" primarily on a camera's screen may, in fact, concentrate the camera operator's re-experience into something that feels more intimate and immediate, thereby nurturing a religiously real re-experience.

In addition, certain spectators may have concerns about seeing a live, "realistic" Passion play performed in a theme park setting. Watching the play through a video camera might alleviate that uneasiness without eliminating the sense of liveness. In his analysis of a performance piece that juxtaposes screen images against a live performer (actor Rick Miller), Peter Cockett argues that,

> the mediatization of the moment engages us by projecting us into the action and simultaneously encourages a critical distance. . . . The mediated image is no less "live" than Miller himself. It creates an alternative perspective on

> the interaction between stage and auditorium that keeps the audience in a state of critical motion.[56]

Using video cameras during "Behold the Lamb" may allow spectators to enter a similar kind of engaged state of critical motion. Here, again, I locate intermediality within the viewer's aisthetic act. The camera not only heightens the performance's energetic dynamic by suspending spectators perceptually between presence and representation, but it also resolves more general apprehensions about representation by giving the viewer a way to mediate the drama's immediacy and use of divine impersonation.

Furthermore, for visitors to HLE who do not attend live theater regularly, the camera's screen may make the experience at "Behold the Lamb" more familiar and, therefore, more resonant. As I have mentioned, borrowing popular media forms and their familiar rhythms is a standard tactic within evangelical dramaturgy. In this case, watching the play by means of a more commonplace media platform might help the spectator's body relax into, and more easily become entrained by, the rhythms of a live performance, thereby prompting resonance. The ability to zoom into expressions and gestures will also multiply the opportunities for motor resonance. And, finally, videotaping the production in some respect commodifies (or, recommodifies) the play, reshaping it into a product that visitors can take home to watch again or share with others. Such commodification is fundamental to evangelical dramaturgy.

This specific visitor act demonstrates how individual visitors/spectators/users can tactically deploy evangelical dramaturgy's strategies in order to personalize their own intimate affective scripts and, consequently, increase the ongoing usefulness of their religious re-experiences. In this case, video cameras give spectators a virtually endless variety of ways to shape the live performance for private consumption. As I have already noted, individual choice and personal agency are fundamental not only to evangelical dramaturgy but also to evangelical theology generally.

"Behold the Lamb" exposes various ways that intermediality can expand the possibilities for generating intimate religiously real re-experiences, especially at large venues. In Chapter Six I return to this idea at greater length when I discuss how megachurches integrate elements like giant projection screens, live rock bands, and smoke and lighting effects into the worship event in order to create intense and immediate devotional encounters, even in a space as enormous as a professional basketball stadium. However, intermedial interventions can also diffuse the energetic dynamic between performers and spectators, and thus hinder the encounter's devotional potential. I would argue that this is the case with the subject of my next chapter—the "Great Passion Play" of Eureka Springs.

4
The "Great Passion Play" and Evangelical Blends

The "Great Passion Play" is staged annually from May through October, five nights a week, in the Ozark Mountains of Eureka Springs, Arkansas. As the program explains, the production is modeled "in form and function" after the famous Passion play in Oberammergau, Germany, "to involve the local community to glorify God."[1] The two-hour play is performed on an open-air three-story-tall permanent set that is the size of two football fields.[2] This set is built into a hillside before a 4,100-seat amphitheater on Mount Oberammergau, thus named by Gerald L. K. Smith, the religious entrepreneur who developed the play as one of various "Sacred Projects."[3] Smith was an ordained minister and political orator especially known for his anti-Semitic views, most openly expressed through the magazine he published entitled *The Cross and the Flag.* In the 1960s, Smith helped revive the struggling town of Eureka Springs through his Sacred Projects, the first of which was the seventy-foot-high Christ of the Ozarks statue on Magnetic Mountain. The statue was completed in 1966 and is visible from four states (Arkansas, Oklahoma, Missouri, and Kansas).[4] This and the other Sacred Projects were developed under the auspices of the Elna M. Smith Foundation, named after Smith's wife. Consequently, as with "Behold the Lamb," the "Great Passion Play" is an evangelical performance event situated within a larger physical and material context that overtly shapes the performance-viewing experience for spectators.

In this chapter, I will continue to examine the strategies that Passion plays use to cultivate an energetic dynamic between spectators and actors. Moreover, I will assert that the "Great Passion Play" tries to generate this energetic relationship in order to serve an overtly political goal. Using the cognitive theory of conceptual blending, I argue that the other Sacred Projects surrounding the "Great Passion Play" prepare spectators to perceive this play in very specific ways that will prompt them to live in a felt blend of evangelical Christian piety and nationalism.

A Sacred Project

Smith claimed that the idea for producing a Passion play came to him during construction of the Christ of the Ozarks statue. As Glen Jeansonne writes:

> According to Smith himself, as he stood on Magnetic Mountain admiring his glistening, half-complete statue, he was struck by yet another inspiration, this time the staging of some sort of Easter tableau. He remembered that the tiny Bavarian village of Oberammergau had been staging a Passion play at ten-year intervals since being spared from famine in 1634. . . . Smith decided that the hollow between Magnetic Mountain and another peak (which he later renamed Mount Oberammergau) was topographically suited for an amphitheatre.[5]

One of the sculptors working on the statue introduced Smith to the writer and director Robert Hyde. As Smith explained in an open letter to the *Eureka Springs Times-Echo,* upon meeting Hyde, he was "impressed by [Hyde's] manner, his integrity, and his dedicated ability. His Christian faith was obvious, but it was not exhibited in sanctimonious or self-righteous form."[6] Planning began soon thereafter, and Smith gave Hyde control over the entire process, which included writing the play, designing and overseeing construction of the amphitheater and set, casting and directing the play, and eventually even playing the role of Christ.[7]

The "Great Passion Play" debuted on 14 July 1968, to a small invited audience. The audience grew by approximately 25,000 annually over the next ten years; the production welcomed its millionth spectator in 1976 and four millionth in 1989.[8] By 2008, over seven million visitors had seen the production.[9] Timothy Kovalcik's 2008 book about the play indicates that by that year there had been three significant script changes and multiple recordings.[10] The production I saw on Saturday, 19 June 2010, was marketed as "The New Great Passion Play," and the program refers to the play as "updated and improved." According to staff members working at the theater, a new script was premiering that summer, making the 2010 text the fifth version of the play.

The 2010 production began with the raising of Lazarus and then moved quickly to the Entry into Jerusalem on Palm Sunday. The Entry is a spectacular scene that includes a host of live animals and supernumeraries. After entering on a live donkey, Jesus performs many miracles, answers various questions posed by the Jewish high priests, and expresses outrage at the market in the Temple; in one crowd-pleasing moment, a furious Jesus upends a market basket that contains about a dozen white doves, which then fly in formation over the audience before disappearing upstage. After these opening scenes, the play focuses a significant amount of time on deliberations among the Jewish priests as they debate how to handle this radical rabbi Jesus. Caiaphas visits Pilate to ask for his intervention, and Pilate's wife cautions him against it. (Pilate's first entrance is another crowd-pleaser; he rides in as part of a procession of Roman chariots pulled by horses.) Unlike Holy Land Experience's thirty-minute "Behold the Lamb," the two-hour "Great Passion Play" gives Pilate a significant role and devotes time to showing disagreement among the Jewish priests.

The play covers most of the major moments in the Passion account: the Last Supper; Judas' betrayal and suicide; Christ's prayers and arrest in the Garden of Gethsemane; the various interrogations of Jesus by Pilate and the Jewish High Council; reactions from the disciples, including Peter's denial; the scourging and sentencing of Jesus; the walk to Calvary, including the Veronica episode; the crucifixion, deposition, and burial; different discussions between the disciples and among the Jewish priests about Jesus' resurrection prophecy; the resurrection; and the encounter between Mary and Jesus at the tomb on Easter morning. However, unlike many Passion plays, this production also depicts Jesus' subsequent appearances to the disciples (including an episode involving doubting Thomas) and his post-resurrection ministry, and it concludes with Jesus ascending into the night sky as Handel's "Hallelujah Chorus" plays over the amplification system. Once Jesus is no longer visible, spectators begin filing out of the theater.[11]

One of the most striking elements of this production is its 400-foot-long set, which concentrates a number of biblical locations onto a replica of a street in ancient Jerusalem. These locations include Pilate's court, the Temple, the Jewish High Council chamber, and the Upper Room. The set extends behind and upstage of this street, and in this area scenes depicting the crucifixion, resurrection, and ascension are staged in more natural settings filled with trees, bushes, and rocks. This part of the set extends around to the left of the audience (stage right) where the raising of Lazarus and Garden of Gethsemane scenes are presented. The trees and other natural elements heighten certain dramatic moments. For instance, as Jesus is praying in the Garden, through the trees spectators begin to catch glimpses of the fiery torches carried by the Roman guards, and suspense builds as they gradually draw closer. This is a gigantic set, but hidden passageways, doors, and paths facilitate very quick scene transitions.[12]

Like the script, the stage has also undergone significant transformations over its lifespan. Locations have changed—for instance, Herod's court used to be a part of the set, but scenes involving Herod were absent from the 2010 production—and the amphitheater initially only seated 3,500 spectators. Various special effects have also been added over time. For example, the ascension in the original production occurred "in an enclosed building" with Jesus "lifted out of sight behind a special screen, which helped hide the wiring."[13] In the 1980s, wires were added to the top of the set so that now Jesus ascends forty feet into the air before he eventually disappears from sight into the trees. Although, despite the tight spotlight, the wires are visible, this ascension still supplies the production with a spectacular closing image. Other elements, such as the many different live animals—camels, donkeys, horses, doves, sheep (the Elna M. Smith Foundation keeps its own flock year-round)—and the "authentic" costumes and props have been important features of the production from the start.

The use of live animals and the attention to "realistic" costumes, props, and settings all aim to give spectators access to the biblical past. In doing so, these elements support evangelical dramaturgy's re-representational goals. Yet, as with "Behold the Lamb" at Holy Land Experience, the actual performance environment has the potential to counteract those goals. While with HLE I suggested this was due to the theme park context, here I would argue that, despite the aesthetic of actuality that the sets and costumes create, the vastness of the stage and amphitheater ultimately undermines the performance's rhythmic potential, thereby hindering possibilities for re-experience.

The stage is incredibly large and, even when you are watching the play from the front row of the amphitheater, the actors look very small as they navigate the set. Although lighting and sound help direct audience attention, at certain points it is difficult to know where to look or how to locate who is speaking, especially since the director makes generous use of simultaneous action. Moreover, because the audience is quite far away, even during intimate scenes, like the Last Supper episode that is staged in an enclosed Upper Room, energy does not concentrate around or emerge from any of the actors. This is also the case with certain key plot points. For instance, the lashing of the whip during Jesus' scourging or the pounding of the nails through Jesus' hands and feet did not evoke the kinds of visible and audible reactions from the audience members around me that these same moments had produced in spectators at "Behold the Lamb." Even with the amplification, these sounds had no tactile dimension. Overall, the play lacked a material, sensual presence.

Notably, the only scenes that possessed a palpable presence were those involving live animals. These moments were almost jarring by contrast, and each time they occurred a kind of energetic rush raced through the audience. Erika Fischer-Lichte maintains, "Animals unfold an almost uncanny 'presence' of the strong order whenever they appear onstage: they seem to cover the entire stage and attract everyone's attention. They steal the actors' show."[14] It seems that by accentuating the live actuality of the performance, these animals could help to cultivate an energetic dynamic within the amphitheater. However, I would argue that in the case of the "Great Passion Play" the live animals instead draw attention to the general absence of felt presence throughout the performance and thus only stoke the spectator's (unrequited) desire for a more intensive, rhythmic relationship with the actors.[15]

Yet, the frustrating lack of materiality of the "Great Passion Play" is not entirely a result of the size of the theater; many theatergoers have sat in the back row of a large house and still felt the physical thrill of a play's liveness and sensed the material presence of the set pieces, props, and actors' bodies. But at the "Great Passion Play," the performance rhythms are severely hampered by the use of a prerecorded script, an example of intermediality that, rather than cultivating an energetic dynamic, undermines it.

Intermedial Dissonance

The "Great Passion Play" has always been a prerecorded production. The music and dialogue are piped over an amplification system, with the performers lip-synching and matching their gestures to the recording. Hyde believed that using a prerecorded script would result in better quality and audibility given the large theater. However, the recorded script also produces a bizarre dislocation. As Dorothy Chansky writes, "The recorded dialogue is often conversational in tone, but the actors' gestures are sometimes bombastic, creating a weird disconnect between the (putative) speaker's body and his or her voice."[16] Thus, it is not the amplification itself that produces a kind of cognitive dissonance; the widespread use of microphones have accustomed many spectators to hearing an actor's voice emerge from speakers and not from the actual speaking body before them, and, as I demonstrated with the performances at HLE, amplifying voices and music does not preclude immediacy and intimacy. Instead, the dissonance results from the odd way the nonspeaking actors try to embody, or pretend to embody, the spoken words. Fischer-Lichte explains how vocality "always also brings forth corporeality. A voice creates all three types of materiality: corporeality, spatiality, and tonality. The voice leaps from the body and vibrates through space."[17] The lack of vocality in the "Great Passion Play" removes a critical element of corporeality from the performance, an absence that likely confuses the spectator's cognitive faculties and subverts possibilities for embodied simulation. This is perhaps why the appearance of live animals, which are not artificially embodying sounds, generates such a delightful energetic charge by comparison.

The prerecording radically alters the performance event's "acoustemology," what Steven Feld calls "the local conditions of acoustic sensation, knowledge, and imagination, embodied in the culturally particular sense of place."[18] Acoustemology helps us recognize the "potential of acoustic knowing, of sounding as a condition of and for knowing, of sonic presence and awareness as potent shaping forces in how people make sense of experience."[19] Both for the actors who create the theatrical space and for the spectators who arrive ready to engage the performance's rhythms, the recorded script disrupts their ability to sense and *make* sense of the world of the play. And, by depriving the theatrical world of an element that is necessary for the "sensuality of emplacement, of making place,"[20] the prerecording fundamentally thwarts possibilities for "religiously real" re-experiences of Christ's Passion.

Therefore, if the "Great Passion Play" were aiming for the same re-representational goals as "Behold the Lamb," I would deem it largely unsuccessful precisely because the prerecording creates a rhythmic and cognitive dissonance that is nearly impossible to overcome. However, like all dramaturgies, evangelical dramaturgy does not have a single unified goal but is deployed in a variety of ways to emphasize certain elements over others depending upon the performance context. I would therefore argue that, rather than cultivating a re-experience of Christ's Passion, the "Great Passion Play" is instead designed to generate a different kind of religiously real re-experience, one that intrinsically links Christian piety to a specific regional identity and nationalistic vision in order to support an explicitly political form of engaged orthodoxy.

Although the terms *nationalism* and *patriotism* are often applied interchangeably, I purposefully use the terms *nationalism* and *nationalistic* to describe the dramaturgical goals of the "Great Passion Play." David Morgan explains that patriotism "faces the openness and contingency of the social compact and regards the nation as a willed, historical, mutable construction" that leaves room for (and is, in fact, dependent upon) dissent. By contrast, nationalism "has a powerful way of erasing or vilifying any other attitude toward the patria" than its own.[21] Furthermore, with respect to material culture, Morgan contends that patriotism "will invest in the flag and other objects and places a power to recall and to honor virtues enshrined in the Constitution and in the heroic deeds of those who champion it." Alternatively, nationalism,

> installs the flag and other objects and places in a national cult in which reverence for the emblems is understood to secure the nation as an earthly expression of divine will and therefore as a domain that cannot allow dissent. The nation itself is thought to be sacramentally deposited in forms that must be regarded as sacrosanct and holy. Such a view will refuse to distinguish between explicitly religious objects, such as the Bible or the Cross, and the American flag.[22]

This kind of nationalistic identity construction recalls Smith's own politics and, as I will demonstrate, directly relates to the purpose of the affective intimate script that the "Great Passion Play" experience produces.

"Christian-Sounding" Voices

In the spirit of Oberammergau's production, the "Great Passion Play" cast of between 200 and 250 people has always been composed entirely of local amateur performers. In addition to promoting an association with the Bavarian play and its long-standing sacred tradition, Smith and Hyde considered an amateur cast critical to the play's pure religious goals. In the early years actors were not paid but were instead allowed to earmark their share of the profits for donation to local churches or charities.[23] As Smith wrote in 1968:

> This will accomplish two great purposes. It will not attract commercially-minded participants, and it will attract Christian people who want only to help present the sacred story, but who are happy to participate in an activity that will accrue some modest financial help to the congregation that they represent. This formula will help assure the participation of sincere Christian people.[24]

From the beginning, Smith and Hyde were attentive to the religious intentions of those who were presenting the Passion drama, recalling tactics similar to those Claire Sponsler identified with respect to the Black Hills Passion play and, perhaps, using these to negotiate similar anxieties about for-profit divine impersonation.[25]

However, not only were Smith and Hyde concerned about the faith of those who would physically impersonate the biblical characters during the show, they also considered religious conviction with respect to the recording. Hyde convinced Smith to hire professional actors and, according to Jeansonne, Smith agreed, "stipulating only that he find actors with 'Christian-sounding' voices."[26] As Smith himself explains,

> Naturally, we were concerned about the voices that were used. They were professional actors dedicated to their faith in Christ who had been recruited carefully by Mr. Hyde with the understanding that they would be rewarded only when, as and if the production made it possible, and then their reward would be very conservative compared to what is ordinarily given actors. Mr. Hyde assured me that no one was asked to speak his voice into the great stereophonic recording unless he was known as a believing Christian.[27]

It appears that Smith may have recognized that it was not simply the text and imagery that communicated the play's sacred message, but that other performance elements, like sound, did as well. Therefore, he wanted every aesthetic feature of the production to emerge from a sincere Christian faith.

However, I also suspect that the recorded voices were intended to create a "Christian" biblical world that sounded like a very specific American community. The 2010 recording had a local, regional sound that, I would argue, for many people carries Christian associations. Most of the voices had Southern accents, many with an Arkansas or Oklahoma dialect. The same was true of the actors on the "Living Bible Tour," another Sacred Project on the Passion Play grounds that I will discuss at length later in this chapter. Some of the actors on that tour not only had local accents but also frequently used nonstandard grammar when speaking "in character"; for instance, the man playing the disciple Peter repeatedly said "the disciples was" and "they was." The local accents and dialect heard in the "Great Passion Play" recording not only serve evangelical dramaturgy's goal to conflate time and place, but for some spectators the familiar sound will also stimulate resonance.

Linda Kintz writes about the long-standing associations in the United States between anti-intellectualism and the South. Like most ethnic, racial, and cultural stereotypes, this one is regularly perpetuated in popular culture, where a Southern accent is often used to fold "regional identity into the codings of class and poor white trash, expressing contempt for all of them."[28] By effectively excluding them from "categories of acceptability," this cultural coding insults a wide range of Americans, a group particularly associated with the "Bible Belt."[29] I believe the "Great Passion Play" recording reappropriates the "southern sound" in order to flip that script. This dramaturgical choice incorporates into the Passion narrative the very "plain folks Americans," to use Kintz's term, who are usually trivialized in, patronized by, or absent from mainstream media culture.[30] As a result, for those spectators who live in or are originally from the region, hearing the central Christian story of salvation reenacted in familiar local dialects, rather than in the typical Hollywood accent, will trigger physical, emotional resonance that not only validates their identity, but that allows them to experience the Passion story in a fresh, unique way. Accent is an affective force that powerfully shapes the spectator's intimate script and its ongoing devotional value. Furthermore, given the prevalent cultural association between Southern accents and the Bible Belt, I suspect that the voices in the "Great Passion Play" register for most people in the audience (consciously or not) as sounding innately Protestant, Bible-believing American. That association may, in fact, be especially true for those spectators who are not from the region or who don't share the accent.[31]

The resonance this dramaturgical choice fosters is a powerful force within the performance's acoustemology. One measure of this was how odd, even disconcerting, the play sounded to my mid-Atlantic, East Coast ear. Most startling was that, to me and my partner, Jesus sounded *exactly* like President Bill Clinton—in accent, tone, and delivery. This reaction suggests how rarely I hear an Arkansas accent in the media; I doubt anyone from the region would have made that same association. This example exposes regional dialect as a compelling affective device that significantly impacts the meaning spectators make from the performance.

This resonance also reveals where the "Great Passion Play" and *The Passion of The Christ* intersect; both cater to a particular insider crowd. As I mentioned in Chapter Three, Timothy Beal claims that *The Passion of The Christ*'s lack of a linear narrative, its use of captions, and the brief flashbacks to Christ's earlier life, which are given largely without context or explanation, are all readily accessible and understandable to a certain Christian audience. While, for other spectators, the film offers "no way into its symbolic world. As a result, they come away alienated feeling like outsiders."[32] Beal surmises that constructing this insider/outsider dynamic "is entirely intentional."[33] Ultimately, the film does not try to indoctrinate new believers but is pointedly—even exclusively—focused on serving a particular insider Christian community. Gibson crafts a film experience that will only resonate with a certain set of believers.

I posit that the regional dialects and accents heard during the "Great Passion Play" function similarly. They are aimed at spectators for whom those sounds will resonate as familiar and therefore represent a dramaturgical strategy designed to cultivate feelings of comfort and belonging within that specific audience. These spectators, usually depicted as outsiders in mainstream culture,[34] are positioned here as insiders. Furthermore, since resonance is a physical sensation, it may give the performance a sensual dimension it otherwise lacks. That sensuality helps to shape an intimate script that aligns a particular regional American identity with the "true" Christian faith. For those spectators who consider themselves members of that regional demographic, this resonant script not only validates the legitimacy of their religious beliefs but may simultaneously encourage those spectators to re-experience a certain nostalgic, idealized American past of shared faith and common values. In doing so, it translates a certain nationalistic vision into an embodied belief.

Dialect and accent are dramaturgical tactics that help the "Great Passion Play" achieve its particular re-experiential goals. However, evangelical dramaturgy is also manifest in other venues and events on the Passion play grounds. Many of these other Sacred Projects also seek to cultivate a nostalgic re-experience of Christian America and, by doing so, prepare the audience for the Passion play. This function is most evident in the Living Bible Tour.

New Jerusalem in Arkansas: The Living Bible Tour

The "Great Passion Play" is situated alongside several other Sacred Projects that frame the performance event for spectators in very specific ways. In addition to the Christ of the Ozarks statue, the 600-acre Passion play grounds is home to a Sacred Arts Museum (originally called the "Christ Only Art Gallery" when it first opened in the late 1960s), a Bible Exhibit that includes 6,000 Bibles in 650 translations, a two-hour Living Bible Tour, the 100-year-old one-room Church in the Grove (relocated to the grounds in 1986), an original section of the Berlin Wall, and the 250-seat "Top of the Mountain Dinner Theater" where a gospel music show led by "The Texans" and a sit-down home-style meal are offered before every Passion play performance. Two short plays are also staged on the grounds each evening before the play: "Parables of The Potter" and "David the Shepherd Boy."[35] The grounds previously included a creationist-themed Museum of Earth History, but that collection has since moved to Dallas, Texas.[36]

These venues encourage spectators to see the "Great Passion Play" through a particular religious mode of spectatorship. All of these exhibits explicitly promote a Christo-centric theology, and many use re-representational strategies to shape the visitor's pre-performance experience into a religiously real re-experience. For instance, characters in the Living Bible Tour and in the two short plays speak directly to visitors "in character" as ancient biblical figures. Also, many of these venues, as well as the concession stands, two gift shops, and Passion play box office, are housed in adobe-style buildings seemingly designed to evoke the ancient biblical world. This is particularly true of the full-size replica of Jerusalem's Eastern Gate that stands across from the amphitheater and marks the beginning of the Living Bible Tour; as the "Great Passion Play" program explains, "Passing through the life-size Eastern Gate replica, you seem to leave the quaint Arkansas village of Eureka Springs behind. Just ahead are scenes from an old world waiting to be discovered."[37] These scenes, like the other Sacred

Projects, are described in the program as opportunities "to get a glimpse of the magnificent man called Jesus."[38]

Yet, the "living" exhibits and other performances do not actually include Jesus himself; instead, they offer visitors a theological and experiential grounding in the narrative of Jesus that prepares them to recognize the full magnitude of the Passion events. In a sense, these pre-performance elements are designed to cultivate anticipation, not just for the "Great Passion Play," but more specifically for the appearance of Jesus in that play, so that, upon seeing "Jesus" in the flesh, spectators will experience fascination. As Tzachi Zamir explains, "We experience fascination when we recognize a force that extends possibilities and is, in this sense, life-amplifying."[39] Acting is a powerful "form of existential amplification" that realizes those possibilities by embodying them, while "the audience takes part in a form of imaginative existential expansion."[40] However, because verbalization is vital to generating this actor-audience dynamic, the recording used in the "Great Passion Play" ultimately thwarts existential amplification. Zamir writes:

> The intensity experienced and/or projected by actors relates to the act *of actually verbalizing* some words and linguistic sequences, relating to the tactile dimension of language. Uttering aloud words . . . affects the speaker differently than mentally reading them; verbalizing them as part of a comprehensive embodiment of the role mobilizes an even more intense experience. The reason is that locked into the words—the consonants and vowels of a well-written dramatic text—is an emotional force that can be released by the actor. In a strong performance, such "energy" is radiated to the audience. (original emphasis)[41]

Due to the prerecorded dialogue, the "Great Passion Play" must rely on means other than the actors' verbalizing bodies in order to cultivate this existential amplification and audience fascination, and thereby expand the spectator's devotional possibilities. I contend that the more intimate and immediate encounters offered around the Passion play grounds, and especially during the Living Bible Tour, are designed to foster fascination. By making the expectation of seeing "Jesus" part of the visitor's intimate script, these other performative events prime spectators to experience fascination when the Passion play begins and, as a result, to experience it energetically.

The first Living Bible Tour begins each day at 10:00 a.m., and new tours start about every fifteen minutes thereafter until 2:00 p.m. This is designed as a walking tour with small groups of guests following a dirt path from station to station; a staff member in a golf cart follows each group to transport people between sites if necessary. The length of the tour is determined by the pace of each individual group, as well as the weather. For example, my group's tour began at 10:30 a.m. and did not end until after 1:00 p.m. Because it was an incredibly hot day and most of the tour is unshaded, staff members had our group pause for a twenty-minute water break at a small concession stand located midway along the tour.

Based upon the website, articles about the tour, and a 2006 DVD version of the tour, it is clear that the tour has changed repeatedly over time. The version I saw included nine stations in the following order: a shepherd and Jack, the cross-back donkey (according to the shepherd, the donkey that led Jesus into Jerusalem became a cross-back at the crucifixion when the shadow of the cross fell across his back and left a mark); a scene with the Samaritan woman who met Jesus at Jacob's Well; an episode at the Passover House; a lengthy scene at the Tabernacle in the Wilderness (the tabernacle has been reconstructed based upon historical evidence) where visitors see the Holy of Holies and learn that the Temple veil that was rent from top to bottom upon Christ's death was "about a foot thick"; an encounter with the Old Testament character Ruth, who expounds upon the biblical analogy of the threshing floor; a conversation with the disciple Peter; an encounter with Moses and the Ten Commandments; a scene with the Virgin Mary; and last, a scene on Golgotha with the disciple John.

The strategies of evangelical dramaturgy are evident throughout the tour, especially with respect to how time and place constantly shift. The scenes are not presented in chronological order but instead flip back and forth between Old Testament and New Testament episodes. Moreover, the actors frequently change tense and voice throughout their presentations. Many begin speaking as themselves in the present tense as they talk about why they stand out in the heat every day offering this performance, before suddenly—and often without any marked transition—they start speaking as their characters. In addition, all of the actors in the Old Testament episodes overtly connect the significance of their stories not only to Jesus but also to the modern present and, oftentimes, to the future End Times. Finally, almost every actor used the scene as an opportunity to personally witness to visitors, and many ended their episodes with a prayer and blessing that began with the phrase, "My prayer for you is." It is clear that the tour functions as a tool for engaged orthodoxy.[42]

These narrative devices are consonant with the circular—simultaneously progressive and retrogressive—mode of reading that many evangelicals employ with the Bible. Therefore, although the cross-temporal shifts may initially seem to erode the tour's claims to authentic replication, I would argue that for many evangelical visitors they may actually enhance the possibility for religiously real encounters. In her discussion of Civil War reenactments, Rebecca Schneider describes how "for those suspicious of linearity" the theatrical elements within reenactments "are not threats to authenticity, but . . . vehicles for access to the transitive, performative, and cross-temporal real."[43] I would argue that this is also the case with the Living Bible Tour.

The Passover House scene illustrates how evangelical dramaturgy governs this Sacred Project. Like all of the episodes, this one included only a single character. A "Jewish" woman stood before the Passover house, talking to us in the modern-day present as we waited for the last members of our group to make their way over from the previous station and settle on benches surrounding the house. Without any noticeable transition, the actress suddenly began speaking "in character" about the Jewish exodus out of Egypt. As she spoke, time and identity became increasingly slippery; sometimes she seemed to be speaking as if her character had traveled with that group of Jews during the biblical exodus, while at other times she referred to this event as something that had happened in the distant past. When she talked about how the Jewish people grew frustrated and began to doubt Moses, she repeatedly slipped back and forth between speaking as if she were a Jew and talking about Jews as a group different from herself. She also pointedly mentioned how, as their skepticism about Moses' leadership increased, the Jews began "murmuring" among themselves. She then remarked, "And we're still murmuring today, right?" Here she spoke as if in the present day, yet she retained her "Jewish" identity. Moreover, it was not clear exactly what she was referencing with this comment. I suspect she was alluding to the "murmuring" of Jewish groups regarding the content of Passion plays, but it remains unclear to me.

After recounting the original Passover story, the woman typologically linked this event to Christ's crucifixion, discussing how the sacrifice of the lamb in the Passover account had prefigured, and then been superseded by, God's singular sacrifice of his son, Jesus Christ. She also asserted that Christ would return, saying, "He is coming back and soon. You'd have to be crazy not to see it." The actress then delivered a personal testimony of her own faith. Like the actor playing John in "Last Supper Communion," this actress also used phrases like "Isn't that right?" to prompt audience responses. Although the audience was far less vocal than the spectators at HLE, various people nodded or said "yes" and "Amen" during her testimony, and her story appeared to move many members of our group. It was also overtly evangelical. At one point, the actress told us we weren't "here just as a tourist," but that each of us had come seeking something "deeper." She also assured us that we were exactly where we needed to be that day. The scene ended with the actress praying that we would each take the gospel out with us "into a broken world" and be a "vessel."

As with all of the episodes along the tour, this scene's script merges past, present, and future into a single encounter. This complicated assemblage is then enhanced further through various material and sensual devices. For example, during the tour spectators meet biblical characters dressed in "authentic" costumes, who stand in or before structures recreated to seem historically accurate to the ancient setting, but who also speak with local dialects and accents. These choices replicate the dramaturgy of the "Great Passion Play" and thus prepare the audience for the evening performance. Moreover, the Living Bible Tour allows spectators to walk through and physically engage a sensual environment similar to the one they will see recreated on the Passion play stage—spectators sit on stone or wooden benches, endure the intense heat of this ancient world, smell the odors in the cross-back donkey's stall, and perhaps even pet Jack's nose. Spectators also travel along the tour in small groups, which makes their encounters with these ancient biblical figures quite personal and intimate. For these reasons, the Living Bible Tour is able to cultivate the energetic dynamic characteristic of evangelical enactment and, thus, to foster religiously real re-experiences of biblical episodes.

The expectation is that guests will visit the other Sacred Projects and take the Living Bible Tour the morning or afternoon before seeing the play; actors along the tour repeatedly reference the Passion play with phrases like "tonight you'll see this" or "remember this bible verse tonight." Consequently, residual traces of the energetic encounters spectators have along the Living Bible Tour—the intimate affective script formed by the tour experience—may intensify and enhance the spectator's subsequent Passion play experience by giving it the viscerality, immediacy, and texture that the large amphitheater and prerecording otherwise inhibit. However, the small communal experience of the tour and the local accents heard along the way may also prime visitors to re-experience the play's nostalgic American vision. The cognitive theory of conceptual blending can help us examine how taking this tour and visiting the other Sacred Projects supply powerful lived experiences designed to engender embodied beliefs that will support the larger ideological goals of the "Great Passion Play" ministry.[44]

Holy Blends

As we interact in and with the world, we reconstruct it into coherent "mental spaces," building these from immediate experiences, as well as from what others have told us about the world. As Gilles Fauconnier and Mark Turner explain, these spaces are "entrenched in long-term memory" and thus connected to schematic knowledge.[45] We "frame" these mental spaces by organizing the elements within them, and the relations between those elements, into "known" packages.[46] This organizing frame "specifies the nature of the relevant activity, events, and participants" in that space. We then create complex meaning by connecting or selectively blending mental spaces into integration networks, and, as we do this, the frames we project into those networks impact how we derive meaning from the blend.[47] This cognitive process is called *conceptual blending*.

As Fauconnier and Turner explain, conceptual blending is "an invisible, unconscious activity" that is "crucial to even the simplest kinds of thought." Moreover, they note that "one of the central benefits of conceptual blending is its ability to provide compressions to human scale of diffuse arrays of events."[48] When conceptual blends are particularly abstract, physical objects and locations can function as material anchors. For example, Fauconnier and Turner discuss how tombstones and cemeteries serve "as material anchors for the blend of 'living with the dead.'" Likewise, churches or other religious spaces can supply material anchors for "spiritual and personal integration networks."[49]

Performances require a sophisticated process of conceptual blending. For instance, when watching a play, spectators make sense of what they see by blending the living actors with their characters' identities. Plays based upon real events—and for evangelical believers, I would put Passion plays into that category—necessitate other degrees of blending. Furthermore, as Fauconnier and Turner assert, "In the case of sensation and perception, our conscious experience comes entirely from the blend—we 'live in the blend,' so to speak."[50] Therefore, spectators at a play not only construct blends, but they also "live in" those blends.[51]

Critically, as spectators live in blends, they do not lose their frame in the real world but instead oscillate between multiple frames in order to construct meaning from the moment-to-moment performance. For example, the actor's real body is critical to the actor/character blend:

> For the spectator, the perceived living, moving, and speaking body is a supreme material anchor. . . . In principle, actors are linked to characters by virtue of performing in the real world actions that share physical properties with actions performed by the characters in the represented world. This allows us . . . to be aware, when we see a play, of more than one framing.[52]

Moreover, certain dramaturgical devices will encourage spectators to shift frames repeatedly. This is the case with the performance text of the Passover House scene, which repeatedly pulls the present "real" world in and out of the blend, thereby creating a complicated network of relations and meaning.

Blending is fundamental to how theater works and from where performances derive much of their meaning; as Fauconnier and Turner contend, theater's "power comes from the integration in the blend," and ultimately "the ability to live in the blend provides the motive for the entire activity."[53] Performative events like the Living Bible Tour also function in this way, prompting visitors to "live in" blends and to develop meaning from their experience inside those blends.

Cognitive theory can therefore help us realize the tremendous sensual power of an event like the Living Bible Tour and how that sensuality may influence meaning construction. Along this tour, spectators not only simulate the actors' activities through their mirror neuron responses, but they also "live in" the biblical world in which those activities take place and will interpret the tour's religious meaning by means of that blend. In addition, the experience of living in the blend helps the spectator produce an intimate script that resolves any confusion or dislocation that the lack of narrative, chronological, spatial, and temporal continuity along the tour might cause. Bruce McConachie argues,

> Cognitive theories suggest that spectators understand the world onstage not as an illusion, but as a different kind of reality when they are living in the blend of performance and mirroring the actions of actor/characters or looking at the setting of a production. Performance, it seems, mixes up our usual categories of actuality and make-believe all of the time.[54]

As I have suggested, this kind of mixing up (of time and place, of presence and representation) is vital to evangelical dramaturgy's re-representational goals and, therefore, one of the reasons why a performative genre like the Living Bible Tour is so effective at generating religiously real re-experience.

Moreover, the Living Bible Tour also highlights another key tactic of evangelical dramaturgy. As Fauconnier and Turner note, a spectator's physical experience at a performance enters the frame and impacts oscillation. During most contemporary theatrical events the real physical-world frame is suppressed, and spectators do not project many aspects of their lived existence at the play into the blend, such as the physical reality of sitting in a seat in a darkened theater closely surrounded by other people, most of whom are usually strangers. Furthermore, during plays spectators are often required to inhibit their natural physical responses, such as their motor and speech powers or the desire to respond to what they see.[55]

This is not the case with most of the evangelical genres I have discussed thus far. The performance events at Holy Land Experience and in Eureka Springs do not take place in darkened auditoriums that suppress the spectator's physical reality. Instead, "Behold the Lamb," the "Great Passion Play," and the Living Bible Tour all constitute outdoor events that leave spectators exposed to the elements, standing, sitting, and sometimes walking in very close proximity to other visitors (who, I would argue, many spectators assume are fellow believers) and also, in some cases, to the actors. In "Behold the Lamb" and the Living Bible Tour, the actors also directly engage spectators and encourage them to participate in the event physically and verbally.

In some respects then, these evangelical performative events recall the medieval tradition of staging outdoor religious performances. During these performances, spectators often stood or sat in public spaces like city streets. They were surrounded by other audience members (who, again, they most likely assumed were fellow Christian believers) and were frequently in close proximity to the actors, oftentimes amateurs. Many of these medieval religious performances also used direct address, anachronisms, and contemporary allusions in order to relate the events onstage to the medieval spectators' lives, just as we find in the Living Bible Tour. Moreover, in many cases it appears the medieval performance dynamic was somewhat interactive, with the audience responding verbally to the characters' actions and words. Consequently, in both the medieval context and the modern evangelical context, the performance conditions draw attention to the spectator's live, physical presence at the religious event, thereby pulling that bodily presence into the blend. Rather than disrupting the blend, I am claiming that this helps cultivate meaningful re-representational blends that serve specific theological or devotional ends.[56] In the case of the Living Bible Tour, spectators live in individualized, immediate, crucicentric religious blends that give biblical literalism a felt texture. Lived experience thus becomes the basis for generating embodied evangelical belief.

"Spheres of Presence" in the Holy Land

Conceptual blending offers us a way to examine the cognitive shape of what Erika Fischer-Lichte calls *atmospheric space*. Atmosphere results from the general impression spectators have of a performance space, and it continues to impact audience perception throughout the entire performance.[57] Drawing upon the work of Gernot Boehme, Fischer-Lichte explains that atmospheres

> pour out into, and thus shape, the space. They neither belong just to the objects or people who appear to radiate them nor to the people who enter a space and physically sense them. They usually constitute the spectators' first sensation on entering the auditorium and enable a very specific experience of spatiality. None of this can be explained by reference to individual objects because atmospheres exist in the interplay of elements and usually form a carefully calculated part of a theatre production.[58]

Atmospheres are therefore "spheres of presence" that "intrude on and penetrate the perceiving subject's body. . . . The spectators are not positioned opposite to or outside the atmosphere; they are enclosed by and steeped in it."[59] A performance's various narrative, rhythmic, and sensual elements together generate an atmosphere—a sphere of presence—that encourages spectators to live in (carefully calculated) cognitive blends from which they will construct complex conceptual meaning.[60]

Accordingly, staging is an inherently visceral act with tremendous cognitive impact. Conceptual blending helps us recognize how the felt charge of an atmosphere can be manipulated dramaturgically to direct audience understanding. This is especially relevant to venues like Holy Land reconstructions, performative sites in which sensual elements aim to encourage visitors to live in a Christian present/ancient Jerusalem blend. Holy Land Experience provides an excellent example of this process. The park's visual and material centerpiece is the six-story high Great Temple, but this structure is surrounded by a variety of other sites: the Upper Room and Calvary Garden Tomb that I described in the previous chapters; The Jesus Boat ("Replica of a boat found in the Sea of Galilee, dating back to the time of Christ"); the Dead Sea Qumran Caves ("Replica of the desert caves where the Dead Sea Scrolls were discovered"); a Wilderness Tabernacle; and a Jerusalem Street Market ("Browse the Middle Eastern marketplace, see the city well, and interact with Jerusalem's own street merchants"). In addition, the entrance gate of the park is "modeled after the Damascus and Jaffa Gates of Jerusalem."[61]

Although park literature advertises the thorough research behind these replicas, a venue like HLE does not actually aim toward historical accuracy.[62] Instead, it operates through geopiety, what Burke Long defines as "that curious mix of romantic imagination, historical rectitude, and attachment to a physical place."[63] Rather than offering an accurate replication of ancient Israel, HLE juxtaposes those "biblical" locales that are most significant to Christians against more familiar—but also blended—spaces, such as "Centurion Treats" and the "Oasis Palms Café" ("Feast on delicious meals in an authentic atmosphere"), or the "Shofar Shop" and "Old Scroll Shop," where Bibles and TBN merchandise are displayed alongside shofars, menorahs, and books about Jewish practices ("Experience first century shopping").[64] Staging choices—such as locating recognizable (and user-friendly) spaces like Oasis Palms Café and Centurion Treats on the pathway between the Great Temple and Calvary's Garden Tomb—may encourage HLE's "affective geography" to comfortably resonate with many visitors.[65]

Perhaps even more resonant is the overall generic model that HLE uses to construct that affective geography: the American theme park. The materials from which the HLE park structures are made, the costumes and props, the lively music piped over loudspeakers throughout the park (in this case, primarily Praise Songs), and even the names of the stores and cafés, all evoke the familiar and accessible theme park genre, an association that the park's location near Disney World significantly bolsters. Collectively, these elements form the park's atmosphere, the "sphere of presence" that penetrates into and resonates through the visitor's body. As a result, visitors know exactly how to engage with and use the HLE space from the moment they drive into the parking lot until they leave later that evening.

Writing about Holy Land reconstructions in the United States, Long asserts,

> Each of these holy lands is a creature of its time and rooted in a particular, transient historical circumstance. Each involves problematic exclusions and inclusions, effaced histories and privileged scenarios, assemblages of nostalgic desire and fantasy, and embodied interpretations of the "true" Bible as well as claims to the truly American.[66]

This is certainly the case with HLE, and conceptual blending can help us further analyze how the visitor's "ideal pilgrimage" to and in this space serves as a powerful foundation for generating embodied beliefs.[67] Visitors to HLE are prompted to live in a theme park/Christian Holy Land blend that is easy to use, contemporary, and, with its Disney-like features, in some respects uniquely American. Their experience navigating and using this familiar, accessible Holy Land constructs an intimate script that is comfortable, comforting, and pertinent. And, like all intimate scripts, it serves to verify the certainty of particular beliefs, in this case the crucial, inviolable importance of Christianity to the Holy Land.

As I noted in Chapter Two, HLE is grounded in a pre-Tribulation apocalyptic theology in which Christianity emerges from, but ultimately supersedes, Judaism; God's relationship to Christians fulfills and replaces the promise he made to the Israelites.[68] Joan Branham contends that HLE crafts the visitor experience using "a strategy of weaving and aggregation that presents Jewish and Christian elements, not in competition or even succession, but as a single congruent organization."[69] Yet, beyond visiting the gift shops and eating establishments, a guest's Holy Land Experience mainly consists of going to various shows and presentations. These performances are signposts for the park experience and are almost all focused on Christianity. Moreover, the most energetically charged moments of the HLE experience occur during "Behold the Lamb" and "Last Supper Communion." The main event at HLE is "Behold the Lamb," and the entire park comes to a halt for this Passion drama; the Praise Songs over the speakers disappear as soon as the performance begins and then resume immediately after it concludes, and no other performances or presentations are staged concurrently. At "Last Supper Communion," visitors are physically isolated from the theme park atmosphere; they enter a space that seemed to me more "historically accurate" and that felt sensually different in many respects from the rest of the park. Here they likely experience one of the most intimate, immediate encounters of their entire day. Attending these two performances were the only times that I felt the rhythmic park elements suppressed and the theme park frame begin to disappear. These events ground the visitor's park experience in synaesthetically rich re-experiences with Jesus.

Most of the other performance events at HLE are also either related to Jesus or specifically Christian in focus. These include "Woman at the Well," "The Empty Tomb," "The Four Ladies Who Loved Jesus," "Forgiven," "We Shall Behold Him," the twenty-minute "Easter Experience" film that plays nearly all day on a loop in the Theater of Life auditorium, and even the "Celebrate Jesus" talent show. Moreover, the only major exhibit in the park is located in the Scriptorium Center for Biblical Antiquities; this fifty-five-minute walk-through tour of the Scriptorium aims to give guests "a dramatic understanding of the history of the Bible, how it parallels the history of civilization, and the impact it has had upon the world."[70] Finally, as I have already noted, Praise Songs play over the loudspeakers around the park, forcibly impacting HLE's acoustemology by infusing the space with Christian-themed rhythms.

There are certainly presentations at HLE that focus on Jewish history and tradition, such as the twenty-five-minute presentations throughout the day in the "Wilderness Tabernacle" and the fifteen-minute "Temples of Israel" presentation on the Temple Plaza. However, in both of these cases the information about Judaism is presented as important precisely because it represents a precursor to Christianity and can therefore help Christians better understand the roots of their religious past. For example, Beal notes that "the Yom Kippur sacrifice performed in the Tabernacle is often interpreted by Christians as a foreshadowing of the eventual sacrifice of God's son, Jesus Christ, for the sins of all humanity. This meaning is explicitly given in the Holy Land Experience performance" in the Wilderness Tabernacle.[71] A description of the Wilderness Tabernacle exhibit on the HLE website confirms this typological approach:

> The presentation offers visitors an understanding about the importance of the rituals and sacrifices offered to God in this sacred place. Learn about the altar of sacrifice, the objects inside the Tabernacle, and the Ark of the Covenant. The Wilderness Tabernacle was designed to move the Israelites closer to God, while also providing a shadow of future glory—the coming of Christ.[72]

Moreover, even when Judaism is not presented through an explicitly supersessionist lens, it is usually commodified—both literally and figuratively—into something that Christians can easily pick up, use, and put down again when no longer needed. For example, staff members throughout the park not only say "Shalom" at every turn, but during presentations like "The Temples of Israel" they also teach guests Hebrew phrases. Park visitors experience Judaism as something that Christians can seamlessly integrate into their faith without contradiction or much effort.

This message is most apparent in the gift shops, where guests can purchase books about Jewish rituals and history, as well as a variety of ritual objects and Judaica souvenirs, at the same time that they buy evangelically oriented DVDs, CDs, books, or a new Bible. I would argue that this easy commodification, coupled with the superficial material presentation of Jewish culture throughout the theme park, prompts visitors to experience Judaism as accessible, but also, to some extent, trivial. Visitors live in a theme park/Christian Holy Land blend that contains very few, if any, meaningfully felt Jewish elements.

Ultimately the park's blend privileges Christianity in ways that reinforce evangelical theology; as in typology, here a Christian frame dominates and organizes the blend. While the blend may initially contain Jewish inputs—the visitor may begin the park experience living in a Jewish/Christian Holy Land blend—as visitors encounter more of the park throughout the day, the Jewish frame begins to disappear and the visitor instead lives in the theme park/Christian Holy Land blend. The high-stakes encounters at HLE—those moments that are difficult to watch, spiritually intense, and emotionally charged—coalesce around Christ; these are the energetic moments I discussed in the previous chapters. In comparison, I contend that the Jewish elements in the space produce largely comfortable, accessible experiences and therefore generate relatively few (if any) energetic, *felt* "meaning-effects."[73] Guests experience Judaism as easy and low-stakes (Jews are chosen and, thus, passive), while they experience Christianity, and specifically the "born again" Christianity that staff members reference frequently during presentations, as the more difficult, felt, and thus meaningful faith (evangelicals make a conscious choice to accept Christ and are, therefore, active). The rhythmic encounter with Holy Land Experience encourages visitors to live in a blend that will instantiate this typological theology as an embodied belief.

The Cross and the Flag

Branham argues that HLE produces "a particular kind of holy land 'experience' connected to Protestant ideals, but also to *American* values, privileging feelings, and the experiential in religious practice" (my emphasis).[74] In addition to the inherently American Disney-esque atmosphere of HLE, an event like the thirty-minute live show entitled "Celebrate America" introduces a nationalistic element into the theme park/Christian Holy Land blend. Moreover, the passive/active distinction I note above may serve to associate evangelical Christianity with U.S. values like free choice and personal agency. However, I contend that, in general, HLE cultivates religiously real re-experiences of Christ that are not fundamentally linked to American identity.

The goals of the "Great Passion Play," and of the Sacred Projects more generally, serve quite different ends that can be traced back to the early history of the Projects. From the start, presenting a particular idealized vision of America was essential to Gerald L. K. Smith's objectives. In his 1968 article about Robert Hyde published in the *Eureka Springs Times-Echo,* Smith wrote,

> I have taken the time to give the reader this detailed summary of the strong family background associations of Mr. Hyde in order that the reading public and those who come to view the great drama will realize that our Foundation did not pick up a fly-by-night dramatist. . . . As I read this summary myself, I am inclined to say, "What an example of family quality! Is this not the substance of which America, as we love it, has been built."[75]

In addition, as I have already noted, Smith's choice to use local, amateur actors recalls a kind of nostalgia for small-town America, one that actors still perpetuate today; in 2005, a twenty-four-year-old teacher, who had been performing in the play since she was in high school, said of the cast, "It's like a family."[76]

Today the Sacred Projects still reflect Smith's political vision, a combination of American nationalism, specific interpretations of family values, and Christian piety. The grounds themselves represent an affective geography that inculcates this ideology. As Long notes, elements like the nostalgia-laden Church in the Grove, the replica of the Liberty Bell, and the section of the Berlin Wall "define the space as Christian, patriotic, and evangelical."[77] In addition, images of soldiers and American flags appear in several of the Sacred Arts Museum's works. Moreover, especially for visitors today, I suspect the isolated location in Eureka Springs contributes to an atmosphere that evokes a particular image of America. The remote setting in the Ozark Mountains, which is not near any major airport or city, requires spectators to drive in order to see the play and visit the other projects. Car ownership and driving are intimately linked to U.S. identity; as Christine Ballengee Morris and James H. Sanders write, the development of the interstate highway system in the 1950s "helped reinforce the romantic notion of the open road as a space where one performs both individual freedom and national pride."[78] Furthermore, for those sitting in the amphitheater, the play's backdrop is the expansive, unadulterated American landscape, entirely natural except for the Christ of the Ozarks statue that is just visible above the treetops. This visual assemblage encourages spectators to live in a blend that reawakens a "Manifest Destiny" spirit. In this blend, spectators experience (for some, re-experience) America and its natural resources as innately Christian.

Collectively, the Sacred Projects encourage visitors to live in a blend that will allow them to re-experience an idealized, nostalgic, Christian America. For certain visitors, living in this blend of nationalistic and evangelical Christian values may come as a welcome reprieve from mainstream American culture and may be the reason some visitors return repeatedly. Stephanie Simon interviewed a number of spectators for her 2005 *Los Angeles Times* article about the "Great Passion Play." One couple from Oklahoma told her they return every year on their anniversary: "We use it to recenter our marriage and our lives. . . . Living in the world we live in, it's easy to get away from your values."[79] More striking with respect to my argument is a comment by Elois Russell, a sixty-seven-year-old from Mineo, Oklahoma, who had attended the play three times. Russell remarked that at the end of the play, "When [Jesus] ascends to heaven, it gives you the same feeling you get when the American flag comes down the street."[80]

Ultimately, living in this "Great Passion Play" blend produces an intimate script that not only verifies the visitor's felt sense of his or her own faith, but that also confirms a certain nationalistic piety that fuses God and Nation, or, as Gerald L. K. Smith would have it, the Cross and the Flag. And, significantly, as is true of all intimate scripts, it can help solve very real problems. In 2005 Anne Grand, a nurse from Baton Rouge, brought her eighteen-year-old son to the play on the day he graduated from army boot camp. As Grand explained, "My biggest fear is that my baby will go to war. . . . If anything should happen to him, I need to know I did everything I could to prepare him."[81]

"Assault on America": Embattled Nationalism

For many conservative evangelicals, the location of the Sacred Projects in Eureka Springs may not only make the need to cultivate this specific blend feel more urgent, but it may also intensify the blend's affective force. In the past twenty years, Eureka Springs has developed into an eclectic tourist town. The downtown's remarkably narrow streets, which zigzag up the sides of steep mountains, are lined with boutiques, cafés, and restaurants, many of them prominently displaying Gay Pride flags. Part Portland, Oregon, part cozy New England town, part Old West,[82] Eureka Springs is now "a funky haven for gay couples, aging hippies, Hell's Angels, and anyone else who feels out of place in the Bible Belt."[83] Therefore, for socially conservative Christians who arrive in Eureka Springs to see the "Great Passion Play," I suspect the Passion play grounds, while less than a ten-minute drive from the center of town, constitute a significant psychic shift from that downtown atmosphere. And for those who do not wish to venture downtown, the Sacred Projects provide them with enough activities and exhibits to fill the morning and afternoon before the show.[84] However, the downtown area also serves as a very powerful reference point that fosters the sense of embattlement that Christian Smith argues "actually *promotes* strong religion" by cultivating "the kinds of felt needs and desires that religion is especially well-positioned to satisfy" (original emphasis).[85] And, in some respect, the re-experiential goals of the Sacred Projects may depend upon the affective force of that embattlement. This relationship was made particularly clear during the pre-performance gospel show at the Top of the Mountain Dinner Theater.

Each night before the Passion Play, visitors can have "a sit down home style meal" in the Top of the Mountain Dinner Theater, followed by a show featuring "the outstanding award winning gospel music of 'The Texans.'"[86] Although not an official Sacred Project, the value package for the Passion Play includes a ticket to the dinner theater. The theater seats 250 people and was nearly full the night I went. Guests sit at long cafeteria tables arranged in a semicircle facing a small stage; upon entering, guests are briskly led to the next set of seats in the closest available row. The night I saw the show, the audience was composed mostly of families, with very few couples on their own; a number of large groups were also in the audience—a few family reunions, a large group of friends in their sixties and seventies (all coupled), and one high school youth group. I would guess the grand majority of audience members were over fifty years old.[87]

"The Texans" is a musical group composed of a husband and wife, their grown son, and two other local musicians/singers. The show starts promptly at 5:00 p.m. with a brief welcome and introduction from the son. As part of this greeting, he explained that "The Texans" consider their show "worship" that would prepare us for the "sermon" we would see later that night—the Passion Play. After this short prelude, dinner was served. There is only one choice for dinner, which is served on cafeteria-style trays; the three beverage options are all nonalcoholic. After the food is cleared away, "The Texans" begin their hour-long show, which is a series of songs interspersed with a few comic interludes. Most of the songs were religious in nature; some were original songs and others Christian standards like "That Old Rugged Cross." The comic bits were painful, mostly because the audience did not seem to react to them. The exceptions were the few times when the banter concerned regional rivalries—much was made of the fact that this "Texan" group was performing in Arkansas, but also very near Missouri and Oklahoma—or when the group referenced Wal-Mart; Wal-Mart is headquartered in Bentonville, Arkansas, a small town in the Ozark Mountains approximately an hour west of Eureka Springs. Although some spectators sang along to the familiar songs, in general the audience was relatively quiet during most of the show.

Given this behavior, the audience response during the last set was striking. At about 6:20 p.m., Sam, the husband/father in the group who also serves as its front man, thanked us all for coming and announced that they were about to close the show with three final songs. The first song was a solo number about a soldier going to war. Coincidentally, a young man in uniform who had just been through boot camp and was about to be deployed to the Middle East was sitting in the audience. Sam referred to him before the song began and asked him to stand up so that we could all thank him for his service with a round of applause; he asked us to do so again after the song. This audience ritual was somewhat ominous given that the song was about a fallen soldier and contained the refrain: "I've made it to Arlington." A number of spectators appeared choked up during the song, and many were wiping away tears when it ended.

The next song was a group number involving the full ensemble. There were a surprising number of costume changes throughout the show, and for this last set the entire group was dressed in red, white, and blue outfits with patterns that evoked the American flag. Before they began singing, Sam explained that this song would address the fact that there is a "mission" in this country to "erase" God from the nation. However, he believes that God and nation are inseparable, and he held up his crossed fingers to underscore this point. This remark prompted a number of audible affirmations and bursts of applause from the crowd. This second song was long, I suspect the longest in the show, and the only one that provoked a lot of active audience response: many cries of "yes," "yea," and other verbal pronouncements, as well as more clapping. The song, whose refrain was "We want America back," contained lines like "take her back from those who have lost control" and "We don't like what she's become." The song included lengthy segments of personal testimony spoken in rhythms reminiscent of charismatic preaching; the music was softer during these sections as the singers described specific things that are wrong with America today.

The wife/mother in the group delivered the longest of these testimonials, and it was paired with a verse about how mothers need to join forces in order to demand change.[88] During her testimony, she specifically denounced the fact that it is acceptable to distribute condoms in public schools while the Gideons can't hand out Bibles, and that "drug addicted," "gun-toting" students are allowed to enter schools, but prayer is banned. All of her examples provoked audible agreement from many members of the audience, especially when, at the climactic moment of her testimony, she loudly condemned the fact that we are forced "to accept abomination" under the guise that it is simply an "alternative lifestyle." This comment prompted the loudest cries and shouts from the crowd, and a few people even jumped to their feet clapping.

The language in this song evoked (spiritual) war and created a militaristic atmosphere in the room that seemed to, as Fischer-Lichte might say, "pour into, and thus shape, the space";[89] I suspect it is no accident that the refrain "We want America back" rhymes with, and thus conjures, the verb "attack."[90] The energetic dynamic in the room dramatically shifted during this second-to-last song. As the intensity of the melody, volume, and language escalated, the audience grew increasingly responsive both verbally and physically. The energy threatened to spill over, and perhaps in some respect it did, since when the song finally ended, the audience clapped wildly, and well over a third of the spectators immediately leapt to their feet; this was the only song to receive a huge round of applause or a standing ovation. With this song—not just the words, but also the heated tone and forceful rhythms—"The Texans" tapped into frustrations seemingly shared by the majority of people in the audience. This song constituted a powerful affective force that directed general feelings of discontent and frustration toward a clear emotional response.

The next and final song also had a nationalistic message, but—honestly—I don't remember it and did not write anything about it in my notes. The energy that surged through the audience during and after "We want America back" left me disoriented and, as a gay person sitting in the audience alongside her partner, even a little bit frightened. I had entered the dinner theater as I tried to enter each of the venues I studied for this project—open to its rhythms and to the embodied beliefs it aimed to cultivate within me. However at no other venue before or after this event did I ever physically feel so much like an "outsider." The strength of the felt dissonance that this particular experience evoked within me was more evidence of the event's potential to function as an affective force.

In the end, the value of the Top of the Mountain Dinner Theater show was not its ability to form a new intimate affective script. Instead, the performance generated its meaning-effects by validating and reinvigorating an affective script of embattled Christianity that already resided within the embodied schemata of many spectators in the audience. As the "worship" that precedes the Passion play "sermon," the dinner theater performance functions like liturgy, radically particularizing and miniaturizing Passion theology into and through an American identity/Christian piety blend.[91] Although other Sacred Projects encourage spectators to live in a similar blend, it is the dinner theater show that most overtly primes spectators—true, only 250 of them maximum each night—to engage the Passion performance, which is played against a nostalgic, idealized American landscape, from inside that blend. In this way the show functions as engaged orthodoxy.

Sarah McNamer writes, "The Passion, as the medieval culture's most potent and pervasive story, clearly functioned as a site of significant cultural work."[92] This is still very much the case today. The Passion narrative is not a blank slate, but as "Behold the Lamb," *The Passion of The Christ*, and the "Great Passion Play" illustrate, it remains a site of cultural work through which artists and spectators distill ideas, inscribe ideology, cultivate emotion, and reinforce values. Cognitive theories of simulation and conceptual blending reveal why performance proves to be such a powerful tool to accomplish these very goals. In the next chapter I will continue to use cognitive theory in order to examine another site of engaged orthodoxy—the 70,000-square-foot Creation Museum in Petersburg, Kentucky.

5

The Creation Museum as Engaged Orthodoxy

Articles in popular media outlets have not only raised awareness about the $27 million Creation Museum, but such press coverage has also imbued the venue with important symbolic value. In a sense, the museum functions as a kind of shorthand—a codeword for conservative Christianity or an emblem of political divisions within U.S. culture and politics generally.[1] Like the "Great Passion Play" and the other Sacred Projects in Eureka Springs, the Creation Museum constructs a cultural paradigm fueled by notions of embattled Christianity and then supplies visitors with a resonant, comforting encounter that validates their position within that paradigm.

The great majority of articles appeared when the museum opened in May 2007, but more recent pieces, such as a 2010 piece in *Vanity Fair,* testify to people's ongoing curiosity about the venue.[2] In my own experience, the Creation Museum prompts more questions from friends and colleagues than any of the other venues I examine in this book. It is not simply the museum's antievolution message that fascinates people. Even more compelling is how the Creation Museum actually conveys that message. By coupling the physical form of a traditional natural history museum with a radical community-based agenda, the Creation Museum empowers and gives public voice to a community that perceives itself as threatened, disenfranchised, and misrepresented by mainstream culture. Using performative tactics, the Creation Museum appropriates both scientific evidence and the natural history museum encounter for the creationist agenda, while simultaneously aligning the creationist identity with characteristics such as intellectual rigor.

As a performance of community, the Creation Museum does—and

probably must—employ the kinds of "discriminatory elements" that John Fletcher suggests are "necessarily present in any expression of community."[3] However, because the museum's performance relies in great part on the premise that the exhibits simply give visitors "the freedom to see what they want to see,"[4] museum employees refract any allegations of discrimination back onto traditional natural history museums, most of which "proclaim an evolutionary, humanistic worldview."[5] For creationist-visitors who approach the Creation Museum believing that "secularized" science's evolutionary narrative has misled and corrupted society, encounters with the museum's space provide them with religiously real re-experiences that supply feelings of stability and certainty, as well as strategies for sustaining—and perhaps enhancing—those feelings in their daily lives. By allowing visitors to "live in" a materially realized re-representational creationist narrative, the Creation Museum transforms belief into meaningful embodied experience. Thus, as with trips to Holy Land recreations, physically engaging the museum space forms an intimate script that can help visitors resolve real-world problems.

Testaments in Brick and Mortar: Creationist Museums

The website Creationism.org lists thirteen creation science centers and museums in the United States.[6] This number is not altogether surprising given statistics on U.S. opinions regarding evolution. In a Pew Research survey released in August 2006, "42% of respondents directly rejected evolution, choosing the option that humans and other living things have existed in their present form since the creation." Among those who said they believe evolution occurred, 21 percent believe it was guided by a supreme being, a view that is roughly the one proposed by the "intelligent design" movement. Only 26 percent of all respondents said they believe in evolution through natural selection.[7] Religion appears to be a significant determining factor with respect to these views; according to the Pew Forum 2008 U.S. Religious Landscape Study, seven in ten members of evangelical Protestant churches, Mormons, and Jehovah's Witnesses reject the evolutionary account.[8]

These figures suggest that creationist centers and museums have a viable audience in nearly half of the nation's population. Admittedly, these venues do not only serve—nor are they exclusively targeted at—evangelical Christians. However, many of them, including the Creation Museum, promote a

Christo-centric creationism founded upon biblical infallibility, a message that likely appeals to many evangelical believers.[9]

Although simpler in design, early creation science museums initiated a critical shift toward employing empirical data as evidence. For example, as the Creation Evidence Museum's website explains, "Dr. Carl Baugh, the museum's Founder and Director, originally came to Glen Rose, Texas to critically examine claims of human and dinosaur co-habitation." When his initial excavations along the Paluxy River "yielded human footprints among dinosaur footprints," Baugh decided "that a museum needed to be established in order to appropriately display this evidence, along with sustained excavations and other areas of scientific research for creation."[10] This museum officially opened in 1984. Today, for only $5 per person, guests can see displays of the museum's most important artifacts and fossils, visit excavation sites, and attend lectures.

Newer venues have maintained this focus on scientific evidence but added more sophisticated exhibits and placed a greater emphasis on "edutainment."[11] For example, in 2001 Kent Hovind, a former public school science teacher turned minister, opened Dinosaur Adventure Land in Pensacola, Florida. Before the park closed suddenly in August 2009, due to Hovind's legal battles with the IRS,[12] guests visited a discovery center and museum, and played interactive games, in order to learn the "truth" about dinosaurs from a creationist perspective. The games were primarily oriented toward children, with each one linking a "science lesson" to a "spiritual lesson."[13] For example, the "Nerve-Wracking Ball" taught kids that a swinging object will never come back higher than the point from which it is released. The game consisted of children standing before a bowling ball dangling on a rope from a tall tree branch. A park guide released the ball and if children didn't flinch when it swung back toward them, stopping just in front of their faces, they had not only learned the science lesson, but also demonstrated "faith in God's laws."[14]

As I noted in Chapter Four, for many years the "Great Passion Play" grounds hosted a creationist-themed museum, the contents of which have since moved to a $2 million facility in Dallas, Texas, called the Museum of Earth History. According to the museum's website, it opened for special tours in July 2011. Similar to Dinosaur Adventure Land, this venue promises to provide "an enjoyable and educational experience exploring the Biblical perspective of Creation and Earth history through the use of scientific displays, artifacts, and historical data."[15] The museum, a joint venture between Christ for the Nations and the Creation Truth Foundation,[16] promotes the idea that "Christians don't have to be afraid of scientific evidence anymore." Until fall 2011, the museum's website was more extensive and contained many more pages and links. A project description on that site claimed that the museum "will be a place that has the courage to display breakthroughs in creation science through lectures, exhibits, multi-media displays, dinosaur fossils, and relics."[17]

These venues constitute one of many high-profile tactics that the contemporary creationist movement has used to gain traction in public debates over science education.[18] As Elizabeth Crooke explains, twentieth-century social movements have typically gone through four stages. An initial period of unrest or agitation is followed by a period of popular excitement that builds feelings of belonging and morale. This general interest then develops into a more formal ideology—"creation science" or "intelligent design" versus simply creationism—before the movement finally becomes institutionalized by means of formal tactics.[19] The presence of large-scale creation science venues—like Dinosaur Adventure Land, the Museum of Earth History, or the Creation Museum—may be an indication that the creationist movement has reached this final institutionalizing phase.

One of the important things that museums offer the creationist movement is cultural validation; as Crooke notes, "the very fact that we tend to ascribe the museum with authority and influence is useful for the social movement."[20] According to a 2001 national survey by the American Association of Museums, 87 percent of Americans "find museums to be one of the most trustworthy or a trustworthy source of information among a wide range of choices. Books are a distant second at 61%."[21] A more recent study corroborates this data. In a 2006 survey of over 1,700 adults conducted on behalf of the Institute for Museum and Library Services, respondents were shown various communication modes and asked to rank the "trustworthiness of display/items or information about them" using a five-point scale, with five being "extremely trustworthy" and 1 being "not at all trustworthy." The average rating for "in-person" visits to museums was 4.62.[22] Furthermore, a museum's authority is particularly empowering because it is demonstrated publicly,[23] a fact that visitors to creationist-themed venues recognize and appreciate. As one guest at Dinosaur Adventure Land remarked, "We've been to museums, discovery centers, where you have to sit there and take the evolutionary stuff. . . . It feels good for [our children] to finally hear it in a public place, something that reinforces their beliefs."[24]

The Creation Museum is the largest and most sophisticated of these venues. When it comes to giving creationists authoritative public visibility, it may even exceed expectations. Run by the Christian ministry group Answers in Genesis (AiG), the Creation Museum uses dinosaurs and fossils to assert the "truth" of biblical history. Ken Ham, a public school teacher from Queensland, Australia, launched AiG in 1979 and is the organization's president. He also founded the museum and serves as its director. AiG's "Statement of Faith" web page begins by listing the organization's two key "Priorities": "The scientific aspects of creation are important, but are secondary in importance to the proclamation of the gospel of Jesus Christ as Sovereign, Creator, Redeemer, and Judge" and "The doctrines of Creator and Creation cannot ultimately be divorced from the gospel of Jesus Christ."[25] This "Statement of Faith" continues with seven points labeled "Basics." For example, the third point states: "The account of origins presented in Genesis is a simple but factual presentation of actual events and therefore provides a reliable framework for scientific research into the question of the origin and history of life, mankind, the earth and the universe." These points are followed by thirteen tenets of "Theology."

AiG's central mission is to disseminate young earth creationism, and the final section of the organization's "Statement of Faith," entitled "General," outlines six core principles of this theory:

> The following are held by members of the Board of *Answers in Genesis* to be either consistent with Scripture or implied by Scripture.
>
> 1. Scripture teaches a recent origin for man and the whole creation, spanning approximately 4,000 years from creation to Christ.
> 2. The days in Genesis do not correspond to geologic ages, but are six [6] consecutive twenty-four [24] hour days of creation.
> 3. The Noachian Flood was a significant geological event and much (but not all) fossiliferous sediment originated at that time.
> 4. The gap theory has no basis in Scripture.
> 5. The view, commonly used to evade the implications or the authority of biblical teaching, that knowledge and/or truth may be divided into *secular* and *religious,* is rejected.
> 6. By definition, no apparent, perceived or claimed evidence in any field, including history and chronology, can be valid if it contradicts the

> scriptural record. Of primary importance is the fact that evidence is always subject to interpretation by fallible people who do not possess all information. (original emphasis)[26]

As I will demonstrate, these central principles, which resonate strongly with the evangelical tenet of biblical infallibility, not only guide the content within the Creation Museum's exhibits but also the manner of their visual and physical display.[27]

The *Creation Museum Souvenir Guidebook* maintains that AiG "is dedicated to proclaiming the Bible's literal history with logical, reliable answers in a skeptical world."[28] The Creation Museum represents the perfect manifestation of this agenda. As Ham's welcome note in this guidebook asserts, the Creation Museum "stands as a monument not only in the physical aspect of brick and mortar, but also in the spiritual as a global testament to the truth of God's Word."[29] Certainly the considerable size of this physical monument has significantly helped to establish its legitimacy and value; the 70,000-square-foot museum and the surrounding grounds cover forty-nine acres in total. However, like Holy Land Experience and the Sacred Projects, the Creation Museum uses various dramaturgical tactics to encourage visitors to feel a sense of intimacy and immediacy that will promote a religiously real re-experience, in this case, a re-experience of the Genesis creation narrative.

"Walk through the Pages of God's Word"

The Creation Museum is located on the Kentucky, Indiana, and Ohio border, seven miles west of the Cincinnati/Northern Kentucky airport; the museum advertises the fact that it is "within a day's drive (650 miles) of almost two-thirds of the U.S. population."[30] According to its online newsroom, the museum had welcomed 1.6 million visitors as of 13 April 2012. Currently, tickets cost $29.95 for adults and $15.95 for children five to twelve. In the past, the museum offered a discounted two-day package, which is what I purchased when I visited the museum in July 2009. Now all tickets are valid for two consecutive days.

The Creation Museum's central attraction is the sixteen-exhibit, two-floor "Museum Experience Walk." Exhibits include a dinosaur dig site, many different fossil and science displays, a journey through biblical history, the Noah's ark construction site, and various point/counterpoint exhibits. Animatronic displays, videos, and short films are scattered throughout this "Experience Walk." In addition, the museum houses a special-effects theater that shows the twenty-two-minute "comic" film *Men in White* every half-hour throughout the day; a dinosaur fossil exhibit that is visually similar to those found in traditional natural history museums; the Stargazer's planetarium (an additional $7.95 with museum admission); various food venues (such as Noah's Café); and the Dragon Hall Bookstore. AiG interprets dragon tales from the Middle Ages as evidence that dinosaurs lived alongside humans. In the Dragon Theater, visitors watch a ten-minute video—"filmed in England at a real castle" and featuring an academic expert who holds a PhD from Harvard—that explains this connection.

The Creation Museum's website promises visitors that the sophisticated special-effects theater and life-size animatronic dioramas will allow them to "experience the Bible and history in a completely unique way—walk through the pages of God's Word and encounter creation, corruption, catastrophe, Christ, the Cross, and consummation through a number of engaging exhibits."[31] The exhibits bring "the pages of the Bible to life, casting its characters and animals in dynamic form and placing them in familiar settings."[32] Museum literature boasts that these state-of-the-art animatronics were created by Patrick Marsh, who also designed the *Jaws* and *King Kong* rides at Florida's Universal Studios theme park, another effort to legitimate the venue's cultural credentials.[33] The museum grounds also contains a botanical garden, picnic areas, and petting zoo.[34] Although these areas are less high-tech, they also offer visitors physically interactive encounters.

The Creation Museum attracts guests, in part, because it promises an empirically based foundation for creationism. Significantly, young earth creationists maintain that those who endorse the evolutionary narrative are simply misinterpreting the scientific data. Therefore, while evidence like fossils proved problematic for earlier generations of creationists, they supply young earth creationists with empirical evidence that corroborates the biblical account of God's plan. Moreover, as Vincent Crapanzano explains, according to many evangelical creationists,

> evolution is not science but philosophy—a worldview whose hypothetical, indeed, fantastical, nature is masked by a series of altogether questionable observations and deductions from these observations that are expressed as though they were scientific certainties. They do not, so they claim, question

> science; they question "bad science," like evolution. They argue that good science, like theirs, confirms the account of creation in Genesis.[35]

It is therefore important to recognize that the Bible is the primary credible source for young earth creationists; although scientific data may support the biblical account, that account's validity does not rely upon such external data. Rather, the relationship between the two operates in the reverse direction; as one museum display proclaims, "The Bible's true account of history gives us the key to interpret the fossils we find in the present." For example, young earth creationists interpret Noah's flood as reconciling many archaeological "mysteries." AiG's *Museum Guide: A Bible-Based Handbook to Natural History Museums* (a 219-page book sold at the Dragon Hall Bookstore for $19.99) explains that the Ark held Noah's immediate family as well as

> two of every kind of air-breathing, land animal and bird (and seven of some). This boat was huge. It was approximately 450 feet (135 meters) long and 45 feet (13.5 meters) tall. . . . All the people and land animals outside the Ark died. The waters were so powerful that tons of rocks and dirt were moved around during the Flood. Plants, animals, and even humans became buried in the muddy sediments. The remains of some of these have been dug up today; they are called fossils. Not all fossils are from the Flood, but most of them are.[36]

The section of the "Museum Experience Walk" devoted to a Noah's Ark reconstruction repeatedly reinforces this flood narrative.

Like fossils, dinosaurs have also been reclaimed by young earth creationists as evidence that confirms the biblical account. The *Museum Guide: A Bible-Based Handbook* explains:

> When talking about the dinosaurs, or any other extinct animal, we must keep some things in mind. First, we know that dinosaurs were real because the Bible says that land animals were created on Day 6, and since dinosaurs are land animals, they were included in this creation (sea and flying reptiles such as pteranodons and plesiosaurs were created on Day 5). We also know that dinosaurs were real because their bones have been discovered and preserved for us to see. Second, we must remember that when God sent the Flood to punish mankind's wickedness, God preserved His creation by sending animals onto the Ark. The various kinds of dinosaurs would have

> also been on the Ark and preserved from the Flood. Dinosaurs could have fit on the Ark, since they were, on average, about the size of a small pony. And God would have preserved the younger representatives of the different dinosaur kinds to reproduce after the Flood. . . . There are many things that could have contributed to the extinction of the dinosaurs, including climate change, starvation, diseases, and hunting by humans and/or other animals (some of the same reasons animals today become extinct!).[37]

Note the careful order of evidence at the beginning of this paragraph: certainty that dinosaurs were real rests primarily on the Bible and only secondarily on the fact that humans have discovered their bones. Similar arguments about dinosaurs and their extinction appear throughout the Creation Museum, particularly in the displays around the Noah's Ark reconstruction and in the dinosaur fossil exhibit.[38]

Dinosaur models—most of them much larger than small ponies—figure prominently in the museum experience from the moment visitors arrive: dinosaur images appear on the museum's entrance gates (see Figure 6), and a dinosaur sculpture outside the museum provides a perfect photo-op. Once inside, dinosaur sculptures and fossil reconstructions greet visitors in the lobby, providing more group photo opportunities, and a large animatronic display of dinosaurs and humans keeps visitors entertained as they wait in line to begin the "Museum Experience Walk" (see Figure 7). Dinosaurs also appear throughout the museum's exhibits: in the Garden of Eden diorama as some of the creatures that Adam named; in displays about humankind's corruption following Adam's sin; as passengers in the Noah's Ark models; and of course, in the dinosaur den and Dragon Theater located at the end of the "Museum Experience Walk."[39] Dinosaur images also appear on most of the museum's promotional materials and merchandise, and are therefore central to the institution's public image.

Although they are not a fundamental part of the Biblical account and only play a minor role within the young earth creationist narrative, these exotic animals are a recurring material presence within and around the museum, oftentimes appearing alongside humans. Dinosaurs not only help to set expectations for the visit, but they also provide a familiar, memorable, and marketable through-line for the museum experience. Moreover, they furnish the spectacle necessary to keep children interested in a museum visit. As Ham asserts, "Evolutionary Darwinists need to understand we are taking the dinosaurs back."[40]

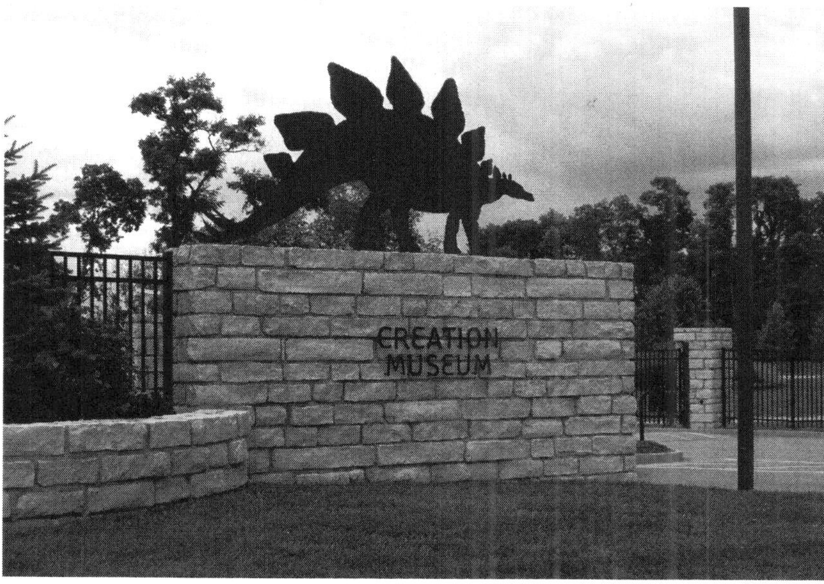

Figure 6. The Creation Museum entrance gates. July 2009. Photo by author.

The Creation Museum publicly co-opts the natural history museum genre, especially its most popular features—fossils and dinosaurs. For creationists who reject the evolutionary narrative of earth science, this appropriation empowers their beliefs while simultaneously neutralizing or curtailing the traditional natural history museum's authority. Elizabeth Crooke contends that independent museums oftentimes develop as part of a social movement's attempt to challenge "the traditional idea of a museum, in the terms of whose story is told, how items are collected and the method of display. By doing so community groups are not only challenging the traditional hegemony of the museum, but are using it for their own purposes."[41] This is certainly one of AiG's objectives. As the museum's press representatives explain, the Creation Museum "counters evolutionary natural history museums that turn minds against Scripture—and Jesus Christ, the Creator of the universe."[42] With the Creation Museum, AiG first appropriates the authority and trustworthiness of the museum genre and then recodes that genre for creationist-believers by offering them a rhythmic, lived experience that resonates with Christo-centric creationist beliefs.

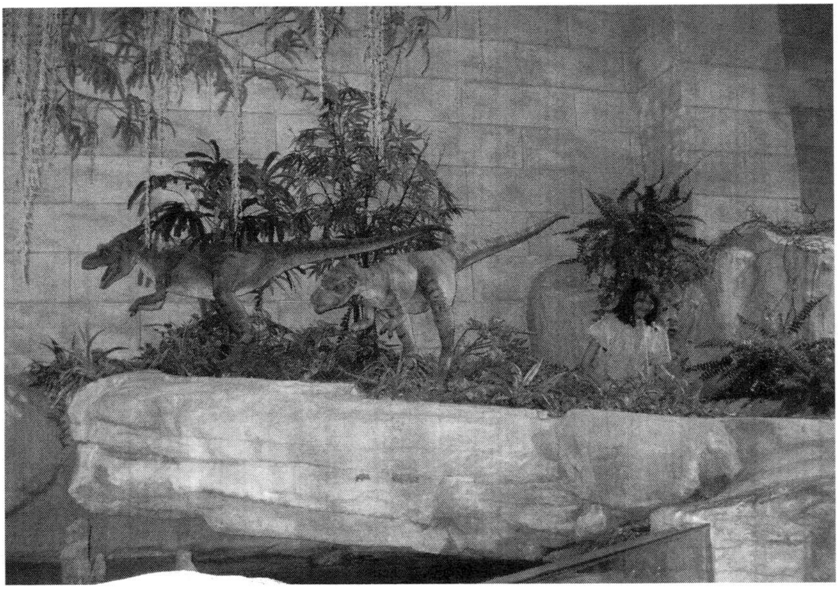

Figure 7. Lobby animatronic display featuring dinosaurs and humans. The Creation Museum. July 2009. Photo by author.

Making Contact with Creationist Certainty

Exhibits in the Creation Museum repeatedly declare that everyone has the same facts, but that people simply draw different conclusions from them. The "Museum Experience Walk" begins with displays in which key points of contention are described as merely a difference of "Starting Points": when interpreting the fossil evidence, people choose either to start from "Human Reason" or to start from "God's Word." According to museum spokespeople, this exhibit is designed to demonstrate that neither side has the upper hand; as explained by Dr. Terry Mortenson, a lecturer and researcher for AiG who holds a doctorate in the history of geology from Coventry University in England, "The very first two rooms of our museum talk about this issue of starting points and assumptions. We will very strongly contest an evolutionist position that they are letting the facts speak for themselves."[43] However, rather than neutral displays of data, these exhibits instead lay a foundation for the museum's larger claims by associating these different "starting points" with contrasting identities, life experiences, and moral consequences.

The first few rooms on the "Museum Experience Walk" depict "secular" scientists as only concerned with evidence in the present, while creationist scientists try diligently to discern what actually happened in the past. The museum presents creationists as insightful, inquisitive thinkers who actively seek knowledge. In doing so, the museum aligns creationists with positively coded characteristics and cultural values, as it simultaneously inscribes the evolutionist identity with certain derogatory traits that contemporary society typically associate with creationists. Thus, the evolutionist is the person who cannot engage in a reasonable and thoughtful debate about the facts and instead blindly follows a "theory" as if it were unquestionable truth.

The format of this opening section seems to suggest that people simply have two possible interpretive frameworks from which to choose—creation science or evolution—and some of the early displays imply a sense of balance by claiming that everyone "interprets" evidence. Nevertheless, language in museum signage and literature situates one of these two options as inarguably superior. For example, the museum's *Souvenir Guidebook* explains:

> Our conclusions about the world are affected by the decision to trust either the words of the *eternal, perfect* God or the words of *temporal, fallible* men. There is an element of faith at work in every interpretation of scientific evidence. . . . Scientists reach different views about the past, not because of what they see, but because of their different starting points. (my emphasis)[44]

The two frameworks clearly differ with respect to the stability and certainty of their starting points. Moreover, although both interpretative systems involve "faith," young earth creationists usually also attach the word *science* to their framework. Some of these language choices may be intended to suggest balance and, thus, to appeal to the non-creationist visitor, but they also undoubtedly privilege the biblical perspective and, therefore, do not contradict the creationist museumgoer's beliefs. I would argue that a kind of bait and switch occurs in this early section of the "Museum Experience Walk." The exhibit initially implies that creationism is simply one of two possible interpretive strategies; however, as the walk continues, creationism emerges as the "correct" and more rational approach to the evidence, with the creationist believer depicted as someone who has logically assessed the available options and thoughtfully chosen biblical "truth" because it makes more sense.

Emphasizing the "common sense" of creation science situates the museum within a particular creationist tradition. For example, Heather Hendershot has examined the films released in the 1950s and 1960s by the Moody Institute of Science (MIS). The MIS was founded in 1945 during the nation's Atomic Age when children were especially drawn to scientific inquiry. Consequently, the MIS's evangelical strategy involved demonstrating the "confluence between science and religion."[45] Hendershot argues that the Institute's films promoted "the natural theology position that God's glory is proved by the physical world, as well as the 'logical,' commonsense assumption that evolution just doesn't make any sense as a means of explaining the world."[46] Like the Creation Museum, these films emphasize "observable" science by highlighting experiments that use tools such as microscopes and telescopes, and in doing so, they "promote the idea that evolution cannot be proven because it cannot be seen."[47] However, while the films and videos that Hendershot examines reinforce these ideas through visual techniques, the museum space offers AiG opportunities to create resonant encounters that will promote those ideas synaesthetically.

For example, the museum uses different tactics to reinforce a distinction between the seemingly open-minded, inquisitive creationist and the rash, illogical evolutionist. Various graphic panels supply visitors with concise, straightforward answers to the questions that evolutionists typically ask when disputing creationism's claims. In one case, a large panel that explains Cain's marriage to his sister begins, "Before jumping to conclusions," and then lists six reasons why this marriage was acceptable in biblical times, among them:

> 1. All humans are related. So whenever someone gets married, they marry their relative.
> 2. One of the most honored men of the Bible, Abraham, was married to his half sister. It wasn't until much later that God instructed the Israelites not to marry close relatives—a principle we follow today.
>
> . . .
>
> 4. The farther back in history one goes (back towards the Fall of Adam), the less of a problem mutations in the human population would be. At the time of Adam and Eve's children, there would have been very few mutations in the human genome—thus close relatives could marry, and provided it was one man for one woman (the biblical doctrine of marriage), there was nothing wrong with close relatives marrying in early biblical history.

In other cases, signs purport to demonstrate through logic how the fossil record supports the creationist account:

> According to God's Word, thorns came after Adam's sin, about six thousand years ago, not millions of years ago. Since we have discovered thorns in the fossil record, along with dinosaurs and other plants and animals, they all must have lived at the same time as humans, after Adam's sin.

The museum journey produces an affective intimate script that solves problems, in part, because displays like these supply evidence-based answers to relevant questions. For young earth creationists, scientific data holds value precisely because (and, in fact, only when) it corroborates scripture.[48] Accordingly, the museum depicts creationists as more scrupulous because they use all of the available "evidence"—scientific data *and* scripture—unlike evolutionists, who only consider part of the evidence.[49]

These divergent characterizations are depicted more comically in the film *Men in White*. In the film's "Enlightenment High School" scene, easily flustered public-school teachers appear distressed by questions that challenge evolution and, in response, they can only spout non sequiturs like "I just think Charles Darwin is wonderful" and "There is no God in the universe." Phrases such as "Don't Question" are written on the classroom blackboard. When one student suggests that he might disagree with the teacher, she replies, somewhat hysterically, "Well then you're in violation of the Constitution of the United States' separation of church and state!" The "Men in White" of the title are two "hip," contemporary angels, Gabriel and Michael (or Gabe and Mike), who narrate the film. In this particular scene, they infiltrate the classroom disguised as students and their repartee with the teachers reveals the shortcomings of evolutionary theory and—accordingly—of non-Bible-based public education.

Gabe and Mike are smug, and I found them quite annoying. But I suspect their sunglasses, comic banter, use of slang, and ability to stand up to (secular) authority figures may appeal to a young generation of museumgoer. Alternatively, the negative depictions of public school teachers and college professors—their geeky outfits, shrill voices, and anxious, uncertain gestures—likely trace a dissonant pattern within most spectators' embodied schemata, a pattern conceptually linked to believing in evolutionary theory. These exaggerated stereotypes therefore serve as powerful affective mimetic elements designed to direct spectators toward certain beliefs and associations. As Jason Byassee explains, in *Men in White* "the battle is presented as a case of free inquiry against tyrannical opponents,"[50] a contest of values that is both culturally relevant and resonant. In this film, as in the museum generally, reason, logic, and the freedom to question are all creationism's allies. Creationists appear evenhanded, rather than fanatical. They are able to discuss the evidence rationally before successfully discrediting evolutionary theory by presenting a more concise, straightforward creationist alternative.

However, AiG is not interested in simply arguing that it is more reasonable or logical to believe the creationist account. Instead, the museum ultimately claims that creationism provides believers with a more comforting and meaningful life. Consequently, the exhibits are designed to produce an intimate script that aligns the creationist narrative with feelings of reassurance and certainty. This goal is similar to what I identified with respect to Holy Land Experience and the "Great Passion Play," and, like those venues, the Creation Museum also employs performative rhythms to achieve it.

For instance, shortly after the "Starting Points" section, museumgoers enter a room containing six panels that recount episodes in history when groups or individuals challenged God's word. Entitled *Attempts to Question, Attempts to Destroy, Attempts to Discredit, Attempts to Criticize, Attempts to Poison*, and *Attempts to Replace*, these panels describe instances when scriptural claims that scientists once rejected were later corroborated by subsequent scientific discoveries: "The Bible implies that most fossils were buried quickly as a result of the worldwide Flood. Nineteenth-century paleontologists argued that fossils were buried slowly. Today, paleontology confirms that fossils were buried rapidly." These panels situate science as the Bible's ally, an even closer ally than the traditional institutional church. A seventh panel, entitled *The Latest Attack: Question Biblical Time*, takes direct aim at modern churches that do not retain a Bible-based message:[51]

> The church *believed* God's Word. Based on the Bible, [Bishop] Ussher calculated creation at 4004 B.C. The church *questioned* it. "Is 6,000 years enough time?" Humanity abandoned it. "Millions of years ago . . ." The philosophers and scientists of the Enlightenment suggested that the universe was not created in six days about six thousand years ago. Christian leaders, not wanting to appear foolish and unscientific, tried to reinterpret the Bible to add millions of years into history. (original emphasis)

According to this exhibit, the Bible provides people with a reliable and accurate account of creation, whereas modern institutions that do not uphold God's word only offer shifting theories that are subject to human speculation and error.

Significantly, the Creation Museum proposes that the dependable certainty creationism offers is not limited to knowledge about the past but also impacts a person's entire philosophy of life and sense of well-being. AiG's *Museum Guide: A Bible-Based Handbook* asserts that naturalist scientists must use principles of causality and analogy to reconstruct the past even though "the best method of reconstruction is to rely on the account of an accurate eyewitness." While "naturalists have no such eyewitness to rely on," creationists have the Bible. Biblical scripture,

> provides a written record of an eyewitness to (who was also intimately involved in) history—the Creator God. This eyewitness cannot lie, so His account is completely trustworthy. We can use this written record as our foundation for understanding the world around us. This will help us to understand why the world is the way it is today and to make sense of where we came from and why we're here.[52]

Large panels installed near the end of the "Starting Points" exhibit endorse this same idea by outlining the larger consequences that are at stake when choosing one's "foundation for understanding the world." On one panel the words "Evolution ~ 14 billion years ago. Human Reason" are accompanied by a long, squiggly line, while the phrases "Creation ~ 6000 years ago. God's Word" appear with a straight, solid line (see Figure 8). These graphics propose two very different experiences—evolution offers wandering ambiguity, while creationism provides a straightforward, confident journey. (Evolution's squiggly line may also evoke the deceptive snake in Eden.)[53]

On the opposite wall, the question "Do different starting points matter in our personal lives?" accompanies photos of people in despair. These images are labeled with questions such as: "Why am I here?" "Am I alone?" "Why do I suffer?" "Is there any hope?" and "Why do we have to die?" A large graphic nearby proclaims, "God's Word Offers Hope." This room takes what visitors might have initially understood as a difference in interpreting scientific evidence and joins it to the museum's central premise—starting from God's word results in a stable, meaningful, and hopeful life, whereas

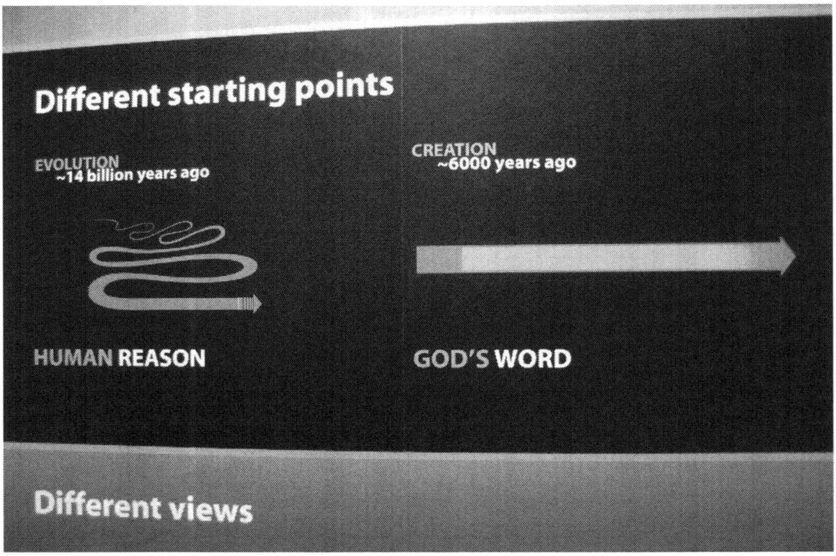

Figure 8. Different Starting Points sign. The Creation Museum. July 2009. Photo by author.

beginning from human reason's claim that we are "only the latest ripple in the endless stream of evolution"[54] eventually leads to (and is, in fact, the cause of) despair, confusion, and suffering.[55]

The museum does not convey this message through language alone. Elements like the squiggly- and straight-line graphics render and reinforce this disparity visually—and, thus, also rhythmically. Using the work of Daniel Stern, Anna Gibbs describes how evidence shows that certain two-dimensional diagrams will reliably elicit "a restricted number of categorical effects ('happy, sad, angry')."[56] This research indicates that certain two-dimensional visuals can evoke not only "the kinematics of gesture" but, in some cases, emotion as well; Gibbs explains, "the same falling line that signals joy departing or deflating will usually be read as sadness."[57] Similar to the relationship between musical cues and emotional production that I discussed in Chapter Three, certain simple diagrams, such as the line drawings in the Creation Museum's Human Reason/God's Word display, can function as affective forces "to incite our own bodies into immediate mimetic response, and, in the same moment, by the same movement, to conscript affects into signification."[58] Consequently, this visual diagram might encourage visitors to physically—and perhaps also emotionally—experience the different consequences that result from accepting an evolutionist "theory" over a creationist "certainty."

Although using empirical data is essential to its mission, this example demonstrates that the Creation Museum articulates and reinforces its larger message by embedding that data within a sensual encounter. Crooke calls museums "contact zones" and claims that when those who have a stake in what is displayed come together in this space "the museum or object as 'contact zone' is animated." Furthermore, she argues that at the core of a museum's significance is the "energy emitted" by the "push and pull" among heritage, interpretation, and display.[59] I interpret this "push and pull" as the visitor's interactive engagement within and with the museum's material, rhythmic features and, therefore, as constituting an energetic encounter, one that ultimately produces a meaningful affective intimate script.

The Creation Museum encourages visitors to understand the differences between an evolutionist and a creationist identity, and the contrasting life experiences these identities offer, by means of their bodies. Because museums, like performances, provide visitors with live sensual encounters, I propose that, like spectators at a play, many visitors will arrive at these spaces in bodies open to the venue's rhythmic possibilities. This may hold especially true for the Creation Museum whose slogan—"Prepare to Believe"—implies as much. Therefore, borrowing the familiar, trustworthy museum motif may prompt many visitors—both believers and skeptics—to enter the space with the open preparedness necessary to generate this embodied understanding. As I have demonstrated, such borrowing is typical of evangelical dramaturgy.

However, some creationists may not initially feel comfortable entering the Creation Museum (perhaps even just subconsciously) precisely because it looks and feels like a typical natural history museum. Accordingly, the prominent animatronic display of dinosaurs alongside humans that greets people in the Creation Museum lobby, as seen in Figure 7, may put those visitors at ease. Moreover, while the inside of the venue looks and feels like a traditional natural history museum, the Creation Museum's exterior design—as other scholars have noted—is reminiscent of the large-scale, modern, "secular" look of a contemporary megachurch.[60] Compare the exterior of the Creation Museum in Figure 9 to Figures 10 and 11, both photographs of different megachurches that I will discuss in Chapter Six. This architectural choice might reassure some spectators, thereby prompting openness to the exhibits and presentations inside. Furthermore, the

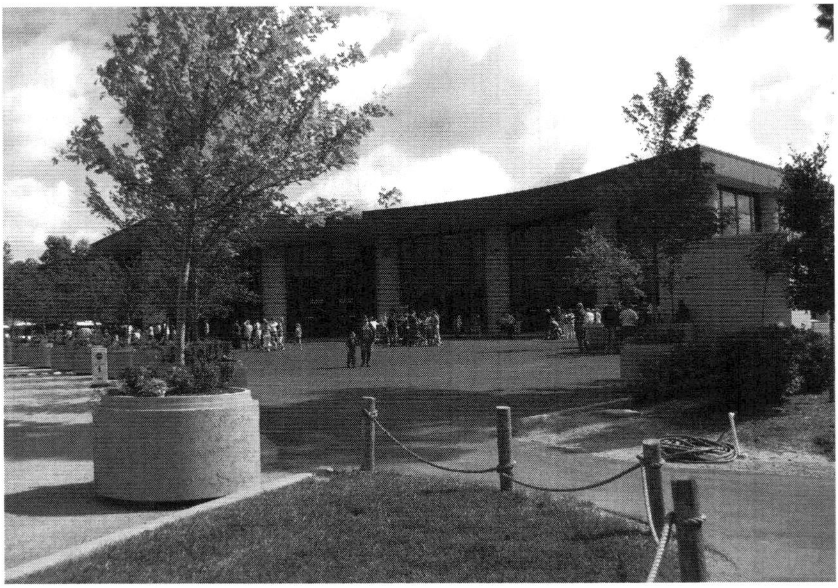

Figure 9. Exterior of the Creation Museum. July 2009. Photo by author.

megachurch motif—like the use of microphones and Praise Songs before "Behold the Lamb" at Holy Land Experience—may encourage certain guests to engage the museum visit as a form of worship. In the case of the Creation Museum, evangelical dramaturgy's appropriation of a popular form (museum and/or megachurch) is quite complicated and proves effective, in part, because this borrowing can be refracted through other evangelical associations and experiences.

Comfortable Creationist Blends

Conceptual blending theory can help us to examine further how bodily interactions with the Creation Museum's material space engender meaning. I maintain that, like a performance, museums prompt visitors to "live in" blends and to derive meaning from their experiences inside those blends. Ham would likely agree that living in the blend is fundamental to how his museum conveys meaning. As he claims, "Parents say even little kids get the

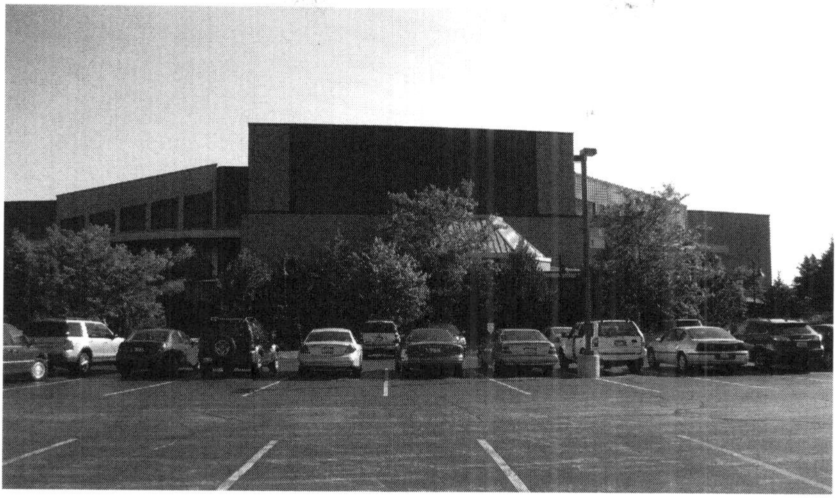

Figure 10. Exterior of Willow Creek Community Church in South Barrington, Illinois. June 2011. Photo by author.

message because they *experience* it" (my emphasis).[61] I interpret the Creation Museum's exhibit spaces as purposefully designed to compel visitors to "live in" specific blends and, thus, to derive meaning from within those blends.

For example, by using the traditional natural history museum walk-through structure, the Creation Museum not only presents the creationist account as a progressive narrative, but it also encourages visitors to "live in" a Bible/science blend consonant with young earth creationism.[62] Tony Bennett notes that as evolutionary thought took hold in the nineteenth century, natural history museums increasingly embodied progressive ideologies. The museum space therefore provided the "context for a performance that was simultaneously bodily and mental"; when visitors followed prescribed routes, the museum's evolutionary narratives "were realized spatially." Bennett claims it was critical that the museum's evolutionary message be "realized or recapitulated in and through the physical activity of the visitor."[63] The museum thus functioned as a performance space whose meaning was generated and reinforced through visitor interactions with it.

The Creation Museum employs a similar performative tactic. The "Museum Experience Walk" blends the typical natural history museum motif,

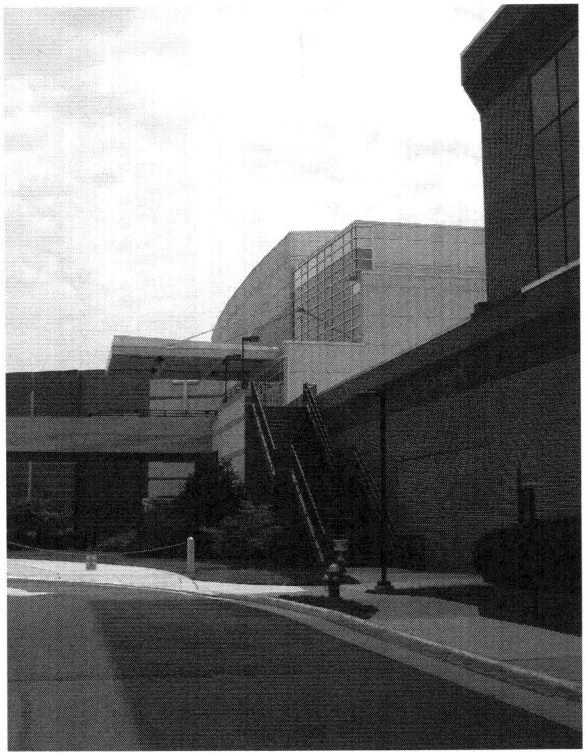

Figure 11. Exterior of McLean Bible Church (Tysons Campus), Virginia. June 2011. Photo by author.

including dioramas, dinosaurs, excavation displays, and quotations from scientists, with the creation account found in the book of Genesis. The traditional material rhythms of the natural history museum verify the authority of the biblical account—or, more accurately, the biblical account validates the museum's authoritative claims. The planetarium and the botanical garden—both spaces culturally legitimated as educational venues—function similarly. As Tracy Davis asserts, physical encounters with displays make "visitors confront the museums' ideologies spatially" while also encouraging "*a conscious performance by the visitor of the meaning of the place*" (original emphasis).[64] This is certainly the case at the Creation Museum, where ambulatory visitors perform the progressive structure of the "Experience Walk" as part of "living in" the Bible/science blend. The venue's power and value derive, in great part, from how it effectively "cements concept to experience,"[65] thus fomenting young earth creationist ideology viscerally.

The progressive walk configuration works particularly well as a creationist tactic because it also draws attention to the problems inherent in trying to put evolution on display, problems seemingly absent from the museum's Bible/science blend. As Bennett explains, curators of natural history museums have always grappled with the fact that "the *processes* of evolution could not themselves be seen—only their outcomes" (original emphasis). Evolution can only be made visible through the "particular narrative ordering" of things, and, even still, it cannot "be made evident at all where sequences were interrupted and discontinuous."[66] The Creation Museum exploits this fact by offering visitors a comforting alternative script; as the *Souvenir Guidebook* explains, "The Creation Museum has designed many of its exhibits in a particular order to emphasize the Bible as the correct starting point."[67] For many Bible-believing creationists, that simple choice of starting point results in coherent resolution. Therefore, while visitors live in the Bible/science blend they experience a whole, unbroken, and progressive creationist narrative that resolves any lingering questions about the past. In other words, as one museum video contends, what is a mystery to scientists "makes perfect sense in a biblical worldview."

The Bible/science blend stands in stark contrast to the experiential blends that traditional science museums typically offer. The very nature of scientific inquiry means that new discoveries usually raise as many questions as they answer. When these questions challenge fundamental concepts—such as notions of consciousness or the self—they very often leave people feeling even more ignorant or uncertain.[68] This seems to be the case with earth science research. As Giovanni Frazzetto explains, while the Judeo-Christian tradition gives humanity "primacy over the rest of nature. . . . Darwinian evolutionary theory places man in the long chain of life, without granting him any privileges over other living species."[69] Consequently, as Umberto Galimberti concludes, for some people the espousal of creationism is not about defending "human dignity in the name of his divine origin" but instead about ensuring humanity's God-given "dominion" over earth.[70]

Studies suggest that traditional museum exhibits on evolution do, indeed, challenge visitors' notions of human authority and dominion. For instance, entrance and exit surveys from an exhibit on evolution at Chicago's Field Museum indicate that, "unprompted, patrons exiting the Field's evolution exhibit reported a strong sense of their own 'fragility' as a species, and many visitors reported feeling very 'small' in comparison with the vast scales of geological time."[71] Evolutionary theory positions nature as indifferent to humankind, a perspective that effectively diminishes humanity's authority and privilege.[72] Since the natural history museum experience reinforces this worldview, it is understandable that many visitors might experience the blends it generates as somewhat discomforting.

Young earth creationism rejects the idea that humanity is insignificant and powerless, finding this view not only "very depressing" but even "cruel and wasteful."[73] As an alternative, young earth creationism foregrounds humankind's importance by making the world, in Stephen Asma's words, "a much smaller place":[74] a 6,000-year-old world created in six days by a God who made mankind in his image and then gave humans preeminence over all other living things. Accordingly, the Creation Museum emphasizes humankind's special relationship with God, as well as humanity's supremacy over all of creation. The brief film shown in the museum's Six Days Theater reminds viewers that God specifically gave humans "dominion" over creation and instructed them to "subdue it." Similarly, visitors to the planetarium watch a largely traditional show about the vastness of space and the cosmos. Yet, at the end, when the audience might typically leave a planetarium show feeling very small in relation to the universe's unimaginable dimensions, the film's narrator explains how God made the special choice to create humankind in his own image to live on Earth. A related idea is expressed more colloquially by Gabe and Mike in *Men in White:* "Hey, folks—life isn't meaningless."

Young earth creationism provides believers with a divinely ordained sense of purpose, and the Creation Museum guest experience reinforces this conceit. Specific rhythmic devices shape the visitor's physical encounter with the museum space in order to prompt guests to live in a reassuring Bible/science blend. However, not every part of the museum functions in this way. Certain exhibits are designed to generate a very different blend, one that not only replicates evolution's wandering uncertainty but also relates that uncertainty to negative moral consequences.

Re-experiencing the Fall of Man

After the exhibit about attacks on God's Word, visitors following the "Museum Experience Walk" enter "Graffiti Alley." As shown in Figure 12, this dimly lit brick alley is covered in a collage of newspaper clippings about issues like stem cell research or the Terri Schiavo case, which in 2005 sparked intense public and legal debates over issues of medical proxy, euthanasia, and end-of-life decision-making. This alley leads museumgoers into the "Culture in Crisis" room. The display on one side of this room shows the model of a church whose wall has been partially demolished by a wrecking ball labeled "Millions of Years." On the opposite wall video monitors are installed to look like the windows of a suburban house. Watching these screens, the museumgoer becomes a voyeur who is privy to each family member's private troubles. One monitor shows a video of two teenage boys in a bedroom. They smoke marijuana as one of them peruses pornography on the Internet. Another monitor shows a teenage girl talking to her friend on the phone about how she is contemplating having an abortion. On a third screen, visitors see the disengaged parents—in the foreground the mother is drinking wine and gossiping with a friend, while in the background the father sits in the living room watching television. Panels around the room suggest that neglecting the Bible results in these cultural "crises." One sign proclaims, "Scripture abandoned in the culture leads to relative morality, hopelessness and meaninglessness."

"Graffiti Alley" and the "Culture in Crisis" room both utilize various synaesthetic elements in order to construct an evolution/social disintegration blend. Cognitive responses, while biological, are also culturally constructed. As Bruce McConachie explains, "the mind/brain is neither 'hard-wired' for certain cultural responses nor is it a 'blank slate' or passive recorder"; instead, "historical cultures narrow and shape nearly all of the aspects of cognition and emotion." Consequently, "attention may be a species-level attribute of human consciousness, but culture helps people to learn what to pay attention to."[75] In "Graffiti Alley" and the "Culture in Crisis" room, culturally coded aesthetic cues create an atmosphere that pours into and shapes the visitor's experience.[76] For example, these rooms are significantly darker and more menacing than the preceding exhibits (see Figure 13). The graffiti-covered brick alley, chaotic soundscape, and dim, red-hued lighting are all meant to make visitors, especially children, feel apprehensive, anxious, or even frightened. Moreover, similar synaesthetic elements reappear later in the "Cave of Sorrows" and "Corruption Valley" exhibits. Photographs and dioramas in the "Cave of Sorrows" depict some of the consequences of humankind's Fall: starvation, murder, pain, genocide. "Corruption Valley," which outlines specific changes wrought by Adam's sin, contains a large, threatening, carnivorous animatronic dinosaur.[77] The sensual reiteration links the "evils" of contemporary culture to Adam's origi-

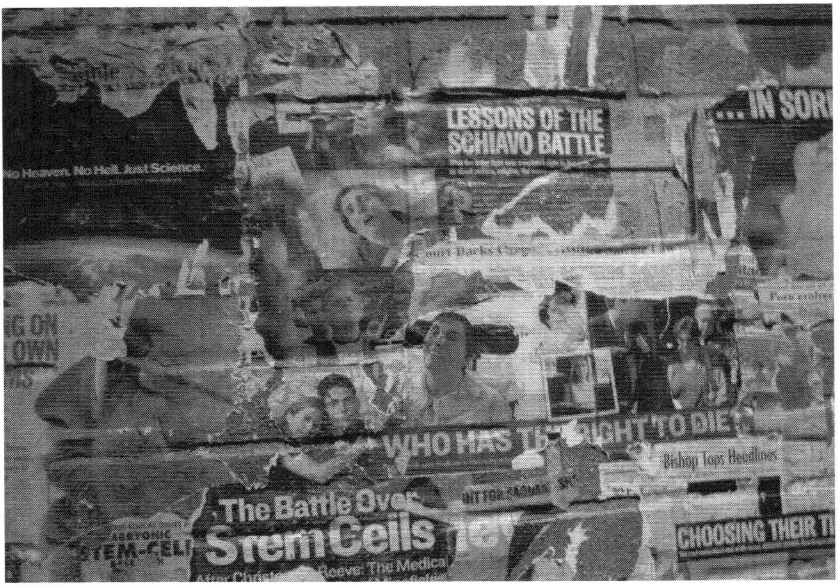

Figure 12. Graffiti Alley newspaper collage. The Creation Museum. July 2009. Photo by author.

nal sin, implying that both result from neglecting God's Word. This echoing embeds within the visitor's body a visceral association between evolutionary theory (identified throughout the museum as the prime example of rejecting God's Word) and life's sufferings.[78] As I have already noted, Erika Fischer-Lichte argues that the atmosphere of a space surrounds and penetrates the spectator's body, thereby causing the entering subject to experience "the space and its things as emphatically present."[79] This kind of presencing supports religiously real re-experience. In this case, the room's atmosphere prompts visitors to re-experience the fall of man but specifically from within an evolution/social disintegration blend.

As with the museum's focus on observable science, this association between evolutionary theory and misery also has roots in an earlier generation of creationist films and videos. Heather Hendershot explains how, according to the 1995 creationist film *When Two Worldviews Collide,* "Evolutionary evangelists . . . advocate premarital sex, physician-assisted suicide, divorce, homosexuality, and abortion."[80] Hendershot suggests that this shift toward

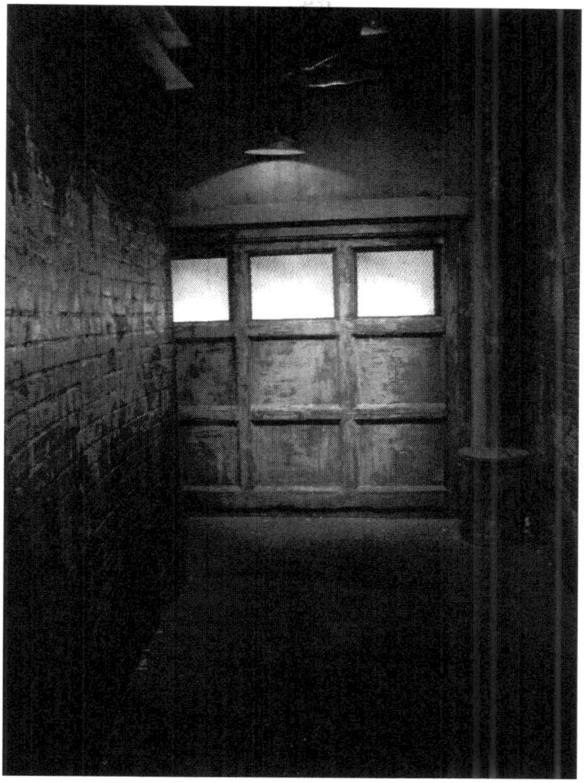

Figure 13. Graffiti Alley leading into the Culture in Crisis Room. The Creation Museum. July 2009. Photo by author.

hot-button topics, which represents a form of engaged orthodoxy, is a recent development within creationist media:

> Contemporary creationist videos, in sum, seem to mirror a key change in evangelical culture since the seventies, and since the demise of MIS, the move toward increasing political engagement. Creationist media now use militaristic rhetoric, repeatedly emphasizing that creationists and evolutionists are engaged in a "battle for the mind."[81]

The Creation Museum operates within this tradition; however, as a physical space it provides AiG with a variety of experientially oriented tactics for promoting that message. By encouraging visitors to live in two opposing sensual blends—Bible/science and evolution/social disintegration—the

Creation Museum experience produces a powerful affective intimate script. This script affirms not only that accepting the Bible's narrative and its salvation message alleviates the distress and suffering of modern life, but also that accepting evolution constitutes (and is essentially inseparable from) rejecting Christianity. As Byassee concludes,

> The message could not be clearer: if you accept anything less than the young-earth creationist view, sooner or later your church will die and you will no doubt become an atheist. On the other hand, if you accept the biblical worldview, things might improve. Insistence on biblical science is just a first step toward renewing the church generally.[82]

From AiG's point of view, choosing between evolution and creationism has wide-reaching consequences.

Like nineteenth-century natural history museums that tried to control the chaos of nature through Enlightenment principles of observation and logic, the Creation Museum attempts to control the chaos and perceived moral disintegration of twenty-first-century life by means of God's Word. The museum is particularly effective at accomplishing this goal because it uses mise en scène, what Martin Seel defines as "the staging of presence." Seel describes artistic mise en scène as a "sensual" process that is "begun or performed intentionally" and presented for an audience.[83] Mise en scène is therefore directly linked to the material, rhythmic elements of a performance; as Fischer-Lichte explains with respect to theater, "By determining performative strategies for generating materiality, the process of staging creates a specific situation into which actors and spectators enter."[84] I contend that the same is true at the Creation Museum.

Ultimately, the Creation Museum "stages" creationist theory, but, importantly, without seeming to do so; as Fischer-Lichte notes, "*mise en scène* unfolds its effects specifically because it is not perceived as staged. The impression of authenticity results from the very background of the careful and thorough staged work."[85] Here, again, we find evangelical dramaturgy challenging any clear separation between theatricality and authenticity. In this case, careful staging may encourage people to live in blends that "feel" natural and genuine, and thus to perceive the conceptual meaning they construct from those blends as incontrovertible and absolute. As Asma notes, "choosing a biblical story of origins brings with it comforting cultural baggage."[86] Such comfort is not only mental or metaphorical. Instead, I would argue that for many visitors the Creation Museum provides actual bodily comfort and a physical reprieve from what they perceive as destructive forces in society. That is one reason the intimate script it generates is so valuable. In addition, a sense of wonder typically accompanies a museum visit; as Lynn Dierking and John Falk's study of the museum experience indicates, "for most visitors feelings of awe exist before the visit, are enhanced during the visit, and persist after the visit."[87] Such feelings can intensify the visitor's affective intimate script and, thus, the emotional meaning it ultimately engenders.

The language used by some reviewers may even validate—if inadvertently—the Creation Museum's ability to achieve its experiential objectives. Writing for the *Chronicle of Higher Education,* Asma admits that "something slowly happens to your criteria of 'reasonableness' the more you become immersed in this creationist worldview."[88] Even more poignantly, in his *New York Times* review, Edward Rothstein asserts,

> Whether you are willing to grant the premises of this museum almost becomes irrelevant as you are drawn into its mixture of spectacle and narrative. . . . For the believer, it seems, this museum provides a kind of relief: Finally the world is being shown as it really is, without the distortions of secularism and natural selection.

And Rothstein also concludes his piece with an image of bodily understanding, proposing that even the skeptic "leaves feeling a bit like Adam emerging from Eden, all the world before him, freshly amazed at its strangeness and extravagant peculiarities."[89] Rothstein hints at the idea that the Creation Museum experience does change (if only temporarily) how visitors subsequently perceive and engage the world, and thus, how they understand it. As with the other genres I have analyzed, the Creation Museum cultivates this kind of embodied knowledge by manipulating the live, rhythmic encounter between user and medium in order to generate a religiously real re-experience.

Bodying Forth a Creationist Identity

In June 2009, scientists attending the North American Paleontological Convention had the option to take a day-trip to the Creation Museum as part of their conference events. One professor on the excursion conceded, "I hate that it exists, but given that it exists, you can have a good time here. They put on a very good show if you can handle the suspension of disbelief."[90] However, as McConachie explains, conceptual blending emphasizes the agency of theatrical spectatorship and thereby challenges the notion that theatergoers or, as I would argue, museum visitors, ever willingly suspend disbelief. Conceptual blending suggests that, rather than ignoring or eliminating inputs, spectators instead engage in "imaginative addition."[91] This notion of imaginative addition in fact correlates to how many evangelicals engage biblical scripture. Crapanzano explains that evangelicals often appear "to be carried away by their enthusiasm, their performance, the power of the Word" to the point where others "might want to liken their condition at such times to Coleridge's notion of 'the willing suspension of disbelief.'" However, he argues that believers "would object to the negative phrasing; they might speak of the willing intensification of belief that constitutes religious faith."[92] In a similar sense, visitors to the Creation Museum are invited to imaginatively add themselves into the material world they see and into the progressive Bible-based narrative that they physically travel through, live in, and, ultimately, perform, as a way to intensify their beliefs.

One reason we visit museums is to have exactly this kind of immediate, intensified experience. Tracy Davis claims that "the spiritual or scientific takes a physical form, and that is the essence and purpose of a museum."[93] That is certainly the case with the Creation Museum, whose purpose is to give both the scientific and spiritual aspects of young earth creationism a palpable, tactile material form. But, importantly, creationist visitors to the museum do not expect to see the Garden of Eden or other episodes from the Genesis creation story represented realistically. Instead, as with Holy Land Experience or the Living Bible Tour, creationist-believers arrive anticipating a re-representation of the biblical narrative that will give them access to the truth of "God's Word" and thereby put them in direct touch with the divinely inspired plan for humankind. Moving through the space generates a re-experience of a different kind than what I identified with respect to Passion plays, but one with a similar religiously real component. Returning to Timothy Beal's language, the Creation Museum re-experience gives visitors a sense of "ultimate reality" and allows them to feel that they have "become a part of it."[94]

The knowledge that emerges from such an encounter is remarkably powerful precisely because it works on and through the visitor's body, a fact we cannot underestimate. Jandos Rothstein maintains that children will leave the Creation Museum wanting more concrete answers, which they will find later in secular science books and classes.[95] Instead, I would argue that while visiting the museum children live in a materially realized creationist world, one that employs exciting scientific evidence and spectacular physical effects (like rumbling seats and water splashing in their faces during a film segment about the biblical Flood) to confirm what family members, church leaders, and the Bible may have taught them. This museum re-experience provides extremely concrete answers and serves to embed creationist belief in the body. Naomi Rokotnitz contends that some performances require spectators to take leaps of faith. Rather than blind faith, this kind of "belief" constitutes "an informed species of decision-making which takes account of—and trusts—embodied knowledge."[96] Like a performance, the Creation Museum shapes belief by first giving the biblical creation narrative physical actuality—a sphere of presence—and then offering visitors the vivid, kinetic, gestalt re-experience of living in it.[97] Bodily knowledge assumes the status of truth, a truth that subsequent encounters with textbooks and science classes won't easily nullify.

Moreover, the museum uses devices that may also connect the creationist identity it constructs to a particular national identity. For example, choosing a starting point underscores the notion of individual choice, a concept that is fundamental to the value-epistemology of modern American culture that Christian Smith describes.[98] In addition, as with the "Great Passion Play," the museum's location in the American heartland (and within one day's drive of much of the country) also aligns it with certain idealized notions of America. Finally, the very idea of humankind as expressly chosen by God parallels the view of America as a New Jerusalem, an idea prevalent among Christians, and particularly evangelicals, since the eighteenth century. Discussing the early twentieth-century debates about Darwinian evolution, and specifically the reaction of Christian fundamentalists like William Jennings Bryan, Hasia Diner notes:

> A core religious belief was that human beings were the crown of creation. And in very American terms, the American was also the crown of creation. But now, reading these accounts of Darwin, one couldn't say that any longer. Darwinism undermined the notion of what it means to be an American.[99]

Creationism not only restores humankind to its "rightful" place of pride in creation, but, for some Americans, it might also reaffirm American exceptionalism and the privileged role of the United States as a New Eden. I would suggest that, in the end, the museum permits visitors to re-experience a nostalgic past in which Protestant, Bible-believing Americans were irrefutably considered the rightful authorities over their nation and its natural resources.[100]

For young earth creationists, this museum endorses a historical narrative that is often marginalized. In this respect, the Creation Museum's aims are akin to those of many living history museums: to give voice and concrete form to the other side of the story; to make people face conflicts in history and understand their consequences; and to help people learn from the lessons of history so that they will act responsibly in the present.[101] Therefore, like many living history museums, a crucial part of the Creation Museum's mission is to inspire change in visitors that will impact their actions after they leave. In other words, it aims to encourage engaged orthodoxy.

The Creation Museum accomplishes this task not only by constructing a clearly defined and reassuring creationist identity for visitors to emulate but also by preparing visitors to body forth this identity once they leave the venue.[102] Scott Magelssen proposes that interactive, role-playing activities in living history museums offer visitors opportunities to rehearse alternative actions that they might then use in the real world.[103] The Creation Museum does not include many hands-on exhibits, but its marketing does imply that visitors will have an intimate, interactive experience: "The area within the museum has been divided into unusually configured spaces that allow for personal interaction with each of the 160 exhibits."[104] Moreover, the museum offers guests other specific ways to "rehearse" responses to evolutionary theory that they can apply later.

First, the museum gives visitors a model creationist with whom they can identify and subsequently emulate. A thoughtful, grandfatherly man narrates nearly all of the short films and videos scattered throughout the museum. His calm, reasonable voice, compassionate demeanor, and Santa Claus–like appearance (complete with a twinkle in his eye) help gain the spectator's trust and confidence. Visitors first encounter this narrator in a video as part of the "Starting Points" exhibit. He introduces himself as a paleontologist who begins his work from the premise of God's Word. Despite this fact, he still maintains a friendship with Kim, a fellow paleontologist who begins from human reason and therefore believes in evolution. The creationist paleontologist returns in subsequent films and videos. He teaches us that dragon legends from the Middle Ages serve as evidence that dinosaurs lived alongside humans. He also narrates the final film in the "Museum Experience Walk" entitled *The Last Adam*. This film is about Christ's crucifixion, and it helps illustrate the paleontologist-narrator's personal journey of faith.

Like signs throughout the museum, this recurring character provides visitors with considered arguments that they could use in future conversations when questioned about their creationist beliefs. But, more important, this figure embodies a composed, informed, and self-assured creationist presence; there is no conflict between his scientific profession and his faith. His appearance and demeanor are also culturally coded, inviting museumgoers—who, in my experience, were predominantly white—to identify with him and find reassurance in his personal history and testimony.[105] Like the accents in the "Great Passion Play," this creationist figure's calm tone and confident gestures may trigger a comfortable and comforting resonance within visitors each time they encounter him. Furthermore, his peaceful verbal and physical rhythms are juxtaposed against the nervous, erratic gestures and expressions of the evolutionist characters, such as the flustered teachers in the *Men in White* film. Those characters will also resonate with spectators as familiar, but not in a comforting or reassuring way.

Mirror neuron research suggests that spectators will simulate the rhythms and gestures of these characters. Evan Thompson explains how the mirror neuron system is one of the different "coupling mechanisms linking self and other at sensorimotor and affective levels" that help to establish empathy.[106] Empathy is not an emotion, but a precondition that leads to other emotional engagements, among them sympathy and antipathy. As Thompson explains, for phenomenologists "empathy is a unique form of intentionality in which we are directed toward the other's experience,"[107] and, consequently, it has a moral dimension. Although empathy is inarguably subjective, individualized, and enculturated,[108] dramaturgical devices can coax spectators toward certain empathetic relationships with characters. By doing so, these devices not only encourage spectators to develop particular feelings for the characters, but they may also impact the spectator's moral experience of those characters. Since these feelings and experiences are traced into the spectator's embodied schema, they also supply a foundation for subsequent action and understanding after the performative encounter. Cognitive science therefore suggests that visitors will simulate the embodied actions of these creationist and evolutionist characters—presented throughout the museum as stark opposites—and that this motor resonance will then influence, in some respect, how the visitor understands these differing identities. I suspect this impact might be particularly acute with younger visitors, who may be more attuned to the characters' physical and vocal rhythms than they are to the specific rhetoric or arguments the characters employ.

During my time in the Creation Museum, I overheard many conversations that indicated, at least to me, that most visitors agreed with the creationist account as it was presented throughout the exhibits. Differences certainly existed, such as those between three people walking to the picnic area who were debating the timing of the Rapture. But in all of the conversations that I heard, it seemed that the fundamental principles of young earth creationism were not under dispute. As I heard one museumgoer remark, "When you see all of this, it just makes sense."

For these visitors, the museum encounter must bolster their faith by offering them facts and arguments that endorse their worldview and that they can draw upon once they return home. Those future experiences are not separate from, but rather an important part of, the Creation Museum encounter. Lynn Dierking and John Falk explain,

> Subsequent experiences, sometimes reinforcing and others not, dramatically contribute to what someone eventually learns from the museum. It is only as events unfold for the individual after the museum visit that experiences that occurred inside the institution become relevant and useful.[109]

This is another reason the narrator figure is an essential component—he allows visitors to "rehearse" vicariously for future conversations with people who do not agree with the creationist account, even furnishing them with scripted sound bites they might utilize. In this way, the Creation Museum helps to cultivate engaged orthodoxy.

The bookstore also facilitates engaged orthodoxy by selling items that commodify creationist belief. These include videos, books, T-shirts, hats, stuffed dinosaurs, buttons, magnets, bumper stickers, jewelry, and postcards. David Morgan analyzes a number of different functions that popular religious objects fulfill for Christians: educating children in the faith, providing daily sacred encounters, maintaining traditions across generations, commemorating important events, protecting those who carry them, and witnessing faith.[110] Most of these functions pertain to the items available in the Dragon Hall Bookstore. But as Alice Rayner argues, an object's material presence can also give "sense to history."[111] I propose that many of the objects for sale at the Creation Museum are designed to "give sense" to sacred, biblical history. When a believer uses one of these objects he or she effectively "touches time in the register of the senses, time that is not separate from the object (as in the effects of time) but incorporated *as* the object in its present" (original emphasis).[112] Purchased in a creationist world, a world housed in a building that may even look like the visitor's home church, the object's user might understand it as imbued with the power and authority of the biblical narrative. And if worn or carried during the actual museum visit, the experience of walking through a creationist-framed world might become incorporated as part of the souvenir's present. The objects sold in the bookstore thereby become material extensions of faith, not only giving sense to history but also giving sense to belief. While the kinetic experiences during a Creation Museum visit enable belief to assume the status of truth, material objects offer visitors another way to carry forth, even body forth, that truth into the world.

Finally, material objects can also play a significant role in mobilizing affect. In her discussion of the souvenirs and T-shirts sold at Teen Mania Ministries' "Acquire the Fire" performance events, Jennifer Williams proposes that "materiality creates the possibility of affect's longevity by affirming the authenticity of the experience after the performance is over, preserving the memory in something material, and creating enduring social networks around those objects."[113] She suggests that in certain evangelical performative contexts, visible and tangible objects help affect to engender and spread ideology, thus rendering ideology "contagious."[114] This link between materiality and affect, which has surfaced throughout these chapters, is especially pertinent to my analysis of megachurches. Williams argues, "It is uncertainty that fuels affect as a motivation and passionate desire," and, consequently, spectacular evangelical performance events, like "Acquire the Fire," allow participants "to purge both affect and ideological uncertainty."[115] I recognize a similar function with respect to megachurches. As I will demonstrate in the next chapter, these large-scale, technologically sophisticated churches use a variety of spectacular tactics in order to generate affective intimate scripts that will direct visitors toward emotional production that can resolve ideological uncertainties.

6

Megachurches

Cultivating Affective Atmosphere

In this final chapter I analyze the evangelical megachurch as a unique, highly visible, and incredibly persuasive performative genre. More specifically, I will demonstrate how each megachurch uses the strategies of evangelical dramaturgy to craft a synaesthetic space and worship experience that will reflect its specific "brand." In his study of the evolutionary origins of religious thought, Pascal Boyer notes that we tend to think about the economic aspects of religion, such as markets, services, and commercial negotiations, "as *consequences* of religious organization rather than as its source" because "we assume that doctrine comes first, and its implementation leads to particular economic and political behavior" (original emphasis). However, Boyer maintains that "some crucial aspects of religious institutions make sense only if we understand what the market for religious services is like, what kind of commodity religious knowledge and ritual constitute."[1] In this respect, religious groups or organizations operate like specialized guilds, deriving their power and influence from the fact that they provide specific services. Yet, as Boyer argues, unlike craftsmen, who "often have no difficulty maintaining exclusive supply, either because other people would not want to perform their dangerous and polluting tasks (gathering garbage, burying the dead, butchering animals, etc.), or because these tasks require technical knowledge and a long apprenticeship," the position of religious specialist is more "precarious" precisely because these individuals often supply services "that could very easily be provided by outsiders."[2]

One way that religious specialists respond to this predicament is by putting forth a doctrine that, among other things, clearly explains the services they offer. "Literate" religious guilds (to use Boyer's term) typically explicate their doctrines by means of texts. As Boyer explains, texts help "to make religious doctrines more coherent, in the sense that all the elements that compose the descriptions of supernatural agents can be brought together for consideration much more efficiently than when they are stored in individual people's memories, in the form of particular episodes."[3] In general, these textual accounts of doctrine are,

> *integrated* (most elements hang together and cross-reference each other), apparently *deductive* (you can infer the guild's position on a whole variety of situations by considering the general principles), and *stable* (you get the same message from all members of the guild). This last feature is particularly important for diffusion. (original emphasis)[4]

This description is certainly relevant to evangelical Christianity. For many evangelical Christians, biblical scripture supplies a doctrine that they consider integrated, deductive, and stable, thereby giving these religious "consumers" a clear idea of what specific services evangelicalism provides.

However, because many Christian denominations—evangelical and otherwise—use this same text, albeit in different ways, establishing and then maintaining one's unique position within the religious marketplace necessitates a more comprehensive form of "branding":

> One solution is to turn the [religious] guild's ministration into a *brand,* that is, a service that is (1) distinct from what others could provide, (2) similar regardless of what member of the guild provides it, (3) easily recognizable by its particular features and (4) exclusively provided by one particular organization. (original emphasis)[5]

As Boyer notes, "there is nothing intrinsically demeaning in saying that some services are offered in the form of a particular brand."[6] Indeed, the close relationship between U.S. evangelicalism and religious consumerism has been a prominent theme throughout this project. As I noted in my Introduction, as early as George Whitefield, American evangelical leaders were reshaping religious media into products that would appeal to "the marketplace."[7]

Boyer is therefore one of many scholars who have analyzed religious trends, and particularly those within evangelical Christianity, through notions of a religious economy.[8] As Shayne Lee and Phillip Luke write, this growing body of research makes "the case for a supply-side analysis of religious vitality."[9] Many scholars now recognize that "religious suppliers carve out a niche in the spiritual marketplace and distinguish their ministries by offering an array of spiritual goods and services that match the tastes and desires of religious consumers."[10] The various genres I have analyzed in the previous chapters are examples of such "goods and services." Therefore, rather than simply examining the phenomenon of religious branding, in this chapter I will consider how, as Boyer asserts, "the creation of recognizable brands of religious services" can directly impact "the kinds of concepts put forth by religious institutions."[11] In other words, I will suggest how branding actually generates doctrine.

Corporate Strategies for "Kingdom Results"

Many evangelical megachurches embrace the notion of branding, and leaders of these institutions are often very transparent about following a business model when formulating their church's mission statement, developing a strategic plan for growth, and building their congregations. These leaders often turn to organizations such as Leadership Network or the Willow Creek Association, which develop and distribute resources designed to help "innovative churches and church leaders better realize their vision and maximize their impact."[12] Although these organizations do not hide their religious motivations and goals, much of the language they use in their materials and on their websites sounds like "corporate speak." For example, Leadership Network's mission statement reads:

> Leaders are always focused on What's Next.
> What is God doing now? How can we join?
> What is the Aha! that we need to move us further?
> Leadership Network was formed in 1984 to work with leaders of innovative churches to explore these questions to generate kingdom results. Believing that meaningful conversations and connections can change the world, Leadership Network seeks to help leaders of innovation navigate the future by exploring new ideas together to find application to their own unique contexts. Through collaborative meetings and processes these leader [*sic*] map future possibilities and challenge one another to action that leads to results. Through our publications, books and online experiences we share

> the learnings and inspiration to others and surface new conversations worthy of exploration.[13]

In addition, some of the more influential megachurch pastors, like Rick Warren, who founded and still leads Saddleback Church in Southern California, spend a fair amount of time on the lecture circuit teaching other pastors about church development techniques. As Warren's biography on Saddleback's website notes,

> He built the Purpose Driven Network, a global alliance of pastors from 162 countries and hundreds of denominations who have been trained to be purpose driven churches. He also founded Pastors.com—an online interactive community that provides sermons, forums, and other practical resources for pastors—including archives of a bi-weekly newsletter that is sent to more than 100,000 pastors and ministry leaders.[14]

Many pastors of newer megachurches, and even of certain Catholic and mainline Protestant congregations, credit these leaders and resources with their own success at church growth and development.[15] For example, in her article on Frank Santora, pastor of Faith Church in New Milford, Connecticut, which was founded in 1983 and now has nearly 3,000 members,[16] Frances FitzGerald writes,

> Santora frankly acknowledges his debt to Warren and many others for the church-growth strategies he practices. . . . Three of Santora's board members head large evangelistic organizations, and Maurilio Amorim, a church-growth consultant, brings him ideas on media and marketing.[17]

Amorim's A-Group is "a full-service marketing, technology, literary and PR firm specializing in Christian and non-profit areas."[18] As with Leadership Network, A-Group communicates its mission through standard corporate jargon:

> Our vision is to offer our clients creative and effective solutions to their branding, technology and communications needs. We work hard to understand their challenges and opportunities. We provide strategic guidance and navigate the marketplace, which has been radically transformed by new technologies.[19]

Amorim describes his company as "a boutique firm that creates a brand for churches."[20] That branding occurs at many levels, including external marketing and weekly bulletin design. However, A-Group also helps pastors select the visual and material elements of their worship services, such as the music, set pieces, and video projections.[21] This suggests that the rhythmic quality of the synaesthetic worship event is critical to how these churches create and maintain their unique brands.

The American megachurch is traditionally defined as "a Protestant church that averages at least two thousand total attendees in their weekend services."[22] Various scholars have analyzed these churches, examining their demographic and growth statistics, programming and outreach strategies, and organizational models, as well as profiling the charismatic individuals who lead some of the more famous megachurches, particularly Rick Warren at Saddleback and Joel Osteen of Lakewood Church in Houston.[23] Although I will certainly touch upon some of these topics in this chapter, my main focus is the physical space of the megachurch, and specifically how the rhythmic worship events that take place in that space not only convey the church's brand but also construct and reinforce specific theological concepts and epistemological assumptions.

I contend that megachurches are not selling a theology, as much as a specific physical encounter with that theology. Michael Hamilton explains that "since the 1950s, denominational divisions have steadily become less important in American church life. . . . At bottom we are all still sectarians; we still prefer to congregate with the like minded. Our new sectarianism is a sectarianism of worship style."[24] A megachurch's worship style generates an experience that fulfills various contemporary needs—such as the desire for stability, reassurance, and personal choice—needs that I have argued other evangelical media also aim to fulfill. And, as with these other genres, megachurches achieve that goal in part by using strategies that shape the point of contact between worshipper and medium. For example, many megachurch sanctuaries contain arena-sized screens, as well as state-of-the-art sound and video projection systems. Anne C. Loveland and Otis B. Wheeler suggest that these elements reflect a shift "from a participatory to a performance-oriented service."[25] However, I contend that in addition to making spectacular services possible, these elements also create synaesthetic worship experiences that draw congregants into an intimate physical relationship with the space and the events that take place in it. Consequently, rather than placing participatory responses and performance-oriented responses at opposite ends of a spectrum, I will argue that the worship style at many megachurches urges visitors to participate actively in a deeply engaged, physical form of devotional performance spectatorship.

I chose megachurches as my closing example because this genre manifests many of the characteristics and dramaturgical strategies I have analyzed in the previous chapters. More specifically, this genre allows me to interrogate further how intermediality, staging, and mise en scène encourage believers to live in conceptual blends that will establish or reinforce specific beliefs by means of the body. Such blending, which begins the moment you pull into the megachurch parking lot, and continues throughout the entire visit, is essential to how these institutions assert their unique identities and "services" within the religious marketplace. Megachurches therefore supply a compelling final example of how evangelical dramaturgy manipulates the live rhythmic encounter between user and medium in order to engender deeply felt religious meaning and to commodify devotional experience.

Defining the Genre: More than Size

Anyone interested in megachurches can read a good deal of published literature on the subject[26] and will find the website www.megachurchmyths.com to be a particularly useful resource. Yet, as Scott Thumma and Dave Travis note in their book *Beyond Megachurch Myths*, "there is no substitute for visiting these churches in person as a way to create your own informed opinions about them."[27] I attended the following services as part of my research: the 11:00 a.m. service at Immanuel Bible Church in Springfield, Virginia on Sunday, 15 August 2010; the 11:00 a.m. worship service at Lakewood Church in Houston, Texas, on Sunday, 10 October 2010 (Pastor Joel Osteen was in England and therefore not preaching that weekend) and again on Sunday, 5 June 2011, when Osteen was preaching; the 9:00 a.m. service at McLean Bible Church (Tysons Campus) in Vienna, Virginia on Sunday, 19 June 2011 (Father's Day); and the 9:00 a.m. service at Willow Creek Community Church in South Barrington, Illinois, on Sunday, 26 June 2011. I also took the guided tour offered daily at The Potter's House in Dallas, Texas, on Friday, 8 October 2010.[28]

These venues reflect my attempt to attend the standard Sunday services at some of the largest and most famous megachurches (Lakewood and Willow Creek), as well as at a couple of less well-known churches. As scholarship and surveys demonstrate, there is no "typical" megachurch; while it is possible to identify trends across these churches and to categorize them based upon various parameters, it is crucial to remember that each is unique. Therefore, although I have tried to account for variety and aimed to avoid sweeping generalizations, my conclusions are necessarily limited not only by my personal experiences but also by my specific choice of venues.

A number of recent surveys supply the most comprehensive data to date on contemporary megachurches: the Megachurches Today 2005 survey (mailed or emailed to a total of 1,836 potential megachurches, with the results based upon the 406 fully completed surveys returned by churches with an average attendance of 1,800 or more); the Faith Communities Today 2005 survey (mailed to a random sample of 3,000 congregations); the Megachurches Today 2000 survey (sent to 600 churches with a total of 153 usable forms collected); the Faith Communities Today 2000 research project (with more than 14,300 participating congregations representing 41 denominations); and the U.S. Congregational Life Survey (with over 300,000 worshippers in over 2,000 participating congregations).[29] Thumma and Travis base most of their conclusions on the data these studies supply. In addition, the Hartford Institute for Religious Research's megachurch reports rely upon these same surveys, as well as two more recent studies: the Megachurches Today 2008: Changes in American Megachurches survey and the June 2009 research report entitled "Not Who You Think They Are: A Profile of the People Who Attend America's Megachurches," which summarizes the results of a survey of 24,900 megachurch attendees.[30]

According to the Hartford Institute, as of September 2008 there were 1,249 megachurches in the United States.[31] This number represents 0.37 percent of the approximately 335,000 congregations of all religious backgrounds operating in the United States at that time (and only 0.39 percent of the 320,000 Christian congregations in the nation).[32] However, since the median average attendance of all Christian congregations is only seventy-five people, studies indicate that 45 percent of people attending Christian worship do so "in churches in the top 10 percent in size."[33] Consequently, as Thumma and Travis explain, "The largest 1 percent of U.S. churches contain [*sic*] at least 15 percent of the worshippers, finances, and staff in America. Across the whole of Protestantism, the largest 20 percent of the churches have around 65 percent of the resources."[34] In addition, the Megachurches Today surveys suggest that weekly attendance at these churches is growing.

The mean weekly attendance at megachurches in 2000 was 3,857 and had reached 4,142 by the 2008 survey.[35]

A summary report written by Scott Thumma and Warren Bird highlights specific trends that are visible across the three Megachurches Today surveys (2000, 2005, and 2008). With respect to theological identity, 65 percent of megachurches in the 2008 study identified with the evangelical label, an increase from 56 percent in 2005. Thumma and Bird explain:

> This labeling of the attenders [*sic*] theological perspective has drastically shifted in 8 years. The vast majority of megachurches have always held a conservative theological position, and this hasn't changed. But what has changed is a turn away from distinctive theological segments within conservative Protestantism toward a "generic evangelicalism." During the past 8 years, nearly 20% more churches chose to describe the theological orientation of the congregation as "evangelical" rather than one of the distinctive variations within conservativism. In some sense the term "evangelical" can be seen as generically encompassing an increasingly broad spectrum of conservative Christians as the subgroup distinctions, such as Pentecostal, traditional, charismatic, etc., are less important or significant.[36]

Interestingly, the studies also reveal a trend toward political moderation; although still politically conservative, in 2008 more megachurches self-identified with a more moderate conservative stance than had previously.[37] The authors of the report conclude:

> This moderated political position may come as a surprise given the large amount of news reports that describe megachurches as right wing bastions of republicanism. While it is indeed true that the majority of megachurch attenders are republicans, this data shows that they are not the arch-conservatives many people portray them as.[38]

It is important to recognize that, rather than surveying attendees directly, this study asked church leaders to identify the political leanings of their congregations. Yet, even given this fact, the results do challenge certain assumptions about megachurch congregants.

As the title implies, in *Beyond Megachurch Myths* Thumma and Travis aim to bust this and other "myths" surrounding megachurches. Admittedly, their book is a Leadership Institute publication, and each chapter ends with a section entitled "Applying What You Have Read," which is intended "to help the readers consider their own church situations and apply a few of the lessons from the chapter to their own congregations."[39] However, for the most part the book is directed at general readers, particularly those with little firsthand knowledge of the megachurch genre, and the authors base their conclusions principally on the evidence supplied by those studies I mention above. *Beyond Megachurch Myths* is therefore a particularly valuable resource for scholars interested in examining the megachurch phenomenon.

One of the first myths that Thumma and Travis refute is the belief that "all megachurches are alike." As they note, many scholars have attempted to classify these churches based upon different variables, most notably size, location (urban, suburban, or rural), and worship style.[40] Alternatively, Thumma and Travis propose a system of four "streams" that takes into account not only size, location, and worship style, but also elements such as mission, culture, organization, leadership, development, history, and ministry.

> The stream or tributary metaphor indicates that while the collection of churches is part of the same river system, there are distinct differences within the internal and external perception of these churches. . . . These streams are in part cultural and stylistic distinctions created to appeal to different audiences. However, these different styles also can reshape a church's organization, format, ministry approach, and entire character of the congregation.[41]

Therefore, in addition to providing a comprehensive categorical system, I consider the streams concept highly compatible with the idea of branding. Thumma and Travis discuss their four streams at length,[42] but I will provide only a brief overview of these categories since, for my purposes, the specific distinctions are less important than the fact that significant differences do exist and that some of these differences signal efforts by megachurches to adapt their brand to reach certain target audiences.

The oldest institutions typically fall into the first stream—"Old Line/Program-based" megachurches. Such a church is located in urban or older suburban areas, usually was established before the current pastor (who most likely has a seminary degree), and often holds a mainline denominational affiliation. The architectural space is typically more traditional, and the worship style is "reverent rather than exuberant."[43] The marketing by these churches focuses on the programs they provide for different age and demographic groups, and the congregation is likely to be of one predominant race—often African-American or Anglo-American. None of the churches I visited fall into this stream.

The "Charismatic/Pastor-Focused" megachurch represents the second stream. Thumma and Travis explain that most churches in this category have a founding or "rapid growth" date from the 1960s to 1980s, reside in older suburban areas of a city, and serve a congregation that is diverse in many respects (race, age, income, religious background, etc.). Although these churches are usually nondenominational, they likely function within a Pentecostal or charismatic tradition. As Jane Lampman explains, "praise songs and the expressiveness of Pentecostal worship, including the lifting up of hands, has spread through Evangelical churches and nondenominational megachurches";[44] this is particularly true of second stream megachurches. However, Thumma and Travis clarify that their use of the term *charismatic* is not meant to suggest "that this type of church is exclusively the province of the Pentecostal/charismatic theological traditions," but instead "that the churches rely greatly on personal 'charisma,' the presence and authority of the senior pastor, for definition and identity."[45]

This is certainly the case at Lakewood Church, which is led by the nationally renowned pastor Joel Osteen. Osteen's father, John, founded Lakewood in 1959. Together, John and his wife Dodie led the congregation and hosted a popular weekly television ministry. Joel, a college dropout with no formal theological training, was running John's media department and had become a successful television producer when his father unexpectedly died in 1999. Joel immediately took over as senior pastor and has since built a ministry empire.[46] As is true of most second stream churches, Lakewood's vision and marketing revolve around Joel's sermons (which are televised and seen by millions of viewers each week), as well as his preaching tours, books, DVDs, and other ministry activities.[47] Thumma and Travis also note that a growing trend in Pastor-focused megachurches "is to build the focus of the ministry not only around the senior pastor but also around their spouse."[48] This is true at Lakewood, first with Dodie and now with Joel's wife Victoria, who is copastor of the church. Victoria actively participates in the church services, leading prayers and delivering short homilies, and often appears alongside Joel in the images used on Lakewood's marketing materials, bulletins, and website. She is also the author of *Love Your Life:*

Living Happy, Healthy and Whole (published by Simon and Schuster) and maintains a blog. Her prominent presence on Lakewood's website is second only to Joel's.[49]

Thumma and Travis note that although the high-profile ministries of the senior pastor are usually what receive the most attention for these churches, if you look more closely you will find "many other ministries at work in the life of the church."[50] Yet, it is this intensive focus on the senior pastor—from people both inside and outside the church—that distinguishes this second stream from the third "Seeker" stream. Although the pastors of some Seeker churches have generated a great deal of publicity, such as Rick Warren or Bill Hybels, founding and senior pastor of Willow Creek Community Church, these leaders usually garner press because of their church's unique mission and worship style, rather than due to their own personal charisma.[51] However, together, the pastors of second and third stream megachurches are those who "tend to get both the most press coverage and criticism" because, as Thumma and Travis explain,

> These [institutions] were the leaders and fast-growth churches of the past few decades, and their leaders have become the spokespersons for much of the religious innovation in the contemporary American religious experience. They are the ones who originally discarded much of the traditional language, symbols, and trappings associated with church architecture and worship from the 1950s.[52]

While second stream megachurches accomplish these goals largely through the personality of a single individual leader, Seeker churches focus their attention on developing new ways "to connect and reach persons outside the faith. The identity they embrace and language they use to describe their church is that this is 'not your typical church.'"[53]

Seeker churches are usually located in suburbs or exurbs and are more likely to be "nondenominational or to be affiliated with an evangelical denomination (although they downplay that connection)."[54] They almost always have a larger percentage of younger attendees and may be quite racially diverse "depending on their target audiences."[55] The worship services at these churches are usually informal and joyful, and many exhibit the same kind of congregational expressiveness that I mentioned with respect to second stream churches.

Unlike Pastor-focused megachurches, Seeker churches usually have a broad leadership base with different individuals running ministries that suit the institution's vision. As I will claim with respect to Willow Creek, arguably these are the most visibly "branded" megachurches. This is likely because, as Thumma and Travis note, "Seeker churches are the churches most strongly influenced by current corporate business practices and values. They have mission and purpose statements and organize much of their staffing according to their functional roles as described in these statements."[56] Many of these churches specifically use corporate strategies to develop those mission statements and to determine what tactics they should employ in order to achieve the goals related to them.

In this respect, Willow Creek epitomizes the Seeker model. As Frances FitzGerald wrote in 2007, "Of all megachurches, Willow Creek, the subject of a Harvard Business School study, must be the most professionally run."[57] From the start, Hybels, who founded Willow Creek in 1975, has considered the "market" he is trying to serve and made decisions about worship style, space, and outreach programs accordingly. As an article in the *Stanford Business Alumni Magazine* explains:

> Prior to founding Willow, Hybels did his own market research in which he asked thousands of people living in the Chicago suburbs why they didn't go to church. They told him they found conventional churches "boring," too focused on money, and irrelevant to their lives. Willow catered to them by offering a church stripped of traditional trappings. There are no stained glass windows or pews in its auditorium, for instance, and worship services aren't structured with liturgies or rituals.[58]

Hybels and other members of the church's leadership have not only maintained this approach over the years, but they have also grown more sophisticated with respect to how they assess the religious marketplace.

For example, Willow Creek's executive pastor, Greg Hawkins, is a graduate of Stanford's Business School and previously worked for McKinsey and Company, a management consulting firm. When Willow Creek opened its new sanctuary in 2003, Hawkins decided to initiate a strategic planning process that involved hiring "a consumer-research expert to measure spiritual growth at Willow Creek and six other churches."[59] The results, which indicated that "one out of four churchgoers—and the most committed of them—felt stalled in their growth or dissatisfaction," prompted Hybels and Hawkins to reassess Willow Creek's "coaching strategies"; at one point, Hybels even suggested that they should create "'customized personal spiritual-growth plans' for everyone in the church."[60] Moreover, the research from this ongoing study—known as Reveal—is now a significant development tool used by other churches. As an article about Hawkins explains, "because so many churches look to Willow for leadership, Reveal is reshaping evangelical Christianity to use mass customization. The Willow Creek Association—the church's huge consulting arm—is urging its 12,000 member churches to use the Reveal tools."[61] The Willow Creek Association has packaged Reveal into various formats, and these are available for purchase through the association's website.[62]

As the Seeker label indicates, leaders of these megachurches are eager to find tools like Reveal that can help them attract new members, especially those who are curious about religion and "seeking" God, but who do not already actively attend a church. In this respect, Seeker churches and "New Wave/Re-Envisioned" churches, the fourth stream, share some characteristics. Like some Seeker churches, fourth stream churches are often multisite and multileader churches, although with less focus on the main campus or senior pastor, as is often the case with Seeker churches. Most New Wave/Re-Envisioned churches were founded after 1990, have grown rapidly in a short time, and are led by pastors under the age of thirty-five. Like second and third stream churches, many of these venues use cutting-edge technology, but to an even greater and more innovative degree; as Thumma and Travis explain, New Wave churches "are significantly more high tech than the other streams, employing sophisticated Web and Internet components throughout the life of the church."[63] However, these churches often reject the "nontraditional language and mindset" of the Seeker approach, instead embracing "overtly traditional, and even ancient, Christian symbols, language, and teaching." Because these churches "desire to embrace the established church tradition on their own terms in new ways, rather than reject and eliminate the old practices," many of them "employ 'ancient-future' techniques to make the worshippers aware of historic Christian creeds and practices, while using highly advanced technology to do so."[64] These megachurches typically have a large percentage of attendees under the age of thirty-five and, because they are in a rapid growth phase, "tend to have physically cramped quarters and much simpler buildings for conducting their ministries."[65] None of the churches I visited fall into this final category.

The United States has a particularly high rate of church attendance. According to a 2010 Gallup poll, 43.1 percent of Americans report weekly or almost weekly attendance at religious services, a number that "is up slightly from 42.8% in 2009 and 42.1% in 2008."[66] A Pew Forum survey indicates that the Jehovah's Witness, Mormon, Evangelical, and Historically Black Church traditions lead the way in service attendance; 58 percent of Evangelicals and 59 percent of Historically Black Church members (many of whose churches likely fall under the evangelical umbrella) report attending church once or more than once a week.[67] Moreover, as I noted above, statistics reveal that a considerable percentage of people worshipping in churches are doing so in megachurches, many of which define themselves through worship style and content, rather than through a specific denominational affiliation. Churchgoing in the United States therefore also reflects the emphasis on choice in American culture generally, something I have touched upon repeatedly throughout these chapters and that also relates to the issue of entrepreneurialism. As Hamilton explains,

> The United States, with the most denominationally divided Christianity of the Western world, also has the highest levels of Christian faith in the Western world. This empirical reality has led some people recently to wonder if the organizational splintering of the American church has not, in fact, been a strength as well as a weakness. The advantage of multiple expressions of Christianity—whether they are based in doctrine or based in worship—is that there is an expression for everyone. Anyone can find a home.[68]

As Hamilton and others have asserted, megachurches are, perhaps, the best illustration of this reality and, consequently, of the tactics that religious leaders employ to create a unique, valuable, and relevant expression that will serve a particular audience of religious consumers.

Hybrid Brands

Churches like Willow Creek and Lakewood fall squarely into a single stream, but that is not always the case. Immanuel Bible Church and McLean Bible Church, both located in northern Virginia, demonstrate how a megachurch can develop a unique brand by employing strategies and features from more than one stream.[69] For example, I would define Immanuel as an "Old Line/Program-Based" church that uses certain Seeker tactics. Immanuel was originally founded in 1964 as a Baptist church but broke off and became nondenominational in 1984. The church has a variety of programs for different demographic groups, and it maintains an elder-centered leadership structure, rather than a pastor-centered structure.[70] However, the worship service is less traditional and features a live band, contemporary Praise Songs, and video projections. Immanuel holds three English-language services on Sundays at 8:00 a.m., 9:30 a.m., and 11:00 a.m., in addition to a Spanish-language service at 12:30 a.m. and another young adult service that meets in the church gym at the same time as the 11:00 a.m. service. The church also has a "cell church"; in 2003, thirty-two members of Immanuel started Gateway Bible Church in Gainesville, Virginia, located about thirty miles west. Gateway's website notes, "From the start, Gateway was commissioned by her 'Mother Church' to be an 'outreach-focused' church."[71] Currently, Gateway's 300-person congregation meets at Gainesville Middle School for its single Sunday service.

Like a Seeker church, Immanuel uses tactics aimed at lowering barriers for first-time visitors: reserved parking at the front of the lot; a sanctuary that looks and feels like a movie theater, with a large projection screen front-center and dimmed lighting; upbeat music playing throughout the lobby and sanctuary before the service. However, this church's pastor delivered the most traditional, Bible-based sermon I heard at any megachurch. According to Thumma and Travis, the 2000 Megachurch survey indicated that only 57 percent of megachurch sermons "always" or "often" include detailed explanations of scripture, while that number was over 70 percent in the 2000 Faith Communities Today survey that includes data from forty-one denominations and faith groups.[72] On the Sunday I visited Immanuel, Bob Hartman, Pastor of Adult Education, delivered a forty-minute sermon in which he unpacked Acts 3:1–4:31 verse by verse through the theme "Confidence Builders."[73] Although other megachurch preachers I heard referenced biblical scripture, Hartman delivered the most exegetical sermon by far.

When Hartman began preaching, everyone around me in the congregation opened their Bibles to the relevant passage. Bibles were also available in the pews, but everyone I saw appeared to be using their own. Hartman also projected the Bible verses on the screen as part of a PowerPoint-type presentation that accompanied his sermon. In addition to the Bible verses, the slides displayed quotations, themes, or images related to his message. Typical of megachurch sermons, Hartman related the scriptural message to everyday life; however, he used excerpts from and references to popular press articles, films, or television only minimally. Instead, as I noted above, he delivered a very Christo-centric and evangelically oriented sermon in which he urged worshippers to have the boldness, confidence, and courage to profess their faith in Jesus Christ. His Bible-based call to spread the gospel of Jesus Christ was also the most challenging sermon I heard with respect to what it demanded of believers. Consequently, although Immanuel's worship style—the auditorium space, music, and technology—would likely appeal to a Seeker audience, I would argue that the sermon, which constituted the largest part of the service, was less "user-friendly." Moreover, even within the auditorium space there are vestiges of a traditional church experience, such as the pews. All of this suggests that despite Immanuel's Seeker service trappings, the church retains a more traditional, "Old Line" core.

McLean Bible Church represents another interesting but very different example of hybridity. Like Willow Creek, McLean follows a "full-service" Seeker model. As Jonathan Mahler writes, contemporary Seeker churches are quite different from "the megachurch of the 1980's, where baby boomers turned up once a week to passively take in a 45-minute service. . . . In many places, they operate almost like surrogate governments, offering residents day care, athletic facilities, counseling, even schools."[74] Radiant Church in Surprise, Arizona exemplifies this model:

> The foyer includes five 50-inch plasma-screen televisions, a bookstore and a café with a Starbucks-trained staff making espresso drinks. (For those who are in a rush, there's a drive-through latte stand outside the main building.) Krispy Kreme doughnuts are served at every service. (Radiant's annual Krispy Kreme budget is $16,000.) For kids there are Xboxes (10 for fifth and sixth graders alone). "That's what they're into," [Pastor Lee] McFarland says. "You can either fight it or say they're a tool for God." The dress code is lax: most worshippers wear jeans, sweats or shorts, depending on the season. . . . Even the baptism pool is seductive: Radiant keeps the water at 101 degrees. "We've had people say, 'No, leave me under,'" McFarland says. "It's like taking a dip in a spa."[75]

Seeker churches like Radiant also differentiate themselves from traditional churches by adopting a more secular-sounding vocabulary, with words like *auditorium* and *campus*.[76] As Mahler notes, "everything about Radiant has been designed to lure people away from other potential weekend destinations."[77] The same could be said of McLean Bible Church.

McLean exhibits many characteristics associated with the Seeker stream.

Even more so than at Immanuel, McLean's church space is designed so that it will feel familiar to new visitors, thereby encouraging return visits that will, hopefully, lead to a serious commitment to the church's many programs and ministries. As Thumma and Travis explain, McLean's main Tysons campus

> has a total of fifty-one acres that include a former National Wildlife Federation property, a 280,000-square-foot multistory building, and a parking deck that holds twenty-five hundred cars. The main auditorium seats twenty-four hundred people, and the campus has a spacious lobby, gym, youth center, community room, adult classrooms, and creative arts space.[78]

When you arrive it feels like you are parking in the garage of the nearby shopping mall. The church also houses a café that is open before services, as well as a small food court. However, despite these everyday amenities, the church's mission is firmly Christo-centric and unapologetically evangelical:

> The vision of McLean Bible Church is to make an impact on secular Washington with the message of Jesus Christ. Metropolitan Washington is a unique place. With over six million people, it is one of the most powerful, educated, and diverse cities in the world. It is also one of the most secularized. We believe that God has assigned a unique role to McLean Bible Church, which is "to impact secular Washington with the message of Jesus Christ." This vision has guided every element of our ministry for over a decade. In Romans 1:16, Paul says, "I am not ashamed of the message of Jesus Christ, for it is the power of God for salvation to everyone who believes." At McLean Bible Church, we believe that a relationship with Jesus Christ is the only thing that can transform a person's life. Our church is unashamedly dedicated to presenting this message, so that every person in Washington is given a chance to understand it and believe.[79]

Worship leaders reinforce this mission verbally during the services, and versions of it appear on much of the literature found throughout the church's lobby and hallways.

Lon Solomon has served as Senior Pastor of McLean Bible Church since 1980, and he usually preaches the Sunday sermon at the main Tysons campus, the location I visited. This campus offers services at 6:30 p.m. on Saturday evenings and at 9:00 a.m., 10:45 a.m., and 12:30 p.m. on Sundays in its main auditorium. In addition, it hosts The Edge, a contemporary "intense band-driven worship" service that also meets at 10:45 a.m., but in Tysons' smaller Smith Center auditorium space.[80] The Edge service includes a live feed to Solomon's sermon in the main auditorium. Solomon is supported by a large Executive Leadership Team composed of the many pastors and ministry leaders who work at McLean's different campuses. Besides Tysons, McLean also has three other "fully functioning" physical campuses around the Washington, DC area, and each holds various weekly services.

In addition to its four physical campuses, McLean hosts two internet campuses and also sponsors Frontline ministry, which offers services at four different venues around the region on Sunday or Monday evenings. McLean's website describes Frontline as "a young-adult expression of McLean Bible Church" that "is dedicated to providing a relevant and authentic worship experience coupled with sound biblical teaching for young adults."[81] The Frontline services, which have a more energetic aesthetic than the Sunday morning services, are led by a younger teaching pastor, currently John McGowan. The services typically draw a younger and more racially diverse crowd.[82] As Thumma and Travis note, "Frontline is distinct from McLean, obviously in terms of age, but also both in worship style and options for social and service involvement. This is a megachurch within a megachurch, but one for a different generation."[83] McLean not only uses tactics common among New Wave churches—internet campuses, a multisite structure, worship services oriented toward a younger demographic, smaller venues—but, in essence, it started a New Wave megachurch within a Seeker church. These strategies help McLean appeal to many different religious consumers simultaneously.

Moreover, McLean's mission and programming are very evangelically minded, which suggests an effort to teach the type of "high-commitment Christianity" that Thumma and Travis associate most strongly with the New Wave stream, but that I also identified at Immanuel.[84] For example, McLean has an Apologetics Ministry Team:

> Apologetics is the area of Christian theology which focuses on the defense of the Christian faith, particularly through the rational justification of Christian belief and doctrines. . . . McLean Bible Church's Apologetic team places a high value on the Church's mission to share the message of Christ so that we can impact secular Washington, DC. For this reason, the MBC Apolo-

> getic Ministry is committed not only to teaching apologetics but also to equipping believers to go out and engage in the conversation for Truth. . . . As one method to meeting this goal, MBC Apologetic Ministry has been offering (and will continue to offer) apologetic information through presentations every third Sunday of the month. In addition to this, the Church will continue to invite guest speakers who are experts in specific areas of defending the Christian faith to speak at the church.[85]

Such programming is a reminder that, although megachurches certainly welcome new believers and encourage all levels of participation, most of them promote a Christo-centric, evangelical theology. That theology is not simply delivered through sermons, literature in the lobby, and small group ministries, but is also reinforced in very powerful ways through the physical space and worship style that attendees encounter when they visit.

The synaesthetic appeal of megachurches is therefore central to both their popularity and their devotional efficacy. According to Loveland and Wheeler, the first generation of contemporary megachurches began to appear in the 1970s, and as they grew these churches tried to reach adults born between the 1960s and 1980s who were raised in a culture that emphasized "visual communication, music, sensations, and feelings," more so than in previous generations.[86] Consequently, many of these churches began integrating elements like Praise Dancing, live music, or full-scale performances into their services. As Thumma and Travis remind readers, over the last two centuries there have been a number of large churches in the United States with the characteristics we now associate with the contemporary megachurch, namely, "charismatic pastors, countless ministries, theatre-style auditoriums, and performance-oriented services"; notable examples include Henry Ward Beecher's Plymouth Church, the Moody Memorial Church, and Aimee Semple McPherson's Angelus Temple.[87] Yet, the rapid growth of these large churches since the 1970s indicates that "there is something distinctive about the last few decades that has promoted the development of so many megachurches. There is a distinct resonance between what megachurches offer and what many contemporary Americans desire."[88] In other words, currently the megachurch brand appeals to a very large segment of the American population. I contend that evangelical dramaturgy may help us to identify and analyze some of the reasons for this tremendous popularity.

The Dramatic Structure of Worship

Attending the standard Sunday morning worship service is the typical way that many new adult visitors first engage with and learn about a megachurch.[89] Accordingly, this service plays a significant role in establishing the church's unique brand. Despite differences in size, geography, and community, all of the megachurch services I attended followed the same basic structure.[90] Significant differences between the services certainly existed, but with respect to overall structure, these differences were largely in degree, not in kind. Moreover, there is evidence that some church leaders may consider this basic structure essential to the overarching megachurch brand.

For instance, the Willow Creek Association's website has a "Service Builder by Willow" page where church leaders can purchase products like music, sermon transcripts, dramatic scripts, and videos/DVDs; some can be downloaded immediately, while products like DVDs and CDs are shipped.[91] The website is organized in a variety of ways. Users can view the titles of services by name and date, or they can search by type (Seeker services, Believer services, GenNeXt services, and Student services).[92] For example, a Seeker service dated 27 July 2009 is entitled "Washed Clean." Clicking on the title brings users to a page that outlines the service's theme and content. The description at the top reads:

> Naaman, a valiant soldier and highly regarded, had difficulty humbling himself before God and obeying the instructions of the prophet Elisha whom he had contacted about curing his leprosy—especially the relatively simple act of washing himself seven times in the Jordan River. When Naaman finally obeyed, he was healed. All too often those who have put their trust in God sometimes face the same reservation of humbling themselves in whatever simple act God has asked us to do. With an emphasis on Willow's upcoming Baptism service, this message reinforces the need to get past the pride and arrogance and to take a step of spiritual courage into the simple, but significant, act of Baptism.[93]

A chart below this description lists the elements included in the service when it originally occurred at Willow Creek.

The "Washed Clean" service begins with a "Walk-In" feature called "Plexiglas Writing Video." It then continues with two songs: "The Time Has

Come" and "Everyday," both written by Joel Houston. Neither of these has a purchase link, but the copyright information is provided.[94] The next element is a "Spiritual Direction" message, originally delivered by Willow's Worship Director, Matt Lundgren. This is followed by another song—"I Give Up" written by Matt and Kristi Lundgren—which is available for preview and immediate purchase. The next section is a reflection entitled, "What is it that you are holding on to today that you need to give up to God?" The service then proceeds with another song, a scriptural reading (2 Kings 5:1–15), the Offering and Announcements, until it finally reaches Hybels's sermon, entitled "Washed Clean." The sermon is available for purchase as a PDF ($10.00), MP3 ($7.00), or audio CD ($10.50). The service then ends with the song "How Great Is Our God," and the outline specifies that "People come forward to receive baptism towels during song."[95]

Other Seeker services on the website include many of the same basic elements and follow a very similar structure. There may be more songs or readings from scripture, and some services include short dramas or the Holy Communion ritual.[96] The Believer services appear to follow a similar model, although they often include a few more traditional songs and may have more songs placed after the sermon.[97] Yet, these differences are relatively small, and therefore Willow Creek's Service Builder website suggests that there is a standard generic format that many megachurch services follow, something apparent during my own visits. Furthermore, once again a synaesthetic devotional experience has been repackaged into a commodity so that it can reach and impact more people than those who are able to travel to the original venue, in this case, Willow Creek Community Church.

There were also certain consistencies with respect to space among the churches I visited. All of the sanctuaries were designed like amphitheaters with tiered seating. Willow Creek and Lakewood had the largest sanctuaries of those I saw. Willow Creek has three levels of seating, an orchestra and two balcony levels, which you reach by escalators or elevators in the lobby. Lakewood is more exceptional given that the church holds its services in the Compaq Center, a sports arena that previously hosted professional teams like the Houston Rockets; as part of its renovations to the space, the church expanded the seating capacity to 16,000.[98] As is true of most indoor sporting arenas, Lakewood's facility is a complicated maze of multiple entrances, escalators, and hallways. Given their expansive dimensions, both Lakewood and Willow Creek have clear signage posted throughout their spaces to help visitors locate specific seating areas, restrooms, and other amenities.

All of the churches utilized greeters in the lobby and at the sanctuary doors. Again, Lakewood provided the most extreme example. The same three people accompanied me on my two trips to Lakewood. On our first visit, after walking through the front doors we were immediately greeted by a friendly staff member who asked if we were new to Lakewood. When we said yes, he handed us off to another staff member, who escorted us efficiently through the facility, pointing out different amenities and features along the way (although too quickly for any of us to remember them later), before leading us down to the floor seating area (or orchestra level) and directing us to seats in the fourth row. The experience felt like a Secret Service escort; and, in fact, our guide was wearing a Secret Service–style earpiece.[99]

All of the other churches had greeters and clearly marked visitor information areas in the lobby. As in many churches, the greeters standing at the sanctuary doors distribute bulletins to worshippers as they enter. Willow Creek was the only exception; there was no bulletin offered at the service I attended. The bulletins used at many traditional churches typically contain an outline of the service, with references to page numbers in a service book and to hymns in a hymnal. The bulletins I received at megachurches functioned quite differently. They offered little to no information about the service format or content, but instead advertised small group opportunities, ministry options, upcoming events, and other activities related to the church culture. Immanuel's bulletin was a small exception; its cover listed the name of the preaching pastor, the title of the sermon, and the scriptural passage upon which it was based, as well as a few of the songs that we would hear during the service. Here, again, we might see evidence of Immanuel's "Old Line" character. McLean's bulletin included the pastor's name and title of the sermon on the cover, but nothing further about the service content. Despite these differences, in every case, rather than a guide to the worship event, the megachurch bulletin primarily functioned as an announcement for the institution's activities, showing attendees the variety of ways they could participate in and benefit from the life of the church beyond the service itself. The bulletin is therefore instrumental to church branding.

This kind of bulletin is also a dramaturgical strategy that supports the larger synaesthetic principles and goals of megachurch worship. The megachurch services I attended were designed so that worshippers could easily commit to, and physically participate in, the event. At traditional churches, oftentimes congregants cling to the bulletin as a guide, referring to it frequently throughout the service to cross-reference content in service books and to see what is coming next; this is especially the case with new visitors. During the actual worship event the bulletin becomes a central focus and, for some attendees, perhaps even a distraction; it offers direction but can also create anxiety for visitors who glimpse unfamiliar events on the horizon or are perplexed by the "insider" terminology (Nicene Creed; Eucharistic Feast; Doxology). Moreover, even when worshippers put down their bulletins, they often remain encumbered by service books or hymnals. Worshippers at megachurches are not tied to such objects, and therefore even first-time visitors can remain physically open to the service itself and completely focused on what is happening in the present moment. Although frequent worshippers may know the overall structure of the service and mentally anticipate what is coming next, their bodies can still remain intent upon the actuality of the live event and their physical presence at/in it.

Other elements also encourage this physical openness and presentness. Every service I attended began with a lengthy musical set—the live band began playing upbeat Praise Music, and worship leaders holding microphones invited the congregation to stand and sing along. These worship leaders guided the congregation through various songs, altogether lasting between twenty and forty minutes. In most cases, the preaching pastor did not appear until after this opening musical segment. The exception was at Lakewood, where Osteen and his wife Victoria came onstage after the first song. The Osteens welcomed the congregation, told attendees that this service would spiritually transform them, and then led everyone in a prayer. This lengthy introduction lasted at least five minutes and the band continued to play softly throughout it. Joel Osteen concluded this segment by explaining that Lakewood's services always begin by "praising God" through music. After assuring visitors that he would return later in the service, he and Victoria took their seats in the front row of the auditorium. This segment served as a kind of teaser for the main event—Osteen's sermon—and clearly reflects Lakewood's "Pastor-Focused" culture. At the other churches, this opening musical section featured members of the pastoral or ministry staff, such as the Creative Arts Ministry team at McLean or the Willow Creek Worship Team.

Rather than using hymnals to follow along with the songs, worshippers in these churches can simply look at the large projection screens in the sanctuary that display the lyrics. Megachurches are known for using these large projection screens; after the vast space itself, these screens are perhaps the key visual signifier of the megachurch brand. These screens, along with the sophisticated sound systems installed in the space, allow worship leaders to control the space's sensory aesthetic strategically. For example, Loveland and Wheeler explain how the acoustical system at Southeast Christian Church in Louisville can make the room "sound smaller" during a sermon and then "'enlarge' it to sound like a cathedral when the Worship Choir sings."[100] Consequently, church leaders do not employ this technology merely to project, amplify, and enlarge, but to craft precise sensual encounters for worshippers.

All of the megachurches I visited made liberal use of their projection screens. Immanuel contains only one screen directly over the chancel area or "stage," while McLean's sanctuary has three screens—one on either side of the stage and another in the middle. The week I visited Willow Creek, the auditorium had two screens that flanked the stage, but in videos of other services at the church there is sometimes a screen in the center, directly over the stage.[101] Lakewood has two screens on either side of the stage and a center screen over the band; this middle screen is sometimes visible, but at other times it is covered by a curtain. A fourth giant jumbotron hangs in the center of the auditorium, as is typical in most indoor sports arenas (Figure 14).

Projecting the lyrics of hymns and Praise Songs onto these screens is not merely a pragmatic choice but one that reflects church culture and that may even promote doctrine. Hamilton argues that using the "overhead projector means that no one needs to be able to read music, everyone is singing in unison, and everyone is—literally—reading off the same page."[102] In this sense, the dramaturgical choice reflects a "democratic" sensibility[103] that may also reinforce the theological tenet that believers have immediate, unmediated, and personal access to God. In addition, as Bo Emerson notes, projections eliminate the need for hymnals, thus allowing worshippers to sing with their heads up.[104] In this posture, the worshipper's body is more open to the rhythms of the event, which enables it to more readily engage with the service's sensual dimensions and, consequently, to experience "flow." The term *flow,* originally used in psychological theories to discuss play, as well as religious and artistic experiences, has been adopted by performance theorists to describe a particular spectatorial mode. As Marvin Carlson explains, during "flow," "reflexivity is swallowed up in a merging of action and awareness, a focus upon the pleasure of the present moment, and a loss of a sense of ego or of movement toward some goal."[105] By allowing attendees to participate physically in the worship event and, thus, to experience the service with un-

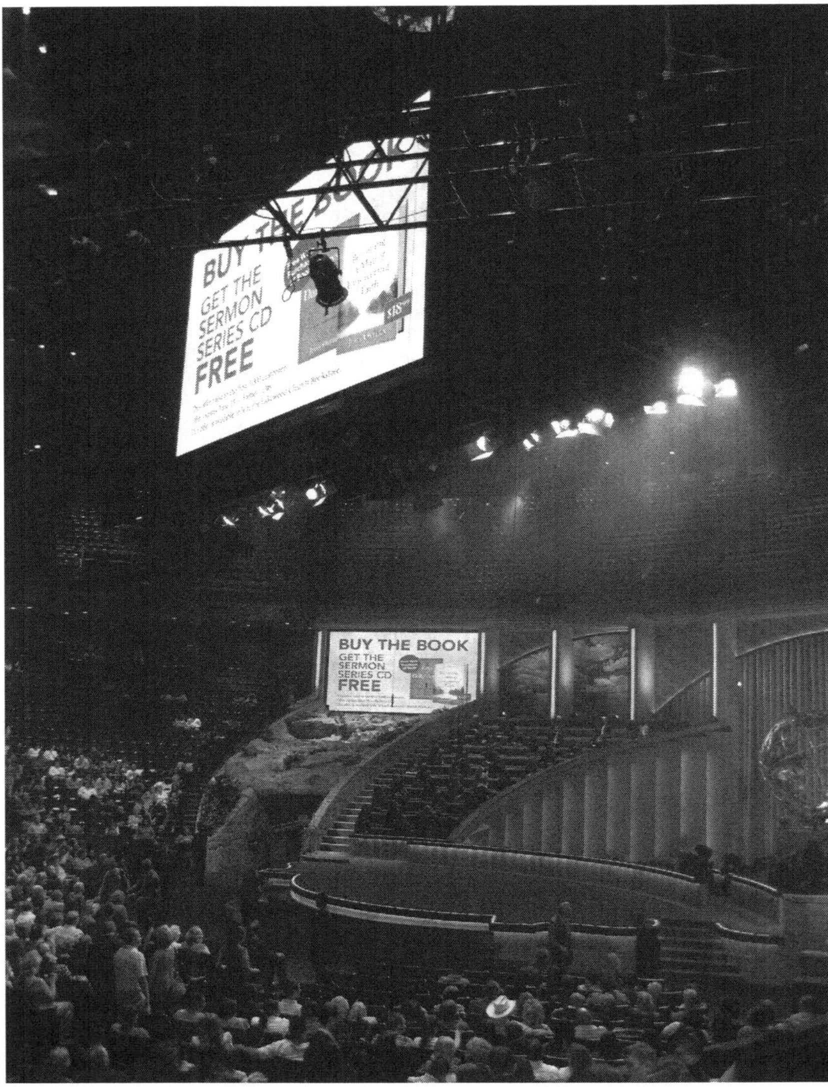

Figure 14. Lakewood Church in Houston, Texas. June 2011. Photo by author.

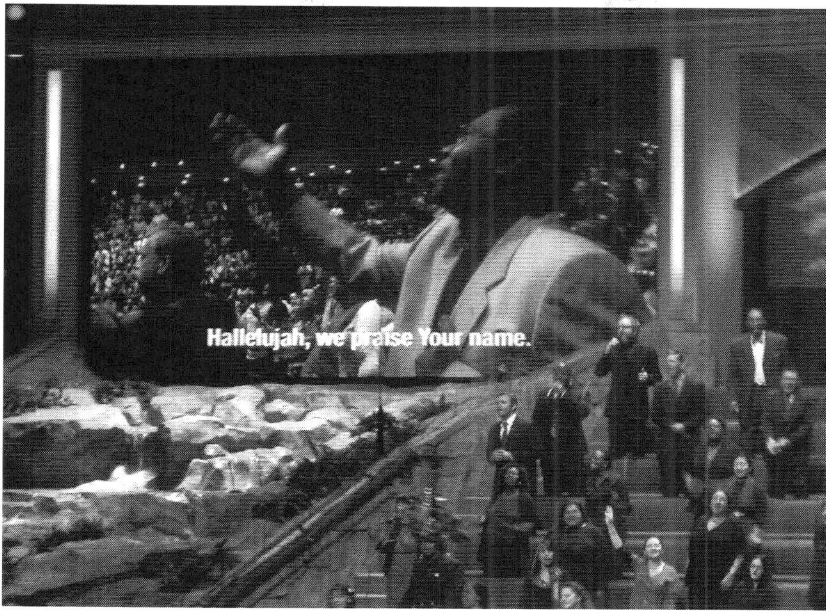

Figure 15. Projection screen with Praise Song lyrics. Lakewood Church in Houston, Texas. June 2011. Photo by author.

encumbered bodies, a dramaturgical choice like projected song lyrics may cultivate devotional "flow." Such an experience may help to foster the kind of deeply engaged awareness and attentiveness that supports evangelical dramaturgy's goals.

This appeared to be the case at the services I attended. In every instance, worshippers stood during the opening musical segment, singing along, clapping, and swaying, although with varying degrees of exuberance and passion. Moreover, as shown in Figure 15, the lyrics on the screens usually appeared as subtitles under live images, typically close-ups of worship leaders, choir members, or fellow congregants. Therefore, even when the songs become repetitive, rendering the lyrics on the screens unnecessary, the projected images continue to draw attention. For example, during my first visit to Lakewood when I was seated in the fourth row, I had an excellent view of the stage and, in essence, no need to watch the screens throughout much of the service. Yet, as my companions and I discussed after the service, all four of us found our eyes repeatedly drawn to the screens, rather than to the live people standing before us. This was also the case in the other churches I visited; even when seated very near the front of the auditorium, I repeatedly found myself watching the screens. Rather than utilizing the spectatorial agency that live performance affords, I remained fixated on the circumscribed narrative presented on the screens.

One reason for this may be the compelling nature of the close-up itself. Also, at Willow Creek and Lakewood particularly, the projections were high-definition images with vibrant, saturated colors; I definitely found myself even more compelled to watch the screens at these two venues. However, this urge to look at the mediated image also recalls my arguments about spectators who choose to watch "Behold the Lamb" through their video cameras and how this act may give the performance more immediacy. In the case of the megachurch service, the screens may take the worship energy projected from the stage—which must extend out to a large, broadly configured congregation in a vast space—and concentrate it, making it more personal and intimate, and thereby heightening the energetic potential of the worship encounter.

The megachurch service thus provides an interesting example for exploring the relationship between hypermediacy and immediacy. As Andy Lavender writes, "Hypermediacy is not simply a question of the multiplicity of sources, images or image systems. It is expressed through simultaneity: two or more sources, images, systems and effects in play at the same time in a shared ecosystem."[106] Although it may seem that a "persistent tension" exists between hypermediacy and immediacy, in fact oftentimes they "work simultaneously,"[107] and Lavender specifically examines performances that display "the mutual play of what might appear to be two distinct media—the screen and the stage—and the ways in which their very co-relation produces effects of immediacy that are deeply involving—more, deeply pleasurable—for spectators."[108] I propose that megachurch services function in this same way.

Using screens in the large, usually unadorned, megachurch sanctuary is therefore a dramaturgical strategy. By shaping the rhythmic relationship between user and medium, these screens cultivate an energetic relationship that serves evangelical dramaturgy's goals. The large television-like screen is also a popular media form that megachurch leaders use to generate a familiar, resonant physical experience that may encourage attendees to open themselves up to the service's theological message. Furthermore, the richly colored, live close-up images presented on those screens add felt texture to the large-scale worship event. That texture particularly clings to the worship leaders, thereby enhancing the energetic dynamic between religious "specialist" and individual worshipper. Lavender could be writing about a megachurch pastor, especially one like Osteen, when he explains,

> the hypermediacy of the staging gives both structure and texture to the event. . . . We are presented with the meeting between the live actor and mediated actor-as-other, seeing the same person as two people and the human figure as both actual and expanded. The actuality of the actor's presence is heightened by the co-presence of his or her mediatized selves, which are themselves staged as part of the theatrical mix.[109]

This same effect occurs during many megachurch services, where the use of screens produces a rhythmic energetic encounter that confirms what worshippers already think, assume, or hope about these worship leaders. In this way, the dramaturgical device helps produce an intimate script that verifies and bolsters the worshipper's religious belief. In addition, because any form of intermediality is an aisthetic act, in this case hypermediacy also directs worshippers into an intimate and immediate way of seeing these religious leaders and, in doing so, traces this particular perceptual mode into their embodied schemata, where it will continue to encourage them to think of these leaders as "larger than life." Consequently, the screens are an important part of the megachurch brand because they help to convey the idea that these particular religious specialists provide something that the average person cannot offer.

Yet equally important dramaturgically are the vivid close-ups of congregants that appear on the screens, delivered by cameramen who either roam through the auditorium or are strategically situated around it. As Anna Gibbs writes,

> the face . . . is an extremely rapid medium of communication, and the televisual close up, especially when it is extreme, enhances its communicative possibilities by drawing our attention to details (trembling lips, rapid eye movements, twitching muscles, and so on).[110]

Seeing close-up shots of congregants, whose expressive faces often display extreme emotional reactions, will trigger spectators' mirror neuron responses and result in simulation. Moreover, music continues to play throughout these worship services thereby underscoring the images. Therefore, as I proposed in my discussion of "Behold the Lamb," the combination of hearing intensely emotive music and seeing images of ardent facial expressions may prompt a kind of emotionally thick motor resonance within worshippers. These images therefore constitute valuable affective forces that skillful camera work, coupled with calculated musical direction, can use to produce a powerful intimate script for congregant-spectators.

Technological enhancements—projected lyrics, close-up images of worshippers and worship leaders, and amplified music—also furnish the worship encounter with degrees of sensuality that call attention to the spectator's own physical presence at and in the live worship event. This physical engagement may counter any inclination toward passivity that the space's large size could otherwise inculcate. I therefore understand these enhancements as dramaturgical devices that reshape the worship service into a synaesthetically rich attraction.

In her article on the "Acquire the Fire" ministry events, Jennifer Williams uses the work of Sergei Eisenstein to consider the relationship between affect and spectacular evangelical performances. For Eisenstein, a theatrical attraction is

> any aggressive aspect of the theatre; that is, any element of the theatre that subjects the spectator to a sensual or psychological impact, experimentally regulated and mathematically calculated to produce in him certain emotional shocks which, when placed in their proper sequence within the totality of the production, become the only means that enable the spectator to perceive the ideological side of what is being demonstrated.[111]

He also specifies that here "sensual and psychological . . . are to be understood in the sense of immediate reality."[112] Consequently, not only is there a material, physical element to Eisenstein's understanding of attraction and its impact on spectators, but that element is sometimes so commanding that it overwhelms the production's other sources of ideology.

Williams argues that certain evangelical events, like "Acquire the Fire," use this "affect of shock" to "rupture" a passive or complacent mode of perception, thereby making spectators physically "vulnerable to ideology."[113] I see a similar effect operating during some megachurch services; lighting and sound production, projected images, and other rhythmic elements impinge upon the worshipper's body so forcibly that they may become that individual's primary basis for meaning creation. However, in this case, I interpret the "shock" of the megachurch attraction as deeply resonant and therefore as producing the pleasurable effects of immediacy that Lavender describes.[114] That pleasure urges visitors to engage a megachurch service in bodies that are open not only to the megachurch experience but also to its ideological message.

Praise Music: Blending and Belonging

As I have already implied, the lengthy musical section that opened all of the services I attended accomplished a number of goals, among them, activating the bodies of congregants by situating them within a sensually overwhelming and highly energized encounter in which they could immediately participate. Worshippers at these services were not passive observers; instead, they were active and essential parts of the mise en scène. In some sense the opening musical set at these services staged the congregation.[115]

There is certainly a range of musical professionalism on display across these churches. Arguably, Lakewood's services exhibit the highest degree of professionalism, practice, and technological enhancement. Lakewood's band is accompanied by a large choir which stands on either side of the stage on graded platforms located near the two screens flanking the stage. A smaller worship team stands downstage and leads the congregation in song. The downstage singers and the choir members wear color-coordinated, camera-ready outfits (Figure 16).

Both Lakewood services I attended began with a "Walk In" element: the auditorium lights dimmed and a video played on the screens. This video is a little over ninety seconds long and its theme is that "God makes beautiful things out of us." It has a dramatic rock beat that builds palpable anticipation within the crowd. Videos of recent services are available on Lakewood's website and, currently, all of them begin with this same video.[116] As the video concludes, an elevator lift upstage center raises the band, which up until that point has been concealed under the stage; smoke effects make this moment quite spectacular. These opening minutes are staged like the beginning of a rock concert, and the congregants respond in kind by jumping to their feet, roaring loudly, and clapping enthusiastically; one service even began with a member of the worship team shouting, "1, 2 . . . 1, 2, 3, 4."[117] Music, videos, lighting, and other effects not only cue worshippers to stand

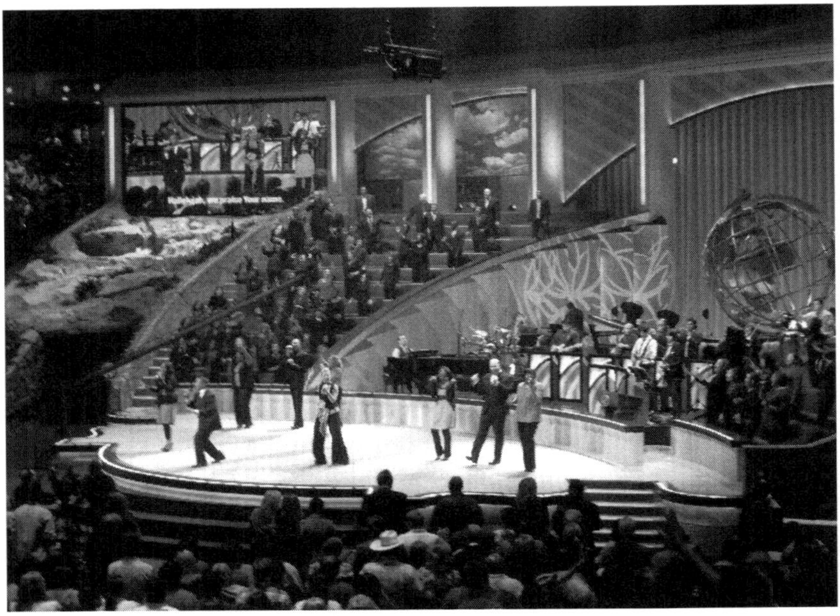

Figure 16. Worship Team at Lakewood Church in Houston, Texas. June 2011. Photo by author.

and become an active part of this momentous, synaesthetically rich event, but together they also set the tone for the service that follows.

Although without as much initial fanfare, all of the other services began quite similarly. Some churches used a "Walk In" element, but in all cases worship officially started when the band and a small team of singers, sometimes accompanied by a choir, began leading the congregation in lively Praise Songs. All of the congregants rose to their feet and began clapping, swaying, and singing along to the music. The Praise Songs used in these services are catchy and easy-to-follow. The melody lines are simple, and the lyrics contain a great deal of repetition, which makes them easy to learn and remember even without the help of the projections. (Similar to after a good Broadway musical, I even found myself humming one of the songs from Lakewood's service days later.) Therefore, in addition to getting the congregation on its feet, moving and clapping along to the beat, Praise Music also keeps worshippers vocally involved in the event.

Like Lakewood, Willow Creek also places a great deal of focus on its band and music, but it utilizes a very different musical aesthetic. At the service I attended, the band consisted of five musicians accompanied by five singers. There was no choir. Although the majority of the congregation appeared to be Caucasian with a significant, but much smaller, Asian constituency, all of the musicians in the band were African American, as were two of the five singers. The rest of the singers appeared to be Caucasian. Of all the praise bands I saw, this one sounded and looked the most contemporary. The singers were all relatively young (perhaps late twenties and thirties), with trendy outfits and fashionable hairstyles; this was certainly the "hippest" praise band I saw. It also played the most complex music. The week I attended, the band played "country worship music," in honor of an outdoor baptism event scheduled for later that afternoon on the church grounds. (The previous week the music had a Blues theme, and the Sunday after my visit the David Crowder band, a well-known Christian group, was coming to lead the service.) In addition, although the band members played the conventional instruments that most Praise bands typically use, such as guitars, drums, and a keyboard, they also incorporated the banjo and fiddle into their program. Furthermore, the songs at Willow Creek were catchy, but the first few had more complicated melodies and more syncopation than those I heard elsewhere. The songs later in the service were a bit simpler melodically, but still more musically complex than those I encountered at other churches. Therefore, like other megachurches, Willow Creek uses music to engage the congregation. However, based upon my visit, as well as the hymns listed on the Service Builder website, it appears that the service music is not standardized to any one particular sound but is based, at least in part, on experimenting with musical genres.

Praise Music is therefore another distinguishing characteristic of megachurches and, as Willow Creek illustrates most clearly, for some churches it is essential to establishing a unique brand. I am not a musicologist and therefore will not attempt a technical analysis of the Praise Music genre. There is a growing body of work by scholars who have specifically analyzed contemporary Praise Music of the kind heard in many U.S. megachurches.[118] Consequently, my goal here will be to suggest how Praise Music supports the goals of evangelical dramaturgy by, among other things, fostering an energetic dynamic within the worship space.

As Robert Woods and Brian Walrath explain, Contemporary Christian Music (CCM) developed out of the Jesus movement of the late 1960s and early 1970s and was further fueled by American cultural trends as well as the charismatic revival that began in the 1970s.[119] Contemporary Worship Music (CWM) is a category of CCM and, as Bert Polman explains, the largest subcategory within CWM is Praise and Worship Music, which is typically led by Praise Teams.[120]

Those who initially tried to transform worship music in response to the CCM movement were hymn reformers who began their work from within the existing musical tradition. However, as Hamilton notes, these reformers "have never been able to develop any real affection for the musical tastes of the ordinary people" and, thus, "still largely remain comfortably inside the taste culture of formal church music."[121] Alternatively, the roots of Praise Music are located in those "revolutionaries" who "began with baby-boom music forms and baby-boom values, and sought to adapt these to the Christian faith."[122] As I have already established, such a strategy is part of a long-standing evangelical tradition of adaptation and, thus, a significant part of the U.S. evangelical brand generally.[123] In this case, Praise Music starts with the sounds, instruments, style, and energy of popular, "secular" musical forms, and then adjusts these to present a Christian message. Hamilton writes that "the starting place for the revolutionaries was secular rock 'n' roll, so they eagerly used guitars and drums, simple accessible lyrics, and the conventions of popular music—simple harmonies, steady rhythm, frequent repetition."[124] This is the tradition currently on display in many megachurches, although the musicians have moved beyond just rock and now borrow from a variety of popular contemporary musical genres.

A crucial feature of these songs is their simplicity, both rhythmically and lyrically. Polman explains that "congregations tend to be uncomfortable with *excessive* syncopation, and certainly object to excessive *and* inconsistent syncopation" (original emphasis).[125] Therefore, popular Praise Songs usually have a simple, catchy melody that quickly entrains the listener's body.[126] The verses are often quite short and the refrains are typically repeated over and over again in performance. Yet because praise bands usually lead these songs, they can afford to have the musical complexity of an artist-oriented pop song in their verses and still remain singable to congregations; Polman writes, "some songs may have syncopated stanzas easily sung by praise teams, with refrains more suitable to the congregation because less complicated rhythmically."[127] This relationship between verse and refrain, combined with the use of instruments like electric guitars and drums, as well as the actual space itself, together result in a secular "concert" aesthetic.

Praise Music is accessible through a variety of venues, including iTunes, making it easy to learn the genre's particular sounds and tropes. Maranatha! Music was founded in 1973 to help give churches around the country access to this new form of worship music, and it remains one of the top three companies that write, record, and market new music to other churches.[128] There are many albums on iTunes by the Maranatha! Praise Band, and these contain some of the most popular Praise Songs. Two songs that I heard during my megachurch visits, "Lord I Lift Your Name on High" and "Blessed Be Your Name," are available on the album *Platinum Praise: Top 20 Praise Songs*, released by Maranatha! in October 2010.[129]

This version of "Lord I Lift Your Name on High" illustrates the typical rock sound that many of these songs borrow. It has a very even melodic line and does not require much vocal range. "Blessed Be Your Name" also appropriates a modern rock motif, but it is quite different and sounds more like a standard country rock song; as one friend remarked, "it could be a duet between Blake Shelton and Carrie Underwood."[130] Therefore, as I suggested with respect to Southern accents in the "Great Passion Play," to some listeners this song might resonate as All-American. These songs are reminiscent of Willow Creek's praise music on the week I visited. The slightly more complicated stanzas are coupled with simpler reprises that are easy for a congregation to remember and then repeat over and over again with increasing confidence. I also heard "Blessed Be Your Name" during the second Lakewood service I attended, but the rendition there was very different from the one included on *Platinum Praise*. As opposed to this slower, country rock recording, Lakewood's band performed the song in a more exuberant and loud rock mode, with heavy use of electric guitar and drums.

Lakewood has also released a number of Praise Music albums. Lakewood's worship leader is Israel Houghton, a Grammy-award winning artist and producer, and this is likely a major factor in the professionalism of the church's worship music performances. All of the musical segments feel like concert productions, with seamless transitions between songs and sharp lighting cues. The performers also have remarkable stage presence, and some are solo recording artists. Two albums, *Cover the Earth: Lakewood Live* (2004) and *Better Than Life: Lakewood Live* (2008), capture the interactive musical dynamic of a Lakewood service; you can hear the congregation in the background clapping and singing along to the songs. The title track on *Cover the Earth* illustrates the typical explosive sound of the opening number at a Lakewood service. "You Are Good" on *Better Than Life* exemplifies the exuberant kind of Praise Song often used during Lakewood's opening musical sections; it has simple lyrics and a repetitive driving rhythm that easily entrains the body. Here, too, listeners can hear the congregation in the background responding enthusiastically.

There are moments in Lakewood's service when the tone becomes more contemplative, as I will discuss later in this chapter. During these sections the energy never deflates or relaxes completely; instead, the musical choices, oftentimes balladlike songs, help to sustain an energetic dynamic within the large space. Two of the songs on Lakewood's *Free to Worship* album (2007) typify this mode: "Free to Worship" and "Mighty to Save." For example, although "Free to Worship" is a slow song, it is not moody or subdued. On the contrary, the song has a melodic vitality that helps to direct the listener's attention and emotional production during the more reflective and introspective moments of the service, such as extended prayer segments or the offering collection. At these times, most congregants are not as physically active and are perhaps even sitting down. A song like "Free to Worship" is therefore used to ensure that attendees are still rhythmically engaged in the worship event. Even more illustrative is *Free to Worship*'s version of "Mighty to Save," during which listeners can hear Osteen delivering a lengthy prayer. This recording effectively demonstrates how the music at Lakewood continues throughout most of the service, underscoring various worship elements and guiding congregants from one segment to the next. Although the use of music at other megachurches is not quite as relentless, it is still employed behind service elements and thus serves as an affective force designed to drive attendees toward certain emotional states.

The sound of these songs, their liberal use of repetition, and the amplification provided by the sound system combine to produce a very physical worship experience. Spectators feel the service working its way into their bodies and are physically entrained by its infectious rhythms; the images of singers and other congregants on the screens further promote entrainment. Therefore, although congregants are surrounded by many people in a vast space, the music enables each person to experience the service on a very personal, intimate, visceral level. Greg Scheer argues that today's Praise Music has "a personal and ecstatic spiritual orientation."

> Today, Evangelical churches don't just sing one praise song; they sing extended medleys of songs that allow enough time for people to enter into a different emotional state. Some people might describe this as "getting into

it" and others as "breaking through" but beneath these phrases we can see the personal and ecstatic goals of the experience.[131]

The Praise Music sound creates an intimate experience that gives the worshipper direct, felt access to God, thereby reinforcing certain epistemological assumptions of evangelicalism.[132] Consequently, Praise Music is a particularly effective device within evangelical dramaturgy, one deployed liberally at megachurches, as well as at venues like Holy Land Experience.

Moreover, Praise Song lyrics reinforce this personalization and the theological concepts it affirms. Scholars writing about Praise Music, as well as critics of the genre, often discuss the "me-centered" lyrics in these songs.[133] For example, these are the lyrics of "Lord I Lift Your Name on High," which is one of the most popular Praise Songs used in congregations today:[134]

Verse: Lord I lift your name on high,
Lord I love to sing your praises,
I'm so glad you're in my life,
I'm so glad you came to save us.
Chorus: You came from heaven to earth, to show the way,
From the earth to the cross, my debt to pay,
From the cross to the grave, from the grave to the sky,
Lord I lift your name on high.
Repeat Verse
Repeat Chorus
You came from heaven to earth, to show the way,
From the earth to the cross, my debt to pay,
From the cross to the grave, from the grave to the sky,
Lord I lift your name on high,
Lord I lift your name on high,
Lord I lift your name on high,
Lord I lift your name on high,
Lord I lift your name on high,
Lord I lift your name on high.[135]

This song illustrates Hamilton's claim that "one cannot sing praise songs without noticing how first person pronouns tend to eclipse every other subject."[136] This characteristic is quite useful for evangelical dramaturgy not only because it focuses the singer/listener on having an immediate, unmediated relationship with God, but also because it validates the notion of personal choice; the singer is choosing to believe, choosing to put his or her faith in God, choosing to lift His name on high. The lyrics do not suggest that someone has prompted the singer to make these choices or that this faith has been passed down through the community, as would the pronouns "we" or "us"; instead, this is a faith defined by individual choice. As I have previously noted, choosing one's faith is not only an evangelical notion but also an American value.

Both Hamilton and Scheer contend that worship style, but more specifically the musical style of a worship service, has become the critical factor in determining a person's church affiliation. Hamilton argues,

> People choose their churches by the type of worship and music they feature. Increasingly, churches sponsor multiple services for multiple musical tastes. Increasingly, we are grouping ourselves with the musically like-minded. This is the root, stem, and branch of the new sectarianism that is flowering in American church life.[137]

Similarly, Scheer writes, "Denominational loyalty has all but eroded, replaced by music style."[138] Here, again, the music in a megachurch provides the attendee with an opportunity to choose one's faith, to break from tradition if necessary and select a religious experience (and, consequently, a doctrine) that is more appealing.

Praise Music is therefore a valuable dramaturgical strategy in many respects. A Praise Music set appropriates the sound and sensual experiences of popular culture to generate a resonant worship encounter that will also promote the church's unique brand. The prevalence of Praise Music throughout the service also makes it easy to commodify and redistribute that experience. For instance, many of Lakewood's CDs, especially the live recordings, replicate the service structure; as I have noted, some even include Osteen's prayers. In addition, the lyrics and the rhythmic experience of Praise Music not only reinforce specific theological concepts and epistemological assumptions, but these features also affirm certain American principles. However, as I have discussed in previous chapters, music is also a particularly powerful tool when it comes to creating affective intimate scripts. The rhythms not only engage and entrain attendees into the worship event, but they add memorable, emotionally rich texture to the embodied schema that the service traces into worshippers' bodies.

Praise Music is critical to making the megachurch experience into an attraction. Beginning the service as a fundamentally theatrical attraction may encourage visitors to open their bodies more willingly and completely to the worship event, one whose rituals and expectations for participation are, in fact, very similar to those of a live concert. At every church I visited, the congregation quickly became a swaying, clapping, and singing unit; many times, I couldn't prevent myself from swaying, clapping, and even singing along. In most cases, congregations also applauded after each song. Unlike the experience at many traditional church services, new visitors to a megachurch are not baffled by when to kneel or stand or bow their heads. On the contrary, the service initially presents itself in the familiar guise of a concert, and most visitors' bodies will reflexively understand how to respond.[139]

I would therefore argue that the opening musical set encourages attendees to live in a concert/worship blend. The amplified music, lighting effects, and projected images all craft a concert aesthetic that supports this blend. Moreover, intense expressions on spectators' faces and arms opened wide are also characteristic of many concert experiences. Initially, the concert frame may be more dominant, and, perhaps, that is the intention. Similar to the Creation Museum's Bible/science blend, here, too, visual and material elements produce a blend that reshapes Christian worship into a culturally acceptable, even desirable, experience for visitors. This may be particularly important for attracting new members, especially Seekers who are not certain what they want theologically, but know that they are yearning for something. As Brian Massumi suggests, yearning is neither an emotion nor an affect, but instead "free-floating affectivity; uncontained ability to affect and be affected. Yearning is a tendency without end; it is unexpiring, unself-consuming."[140] I propose that this "tendency without end" is what Seekers feel, and that the concert/worship blend aims to transform that yearning into a more concrete feeling—the desire to belong—before immediately satisfying that desire. Music is vital to this process because the familiar rhythmic and melodic tropes of popular music help to give that yearning a clearly defined emotional shape, and then the lyrics supply the remedy: God.[141]

The notion of belonging is often built into the mission and goals of megachurches. For example, a postcard in McLean's lobby reads:

> We know that McLean Bible Church is a big place. We also know that in the fast-paced, busy environment in Washington, DC, it can be hard to find an authentic community, where you feel like you belong. That's why we have small groups. Come join us and find a safe place to be yourself, be accepted, and be inspired to grow in your relationship with Jesus Christ. Learn more about small groups and sign-up to join. Visit the Connect Room after any McLean service or visit us online at www.mcleanbible.org/belong." (original emphases)[142]

Willow Creek promotes a similar idea in its welcome literature:

> Welcome to Willow Creek Community Church, where our doors are open to people from all backgrounds, regardless of where they are on their spiritual journey. If you're new to Willow Creek or are considering joining us for a service, we hope you'll find a place where you are warmly welcomed and feel at home.[143]

Willow Creek's literature also emphasizes the many ways it can help people "connect" with one another.[144] But even at less overtly Seeker-oriented churches, the opening musical segment promotes a concert/worship blend that aims to instantiate in all attendees a powerful felt sense of belonging, a feeling that they will then attribute to the presence of God. The sensual experience within the worship/concert blend is meaningful precisely because it seems to fulfill certain (perhaps inarticulable) felt needs; the music's affective force moves worshippers from yearning to secure belonging. Returning to Stephen di Benedetto, we can therefore recognize Praise Music as one of the more prevalent tactics used within the megachurch's performance sensorium to invite attendants to live, feel, and belong to a larger community.[145]

Mission and Message

The musical opening at these services is sometimes interspersed with other elements that begin to introduce church doctrine more explicitly, if still sometimes subtly, into the worship event. Both Immanuel and Willow Creek projected scriptural passages onto the screens during the opening musical set. Immanuel only interrupted the praise singing once—a lengthy passage from Revelation appeared on the screen and, as more muted music played in the background, the worship leader asked the congregation to read the scripture aloud with him. Then the congregation returned to singing. At Willow Creek the singers paused a few times between songs to gaze at scriptural passages displayed on the screens, and the musicians underscored these moments with a quieter musical line. However, the Praise Song leaders did not actually read the passages aloud, nor did any of the congregants seated around me.

At McLean, the musical set was divided into two distinct parts. After a few opening songs, Pastor Solomon entered and the band exited offstage. This was quite different from when the Osteens appeared onstage after the opening song in Lakewood's service. In that case, the band continued playing, thus integrating Joel and Victoria into the musical set. At McLean, Solomon appeared a bit later into the service and had the stage entirely to himself. He briefly welcomed congregants and asked us to greet one another, before inviting us to sit. The auditorium suddenly darkened, and a short, professionally made video with a Father's Day theme played on the center screen. After the video, the lights were brought up slightly. Congregants remained seated as they listened to a member of the worship team sing a solo number. As the song ended, the lights went back up to full, and the entire worship team returned to the stage to lead the congregation through three more lively Praise Songs. Between these songs, scriptural passages appeared on the side screens. As at Willow Creek, the singers merely paused to look at them for a few moments, giving the congregation time to read them silently, before moving on to the next song; nobody onstage or in the congregation appeared to read them aloud.

At every megachurch service I attended, the preaching pastor came onstage at the end of the Praise Song set, marking the transition to the second section of the service. The content of this middle section varied somewhat between the churches. At McLean and Immanuel, the pastor made announcements, led the congregation in a prayer, and then signaled for the offering to begin. Willow Creek followed a similar structure, although the offering began immediately after the opening Praise Songs and was collected during the lengthy announcements section. In all of these cases, "stagehands" brought out lecterns for the pastors to use. At Willow Creek a "prison cell" set piece was also arranged upstage as the pastor spoke.

The week I visited Willow Creek, Pastor Darren Whitehead preached because Hybels had suffered a concussion the previous day. After delivering announcements about church-sponsored mission trips and other upcoming events, including a Global Leadership Summit hosted by Willow Creek that featured high-profile speakers such as Howard Schultz (chairman, CEO, and president of Starbucks Corporation) and Michelle Rhee (founder and CEO of StudentsFirst; former chancellor of D.C. Public Schools), Whitehead offered a brief preview of his sermon. He explained that because that afternoon's baptism event would focus on new beginnings, his sermon would concentrate on "What God has delivered us from." As Whitehead spoke, two instrumentalists and two singers reentered. Whitehead then left the stage, the lights dimmed, and a video played on the two screens as the worship team provided live musical accompaniment. The video showed images of people who had overcome difficulties—divorce, abuse, addiction—through faith in Jesus. As at McLean and Lakewood, the video was exceptionally well produced.

Although each church I visited handles this middle section of the service somewhat differently, I contend that it serves a similar purpose in every case. As Thumma and Travis note,

> It is important to remember that the use of creeds and recited prayers (such as the Lord's Prayer) are as teaching and modeling tools to instruct congregants in the facts of the faith. Today's megachurches use other methods, such as video slides, the Apostles' Creed set to music and sung, and multiple displays of the church's vision and values expressed in contemporary slogans, to teach those principles in ways that connect better with today's attendees.[146]

The middle section of the service is where such teaching begins to take place. Elements like announcements, prayers, and short videos give attendees a clearer idea of the church's specific theological message and ministry goals. Thanks to the resonant musical opening, worshippers may greet this middle section in bodies that are open and amenable to those church-specific messages. Church leaders only begin to present these creeds and doctrine explicitly once they suspect that people are more inclined to accepting them.

Lakewood's middle section—between the opening praise singing and the sermon—was the longest and most distinctive. It also demonstrates how Lakewood capitalizes on the sense of belonging that the lengthy, energetic musical set and consequent concert/worship blend aim to instill. The first time I visited Lakewood the preaching pastor was Marcos Witt, currently the associate pastor for the Hispanic congregation of Lakewood in Houston. This service was structured a bit differently from the one I attended in June 2011, at which Osteen preached. I have watched a number of Osteen-led services on Lakewood's website, and all of these conform to the structure of the service I attended in June 2011. Therefore, I will focus my analysis on the structure and content of that service since I believe it is more typical of Lakewood's worship brand.

After about forty minutes of praise singing, Osteen returned to the stage to lead the congregation in a lengthy prayer of between four and five minutes. He then invited anyone in pain or need to approach one of the many prayer partners who were standing throughout the Compaq Center. These prayer partners, among them Joel and Victoria, are ready to pray with congregants one-on-one. This prayer partner section was underscored by one of the slower, balladlike Praise Songs I described earlier. Although Osteen invites people to sit during this prayer section, many worshippers in the congregation remain standing—hands up, swaying, and singing along. Many have their eyes closed and wear intense, emotional expressions. At both services I attended, many people in the congregation wept during this section. These included people who went up for prayers, as well as many who did not.

This prayer partner segment is the affective center of the Lakewood service. Although the dramatic structure of the service positions Osteen's sermon as the climax, the opening Praise Songs are intended to prime congregants so that they will actively participate in this prayer ritual and, as one of the singers proclaimed, "receive what God has for you today."[147] The music and projected images of people praying are affective forces that encourage other worshippers toward certain emotional responses. Close-up shots give viewers intimate access to the zealous and concentrated expressions of those people praying one-on-one, as well as of people standing in the audience—many with tears streaming down their cheeks. This live "film" is underscored by music that may, as I have argued, trigger an emotionally dense motor resonance in both the congregants in the auditorium, as well as those spectators watching on their televisions.[148]

As this section draws to a close, the music grows louder and stronger, almost insistent, as the congregation and Praise Team repeat the song's refrain over and over again. The images on the screen begin to change; close-ups of smiling faces and images of congregants hugging their prayer partners now appear. The music and projections guide the congregants through a vicarious journey from pain and struggle to relief and peace achieved through prayer. Once everyone is back in their seats, the musicians shift to a more energetic, lively Praise Song. The lights, which were dimmed during the prayers, are bright once again. And, suddenly, the tone and energy in the auditorium turn celebratory.

Although this prayer partner section only occurred at Lakewood, it offers a vivid illustration of how the megachurch service actively tries to serve the worshipper's needs. The dramatic structure, projected close-ups, music, and lighting choices all help to construct an affective intimate script that aims to solve people's problems; personal troubles and concerns are purged through prayer. Moreover, as I discussed with respect to the moment of touch in "Last Supper Communion" at Holy Land Experience, here, too, touch makes the ideological message—in this case, that with God's love we can overcome all problems—concrete, giving it form and substance. Although the touch at "Last Supper Communion" occurs in a more intimate environment with every spectator experiencing it directly, it is also quite brief. At Lakewood, the touch of the prayer partner lasts much longer and is captured on the screens for the rest of the congregants to see (and simulate). In this way, the screen images allow the touch and its ideological content to echo through the congregation.[149]

A highly participatory service element like this prayer call may be especially necessary at Lakewood. In order for the service to remain relevant and useful it must produce an intimate script that serves both the large, disparate audience physically present in the enormous Compaq Center, as well as the millions of television viewers. The prayer call accomplishes this by making the transformative spiritual work of Lakewood visible and, in some respect, tangible. The televised close-up images of intense praying followed by joyful relief allow all spectators to take—and simulate—that same journey, and thus to experience a sense of resolution. Consequently, the combination of images and music may help foster a powerful energetic worship dynamic not only for every person in the live congregation, including those standing in the very back rows of the audience, but even for those viewers watching at home.

The Sermon

As I have stated, the dramatic climax of the megachurch service is the sermon. The sermon continues to introduce attendees to the church's specific theological message, although in a more overt fashion. Understandably, the preacher's style and choice of content differed significantly between the churches I visited, making the sermon another significant branding device.

A great deal of criticism leveled at megachurches concerns the sermons, much of it directed at preachers at venues like Willow Creek, Saddleback, and Lakewood. As FitzGerald notes, some evangelical pastors and scholars have charged the leaders of such venues "with preaching a Christianity lite" message that is "'me-centered,' rather than God-centered." They argue that this theology "proposes that people are basically good, rather than essentially sinful and in need of salvation. . . . That the Scriptures help to heal pain and bring self-fulfillment, but in doing so they are suggesting that the Bible is true just because it works."[150] Many accuse Osteen, in particular, of offering a message that is "light on theology."[151]

This is another myth that Thumma and Travis aim to debunk in their book, claiming that "most megachurches present a serious, high-commitment Christian message" and have "belief statements on paper and in practice that are clearly in line with orthodox Christian doctrine."[152] They maintain that the confusion arises due to the presentation of the message:

> Megachurches express the message in forms that use conversational language, images, and examples that resonate with contemporary culture. A pastor may quote from a historical figure or serious theological literature, but it is much more likely attendees will hear quotes from current news, movies, and television to appeal to a broad contemporary audience.[153]

This was certainly the case at some of the churches I visited.

I have already noted that Immanuel Bible Church in Virginia offered the most challenging, evangelistic, and Bible-based "teaching" sermon of those I heard. Pastor Hartman used a PowerPoint presentation to lead congregants through that week's Bible passage and the seven "Confidence Builders" around which he had organized the sermon. During the sermon, the screens never veered from this presentation to show live images of Hartman's face or of the congregation; instead, the slides kept congregants focused on the biblical exegesis. Everyone around me was following along in their personal Bibles, and the bulletin contained a sheet of paper that said "The Book of Acts" at the top, with spaces to write the date, pastor, and title underneath. The rest of the page was lined for note taking. The sermon at Immanuel felt like a Bible study, and the congregation treated it as such.

Surveys indicate that megachurch sermons have "higher rates of the use of personal stories or firsthand experiences, illustrations from contemporary media such as magazines, newspapers, television, or movies, and practical advice for daily living" than do sermons at other mainline Protestant or Catholic churches.[154] Hartman did use personal anecdotes and contemporary examples to relate the scripture to people's lives today, but he also used more references to evangelical tenets and beliefs than did any of the other preachers I heard. For example, he discussed Israel's rejection of Christ and how the Rapture will only occur once Jews in Israel begin to accept Jesus as their Savior; Hartman referred to the Rapture as an event we should actively anticipate. In addition, when outlining his third Confidence Builder—"Expect victory over death"—Hartman explained that death is often used as the ultimate threat to evangelists. However, since death does not actually kill true believers, evangelists really have nothing to fear when spreading the gospel message. He also promoted courses, particularly one offered by Answers in Genesis, that would help prepare believers "to be like Peter and spread the Gospel."

This sermon was not Seeker-oriented; Hartman did not deliver a particularly "user-friendly" message. Instead, he challenged listeners to step out of their comfort zones and step up for Christ. The use of recognizable everyday media forms (large screens and PowerPoint slides), as well as the theaterlike space, may have helped to reinforce the confidence of current believers, especially those who had strayed from the church or were looking for ways to reaffirm their faith. The large congregation, as well as the affective journey leading up to the sermon, reminded those believers that they were not alone in their faith and may have prompted them to feel like they belonged to something everlasting and true. Overall, this service deployed the strategies of evangelical dramaturgy in order to help visitors re-experience membership within an ideal Christian community—perhaps a community they nostalgically recall from childhood or one they have imagined in moments of yearning. In this respect, Immanuel's service functioned very much like the dinner theater show before the "Great Passion Play." The music and other rhythmic devices initially built affective momentum and cultivated a sense of community. Then, through the final element—the sermon—the service event purposefully directed attendees toward a specific and somewhat rigid ideological message and purpose.

Pastor Solomon's sermon at McLean functioned quite differently. He also used a PowerPoint presentation with slides that displayed key points and various quotations from contemporary media. However, at McLean these slides only appeared on the center screen; the two side screens continued to display live images of Solomon or, at times, of congregants in the auditorium. In this case, close-up images of facial expressions and gestures accompanied the textual content, a combination that significantly influenced the affective intimate script.

In honor of Father's Day, Solomon's sermon was entitled "The Price of Being an Effective Father," and it was, in great part, a "wake-up call" for fathers in the audience. Solomon's overarching message was that many men struggle to be effective fathers because, as he said, "being an effective, godly father is one of the most demanding jobs in all the universe." Similar to Hartman, Solomon logically organized his sermon around four main points, in this case, four "key prices" that come with being an effective father. According to Solomon, an effective father "Cultivates a deep personal relationship with Christ," "Invests large amounts of time in his children," "Confronts his children," and "Speaks words of blessing and affirmation over his children." Solomon initially noted that these four prices simply confirm what the Bible already tells us to be true and, as he outlined each price in great detail, he casually mentioned scriptural passages relevant to each. For instance, he quickly read three verses—Ephesians 6:4, Hebrews 12:9, and 1 Thessalonians 2:11—when discussing the third price of confrontation.[155] However, in order to substantiate his points, Solomon primarily relied upon quotations or statistics from recent studies and articles published in sources like *Time, Washingtonian,* and *USA Today.* His conclusion used humor to remind fathers of the sacrifices that come with effective fathering, such as taking the kids to a local theme park rather than enjoying a relaxing vacation in Tahiti. The slide that accompanied this point juxtaposed a picture of a beautiful beach against a picture of a son and his father on a children's amusement park ride, with the father uncomfortably squeezed into the tiny seat.

The style and content of Solomon's sermon would likely appeal to a Seeker crowd. By employing popular media references, contemporary examples, and personal anecdotes of his own experiences as a father, Solomon helped the audience recognize how the message related to them personally. He presented that message rationally, in a tone that was firm but fair. Moreover, Solomon frequently reminded the fathers in the audience that he was simply outlining a current social problem, the significance of which he substantiated with evidence (statistics and scientific data found in well-known media outlets, rather than in obscure scholarly journals), and then offering them a clear, logical solution. That solution has "prices," but Solomon also explained the rewards that one received if he accepted those prices. However, at no point did he suggest that anyone *must* accept this solution. On the contrary, he repeatedly remarked that each father had to make a personal choice about how to respond to this information.

This strategy is quite similar to what I identified in the Creation Museum. Solomon's sermon offered evidence, but the listener was given the choice of what to believe and how to respond. The connection to a Christ-centered message was present, but it did not dominate the theme. However, as in the Creation Museum with its different Starting Points, Solomon situated belief in the gospel message of Christ as the foundational premise upon which his argument rested. The four prices he outlined are hard for any father to bear, but Solomon made it very clear when discussing the first price that fathers can *only* gain the necessary "wisdom," "tenacity," and "self-control" to do so through the "power of Christ." If you begin from that starting point, you can handle the other three prices and, ultimately, become an effective father. However, without faith in Christ, you have little hope of achieving this incredibly difficult goal.

Here, again, a megachurch service used tactics of evangelical dramaturgy (a familiar comforting space; resonant music, language, cultural references, and visual devices; close-up shots of expressive faces) to construct an intimate script designed to resolve congregants' problems. For some attendees, that problem may have originally lacked clear definition before the service—perhaps it was just the yearning for a better home life or a better relationship with their children—but the sermon gave it emotional shape. The sermon also situated the resolution as contingent upon a particular Christo-centric theological conceit. Yet, critically, Solomon described the decision to accept this framework and its solution as a matter of personal choice; when a father is ready to change, this is one way he might choose to do so. As I have argued, the perception of individual choice is an important feature of evangelical theology and, thus, of evangelical dramaturgy.

The visual style of Pastor Whitehead's sermon at Willow Creek was somewhat similar to Solomon's presentation. Whitehead delivered a Bible-based sermon in which he led the congregation through 1 John 1:5–10, 1 John 2:1–2, and 1 John 3:1 verse-by-verse.[156] Visitors who did not bring their own Bibles could borrow one from bookcases in the lobby or in the back of the auditorium. During the sermon, both screens usually displayed live images of Whitehead, oftentimes close-up shots of his face, which was unambiguously expressive. Occasionally the screens showed PowerPoint-type slides with Bible verses or relevant images and passages. However, the majority of the time the screens focused the audience's attention on Whitehead himself. Since Hybels usually delivers the Sunday message, this pastor-focused production style is not surprising.

The sermon's theme was very Christo-centric: Christ's sacrifice on the cross paid for humankind's sins. Occasionally Whitehead wove a bit of interesting history into his sermon. For example, he explained that *tetelestai*, the word Christ speaks from the cross that is usually translated as "it is finished," was actually a legal term meaning "paid in full." This reference to the original language is fundamental to the historico-grammatical approach that many literalists use when reading scripture; as Vincent Crapanzano explains, this "method of exegesis . . . focuses on the original language or languages of the text and its historical situation."[157] Throughout the sermon, Whitehead also discussed issues such as self-deception, confession, and atonement. Like Solomon and Hartman, he built a compelling, rational argument, using the Bible verses themselves as his outline. Yet, like Solomon, he also relied heavily on anecdotes, stories, and contemporary examples. Furthermore, the first two-thirds of the sermon was somewhat challenging theologically, since it focused firmly on Christ's sacrifice on the cross and the believer's need to acknowledge and confess his or her sins in order to receive the rewards of that act.

However, Whitehead shifted into a more affective mode for the last section of his sermon. He concluded with a lengthy "true" story about a girl named Jodi who stole from her parents and ran away from home to go to the big city, leaving behind a churchgoing family and community. She became involved with a man who turned out to be a drug dealer, moved in with him, and eventually became addicted to heroin. After a few months, she started selling her body to pay for this habit. When, after another few months, she became infected with a sexually transmitted disease, her boyfriend kicked her out, saying, "You disgust me." Jodi used the rest of her money to buy a bus ticket that would take her to a new place so that she could start fresh. Since the bus happened to be traveling through her hometown, she called her parents, whom she had not seen or spoken to for about a year, and left a message for them explaining that she would be passing through the next day and would love to see them briefly at the bus station. However, after she hung up the phone, she held out little hope that they would actually show up.

Arriving in her hometown the following day, Jodi assumed nobody would be there to see her, but she got off the bus anyway to stretch her legs. As Whitehead recounted, when she stepped off the bus "a roar went up." There, standing in the bus station, was the entire town and, hanging overhead, a banner that read "Welcome Home Jodi." Her parents ran to her and held her. When she tried to apologize they stopped her, explaining that there was no time to talk because they all needed to rush her home to the party that they had planned in her honor.

This story functioned as a compelling affective force. The close-ups of Whitehead, who appeared as if he might begin crying near the end of the tale, forcefully directed the emotional production of the audience. The sermon began as biblical exegesis, but it ended with an emotionally wrought story that is reminiscent of the prodigal son parable from the Gospel of Luke, while also sounding like a generic tale recognizable to anyone familiar with contemporary television or film. It therefore resonates with committed Christians and Seekers alike.

As Whitehead neared the end of this story, his voice grew louder and more urgent, even fraught, thereby reigniting in the congregation the energy that the Praise Music had initially sparked. Whitehead then immediately honed this energy into a communal physical ritual. Notions of imprisonment and freedom recurred throughout Whitehead's sermon, and, during those moments, he used the large prison set piece that stood behind him onstage as a kind of prop. He concluded the story about Jodi by linking it back to the "paid in full" theme and explained that the baptism event later that afternoon would provide people with an opportunity to break free from imprisonment; no matter what anyone had done—even if they had sunk as low as Jodi—Christ had still paid for their sins "in full," and adult baptism was the way to demonstrate a wholehearted personal acceptance of Christ's gift. Whitehead then invited everyone who had signed up for that afternoon's baptism to come onstage and walk through the open doors of the prison set piece. As these individuals passed through the prison doors, a staff member handed them a towel, which they would use that afternoon and could then keep as a memento of the experience, before directing them to stand in groups on either side of the stage, facing the congregation. The cameras remained focused on the prison and as each person walked through it the congregation applauded loudly.

During this ritual, the Worship Team led the congregation in the song "Amazing Grace (My Chains are Gone)," a popular Praise Song mash-up that is also included on Maranatha!'s *Platinum Praise* album. This song begins with the familiar lyrics and melody of "Amazing Grace": "Amazing grace / How sweet the sound / That saved a wretch like me / I once was lost, but now I'm found / Was blind, but now I see. / 'Twas grace that taught my heart to fear / And grace my fears relieved / How precious did that grace appear / The hour I first believed." Using this time-honored hymn evoked the long-standing significance of the baptism ritual and likely also resonated with those Seekers who had experienced a traditional church upbringing. After establishing that familiarity and sense of tradition, the song transitions into a more contemporary refrain whose lyrics are quite relevant to the baptism theme: "My chains are gone / I've been set free / My God, my Savior has ransomed me / And like a flood His mercy rains / Unending love, Amazing grace." Sometimes the worship team returned the congregation to the "Amazing Grace" verses, but the majority of the song was devoted to repeating this refrain. The congregants sang these lines over and over again, the intensity and volume increasing as more people approached the stage.

After everyone in the congregation who had already signed up for the afternoon baptism completed this ritual, Whitehead invited anyone else who now wanted to dedicate themselves to Christ to also walk up on stage and pass through the prison doors. (He promised that they could still sign up for the afternoon baptism as well.) Whitehead explained that the ministers and people of Willow Creek believe that baptism needs to be a personal, purposeful choice; therefore, even if someone had been baptized as an infant or child, he encouraged that person to get rebaptized now as an adult. Many people in the congregation chose to participate in this public act, a ritual very similar to an altar call.[158] The congregation's singing and applause were even louder and more enthusiastic for these people. The screens displayed close-up shots of their faces, and many of them were crying. People in the audience were also crying, and I noticed many people in the lobby still wiping away tears after the service.

A combination of dramaturgical devices—the emotional story of Jodi as prelude, the resonant music with relevant lyrics whose volume and tone intensified as more people approached the stage, the high-definition close-up shots of expressive faces—created an energetic space. Just as I claimed with respect to Lakewood's prayer partner segment, here, too, the dramatic structure and rhythmic features enabled the service to function as a powerful affective force that urged congregants toward a concrete, physical act of religious commitment, which they either performed themselves or watched on the screens (and simulated). Furthermore, despite the challenges and stipulations that the sermon initially posed, Willow Creek's service ultimately constructed an intimate script that seemed to offer a clear and relatively undemanding solution to congregants' problems.

"I will never be the same, never, never, never"

Like other evangelical genres, the megachurch service uses a variety of sensual devices to create a synaesthetic, rhythmic encounter that will offer the user a felt sense of stability and reassurance. Each megachurch alters the tone, structure, and style of the service to fit its particular consumer-visitor. The examples above demonstrate that the sermon is also adapted to reflect the church culture and to meet the needs of a certain audience. However, at a Pastor-focused church like Lakewood, the sermon plays a particularly important dramaturgical role when it comes to establishing the megachurch's unique brand.

Even more so than at Willow Creek, the sermon at Lakewood feels like a dramatic climax. The service that precedes it is highly energetic, and Lakewood's congregation, singers, and choir were, by far, the most exuberant ones I encountered. The sermon section begins about an hour into the service, but before Osteen's sermon, Victoria often delivers her own mini-sermon or homily. This occurs after the celebratory song that follows the prayer partner section. When I visited, Victoria explained that Lakewood had dedicated that week to families. She discussed how families needed to devote themselves to God by making an "agreement" with Him. She used a number of metaphors to convey her message; for example, she described how parents must use this agreement to "bind" evil things that try to interfere with their children and that when family members stray from this agreement parents should cover them "with blankets of love." After about ten minutes, she led the congregation in a lengthy prayer for families. She then asked everyone to give their tithes to the Lord, and the band played another song as staff members gathered the offering.

The palpable energetic relationship established by the praise singing and prayer partner segment was still active when Victoria took the stage, and her homily began to focus that energy toward a God-centered message of faith. However, despite the concrete metaphors she used, the message itself was rather vague. Victoria never explained what specific points there might be in this "agreement" or what dedicating oneself to God actually involved. This is the kind of "theology lite" that critics of megachurches often mention, and it was also apparent in Joel's sermon, which immediately followed the offering. Therefore, unlike the three other sermons I have analyzed, all of which followed a logical structure to convey a clear message, the sermons at Lakewood—both Victoria's and especially Joel's—use very different tactics to craft an intimate script that will offer congregants relevant felt solutions.

After greeting the crowd, both those in the auditorium and the viewers at home, Osteen typically opens with a short funny anecdote. Following this, he officially begins his sermon with a communal ritual. He asks everyone to hold up their Bibles and to speak aloud a kind of "creed" that is displayed on the screens. Together, Osteen and the congregation declare:

> This is my Bible. I am what it says I am, I have what it says I have, I can do what it says I can do. Today, I will be taught the Word of God. I boldly confess; My mind is alert, My heart is receptive, I will never be the same. I am about to receive the incorruptible, indestructible, ever-living seed of the Word of God. I will never be the same, never, never, never, I will never be the same, in Jesus' name. Amen.

This creed is also posted on Lakewood's website and, notably, was not uttered at the first service I attended when Osteen was out of town and Pastor Witt preached in his place.[159]

From my perspective, the vast majority of people around me in the auditorium participated in this vocal and physical ritual, a powerful moment of staging that directs the congregation's attention on Osteen and the message he is about to deliver. Here, again, the visitors are critical elements of the mise en scène. However, despite this introduction, Osteen's was the least Bible-centric sermon I heard. This is also true of the many sermons by Osteen that I have watched on Lakewood's website. Although he typically mentions a verse or biblical example now and again, Osteen does not focus on the scripture itself. Instead, his message is almost always about what personal dedication to that scripture can achieve in people's lives. Yet, as with Victoria's "agreement," Osteen only vaguely alludes to what exactly that dedication entails. For example, the week I attended, the sermon theme was weariness, and Osteen talked about the rewards people will receive if they push through the weariness that tests them every day. According to the sermon, people are able to push through that weariness by simply having faith that God will eventually reward them, not by commitment to any specific doctrine or biblical command.

Listening to Osteen's sermon therefore feels very similar to attending a self-help lecture. In the sermon I attended, Osteen offered us new ways to think about and mentally overcome our daily problems, such as the loss of a job, divorce, or illness. He instructed us to tell our problems "you're no match for me" because we can take hold of God's strength. He reminded us that, in order to overcome weariness, we must talk to ourselves in "the right way." Rather than thinking about the long journey, which seems impossible, we should instead only focus on today and the present moment. He assured us that God had "set an end to [our] problems" and would give us the strength to make it through today. And then he promised us that tomorrow God would give us the strength to overcome that day's adversities. Although Osteen typically mentions God quite a bit in his sermons, he usually does not spend time explaining specific theological tenets or beliefs, nor does he regularly discuss the requirements of belief in God. Note that the "This is my Bible" creed includes the phrase "I boldly confess," but it remains unclear what exactly people are confessing.[160] As Osteen himself admits, in order to reach the "everyday person" he avoids being "too religious."[161]

Given the lack of biblical exegesis in the sermon itself, the "This is my Bible" creed is somewhat extraordinary. First, holding up the physical Bible serves to connect the sermon to scripture; as Crapanzano explains, biblical literalism has a tendency to give tremendous symbolic value to the material Bible as book. Thus, like biblical literalism itself, this gestural element of the creed ritual "exploits . . . the materiality of the sign."[162] In addition, like Praise Songs, the "This is my Bible" creed is replete with first-person singular pronouns and begins as an affirmation of the speaker's individualized faith—this is *my* Bible, not *our* or *the* Bible—and of personal self-worth. The speaker then sets an intention to remain open and receptive to Osteen's message and, importantly, to accept it as the "incorruptible, indestructible, ever-living seed of the Word of God." The "This is my Bible" creed collapses Osteen's and God's words into a single entity. Furthermore, the speaker sets a firm and unwavering goal—or, perhaps, it is even a promise—to be permanently transformed by this message. Lifting their Bibles and speaking these words is a performative act that helps congregants greet Osteen's sermon in a particularly amenable physical and mental state, prepared to hear Osteen's message *as* the Word of God.

This elision is enhanced by the fact that Osteen seemingly works only from notes, and his sermons have far less structure than any of the others I have analyzed; both he and Victoria can actually become quite repetitive. Osteen's sermons therefore have a spontaneous quality that, to some congregants, may suggest that the Holy Spirit is speaking directly through him.[163] Consequently, rather than logic, Osteen's sermons function primarily through his physical, bodily presentness and, specifically, his face. Even without sound, I suspect viewers would understand the emotional journey that his sermons describe simply by watching his big, broad, and unambiguous facial expressions. His sermons impact people by the reality of his actual presence and by the simulation that his particular speaking style affords.

These elements contribute to Osteen's imposing charisma and stage presence, which the cameras that remain focused on his face for most of the sermon pull into high relief. These forces play a vital role in fostering an energetic dynamic between Osteen (the religious specialist) and each individual attendee/viewer. Jane Goodall distinguishes charisma from presence, saying:

> Charisma needs to be understood in a longitudinal sense, as a heightened life force that animates a whole career and fuels the trajectory of a sustained mission in the world. Presence is an expression of life force in the moment, so that the moment itself is transformed in a way that has an impact on all who witness it. Its very transience is a factor in its uncanny potency.[164]

This definition of charisma certainly pertains to Osteen, whose life force animates much more than any momentary encounter. Yet, I would suggest that, particularly for those congregants in the Compaq Center, the live images of Osteen that are projected during his sermon help to concentrate his charisma into a potent form of stage presence. As Goodall writes, "the stage actor radiates, the film actor concentrates";[165] during a service, and especially his sermon, Osteen does both simultaneously. The concurrent use of live screen images is an evangelical dramaturgical device intended to prompt the kind of generative double-vision of presence and representation that will cultivate an energetic relationship between performer-pastor and spectator-believer.

Moreover, Goodall asserts that "the charismatic leader and the actor with presence have in common a capacity to communicate with a peculiar intimacy to the individuals massed as their audience."[166] Osteen's power as a preacher derives largely from his ability to engender that sense of "peculiar intimacy" within all of the live spectators in the Compaq Center and, simultaneously, within the television audience. In this case, that combination of immediacy and intimacy, of presence and representation, produces a re-representational re-experience that puts congregants in direct, physical, felt contact with the "incorruptible, indestructible, ever-living seed of the Word of God." The specific dramaturgy that governs Lakewood's service is essential to achieving this goal.

During his sermon, Osteen's tone and expressiveness prompt congregants to underscore points of his message with verbal affirmations and applause. These grow more frequent and exuberant toward the end of the sermon, and they help Osteen transition to his customary conclusion in which he invites congregants to affirm their faith publicly. At the end of every sermon I have watched, Osteen asks the audience to repeat the following prayer after him: "Lord Jesus. I repent of my sins. Come into my heart. Wash me clean. I make you my Lord and Savior." He then opens his eyes, looks out at the audience, and explains that "if you prayed that simple prayer we believe you got born again." He then encourages people to "get in a good bible-based church" and to keep God first in their hearts.[167] This is more concrete guidance than he has offered thus far, but it is still relatively vague.

For new visitors, it may be shocking to discover that simply repeating this prayer with Osteen constitutes being "born again," and, indeed, as my previous chapters demonstrate, many evangelicals would disagree with this definition of spiritual new birth. Osteen has constructed a welcoming, inclusive theology with very low barriers to entry. Yet he does suggest that the stakes are high. His next prayer typically includes a version of the following passage:

> With our heads bowed in prayer, let me ask you an important question. If your heart stopped beating in the next couple of minutes, are you at peace with God? Do you know where you'd spend eternity if you died a moment or two from now? If not, I would love to pray with you. I'm not here to condemn anybody. I'm here to help you find a new beginning. And I know that comes from a personal relationship with Jesus Christ.

Osteen then invites anyone who is not at peace with God, or who needs a fresh start, to stand up and "accept the free gift of Christ's salvation." He admits that it might be embarrassing to stand up in front of this large crowd, but he asks attendees to "be bold" and to demonstrate to God that they are not ashamed of Him.

At some services, Osteen hammers home this point for a number of minutes, rallying the audience with phrases like "Don't put it off!" As people begin standing, he usually instructs the audience to clap for these people and to thereby encourage other people to also "take that step of faith." As at Willow Creek, the momentum of this "altar call" is fueled, in part, by intensifying musical underscoring as well as applause and verbal affirmations from the congregation; Lakewood, however, replays this same ritual every week. At some point, when enough people are standing, Osteen declares, "The angels are rejoicing in the heavens right now" and then asks everyone to pray the "born-again" prayer once more: "Lord Jesus. I repent of my sins. Come into my heart. Wash me clean. I make you my Lord and Savior." As the service comes to an end, Victoria typically joins Joel onstage. After asking people to "Give us at least a year of your life and, we promise you, you'll never be the same," he concludes with a final blessing over the congregation. The band begins a lively final Praise Song, and people begin streaming out of the auditorium.

Given the very general concepts that Osteen usually works with in his sermons, such as growing weary in the face of life's troubles, I suspect that most people find something in his sermon that relates to their specific situation.[168] The final moments of the service are designed to offer listeners a way to begin solving those problems. True, the end of Lakewood's service becomes increasingly urgent as, suddenly, Osteen tells audience members what is at stake—their eternal souls. His expressive voice and face, as well as the music, help attendees to feel that urgency. But the service also provides visitors with a relatively easy way to begin addressing this issue; the first step is to put your faith and trust in God, and some people, just by speaking the "born-again" prayer, may have inadvertently already done so. Admittedly, subsequent steps remain unclear, but articulating those is the goal of Lakewood's small group ministries, not of the main service event. Instead, the purpose of the weekly worship experience is to produce a potent affective intimate script that will give visitors a felt sense of stability and reassurance. Moreover, it is a script that changes only slightly from week to week and, therefore, one to which they can return repeatedly. Like the medieval texts that Sarah McNamer describes, the Lakewood service offers the user an opportunity for "performative iteration" and, therefore, provides the individual worshipper with a valuable tool for his or her long-term process of belief-making.[169]

"A Feeling of Fullness": Aesthetic Worship

For some worshipers a megachurch service may constitute the kind of liminal experience that Erika Fischer-Lichte defines as aesthetic:

> While I will label those liminal experiences aesthetic which make the journey the goal, the liminal experiences which use the journey to reach "another" goal are non-aesthetic. Such goals could consist of a socially recognized change of status; the creation of winners and losers or communities; the legitimization of claims to power; the creation of social bond; entertainment. That is to say, aesthetic experience concerns the experience of a threshold, a passage in itself; the very process of transition already constitutes the experience. . . . It depends on the individual's perception whether they are concentrating on the liminal state into which their perception has led them or whether they are experiencing it as a transition to a specific goal.[170]

This is what some critics identify as the potential pitfall of megachurch worship: it becomes an aesthetic experience—an end in itself—rather than an impetus toward other (the implication being, more meaningful) goals. As Thumma and Travis note, many critics "feel that the Megachurch movement is driven by the 'Sunday show'—its spiritual spectacle. . . . In the critics' view, this experience overwhelms congregants with comfort and functionality but does not lead to the true worship of God."[171]

However, evangelical dramaturgy recognizes the tremendous devotional value inherent within that sensuous, rhythmic threshold experience. Worshipping in these hypermedial spaces can provoke the kinds of transformations that "create physiological, affective, energetic, and motoric changes to the body," transformations that Fischer-Lichte argues allow spectators to perceive, and thus experience, "entirely ordinary bodies, actions, movements, things, sounds, or odors . . . as extra-ordinary and transfigured."[172] This visceral liminal state fosters immediacy within the hypermediated and, consequently, the intense pleasure that accompanies "contact with something that matters, something that affects you."[173] For this reason, the hypermedial megachurch service may indeed be enough for many worshippers; Jay David Bolter and Richard Grusin suggest that hypermediacy can "create a feeling of fullness, a satiety of experience, which can be taken as reality."[174]

Megachurch pastors like Bill Hybels and Rick Warren might agree. However, as FitzGerald notes, these leaders maintain that "the first step is to capture their attention and to deal with their 'felt needs,' as Jesus did when he healed the sick. But that is only the first step."[175] As with the Creation Museum, the affective, intimate script that megachurch services produce can satisfy the believer's spiritual, psychic, and visceral needs in the moment-to-moment experience. However, after those immediate needs are fulfilled, megachurch leaders hope that this initial positive experience—this feeling of fullness—will mark just the beginning of a more intensive, long-lasting relationship.

And, significantly, the genre works especially well for new visitors who are seeking something but are unclear exactly what it is; for those visitors who are experiencing the "unexpiring, unself-consuming" yearning that Massumi describes. The service, and particularly the sermon, gives that indistinct yearning focus and direction, reshaping it into a specific desire that faith in God can satisfy. For these visitors, a megachurch service produces an affective intimate script that supplies both a clear problem and an immediate solution for it. This alone might encourage repeat attendance that eventually develops into longer-lasting engagement.

Familiar Spaces

Living in the blend involves oscillating between multiple frames in order to construct meaning from the moment-to-moment performance event, as I discussed in Chapter Four. A productive shifting between frames can occur when people are "living in" the blend, particularly when that blend is constructed from sources that appear to be extremely different. There are many kinds of integration networks that humans create through conceptual blending, but Gilles Fauconnier and Mark Turner contend that the most sophisticated and generative of these are double-scope networks. Theatrical events require spectators to develop quite advanced double-scope blends. Fauconnier and Turner explain that in double-scope networks "both organizing frames make central contributions to the blend, and their sharp differences offer the possibility of rich clashes. Far from blocking the construction of the network, such clashes offer challenges to the imagination; indeed, the resulting blends can be highly creative."[176] Consequently, double-scope networks constructed from two widely unrelated inputs will oftentimes produce "extraordinarily rich emergent meaning."[177] I maintain that one reason Seeker churches are compelling—not just their services, but the entire visitor experience—is because they inspire rich, creative meaning through this kind of conceptual blending.

As I have already noted, Willow Creek was the church I visited that subscribes most closely to the "full-service" Seeker model. It was also the most visibly branded church I visited. Its central campus is located in South Barrington, an affluent northwestern suburb of Chicago. Parking is a major concern for many megachurches, and each venue uses different strategies to guarantee that parking does not become an obstacle to attendance. As I noted, Immanuel reserves sections at the front of its lot for new visitors, and McLean has a multilevel parking garage. At all of the churches I visited, police officers directed traffic out of the parking lots after the services. Willow Creek has two large parking lots near the church entrances, as well as various satellite lots. The website advises new visitors to "Enter the Fast Trac Parking lot from the Barrington Road entrance and a shuttle will take you directly to the E entrance conveniently located near the Main Auditorium. Shuttles operate one hour before the service and one hour after the service concludes."[178] To local commuters, especially those who use the Chicago-area transit system regularly, this language probably sounds familiar and conveys expedience and efficiency. Therefore, even before arriving at the church, new visitors have a sense that Willow Creek is catering to their physical, everyday needs.

The Willow Creek brand is modern and suburban. Warm, natural hues complement the large windows in the lobby and auditorium, which look out onto the expansive, meticulously landscaped grounds complete with waterfalls. The lobby contains the Harvest Food Court and Dr. B's café; Dr. B's looks similar to a Starbucks cafe (see Figure 17). Before and after services, worshippers can purchase coffee, breakfast, or snacks, and then enjoy them while sitting in the adjoining 800-seat atrium.[179] The lobby also contains banks of computer kiosks where visitors can search for information about Willow Creek and its programming (Figure 18).

Willow Creek's lobby merges the familiar experience of a Starbucks visit with the crisp efficiency of a modern conference center. The space feels new,

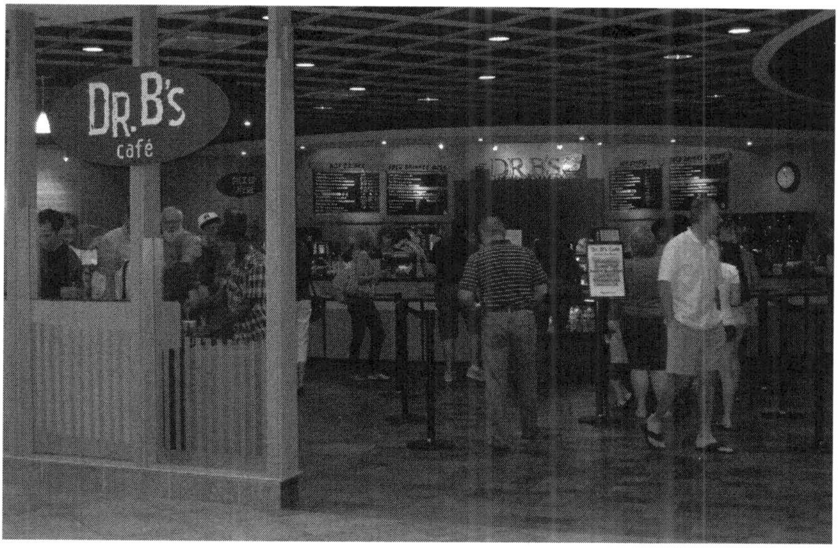

Figure 17. Dr. B's café. Inside Willow Creek Community Church in South Barrington, Illinois. June 2011. Photo by author.

but not overly shiny; modern, but not urban; inviting, but without being pushy. Willow Creek's website proclaims:

> Our doors are wide open to everyone, regardless of their background. What most people usually notice is the large number of people who attend services and our size. But don't let our size overwhelm you—size has benefits. You can blend in if you like, but we make it easy to get connected.[180]

The culture allows visitors to engage this familiar space on their own terms. There is also nothing in the lobby that appears overtly religious, except for the occasional bookcase of Bibles. I suspect some people could walk through the space and never realize it was a church. This is critical to the Willow Creek brand.

The entire Willow Creek space, not simply the auditorium, is designed to feel familiar and, thus, to resonate with visitors. The congregants themselves are an important part of this aesthetic, and they purposefully stage themselves in ways that will create a particular kind of atmospheric space.

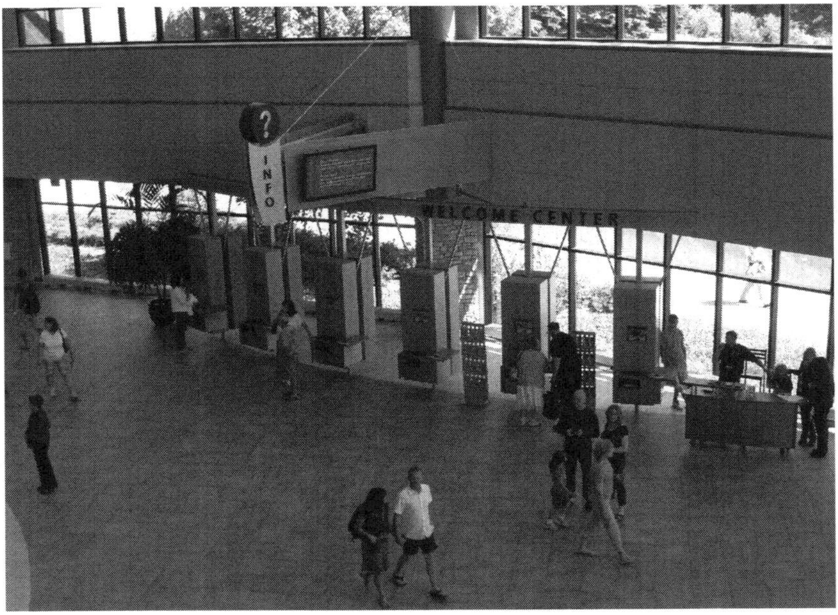

Figure 18. Lobby of Willow Creek Community Church in South Barrington, Illinois. June 2011. Photo by author.

Although some parishioners dress up for worship, others arrive in much more casual attire, such as jeans and T-shirts. In addition, people do not noticeably alter their bodies, voices, or demeanor when they walk into the sanctuary, as is often the case at traditional churches. Some critics of contemporary megachurches disparage this fact; Eddie Gibbs, a professor of church growth at Fuller Theological Seminary, explains how "worship that degenerates into a casual overfamiliarity is both presumptuous and embarrassing to those who see God from a transcendental perspective."[181] However, megachurch leaders and members contend that God is "constantly intervening in the everyday lives of human beings. And he could be encountered anywhere, not just in church."[182] Integrating everyday synaesthetic elements into the church space creates a memorable, felt experience that helps to embed this particular theological message and epistemological assumption into the worshipper's body.

As with Holy Land Experience or the Creation Museum, the fact that even the exterior of many megachurch buildings looks familiar and not disconcertingly "religious" might encourage certain people to arrive at worship in bodies that are more open to the religious messages delivered inside (see Figures 10 and 11 in Chapter Five). Consequently, at a church like Willow Creek the entire campus space prompts a productive shifting back and forth between frames—from the familiar everyday to the extraordinary sacred, and back again. Initially there may be no confusion between the two felt experiences; they work symbiotically but do not merge entirely into a solid blend. Based upon previous experiences at or knowledge of worship in traditional churches, many new visitors will likely decompress the blend often and remain more aware of the everyday frame. But repeated interactions with the space may transform the visitor's conceptualization of worship, thereby enabling the sacred frame to exert a more prominent influence over the blend, until, finally, visitors live in a sacred/secular megachurch blend.

I would argue that megachurch proponents and critics both recognize that visitors who engage these spaces "live in" a sacred/everyday blend. However, to their advocates, integrating cafés and gyms into megachurches does not desacralize the spiritual; on the contrary, including these familiar elements in the church space sanctifies the mundane while also teaching worshippers a new and devotionally valuable aisthetic practice. Megachurch leaders believe accessibility represents only the first step toward achieving larger evangelical goals. As Jonathan Mahler explains, Seeker church leaders typically have long-term plans for their congregations that involve "much more than playing video games and eating doughnuts." Radiant's founder Lee McFarland admits that "his hope—his expectation, really—is that casual worshippers will gradually immerse themselves in Radiant's many Christ-based programs . . . until they have eventually incorporated Christian values into every aspect of their lives."[183] Worded somewhat differently, "living in" a megachurch's blend will embed within a congregant's body patterns of faith that, rather than rejecting the mundane or everyday, instead reshape these secular rhythms into sacred expressions of Christian faith. Ultimately, the megachurch visit produces an embodied schema that promotes this new epistemology.

Finally, by carefully constructing a "blended" environment, megachurches, especially spaces like Willow Creek or Lakewood, stage the visitor without them necessarily realizing it. As with all venues, design choices direct visitors to interact with certain material elements, to navigate the space in particular ways, and to conduct themselves in a specific fashion, while at the same time seeming *not* to force anything upon them. As with all spaces, choice is contingent. For this reason, spatial design functions as a valuable tool for evangelical dramaturgy because it circumscribes visitors without seeming to do so. Similar to the Creation Museum's "Museum Experience Walk," as visitors move through and interact with the megachurch space, they also trace certain concepts—choice, modernity, familiarity—into their bodies. The lobby is therefore an especially powerful device, because it incorporates these concepts into visitors' embodied schemata even before the worship event begins. As a result, worshippers may then understand and interpret the service, including the sermon message, through those same concepts. In this respect, the megachurch's spatial design, along with the other dramaturgical choices—a live band, Praise Music, projection screens, microphones, roving cameramen, lighting and smoke effects—create a "felt," tangible brand. And the visitor's experience of that brand—of living in the blends through which that brand is constructed—may, ultimately, generate doctrine.

Lavender contends that, in many instances, the effect of hypermedial mise en scène has "less to do with the direct production of meaning and more to do with the production of a (meaningful) texture to the event."[184] That texture serves as a valuable basis for subsequent meaning construction. The same is true here. Certainly many megachurch leaders are committed to an evangelical, Christ-centered theology.[185] Yet, I maintain that they also know many visitors will initially return to their church not because of its specific theological message but because of the resonant texture of the megachurch event. This event begins long before the service itself, the very moment visitors pull off the road and into the church parking lot, and it continues until they drive away again.

Since I began my first chapter with a medieval example, it seems fitting to end this study with a similar comparative case. As I have argued elsewhere, despite its obvious differences, the medieval parish church may offer us insight into the devotional form and function of the contemporary megachurch.[186] The medieval parish church played an important role in the daily lives of the laity. The civic geography of medieval towns was often determined by the location of parish churches, and the parish was one of the many communities in which each Christian layperson counted him- or herself a member. Similar to the megachurch, the parish church also constituted a powerful force because it fulfilled a number of the laity's needs by providing social services; although it was a religious institution, its influence extended far beyond sacred parameters. However, I am particularly interested here in the parish church space, which, like the megachurch space, provided worshippers with a powerful rhythmic devotional experience.

Most parish churches in the Middle Ages were full of sculptures, hammerbeams, painted windows, carved bench ends, vestments and altar cloths, liturgical vessels, candles, and various other decorations. In other words, they constituted incredibly rich material spaces. The rhythms of these spaces extended out, toward the visitor, thereby implying a degree of devotional accessibility.[187] As with the contemporary megachurch, this medieval worship space traced an embodied schema in visitors that promoted certain epistemological assumptions related to knowledge of God.

As various scholars have shown, medieval laypeople were in control of many aspects of their parish churches, but particularly of their material features and, thus, of their devotional rhythms. As Katherine French explains,

> The laity's involvement in their parishes went well beyond attending the liturgy and paying tithes. Episcopal mandate also required them to maintain the nave and churchyard and to supply various liturgical items such as mass books, candlesticks, and chalices, while the clergy took care of the chancel.[188]

Laypeople commissioned many of the images that filled these churches (stained-glass windows, small and large sculptures, wooden carvings), donated silver plate and religious books to the altars, and covered statues of saints in their own clothing, jewelry, and rosaries. Lay parishioners also stood in codified areas of the church during worship, thus staging themselves as part of the service's mise en scène, an act that often also reinscribed various social and political hierarchies. Laypeople sometimes staged dramatic performances inside or outside their churches; even their funerals, especially those of the wealthy, were spectacular, synaesthetically rich, and performative church events. Moreover, laypeople paid to have services and prayers said for themselves or family members in the church, thereby filling the space with sounds. And they paid to keep the candles that stood before images and the altar, and that illuminated the space, continually burning.

This was a space over which the laity exerted a tremendous amount of sensual, rhythmic control. It was the laity who determined the felt sense of the medieval parish church, who crafted its atmospheric space, who used elements that engaged all of the senses to establish each church's unique brand. They are also the ones who brought their everyday materialities into the space—their own prayer books, clothing, jewelry—and made these an integral part of the synaesthetic worship experience. In this respect, the medieval laity also lived in an everyday/sacred devotional blend whenever they engaged their parish churches.

Many of these same things are true of the contemporary megachurch, as I have demonstrated in this chapter. In the end, most megachurches are lay-oriented and lay-controlled enterprises. These churches are often led by pastors who are, in fact, themselves "laypeople" with no formal theological training.[189] In addition, lay ministers, worship leaders, and elders often play significant roles in the life of the church. Moreover, it is the laity—the religious consumers—who exert the most control over the atmosphere and determine the brand. While medieval laypeople exercised their control directly, modern laypeople wield their control by means of consumption. Furthermore, in both cases the church's actual space is a visual, sensual, rhythmic testament to what laypeople want from their religious institutions and what they feel is important to their devotional lives. For example, I find it revealing that both the medieval and contemporary spaces try to address the laity's needs and desires by constructing everyday/sacred worship blends that erase any felt separation between faith and daily life, between the public and the private. And, significantly, in both contexts the church is more than a "Sunday morning" space but is instead an institution that provides an array of social services that laypeople can turn to throughout the week.

Consequently, although the contemporary megachurch is known for its large size, modern appeal, Protestant affiliation, and technological sophistication, in many ways its tactics and purpose are not that different from those of the small, medieval, pre-Reformation parish churches around which many medieval laypeople constructed their lives. Accordingly, we might learn new things about the value that megachurches hold for evangelical believers today by considering the role of the parish church in the medieval layperson's life—not simply the theological, social, and political aspects of that role but also its synaesthetic and rhythmic elements. As I noted near the beginning of this chapter, Thumma and Travis argue that the rapid growth of megachurches since the 1970s suggests "a distinct resonance between what megachurches offer and what many contemporary Americans desire."[190] I am proposing that the megachurch phenomenon may mark a desire to return to a medieval past, a time when the lives of most individuals and communities revolved around the parish church, and the church was fully integrated into and guided daily life. Significantly, it was also a time when a church not only served the social and devotional needs of its members but, through its physical, material space, also aimed to address the laity's felt needs.

Coda

Throughout this project I attempted to understand U.S. evangelicalism by physically engaging its dramaturgy. I tried to open myself up to unfamiliar—sometimes uncomfortable—affective scripts in order to experience the felt solutions they are designed to offer and, thus, in Timothy Beal's words, to find my way "into the other's story."[1] None of the individual performative devices I have discussed throughout these chapters is specific to evangelical dramaturgy; elements such as live recreations, commodification, or elisions of past and present certainly appear in other theatrical traditions and contexts. My goal therefore has not been to argue that the tactics of evangelical dramaturgy are unique to the performative culture of American evangelicalism but instead to examine how genres made for and by evangelical believers today use these strategies to create live encounters that will satisfy the devotee's immediate needs.

As I was finishing this project I began reading Jill Lepore's *The Whites of Their Eyes: The Tea Party's Revolution and the Battle Over American History* and was struck by similarities between the Tea Party tactics that Lepore describes and the strategies I had identified within evangelical dramaturgy.[2] Some correlations are obvious, such as the effort to define the United States as a Christian nation founded on Christian principles,[3] a concept that some evangelical genres I have analyzed, like the Sacred Projects, emphasize more than others. However, other parallels, such as the skillful manipulation of time to craft reenactments, may suggest a more fundamental similarity between evangelical dramaturgy and the Tea Party's dramaturgy.

For instance, Lepore suggests that the Tea Party's Revolution is not "just another generation's story" but is instead "more like a reenactment."[4] Yet rather than simply returning to an ideal American past, this particular form of reenactment tries to reshape the relationship between past and present. The Tea Party leaders do not evoke the Founding Fathers in order to draw an analogy to our present circumstances but to achieve something far more literal; according to Lepore, they are not proposing that "our struggle is like theirs," but rather that "we are there" or "they are here."[5]

> To say that we are there, or the Founding Fathers are here . . . is to subscribe to a set of assumptions about the relationship between the past and the present stricter, even, than the strictest form of constitutional originalism, a set of assumptions that, conflating originalism, evangelicalism, and heritage tourism, amounts to a variety of fundamentalism.[6]

This reference to heritage tourism alongside originalism and evangelicalism underscores that fact that the Tea Party is an inherently performative movement that uses events, props, costumes, accents, and role-playing to gain widespread visibility and to assert its positions within a larger cultural conversation. In this respect, the Tea Party's strategies are closely related to those of evangelical dramaturgy, which uses performative tactics to generate re-representations. The user's resonant, felt experience of those re-representations not only functions as testimony to their reality but also allows the user to re-experience the past historical event. Tea Party events may aim to cultivate this same type of historical re-experience.

Moreover, I could not help but recall the Creation Museum's use of the Genesis account and its characterization of "secular science" when reading Lepore's assertion that "the telling of history is, by its very nature, controversial, contentious, and contested; it advances by debate. This doesn't make history squishy, vague, and irrelevant. It makes it picky, demanding, and vital."[7] Similar to scientific discoveries, the evidence we uncover through historical research often raises more questions than it answers, making the historical narrative more, rather than less, complicated. This leads to further uncertainty rather than to greater stability.

In general, academic historians have not been particularly focused on helping the general public recognize the value and necessity of a critical, complicated historical narrative. As Lepore notes, "for much of its history, the American historical profession has defined itself by its dedication to the proposition that looking to the past to explain the present—and especially to solve present-day problems—falls outside the realm of serious historical inquiry."[8] Consequently, academic historians' "inability to write for general readers" and "unwillingness to examine the relationship between the past and present" have not only served to widen the gap between academic and popular history (and between their, at times, quite different ways of defining evidence), but, according to many critics from both inside and outside the academy, the scholarly approach to history has also failed "to provide a narrative synthesis, to tell a big story instead of many little ones."[9] That failure has, in Lepore's words, "left plenty of room for a lot of other people to get into the history business."[10]

The Tea Party has done exactly that. As Lepore explains, the Tea Party's approach to history "has no patience for ambiguity, self-doubt," and, like the historical perspective I identified at the Sacred Projects, it functions, in great part, through "nostalgia for an imagined time . . . less riven by strife, less troubled by conflict, less riddled with ambiguity, less divided by race."[11] As a result, when faced with contemporary crises or problems the movement supplies a clear and definitive answer: "We have forsaken the Founding Fathers."[12] In addition, Lepore maintains that the Tea Party professes a form of historical fundamentalism in which

> certain historical texts—"the founding documents"—are to be read in the same spirit with which religious fundamentalists read, for instance, the Ten Commandments; that the Founding Fathers were divinely inspired; that the academic study of history (whose standards of evidence and methods of analysis are based on skepticism) is a conspiracy and, furthermore, blasphemy; and that political arguments grounded in appeals to the founding documents, as sacred texts, and to the Founding Fathers, as prophets, are therefore incontrovertible.[13]

As Lepore's comparison implies, this way of reading historical and legal texts is closely related to Fundamentalist literalism's construction of a "biblically constituted history," a parallel that Vincent Crapanzano analyzes.[14] We might then consider the Tea Party as a performative response to the fact that, as Crapanzano asserts, "history as a source of understanding and explanation, not to mention of perspective and solace, seems to have played a diminishing role" in American lives, with "'historical events' . . . mechanically filed away in empty chronologies or poorly articulated periods," rather than "integrated into vital and meaningful trajectories."[15] The Tea Party aims to construct a more meaning-rich historical narrative, and, thus, the movement's tactics and objectives are akin to those of evangelical dramaturgy—to craft re-experiences that eliminate ambiguity and self-doubt by providing straightforward, certain, and deeply resonant solutions.

The Tea Party also returns us to the issue of entrepreneurialism, specifically the importance of fostering small "entrepreneurial" opportunities for meaning-making within larger environments that might otherwise feel impersonal and promote anonymity. The atmospheric space of many Tea Party events generates the impression of a local, antiestablishment movement fueled by ordinary citizen-volunteers. This grassroots "sphere of presence" significantly impacts how people perceive the movement and its agenda, even though, as many journalists have demonstrated, the Tea Party is not, in fact, a truly grassroots movement.[16] As Frank Rich noted in an August 2010 op-ed piece about the Tea Party,

> There's just one element missing from these snapshots of America's ostensibly spontaneous and leaderless populist uprising: the sugar daddies who are bankrolling it. . . . You've heard of one of them, Rupert Murdoch. The other two, the brothers David and Charles Koch, are even richer, with a combined wealth exceeded only by that of Bill Gates and Warren Buffett among Americans.[17]

As Jane Mayer reported in the *New Yorker:*

> The Kochs operate oil refineries in Alaska, Texas, and Minnesota, and control some four thousand miles of pipeline. Koch Industries owns Brawny paper towels, Dixie cups, Georgia-Pacific lumber, Stainmaster carpet, and Lycra, among other products. *Forbes* ranks it as the second-largest private company in the country.[18]

The Tea Party's visibility and organizational strategies are therefore indebted to larger corporate entities. Nonetheless, these associations remain in the background and do not perceptibly intrude upon the movement's sphere of presence. For example, the Americans for Prosperity Foundation, an organization that David Koch founded, organizes and funds Tea Party events around the country. Describing one such event held in Texas in July 2010, Mayer writes:

> An advertisement cast the event as a populist uprising against vested corporate power. "Today, the voices of average Americans are being drowned out by lobbyists and special interests," it said. "But you can do something about it." The pitch made no mention of its corporate funders.[19]

I would therefore argue that despite various articles explaining its corporate ties, many people—both supporters and detractors among them—still (even just subconsciously) perceive the Tea Party as a spontaneous, community-based movement because it uses language and tactics—hosting small-scale training sessions, organizing local demonstrations, canvassing voters, generating petitions, raising funds through many different small organizations, creating a virtual network through social media—that engender the felt sense of a grassroots, anticorporate, and, thus, entrepreneurial political movement. Consequently, even the larger Tea Party events can be experienced as intimate, resonant encounters that promote notions of individual choice and agency, national ideals upon which Tea Party politicians subsequently draw.

Throughout these chapters I have been cautious about eliding evangelicalism with political conservativism. Not all evangelicals are politically conservative, and certainly not all conservatives are Christian evangelicals. But Lepore's analysis gave me pause. There is definitely overlap between the Tea Party and the evangelical Christian community.[20] Perhaps the reason many evangelical Christians are attracted to this political movement's message is because the Tea Party is using resonant strategies—not simply familiar ways of talking about trustworthy evidence and reliable documents, but also of conceptualizing the relationship between past and present, of crafting felt narratives about contemporary culture, of challenging distinctions between sacred and secular, and of eliminating ambiguity by means of synaesthetic, performative encounters.

It seems the Tea Party is, indeed, employing strategies from evangelical dramaturgy to construct both its message and the performative events that promote it. A person's familiarity with and previous experience of that dramaturgy may then determine whether they find the Tea Party physically reassuring or disconcerting; here, again, the productive tension and interplay between "making belief" and "belief making us" is evident. Therefore, in order to understand exactly why this movement is appealing, it is necessary to recognize that religious beliefs and experiences, as well as the epistemological assumptions they promote, do not passively stand beside the Tea

Party's message and its delivery, but instead infuse them, determining and shaping the very language (verbal and sensual) used within that movement's mode of performance.

However, perhaps more challenging is that constructively analyzing the Tea Party also requires examining affect as a formative element within U.S. political discourse generally. Janet Jakobsen and Ann Pellegrini have argued that the traditional U.S. "secularization narrative . . . identifies secularism with modernity and asserts the privatization of religion as key to civil peace." As a result, the visible public presence of religious groups—particularly those that elicit strong emotional responses from followers—are typically viewed by secularists "as dangerous anti-modern throwbacks" and approached apprehensively.[21] Accordingly, secular discourse has largely ceded the language of affect to religion, a bifurcation that, as Pellegrini explains, has hindered secularism's ability to engage affective experience productively:

> In secular thinking religion is the place where affect is most solicited, most contained (privatization), and most stigmatized. . . . It is not that religion is "just" a matter of affect (far from it). It is rather that in Christian secular framings, the identification of feelings with religion; or of religion *as* feelings, nothing more than feelings; or—if there is to be something more—of religion as irrational belief blocks us from identifying what feelings the secular mobilizes and draws upon. For starters: hope, fear, anxiety, terror.[22]

Consequently, U.S. secular discourse, especially secular political discourse, has largely failed to rigorously and judiciously analyze how people (including secularists) perceive and interpret political principles through felt affective scripts and, thus, to appreciate affect as a legitimate and valuable mode of world-creation and meaning-making.

For example, in an article about religious advertising during the 2012 U.S. presidential primary race, Jeremy Peters describes how

> politicians have long employed coded language in their messaging targeting religious conservatives, a practice often derided as dog-whistle politics for its ability to stir emotions among those who are in-the-know while passing undetected over others. Sarah Palin has often referred to her support from "prayer warriors," a term known among evangelicals as those who engage in battle with Satan.[23]

However, rather than surreptitiously using "code words," Ross Douthat suggests that we might instead understand these politicians as "employing the everyday language of an America that's more biblically literate than the national press corps."[24] Rather than dismissing affective political strategies as merely emotional ploys, it is necessary to interrogate them as legitimate, meaningful tactics.

I interpret William Connolly's 2008 book *Capitalism and Christianity, American Style* as an attempt to undertake this kind of critical work. Although I find Connolly's arguments too polemical at times, I am compelled by what he calls the evangelical-capitalist resonance machine. Connolly examines "how revenge themes have become incorporated into one wing of Christianity today and how they resonate with exclusionary drives and claims to special entitlement running through the cowboy sector of American capitalism."[25] Because "the spirituality of each constituency amplifies that of the other, even as their creeds vary," the result is an evangelical-capitalist resonance machine.[26] This resonance machine is effective, in part, because it promises "solace in the church and the family," while also "fomenting an aspirational politics."[27]

The powerful efficacy of this resonance machine is on display in a company like Wal-Mart. Bethany Moreton examines how "the world's largest company" won "hearts and minds to the case of corporate capitalism in the old heartland of anticorporate agitation."[28] Wal-Mart accomplished this feat, in great part, by developing a "service ethos" that "imbued shopping with 'family values.'"[29] Thus, by removing "several traditional stumbling blocks for Christian devotees of consumption," Wal-Mart not only "transformed itself into a national Christian icon," but it also constructed a "mode of shopping" that resonated with evangelical values and needs.[30]

As this example helps illustrate, the resonance that Connolly describes is not simply conceptual or metaphorical. Building from Linda Kintz's work, Connolly argues that "patterns of rhythm, resonance, dissonance, and reverberation not only play a role within cultural life, but . . . they also forge subdiscursive modes of communication between us and other parts of nature."[31] In other words, the solace and aspiration this evangelical-capitalist resonance machine affords are felt experiences that supply meaningful and applicable affective scripts. For example, in the case of Wal-Mart, the shopping experience generates a very real, felt affective script that defines "mass buying" as "procuring humble products 'for the family,'" and that situates Wal-Mart "managers, employees, and customers . . . as Christian servants."[32] That script not only helps to "make mass consumption safe for the white Protestant heartland,"[33] but it also provides Christian shoppers with a simple, daily opportunity to express their religious identity in the public marketplace. I therefore find Connolly's arguments about an evangelical-capitalist resonance machine relevant to my own claims about evangelical dramaturgy and, particularly, to how evangelical dramaturgy might help us examine affect in public political discourse.

Pellegrini suggests that the recent turn to affect in scholarship may, in fact, signal "a desire for the forms of world-making and plenitude and excess that have otherwise been set down as religion's provenance."[34] Such desire certainly has a political dimension, and therefore it may also represent a longing to engage with and create space for a wider array of feelings within certain arenas of political dialogue and activism. The Tea Party may indicate that evangelical dramaturgy contains political power precisely because it generates felt re-experiences—affective scripts—that immediately and concretely respond to a longing for belief, in this case, a belief in the U.S. imaginary.[35] That longing is certainly felt by people across the political spectrum; however, because political secularism typically relegates affect to the religious sphere, I would argue that U.S. liberal secularism has often failed to offer its own vital and meaningful trajectories in response to that longing.[36]

Rebecca Schneider concludes her book on reenactment by analyzing certain politically oriented performances that make "matters of *affective affiliation* gain in complexity" by shifting "time, space, and bodies according to contingencies and complicities of privilege, politics, and power" (my emphasis).[37] These reenactments, whose "strange anachronisms of cadence and syntax trouble sensibility," function through what she calls "queer time."[38] Schneider maintains that queer time could begin to help answer "the question of how to effectively protest government and multinational corporate actions under neoliberal global capital [that] has flummoxed the Left across the Bush era (and beyond)."[39] In other words, these performance reenactments can produce affective scripts that may help solve problems of political agency and activism in the present.

This political efficacy is due, in great part, to "a particular U.S. relationship to memory and futurity" that reads past against/as future: "The future is America's geography of revision, and it's up ahead that America's past (the future's past) will be (re)encountered among the (so-called) living. Indeed, the sense that the past is a future direction in which one can travel . . . is familiar."[40] Schneider therefore views queer time as a powerful political instrument because it "reminds us of a durational 'now' for political action." She writes, "The turn to the past as a gestic, affective journey through the past's possible alternative futures . . . bears a political purpose for a critical approach to futurity."[41] It is precisely because queer time rejects linear historical chronology, situating the past before us *as* future, that it can ignite new modes of active political response.

According to Schneider, reenactment is a crucial way that people engage with and actualize this idea that history "remains before us."[42]

> History is not remembered (America has no reminiscence) as it was, but experienced as it will become. It must be acquired, purchased, begun again and again. A nation of futurity is here, still, a nation without reminiscences—unless reminiscence is relived as NOW, acquired (purchased even, copyrighted) as affective "present time" experience, beginning again.[43]

By creating encounters in which different temporal moments touch one another, performance reenactments can generate previously unrecognized resonances across historical moments, resonances that will supply spectators with felt political urgency about the present.

I see a direct relationship between queer time's way of understanding/experiencing history and evangelical dramaturgy. This is somewhat understandable given the connections between evangelicalism and American identity that I outlined in my Introduction. However, I find the correlations particularly striking given my analysis of the Tea Party and the specifically liberal political performances that Schneider analyzes to illustrate queer time. Evangelical dramaturgy may therefore reveal places where American evangelicalism and U.S. secular discourse touch—where they share modes of meaning-making and degrees of longing. Moreover, it might reveal that in order to generate momentum that results in true long-term change, political discourse must not only trigger affect, but it must also construct vital, meaningful trajectories that offer relevant affective scripts for future action. Accordingly, evangelical dramaturgy not only offers us ways to analyze and understand evangelicalism, but it may also help us to examine affect's place in U.S. political and cultural longing more generally.[44]

***

While working on this project, I discussed my various research trips with many different professional colleagues and friends. Nearly everyone responded with curiosity mingled with some combination of fear, anxiety, and hostility, in many cases, very fervently expressed. Although most colleagues asked many questions and wanted to hear more about the different evangelical venues I visited, they also reacted quite cautiously to my own personal interest in and affective responses to these places. Many said they hoped I wouldn't be "converted" or "won over" by these encounters.[45] Crapanzano noted a similar reaction among his friends and colleagues: "Nearly everyone who showed interest in my research asked me, sheepishly, apologetically, but with consuming curiosity, whether or not I had ever been tempted—that was the word they most frequently used—by Fundamentalism."[46] Although often, if not always, said in apparent jest, I found the frequency of such comments noteworthy, especially since they were typically accompanied by remarks (usually zealous) about the ridiculous and absurd premises of venues like the Creation Museum and Holy Land Experience. After a while I began to wonder why, if these venues were so ludicrous, these same colleagues implied that I could be tempted or converted by them. I don't believe any of these colleagues consider me particularly naive or gullible. Rather, I think their reactions—like those that Crapanzano recounts—suggest certain contradictory (and uneasy) impulses within U.S. secular discourse when it comes to affective religious experience. Perhaps evangelical dramaturgy can offer us a critical framework for addressing these inclinations and, thus, for productively examining affect, both in religious contexts and elsewhere.

Pellegrini admits to feeling a kind of "affect envy" during her research into evangelical Hell Houses. Like her, I must "acknowledge my own envy—not fear, not repugnance—for the affective surplus on display"[47] at the venues I visited. I do not believe this feeling distorted my critical lens. Alternatively, I would suggest that integrating such responses into this research has helped me recognize the value of meaningful, vital trajectories within any secular/political/religious belief system, as well as the importance of developing conscientious ways to speak and write about that value critically.

Notes

Introduction

1. Frank Rich, at the time the cultural commentator for the *New York Times,* is often attributed with opening the mainstream public debate about the film with his 3 August 2003 article in the *International Herald Tribune* entitled "Mel Gibson's Martyrdom Complex." This was followed by an array of *New York Times* pieces that Rich devoted to Gibson's film during the months preceding and following its release. Among the many other reviews and articles related to the film, see A. O. Scott, "'The Passion of the Christ': Good and Evil Locked in Violent Showdown," *New York Times,* 25 February 2004; Peter J. Boyer, "The Jesus War," *New Yorker,* 15 September 2003, 58–71; Jon Meacham, "Who Killed Jesus?" *Newsweek,* 16 February 2004, http://www.newsweek.com/2004/02/15/who-killed-jesus.html#; David Gates, "Jesus Christ Movie Star," *Newsweek,* 8 March 2004, http://www.newsweek.com/2004/03/07/jesus-christ-movie-star.html; Maureen Dowd, "Stations of the Crass," *New York Times,* 26 February 2004, op-ed; Kenneth Turan, "A Narrow Vision and Staggering Violence," *Los Angeles Times,* 24 February 2004, http://www.latimes.com/et-passion24-2004feb24,0,6930255.story; Richard Corliss, "Holy Hypocrisies," *Time,* 27 February 2004, http://www.time.com/time/columnist/corliss/article/0,9565,596038,00.html; Corliss, "Movies: The Goriest Story Ever Told," *Time,* 1 March 2004, http://www.time.com/time/magazine/article/0,9171,993485,00.html. The website *The Text This Week,* which features a wide variety of resources for study and liturgy, has a bibliography of articles published about the film by scholars, critics, and religious leaders from across the globe: *The Text This Week,* "'The Passion of the Christ' Mel Gibson Movie—Articles, Study Guides, & Opinions," http://www.textweek.com/response/passion_movie.htm.

2. Timothy K. Beal and Tod Linafelt, "Introduction," in *Mel Gibson's Bible: Religion, Popular Culture, and* The Passion of the Christ, ed. Beal and Linafelt (Chicago: University of Chicago Press, 2006), 3.

3. See Marcia Kupfer, "Introduction," in *The Passion Story: From Visual Representation to Social Drama,* ed. Kupfer (University Park: Pennsylvania State University Press, 2008), 4. See also Mark C. Taylor, "The Offense of Flesh," in *Mel Gibson's Bible: Religion, Popular Culture, and* The Passion of the Christ, ed. Beal and Linafelt (Chicago: University of Chicago Press, 2006), 139–52, and Debra Taylor Cashion, "The Man of Sorrows and Mel Gibson," in *Tributes in Honor of James H. Marrow: Studies in Painting and Manuscript Illumination of the Late Middle Ages and Northern Renaissance,* ed. Jeffrey

Hamburger and Anne Korteweg (Turnhout: Brepols, 2006), 139–45. For the development of crucifixion and Passion iconography, see Rachel Fulton, *From Judgment to Passion: Devotion to Christ and the Virgin Mary, 800–1200* (New York: Columbia University Press, 2002).

4. As Timothy Beal notes, although some scholars and religious leaders from other traditions hoped Gibson's film would offer "'teachable moments' and opportunities for interreligious dialogue," it largely proved baffling to non-Christians. Beal, "They Know Not What They Watch," in *Mel Gibson's Bible: Religion, Popular Culture, and* The Passion of the Christ, ed. Beal and Linafelt (Chicago: University of Chicago Press, 2006), 199.

5. Kupfer, "Introduction," 19.

6. Taylor, "Offense of Flesh," 140.

7. Margaret Miles, *Seeing and Believing: Religion and Values in the Movies* (Boston: Beacon Press, 1996), 46.

8. Ibid., 45.

9. Among them: *On "The Passion of the Christ": Exploring the Issues Raised by the Controversial Movie,* ed. Paula Frederickson (Berkeley and Los Angeles: University of California Press, 2006); special edition on "Mel Gibson's *The Passion of the Christ,*" *Journal of Religion and Society* 6 (2004); *Re-Viewing the Passion: Mel Gibson's Film and Its Critics,* ed. S. Brent Plate (New York: Palgrave Macmillan, 2004); *Mel Gibson's* Passion: *The Film, the Controversy, and Its Implications,* ed. Zev Garber (West Lafayette: Purdue University Press, 2006); *Mel Gibson's Bible: Religion, Popular Culture, and* The Passion of the Christ, ed. Beal and Linafelt (Chicago: University of Chicago Press, 2006); and various essays in *The Passion Story: From Visual Representation to Social Drama,* ed. Marcia Kupfer (University Park: Pennsylvania State University Press, 2008).

10. John Fletcher, "Tasteless as Hell: Community Performance, Distinction, and Countertaste in Hell House," *Theatre Survey* 48, no. 2 (2007): 313–14.

11. Margaret Miles, "The Passion for Social Justice and *The Passion of the Christ,*" in *Mel Gibson's Bible: Religion, Popular Culture, and* The Passion of the Christ, ed. Beal and Linafelt (Chicago: University of Chicago Press, 2006), 121–22.

12. Ibid., 122. Miles asserts, "There is a contradiction between entertainment (passivity)—the condition in which movies are viewed—and religious engagement that requires viewers' imaginative participation (activity)" (123).

13. Beal, "They Know Not What They Watch," 200–201.

14. In Chapter Three I discuss how this film produced certain tropes that still circulate through evangelical media and will argue that these reveal the film's ongoing relevance among believers. Kupfer writes, "With statements like 'to see the *Passion* is an act of worship,' not to mention profusions of tears, moviegoers reenacted affective dispositions." She also notes examples of the movie provoking more active responses: "a Texas man, for example, confessed to a long unsolved murder." Kupfer, "Introduction," 238, n. 30. Many of the articles in *Mel Gibson's Bible: Religion, Popular Culture, and* The Passion of the Christ recount evidence of the film's devotional efficacy. See especially Beal, "They Know Not What They Watch," 199–204; Robert M. Franklin, "*The Passion* in Black and White," 195–97; George Smiga, "The Good News of Mel Gibson's *Passion,*" 21–28. See also Jody Eldred, *Changed Lives: Miracles of the Passion* (Eugene, OR: Harvest House, 2004), which recounts "stories of people whose eternal destinies had been miraculously rerouted" by Gibson's film (10). There is also a companion DVD of the same title that was released by Good Times Entertainment.

15. Donnalee Dox, "The Willing Sustenance of Belief: Religiosity and Mode of Performance," *Journal of Religion and Theatre* 8, no. 1 (2009): 41, http://www.athe.org/associations/12588/files/Dox.pdf.

16. Taylor discusses the film's theological appeal to Protestants throughout "Offense of the Flesh." Beal also discusses the film's appeal for both Catholics and evangelicals in Beal, "They Know Not What They Watch," 199–204.

17. A publication such as *A Guide to The Passion of The Christ*, published by the Catholic Exchange Press, illustrates this distinction. The introduction to this guide specifically notes, "In terms of effecting conversions and motivating people to weed out sin from their lives—which is what meditating on the Passion is all about—our evangelical brothers and sisters have been an inspiration. But can their theology adequately mine such cinematic gems as the Last Supper flashbacks or the deeply Marian themes presented in the movie?" Consequently, the book fulfills a mediating role by providing "answers to some of the many questions critical to a full understanding of authentic Christianity—questions *The Passion of The Christ* will most certainly raise," particularly because so many people, even those raised as Christians, "have not received an education in the Faith that equips them to *see* those connections, which are quite real and are, in fact, delineated for us in the teaching of the Church." *A Guide to The Passion of The Christ: 100 Questions about* The Passion of The Christ (Encinitas, CA: Catholic Exchange Press, 2004), 2, 3, original emphasis. While the priesthood and institutional church often function to mediate the relationship between laity and God within Catholicism, most evangelical denominations resist the need for such intercession. This is particularly apparent with respect to Bible-reading practices among evangelicals, something I will discuss later in this Introduction and in Chapter One.

18. Deidre Sklar, "Unearthing Kinesthesia: Groping among Cross-Cultural Models of the Senses in Performance," in *The Senses in Performance*, ed. Sally Banes and André Lepecki (New York: Routledge, 2007), 43.

19. Randall Balmer, *The Making of Evangelicalism* (Waco, TX: Baylor University Press, 2010), 2. For a lengthier definition, see Balmer, *Encyclopedia of Evangelicalism* (Waco, TX: Baylor University Press, 2004), 244–48.

20. In this respect, I am attempting a similar goal as do Shayne Lee and Phillip Luke Sinitiere in their book *Holy Mavericks*, in which they aim to demonstrate evangelicalism's "tremendous diversity and complexity." See *Holy Mavericks: Evangelical Innovators and the Spiritual Marketplace* (New York: New York University Press, 2009), 8.

21. Thanks to Ann Pellegrini for her thoughts on this "creative tension."

22. Vincent Crapanzano, *Serving the Word: Literalism in America from the Pulpit to the Bench* (New York: New Press, 2000), 181.

23. Quoted in Crapanzano, *Serving the Word*, 162. From Susan Harding, "The Gospel of Giving: The Narrative Structure of a Sacrificial Economy," in *Vocabularies of Public Life: Empirical Essays in Symbolic Structure*, ed. R. Wuthnow (London: Routledge, 1992), 39–56.

24. William E. Connolly, *Capitalism and Christianity, American Style* (Durham: Duke University Press, 2008), 56. Connolly employs the term *resonance machine* throughout his study. I will return to his arguments about the relationship between conservative evangelicalism and U.S. capitalism later in this chapter and again in the Coda.

25. Linda Kintz, *Between Jesus and the Market: The Emotions that Matter in Right-Wing America* (Durham: Duke University Press, 1997), 6–7. Certainly this familiarity can also be used for less productive, even destructive, purposes, something I also address in this book.

26. Stephen M. Hoover, "The Cross at Willow Creek: Seeker Religion and the Contemporary Marketplace," in *Religion and Popular Culture in America*, ed. Bruce David Forbes and Jeffrey H. Mahan (Berkeley: University of California Press, 2000), 147.

27. Ibid.

28. Significantly, Western scholars today seem more willing to accept a symbiotic relationship between popular culture and religious belief when it concerns non-Western religious theater, readily acknowledging that popular images and performances function as a vital part of religious traditions like Buddhism and Hinduism. One reason for this may be because Western scholars envision Eastern religions as free of these very Western socio-cultural binaries. Phillip Zarrilli raises a related point at the beginning of *Psychophysical Acting: An Intercultural Approach after Stanislavski* (London: Routledge, 2009), 5–6.

29. Just a few examples include Bruce L. Shelley and Marshall Shelley, *The Consumer Church: Can Evangelicals Win the World Without Losing Their Souls?* (Downers Grove, IL: InterVarsity Press, 1992); Miles, *Seeing and Believing;* Kintz, *Between Jesus and the Market; Media, Culture, and the Religious Right,* ed. Linda Kintz and Julia Lesage (Minneapolis: University of Minnesota Press, 1998); David Morgan, *Visual Piety* (Berkeley: University of California Press, 1998); Colleen McDannell, *Material Christianity: Religion and Popular Culture in America* (New Haven: Yale University Press, 1998); *Religion and Popular Culture in America,* ed. Bruce David Forbes and Jeffrey H. Mahan (Berkeley: University of California Press, 2000); Amy Johnson Frykholm, *Rapture Culture:* Left Behind *in Evangelical America* (Oxford: Oxford University Press, 2004); Randall Balmer, *Mine Eyes Have Seen the Glory: A Journey into the Evangelical Subculture in America* (Oxford: Oxford University Press, 1989; 4th ed., 2006); David Morgan, *The Lure of Images: A History of Religion and Visual Media in America* (London: Routledge, 2007); *Understanding Evangelical Media: The Changing Face of Christian Communication,* ed. Quentin Schultze and Robert Woods Jr. (Downers Grove, IL: InterVarsity Press, 2008); David W. Stowe, *No Sympathy for the Devil: Christian Pop Music and the Transformation of American Evangelicalism* (Chapel Hill: University of North Carolina Press, 2011).

30. In Chapter Six I discuss how critics of large, multimedia churches, commonly called *megachurches,* often raise this very issue.

31. Heather Hendershot, *Shaking the World for Jesus: Media and Conservative Evangelical Culture* (Chicago: University of Chicago Press, 2004), 1.

32. D. G. Hart, *That Old-Time Religion in Modern America: Evangelical Protestantism in the Twentieth Century* (Chicago: Ivan R. Dee, 2002), 175.

33. Nathan Hatch writes that the expansion and reshaping of evangelicalism in nineteenth-century America happened through "common people who moulded it in their own image and who threw themselves into expanding its influence." Hatch, *The Democratization of American Christianity* (New Haven: Yale University Press, 1989), 9.

34. Ibid.

35. For work on early nineteenth-century evangelical publishing, see David Paul Nord, "The Evangelical Origins of Mass Media in America, 1815–1835," *Journalism Monographs,* no. 88 (May 1984): 1–30; *Faith in Reading: Religious Publishing and the Birth of Mass Media in America* (New York: Oxford University Press, 2004). Hatch discusses twentieth-century evangelical radio broadcasting in *Democratization of American Christianity,* 217.

36. Hatch, *Democratization of American Christianity,* 210.

37. Exceptions certainly exist, among them Dox, "Willing Sustenance of Belief"; Timothy Beal, *Roadside Religion: In Search of the Sacred, the Strange, and the Substance of Faith* (Boston: Beacon Press, 2005); Dorothy Chansky, "North American Passion Plays: 'The Greatest Story Ever Told' in the New Millennium," *TDR* 50, no. 4 (2006): 120–45; Kevin J. Wetmore Jr., "Intelligent Design (after Julie Taymor): Opposing Darwinism in The Crystal Cathedral's *Creation: Once Upon All Time,*" *Journal of Religion and Theatre* 6, no. 2 (Fall 2007): 124–39, http://www.athe.org/associations/12588/files/wetmore2.pdf;

and Jennifer Williams, "Acquire the Fire: Affect, Ideology, and Contagion in Evangelical Performance," *Journal of Religion and Theatre* 7, no. 1 (2008): 20–34, http://www.athe.org/associations/12588/files/Williams.pdf. See also John Fletcher's forthcoming book that examines evangelical outreach through the lens of activist performance: *Preaching to Convert: Evangelical Outreach and Performance Activism in a Secular Age* (Ann Arbor: University of Michigan Press, forthcoming). In addition, I would say an exception to this observation is Hell Houses, Christian-themed haunted houses that present images of "sin." Many scholars have published work on these performative events, such as Fletcher, "Tasteless as Hell," 313–30; Ann Pellegrini, "'Signaling Through the Flames': Hell House Performance and Structures of Religious Feeling," *American Quarterly* 59, no. 3 (2007): 911–35; and Kevin J. Wetmore Jr., "The Devil Is an Ass: Radical Evil Redefined as Ridiculous Evil from the English Renaissance to Contemporary Hollywood," *Journal of Religion and Theatre* 9, no. 1 (2010): 28–40, http://www.athe.org/associations/12588/files/Wetmore.pdf. I have also attended various conference presentations on Hell Houses and chaired a session devoted entirely to Hell Houses ("Highway to Hell House: Performing Those Damned Christian Identities in Local, National, and Virtual Venues") at The Association for Theatre in Higher Education's 2011 conference. Although I visited Hell Houses as part of my research, I do not examine these venues in this project.

38. There are some exceptions. For instance, Dorothy Chansky discusses this play in "North American Passion Plays," 120–45, and Claire Sponsler discusses American Passion plays generally, although not this one specifically, in Chapter Five of *Ritual Imports: Performing Medieval Drama in America* (Ithaca: Cornell University Press, 2004), 123–55. This and other contemporary Passion Plays (such as the annual play in Union City, New Jersey, that completed its ninety-eighth season in 2012) are more regularly covered by the mainstream press. For example, a piece about a Passion Play presented annually for the last two decades in Wauchula, Florida, recently appeared on the front page of the *New York Times:* Dan Barry, "A Passion Play Endures as a Seasonal Miracle," *New York Times*, 20 April 2011.

39. Joan R. Branham, "The Temple that Won't Quit: Constructing Sacred Space in Orlando's Holy Land Experience Theme Park," *Crosscurrents* 59, no. 3 (2009): 358–82; Burke O. Long, *Imagining the Holy Land: Maps, Models, and Fantasy Travels* (Bloomington: Indiana University Press, 2003), 70–87; Beal, Chapter Two of *Roadside Religion*, 46–70; Ronald Lukens-Bull and Mark Fafard, "(Re)Creating Israel in Christian Zionism," *Journal of Religion and Society* 9 (2007): 1–20, http://moses.creighton.edu/JRS/2007/2007-16.pdf.

40. The Pew Forum on Religion and Public Life, "Summary of Key Findings," http://religions.pewforum.org/reports.

41. The Pew Forum on Religion and Public Life, "Affiliations," http://religions.pewforum.org/affiliations. Historically Black Protestant Church statistics broke down as Baptist (4.4 percent), Methodist (0.6 percent), Nondenominational (<0.3 percent), Pentecostal (0.9 percent), Holiness (<0.3 percent), and Protestant nonspecific (0.5 percent).

42. Of those listed as unaffiliated, Atheists accounted for 1.6 percent and Agnostics 2.4 percent; 12.1 percent are listed as "Nothing in particular." For the complete breakdown of all affiliations, see The Pew Forum on Religion and Public Life, "Affiliations," http://religions.pewforum.org/affiliations.

43. Institute for the Study of American Evangelicals, "Defining Evangelicalism," http://isae.wheaton.edu/defining-evangelicalism/.

44. Institute for the Study of American Evangelicals, "Evangelicals and the End Times," http://isae.wheaton.edu/defining-evangelicalism/evangelicals-and-the-end-times/.

45. National Association of Evangelicals, "What is an Evangelical?" http://www.nae.net/church-and-faith-partners/what-is-an-evangelical.

46. As cited earlier, Balmer, *Making of Evangelicalism,* 2.

47. National Association of Evangelicals, "What is an Evangelical?" http://www.nae.net/church-and-faith-partners/what-is-an-evangelical.

48. Crapanzano, *Serving the Word,* 7.

49. Ibid., 63.

50. "They recognize that it is only through continual Bible study that they can enrich their understanding and, thereby, enrich their own lives." Crapanzano, *Serving the Word,* 71.

51. Hatch, *Democratization of American Christianity,* 5. As with popular culture, Hatch claims that this democratic Christianity distinguishes the United States from other industrialized democracies.

52. See Jonathan Sarna, *American Judaism: A History* (New Haven: Yale University Press, 2004); Sefton Temkin, *Isaac Mayer Wise: Shaping American Judaism* (Oxford: Oxford University Press, 1991); Max May, *Isaac Mayer Wise The Founder Of American Judaism: A Biography* (New York: Knickerbocker Press, 1916).

53. Harry Stout, *The Divine Dramatist: George Whitefield and the Rise of Modern Evangelicalism* (Grand Rapids, MI: William Eerdmans, 1991), xx.

54. Ibid., xiv. I will discuss the popularity of the lay preacher and congregational leader in greater detail in Chapter Six when I analyze megachurches.

55. Hatch, *Democratization of American Christianity,* 6.

56. Ibid., 7.

57. I address this issue in more depth as part of my analysis of the "Great Passion Play" of Eureka Springs in Chapter Four.

58. Hatch, *Democratization of American Christianity,* 4. Hatch argues that this form of religious populism, which reflects ordinary people and is led by "the charisma of democratic movement-builders, remains among the oldest and deepest impulses in American life" (5).

59. Wade Clark Roof, *A Generation of Seekers: The Religion of the Baby Boom Generation* (San Francisco: HarperCollins, 1993), 67.

60. Christian Smith, *American Evangelicalism: Embattled and Thriving* (Chicago: University of Chicago Press, 1998), 24. Smith's analysis is based upon data collected over a fifteen-month period from 1995 to 1996. His team used a variety of research methods, including "semistructured, two-hour, face-to-face interviews with 130 churchgoing Protestants" in six states across the nation, a random telephone survey chosen from all Americans, further in-depth face-to-face interviews with 178 evangelical Christians from twenty-three different states, and various other interviews and follow-up surveys. Smith outlines his "extensive, multimethod data-gathering effort" on page 17 of *American Evangelicalism.*

61. Hatch writes, "Believing they have little reason to trust scholars and experts to clarify important religious and ethical issues, religious populists spend their time rallying the faithful and inviting them to arbitrate complicated religious and moral questions for themselves. In this sense, the people continue to serve as custodians of their own beliefs, communicating them in understandable terms." *Democratization of American Christianity,* 218.

62. Connolly, *Capitalism and Christianity,* 47.

63. Bethany Moreton, *To Serve God and Wal-Mart: The Making of Christian Free Enterprise* (Cambridge: Harvard University Press, 2009), 250. Regent University's mission statement reads, "Regent University is one of the nation's leading academic centers for Christian thought and action, with a multitude of graduate and undergraduate pro-

grams available worldwide. Our academic standards are high and our programs rigorous, but what sets Regent apart is our mission to prepare capable men and women to excel both in mind and spirit. Our students, faculty and administrators share a calling, founded on Biblical principles, to make a significant difference in our world." Regent University, "About Us," http://www.regent.edu/about_us/.

64. Ibid., 160, 250.

65. Connolly, *Capitalism and Christianity,* 109. Moreton argues that for a certain Christian constituency, "faith in God and faith in the market grew in tandem, aided by a generous government and an organized, corporate-funded grassroots movement for Christian free enterprise. . . . Although free-market economic theories captured the hearts and minds of elite policymakers in the later twentieth century, the animating spirit of Christian free enterprise shaped the outcome." *To Serve God and Wal-Mart,* 5. For an interesting look at the relationship between contemporary U.S. evangelicalism and economics, see Robert E. Nelson, *Economics As Religion: From Samuelson to the Chicago School and Beyond* (University Park: Pennsylvania State University Press, 2001).

66. Crapanzano, *Serving the Word,* 338.

67. Ibid., 33. This issue is related to liberal secularism and its own ties to a Protestant worldview, something I briefly discuss in the Coda. See also Janet R. Jakobsen and Ann Pellegrini, "World Secularisms at the Millennium: Introduction," *Social Text* 64 (2000): 1–27, and *Secularisms,* ed. Jakobsen and Ann Pellegrini (Durham: Duke University Press, 2008); Ann Pellegrini, "Feeling Secular," *Women and Performance: A Journal of Feminist Theory* 19, no. 2 (2009): 205–18.

68. Crapanzano also notes "a parallel between the hero in a world destined by God and 'America' as it was conceived of in nineteenth-century Protestant historical consciousness." *Serving the Word,* 358, note 5.

69. Stout, *Divine Dramatist,* xvi.

70. Stout writes, "Like no preacher before, and perhaps since, he demonstrated that the passions *could* be as effective an anchor of evangelical preaching as the intellect. Beyond that, a passion-based ministry was able to compete with the growing range of goods and services in the public square." *Divine Dramatist,* xx, original emphasis.

71. Smith writes, "Contemporary evangelicalism inhabits a pluralistic, competitive religious economy, on which it has very successfully capitalized. . . . Evangelicalism exhibits a tremendous fluidity with which it generates entrepreneurial leaders who promote an immense variety of religious products." *American Evangelicalism,* 86.

72. Ibid., 43; as quoted, 44.

73. Frykholm discusses the significance of daily prayer among the *Left Behind* readers she interviewed: "Popular among readers I interviewed are texts like *One Year Bible* and *Daily Bread.* These texts organize the Bible into short passages that provide structure for the significant Protestant practice of 'daily devotions.' . . . By reading the Bible day after day, year after year, readers strive to intertwine the Bible with their everyday lives. They memorize certain verses or passages that they can repeat to themselves as forms of prayer in times of crisis or need. Biblical words take root in thought and speech." *Rapture Culture,* 110. Also, the websites for many of the venues I analyze offer daily devotions,for example, Holy Land Experience, "Daily Devotion," http://www.holylandexperience.com/resources/daily_devotion.html and Answers in Genesis, "Devotions," http://www.answersingenesis.org/devotions/devotions.asp. All of the venues also sell a variety of daily devotional resources.

74. Kintz, *Between Jesus and the Market,* 33. Frykholm suggests something similar about the impact of daily Bible study: "The words of the Bible become ingrained in readers' minds and very often sprinkled into speech. Readers use biblical texts to frame

and understand their everyday lives and to guide particular actions." *Rapture Culture,* 111.

75. This is directly related to the mode of biblical interpretation that Crapanzano describes: "Most evangelicals . . . insist that the act of interpreting their experiences through Scripture actually changes the way they experience and even perceive the world. . . . With this profound cognitive, emotional, and spiritual reorientation comes the transformative role of interpretation through Scripture of experience. In evangelical terms, the reborn have surrendered to the Word and are being sanctified. In philosophical terms, the interpretation of experience is immediately realized in the experience itself, at least in its articulation." Crapanzano, *Serving the Word,* 123.

76. Kintz, *Between Jesus and the Market,* 33. Crapanzano discusses the sensual language that some evangelicals use to describe their experiences with scripture. One man he interviewed remarks, "I remember reading the New Testament and finding how sweet its words were, how delicious, how soothing, how comforting. . . . Now I am chewing on things that I used to love, and I spit them out and say they taste horrible. And I chew on other stuff that I used to hate, and now it tastes wonderful. It's the Word of God that did that." *Serving the Word,* 114.

77. Naomi Rokotnitz, "'It is required/You do awake your faith': Learning To Trust the Body Through Performing *The Winter's Tale,*" in *Performance and Cognition: Theatre Studies and the Cognitive Turn,* ed. Bruce McConachie and F. Elizabeth Hart (New York: Routledge, 2006), 140.

78. For an overview of cognitive theory and its impact on philosophical inquiry, see Evan Thompson, *Mind In Life: Biology, Phenomenology, and the Sciences of the Mind* (Cambridge: Harvard University Press, 2007), and Shaun Gallagher and Dan Zahavi, *The Phenomenological Mind: An Introduction to Philosophy of Mind and Cognitive Science* (London: Routledge, 2008).

79. Hart, *That Old-Time Religion,* 189.

80. Kintz maintains that "the charismatic religions and regional cultural differences of the American South, Midwest, and West have never fit comfortably into a European model that saw reason to be opposed to feeling in a binary that privileged the unemotional, supposedly objective perspective. . . . In part because of secular analyses that have too often coded feeling and spirituality as irrational and feminized, religious conservatism and its understanding of media have been able to appropriate feeling in the interests of masculine privilege in a way that often leaves their secular critics unable to understand quite what happened. Part of what happened is that absolutist Christianity has situated meaning in the heart of Christ rather than the head of Man, continuing a rhetorical tradition that has long been a part of American religious discourse." Although she situates this relationship between emotion and reason as part of American religious culture, she still claims that it resides in "an imaginative space too many academics seem unable to enter," a space she associates with small-town America. *Between Jesus and the Market,* 18, 20.

81. In fact, in my Coda I specifically address the relationships between certain political strategies and U.S. evangelical practices.

82. The authors of *Religion and the Culture Wars* argue that the culture wars conflict is distinctly religio-political in nature, with the Christian Right located principally among evangelicals. See John Clifford Green, James L. Guth, Corwin E. Smidt, and Lyman A. Kellstedt, *Religion and the Culture Wars: Dispatches from the Front* (Lanham, NY: Rowman and Littlefield, 1991), 2. For the term *culture wars,* see James Davidson Hunter, *Culture Wars* (New York: Basic Books, 1991).

83. Kintz, *Between Jesus and the Market,* 55. Lawrence Grossberg, *We Gotta Get*

Out of This Place: Popular Conservatism and Postmodern Culture (New York: Routledge, 1992).

84. Kintz, *Between Jesus and the Market,* 61. Here she is quoting Grossberg, *We Gotta Get Out of This Place,* 86.

85. Kupfer, "Introduction," 8. For more complete discussions of these trends in Passion imagery, see Fulton, *From Judgment to Passion;* Paul Binski, *Becket's Crown: Art and Imagination in Gothic England, 1170–1350* (New Haven: Yale University Press, 2004); *The Broken Body: Passion Devotion in Late Medieval Culture,* ed. Alasdair MacDonald, Bernhard Ridderbos, and R. M. Schlusemann (Groningen: Egbert Forsten, 1998); Sarah Beckwith, *Christ's Body: Identity, Culture and Society in Late Medieval Writings* (London: Routledge, 1993).

86. Sarah McNamer, *Affective Meditation and the Invention of Medieval Compassion* (Philadelphia: University of Pennsylvania Press, 2010), 12.

87. Ibid., 47–50.

88. David Morgan, "Catholic Visual Piety and *The Passion of the Christ,*" in *Re-Viewing The Passion: Mel Gibson's Film and Its Critics,* ed. S. Brent Plate (New York: Palgrave Macmillan, 2004), 85. Related points are made in essays in the collections and journal issues devoted to Gibson's film that I cite in note 9.

89. Taylor, "Offense of Flesh," 140.

90. Jill Stevenson, *Performance, Cognitive Theory, and Devotional Culture: Sensual Piety in Late Medieval York* (New York: Palgrave, 2010), 151–63; "The Material Bodies of Medieval Religious Performance in England," *Material Religion: The Journal of Objects, Art, and Belief* 2, no. 2 (2006): 204–32.

91. For example, U.S. evangelicalism operates through a model of embodied perception akin to the models outlined in the most prevalent medieval perceptual theories, both of which are supported by research in cognitive theory. Work on medieval theories of perception and its impact on devotion includes Robert Scribner, "Popular Piety and Modes of Visual Perception in Late Medieval and Reformation Germany," *Journal of Religious History* 15 (1989): 448–69; Michael Camille, "Before the Gaze: The Internal Senses and Late Medieval Practices of Seeing," in *Visuality Before and Beyond the Renaissance,* ed. Robert S. Nelson (Cambridge: Cambridge University Press, 2000), 197–223; Suzannah. Biernoff, *Sight and Embodiment in the Middle Ages* (New York: Palgrave, 2002); Patricia Cox Miller, "Visceral Seeing: The Holy Body in Late Ancient Christianity," *Journal of Early Christian Studies* 12, no. 4 (2004): 391–411; Suzannah Biernoff, "Carnal Relations: Embodied Sight in Merleau-Ponty, Roger Bacon and St Francis," *Journal of Visual Culture* 4, no. 1 (2005): 39–52. I discuss the similarities between medieval and cognitive theory models of perception in *Performance, Cognitive Theory, and Devotional Culture,* 15–44.

92. Just a few examples include Gail McMurray Gibson, *The Theater of Devotion: East Anglian Drama and Society in the Late Middle Ages* (Chicago: University of Chicago Press, 1989); Hans Belting, *The Image and Its Public in the Middle Ages: Form and Function of Early Paintings of the Passion,* trans. M. Bartusis and R. Meyer (New Rochelle, NY: Caratzas, 1990); Eamon Duffy, *The Stripping of the Altars: Traditional Religion in England, 1400–1580* (New Haven: Yale University Press, 1992); Corine Schleif, "Hands That Appoint, Anoint and Ally: Late Medieval Donor Strategies for Appropriating Approbation Through Painting," *Art History* 16, no. 1 (March 1993): 1–32; Henk Van Os, *The Art of Devotion in the Late Middle Ages in Europe, 1300–1500,* trans. Michael Hoyle (Princeton: Princeton University Press, 1995); Seth Lerer, "'Representyd now in yower syght': The Culture of Spectatorship in Late-Fifteenth-Century England," in *Bodies and Disciplines: Intersections of Literature and History in Fifteenth-Century En-*

gland, ed. Barbara Hanawalt and David Wallace (Minneapolis: University of Minnesota Press, 1996), 29–62; Claire Sponsler, *Drama and Resistance: Bodies, Goods, and Theatricality in Late Medieval England* (Minneapolis: University of Minnesota Press, 1997); Brian Spencer, *Pilgrim Souvenirs and Secular Badges* (London: Stationery Office, 1998); Katherine French, *The People of the Parish: Community Life in a Late Medieval English Diocese* (Philadelphia: University of Pennsylvania Press, 2001); Sarah Beckwith, *Signifying God: Social Relation and Symbolic Act in the York Corpus Christi Plays* (Chicago: University of Chicago Press, 2001); Mark Amsler, "Affective Literacy: Gestures of Reading in the Later Middle Ages," *Essays in Medieval Studies* 18 (2001): 83–110; Victor I. Scherb, *Staging Faith: East Anglian Drama in the Later Middle Ages* (Madison: Fairleigh Dickinson University Press, 2001); Kathleen Kamerick, *Popular Piety and Art in the Late Middle Ages: Image Worship and Idolatry in England, 1350–1500* (New York: Palgrave, 2002); Richard Marks, "An Age of Consumption: Art for England c. 1400–1547," in *Gothic Art for England, 1400–1547*, ed. Richard Marks and Paul Williamson (London: V&A Publications, 2003), 12–25; Eamon Duffy, "Late Medieval Religion," in *Gothic Art for England, 1400–1547*, ed. Richard Marks and Paul Williamson (London: V&A Publications, 2003), 56–67; Herbert L. Kessler, *Seeing Medieval Art* (Ontario: Broadview Press, 2004); Jeffrey F. Hamburger, *The Visual and the Visionary: Art and Female Spirituality in Late Medieval Germany* (New York: Zone, 1998); Susan Foister, "Private Devotion," in *Gothic Art for England, 1400–1547*, ed. Richard Marks and Paul Williamson (London: V&A Publications, 2003), 334–36; Eamon Duffy, *Marking the Hours: English People and Their Prayers, 1240–1570* (New Haven: Yale University Press, 2006); Sarah Rees Jones and Felicity Riddy, "The Bolton Hours of York: Female Domesticity, Piety and the Public Sphere," in *Household, Women and Christianities in Late Antiquity and the Middle Ages,* ed. Anneke B. Mulder-Bakke and Jocelyn Wogan-Browne (Turnhout: Brepols, 2006), 215–60; Pamela King, *The York Mystery Cycle and the Worship of the City* (Cambridge: D. S. Brewer, 2006); Jessica Brantley, *Reading in the Wilderness: Private Devotion and Public Performance in Late Medieval England* (Chicago: University of Chicago Press, 2007); Sarah Stanbury, *The Visual Object of Desire in Late Medieval England* (Philadelphia: University of Pennsylvania Press, 2008).

93. Frykholm, *Rapture Culture,* 179.

94. Ibid.

95. I discuss these practices throughout *Performance, Cognitive Theory, and Devotional Culture,* especially on pages 45–113. Also, see the many sources I list in note 92 above.

96. Frykholm, *Rapture Culture,* 40.

97. Ibid., 102.

98. Another notable example is the website GodTube, a Christian-oriented version of YouTube. The description on GodTube's homepage is very evangelically minded: "Godtube.com is a video sharing platform offering online Christian videos with faith-based, family friendly content. Popular video sections on GodTube include; Christian bands and singers in Christian music videos, Christian comedians, funny video clips, cute videos featuring kids and animals, inspirational videos. Be inspired in your walk with Jesus Christ and grow in your knowledge of the Bible with videos highlighting Bible verses by topic." GodTube, "Homepage," http://www.godtube.com/.

99. I am inspired by work like Nicole Klan's "Margery Kempe and Pentecostalism," *Religion and Literature* 42, nos. 1–2 (2010): 163–84, and other essays in this journal issue, for their attempts to demonstrate the ways in which medieval studies offers us a productive point of contact and, more significantly, a responsible language for seriously and critically investigating contemporary religion.

100. Anne Clark, "Why All the Fuss about the Mind? A Medievalist's Perspective on

Cognitive Theory," in *History in the Comic Mode: Medieval Communities and the Matter of Person*, ed. Rachel Fulton and Bruce Holsinger (New York: Columbia University Press, 2007), 170–81.

101. Rebecca Schneider, *Performing Remains: Art and War in Times of Theatrical Reenactment* (London: Routledge, 2011), 36.

102. Ibid., 35.

103. Carolyn Dinshaw, *Getting Medieval: Sexualities and Communities, Pre- and Postmodern* (Durham: Duke University Press, 1999), 54.

104. Schneider theorizes "the body as an archive." *Performing Remains*, 37.

105. Thanks to Ann Pellegrini for pointing out this connection.

106. Shelley and Shelley, *Consumer Church*, 14–16; Fletcher, "Tasteless as Hell," 314–16.

107. Hendershot, *Shaking the World for Jesus*, 3–4, 8.

108. Dox, "Willing Sustenance of Belief," 43.

109. Zarrilli, *Psychophysical Acting*.

110. Analyzing prayers as experiences, Fulton attempts to "use" medieval prayers herself as one mode of inquiry. She writes, "It is extremely difficult, if not impossible, to handle such artifacts as prayers without experiencing something of their intended effect. Some readers may find this unsettling, not what they are used to in reading an academic article." Fulton, "Praying with Anselm at Admont: A Meditation on Practice," *Speculum* 81, no. 3 (2006): 707.

111. Beal, *Roadside Religion*, 12. See also Robert Orsi's related claims about how religion is studied and engaged by secular academics. Orsi, "Snakes Alive: Religious Studies between Heaven and Earth," in *Between Heaven and Earth: The Religious Worlds People Make and the Scholars Who Study Them* (Princeton: Princeton University Press, 2005), 177–204.

112. Beal, *Roadside Religion*, 12–13.

Chapter 1

1. Simon Shepherd, *Theatre, Body and Pleasure* (London: Routledge, 2006), 36–37.

2. Ibid., 85.

3. Ibid., 94–95.

4. Ibid., 85.

5. Jill Stevenson, *Performance, Cognitive Theory, and Devotional Culture: Sensual Piety in Late Medieval York* (New York: Palgrave, 2010).

6. Jennifer Garrison, "Mediated Piety: Eucharistic Theology and Lay Devotion in Robert Mannyng's *Handlyng Synne*," *Speculum* 85, no. 4 (2010): 899.

7. Ibid., 895.

8. Ibid., 895–96.

9. Ibid., 896.

10. Ibid.

11. Shepherd, *Theatre*, 37. Although I think Mannyng's choice here is purposeful, Shepherd does note that "there might not be conscious intention on the part of the makers of the work. They may be unconsciously operating within their own ideological constraints as to what is practical or proper" (37).

12. Cathy Turner and Synne K. Behrndt, *Dramaturgy and Performance* (New York: Palgrave Macmillan, 2008), 36.

13. As Sarah McNamer writes, "This horizon of expectations not only operates in the production of individual texts; new literary genres arise out of its hidden im-

peratives." *Affective Meditation and the Invention of Medieval Compassion* (Philadelphia: University of Pennsylvania Press, 2010), 61. Here McNamer is using a concept developed by Hans Robert Jauss in *Toward an Aesthetic of Reception* (Minneapolis: Minnesota University Press, 1982), 76–109.

14. Turner and Behrndt, *Dramaturgy and Performance*, 36.

15. Evan Thompson, *Mind In Life: Biology, Phenomenology, and the Sciences of the Mind* (Cambridge: Harvard University Press, 2007), 358. Francisco J. Varela first outlined this approach in "Neurophenomenology: A Methodological Remedy for the Hard Problem," *Journal of Consciousness Studies* 3 (1996): 330–50. As Shaun Gallagher and Dan Zahavi explain, *neurophenomenology*, as defined by Varela, originally signified "an approach to the neuroscience of consciousness that incorporates the phenomenological methodology outlined in the Husserlian tradition. In recent years, however, the term has been used in a much looser sense to signify any kind of appeal to first-person data in combination with data from neuroscience." *The Phenomenological Mind: An Introduction to Philosophy of Mind and Cognitive Science* (London: Routledge, 2008), 41. They also explain various changes that have motivated "a reconsideration of phenomenology as a philosophical-scientific approach," among these the notion of "embodied cognition," which took hold in the 1990s, and the progress in neuroscience (5).

16. Thompson, *Mind In Life*, 14.

17. Mark Johnson, *The Meaning of the Body: Aesthetics of Human Understanding* (Chicago: University of Chicago Press, 2008), xi.

18. Ibid., ix.

19. Mark Johnson, *The Body in the Mind* (Chicago: University of Chicago Press, 1987), 19, 205; Vittorio Gallese, "Embodied Simulation: From Neurons to Phenomenal Experience," *Phenomenology and the Cognitive Sciences* 4, no. 1 (2005): 23–48.

20. Johnson, *Body in the Mind*, 20. Here Johnson is using Ulric Neisser's definition of schema.

21. Ibid., 21.

22. Ibid., 175.

23. Tobin Nellhaus, "Performance Strategies, Image Schemas, and Communication Frameworks," in *Performance and Cognition: Theatre Studies and the Cognitive Turn*, ed. Bruce McConachie and F. Elizabeth Hart (New York: Routledge, 2006), 83.

24. Ibid., 82.

25. Paul Soukup argues that the core tenets of evangelical theology—in particular the emphasis on the believer's personal relationship with God—have "consequences for communication, media use and media study." Soukup, "Considering a Catholic View of Evangelical Media," in *Understanding Evangelical Media: The Changing Face of Christian Communication*, ed. Quentin Schultze and Robert Woods Jr. (Downers Grove, IL: InterVarsity Press, 2008), 269.

26. Stephen M. Hoover, "The Cross at Willow Creek: Seeker Religion and the Contemporary Marketplace," in *Religion and Popular Culture in America*, ed. Bruce David Forbes and Jeffrey H. Mahan (Berkeley: University of California Press, 2000), 150.

27. Ibid., 150. Hoover describes these media as "tactile, visual, embodied, and 'effervescent'" (151).

28. One issue that sometimes creates friction between different evangelical denominations is the role of personal experience. Although Fundamentalists "strive for a personal relationship with Jesus," many are quite skeptical of religious practices—particularly those associated with Pentecostalism—that appear "to give greater credence to experience than to doctrine and the careful reading of Scripture." Vincent Crapanzano, *Serving the Word: Literalism in America from the Pulpit to the Bench* (New York: New Press, 2000), 146, 41. While most evangelicals are suspicious of religious

experiences that are not guided and cultivated through Bible-based spiritual approaches, I will argue that the media forms I examine in this study suggest a more ready acceptance of personal faith experiences by less Fundamentalist evangelicals. Indeed, some of the venues I visited draw a more Pentecostal audience, and I discuss Pentecostalism in Chapter Two. In a sense then, evangelical dramaturgy is a reaction to both mainline Protestant and Fundamentalist evangelical attitudes concerning the authority of individual, somatic religious experience.

29. Cloud Ten Pictures, "Plans for Big Budget Left Behind Remake," 13 October 2010, http://www.cloudtenpictures.com/site2/news_article.php?id=42.

30. Left Behind, "General FAQ," http://www.leftbehind.com/07_media_pr/faq_general.asp.

31. Cloud Ten Pictures, "Plans for Big Budget Left Behind Remake," 13 October 2010, http://www.cloudtenpictures.com/site2/news_article.php?id=42.

32. Cloud Ten Pictures: Left Behind The Next Film, "Homepage," http://leftbehind4.com/.

33. Left Behind, "Author's Corner: Jerry B. Jenkins," http://www.leftbehind.com/03_authors_testimonials/authors_corner.asp.

34. Left Behind, "Author's Corner: Dr. Tim LaHaye," http://www.leftbehind.com/03_authors_testimonials/bio_lahaye.asp. Heather Hendershot explains that LaHaye and his wife Beverly have been leading figures in the Moral Majority and are "known among politically involved evangelicals for supporting laws that ban pornography, homosexuality, and abortion" and for their efforts "to establish 'decency standards' for the entertainment industries." However, she also notes that LaHaye has been able to keep this "fringe" identity somewhat separate from the book series: "LaHaye has succeeded . . . in mainstreaming his ideas and dulling their conspiracy theory edges. Secular reviewers have not identified LaHaye as part of a 'lunatic fringe.'" Hendershot, *Shaking the World for Jesus: Media and Conservative Evangelical Culture* (Chicago: University of Chicago Press, 2004), 191–92.

35. Left Behind, "End Times," http://www.leftbehind.com/02_end_times/. According to the website, each week members receive *Interpreting the Signs*, an online newsletter featuring articles by Tim LaHaye, Jerry Jenkins, and other End Times scholars, as well as access to exclusive online message boards where members "can discuss these important issues with fellow Christians."

36. Recently, End Times theology briefly entered the mainstream spotlight—as it has, periodically, over the centuries. Harold Camping, a self-taught Bible scholar, predicted that 21 May 2011 would be Judgment Day. Those who subscribed to his prophecy started a media blitz. For example, in New York City signs appeared in subway cars and stations, and on street corners. In the weeks before 21 May, some believers came to New York to distribute Bibles at street fairs with many lingering in public spaces like Times Square and carrying signs announcing Judgment Day. On Friday, 20 May, local television stations carried stories about the movement. For a brief overview, see Ashley Parker, "Make My Bed? But You Say the World's Ending," *New York Times*, 20 May 2011. Not surprisingly, various performance venues and bars around the city planned Rapture-themed parties, such as "It's the End of the World! Rapture and Floating Cabaret" at Galapagos Art Space in Brooklyn. See also Laurie Essig's article in which she comments upon this recent Rapture phenomenon, "No Rapture, but the End Days Are Upon Us," *Chronicle of Higher Education*, 23 May 2011. In addition, a popular belief that the Mayan calendar indicates that 21 December 2012 is a kind of "Doomsday" has also increased interest in Apocalyptic prophecy.

37. Timothy Beal gives a brief overview of these in *Roadside Religion: In Search of the Sacred, the Strange, and the Substance of Faith* (Boston: Beacon Press, 2005), 65–66.

For a more detailed explanation, see Paul Boyer, *When Time Shall Be No More: Prophecy Belief in Modern American Culture* (Cambridge: Harvard University Press, 1992).

38. Beal, *Roadside Religion,* 65.

39. Boyer, *When Time Shall Be No More,* 88.

40. Post-tribs believe the Rapture will occur after the Tribulation, while pre-wrath theology argues "that the faithful will undergo the first part of the tribulation, inflicted by the Antichrist . . . but will not undergo the ultimate divine wrath and judgment on Earth." Beal, *Roadside Religion,* 65–66.

41. Tim LaHaye and Jerry B. Jenkins, *Left Behind: A Novel of the Earth's Last Days* (Carol Stream, IL: Tyndale House, 1995), 265. This is the first book in the series.

42. Ibid., 344.

43. Ibid., 187.

44. Mark Amsler, "Affective Literacy: Gestures of Reading in the Later Middle Ages," *Essays in Medieval Studies* 18 (2001): 83.

45. Ibid., 84.

46. Tyndale House, "Tyndale Repackages 'Left Behind' Titles for New Generation of Readers," 7 March 2011, http://mediacenter.tyndale.com/downloads/press_kits/LBRepackagePR.pdf.

47. Similar arguments about materiality could be made for readers accessing the book on their Kindles, Nook Readers, or iPads. In fact, those technologies may help to lower the barrier to entry for those readers who might otherwise be hesitant to read the books in public.

48. Linda Kintz, *Between Jesus and the Market: The Emotions that Matter in Right-Wing America* (Durham: Duke University Press, 1997), 7.

49. Kintz uses the notion of resonance in a specifically political way to interrogate the emotional appeal of "conservative cosmology." Although evangelical dramaturgy is not apolitical, as I discuss briefly at the end of this chapter and in more detail in subsequent chapters, I am expanding Kintz's definition beyond the exclusively political context she uses. *Between Jesus and the Market,* 6.

50. Ibid., 7.

51. Left Behind, "Products," http://www.leftbehind.com/01_products/browse.asp?section=Books.

52. Amy Johnson Frykholm discusses the prevalence of this throughout *Rapture Culture:* Left Behind *in Evangelical America* (Oxford: Oxford University Press, 2004).

53. Here I am referencing the concept of mattering that Kintz employs and that I mentioned in the Introduction. See Kintz, *Between Jesus and the Market,* 55–61.

54. Sarah Beckwith, *Christ's Body: Identity, Culture and Society in Late Medieval Writings* (London: Routledge, 1993), 49–50.

55. Donnalee Dox, "The Willing Sustenance of Belief: Religiosity and Mode of Performance," *Journal of Religion and Theatre* 8, no. 1 (2009): 30, http://www.athe.org/associations/12588/files/Dox.pdf.

56. Ibid. In another article on a related theme, Dox asserts, "The theological centrality of Christ's human body . . . posits the human body as an irreducible testament to divine *logos.* Hence, Aristotelian-influenced, post-Renaissance theories of representation, mimesis, theatricality, and postmodern performativity fall short of illuminating how medieval 'liturgical drama' was understood to work." "Ceremonial Embodiment: The Problem of 'Liturgical Drama,'" *Ecumenica* 3, no. 2 (2010): 38.

57. Translation and transcription reprinted in Nils Holger Petersen, "Devotion and Dramaticity in the *Bordesholmer Marienklage* (1476)," in *Dies est leticie: Essays on Chant in Honour of Janka Szendrei,* ed. David Hiley (Ottawa: Institute of Medieval Music, 2008), 416. Original Latin: "Incipit planctus deuotissimus beatissime Marie

virginis cum misericordissima et deuotissima nota. Planctum istum facit beata virgo Maria cum quattuor personis deuotis deuotissime bona sexta feria ante prandium in ecclesia ante chorum in loco aliquantum eleuato vel extra ecclesiam, si bona est aura. Planctus iste non est ludus nee ludibrium, sed est planctus et fletus et pia compassio Marie virginis gloriose. Et quandocunque fit a bonis et deuotis hominibus, in genere siue in specie valde prouocat homines circumstantes ad pium fletum et ad compassionem, sicut facit sermo deuotus bona sexta feria de passione domini nostri Jhesu Cristi." Transcription in Petersen, "Devotion and Dramaticity,"414–15. The original text is found in the manuscript Eel Universitatsbibliothek, Cod. Ms. Bord. 53, ff. lr–2r.

58. Petersen, "Devotion and Dramaticity," 422.

59. Ibid., 427.

60. Dox, "Willing Sustenance," 30.

61. Ibid., 30–31.

62. As defined by David Bebbington, crucicentrism is "a stress on the sacrifice of Jesus Christ on the cross as making possible the redemption of humanity." Quoted by National Association of Evangelicals, "What is an Evangelical?" http://www.nae.net/church-and-faith-partners/what-is-an-evangelical.

63. Dox, "Willing Sustenance," 31.

64. Beal, *Roadside Religion,* 41.

65. Doing so only underscores the fact that, as Erika Fischer-Lichte notes, "an absolute opposition between 'presence' and 'representation' is not sustainable." *The Transformative Power of Performance: A New Aesthetics,* trans. Saskya Iris Jain (2004; London: Routledge, 2008), 147.

66. Ibid., 148.

67. Ibid., 150.

68. Hoover, "Cross at Willow Creek," 156.

69. Rebecca Schneider, *Performing Remains: Art and War in Times of Theatrical Reenactment* (London: Routledge, 2011), 2, 9.

70. Ibid., 53.

71. Ibid., 3, 53.

72. Crapanzano, *Serving the Word,* 181.

73. Beal, *Roadside Religion,* 60.

74. Ibid., 67. This apocalyptic expectation is often deployed in the service of supersessionist or teleological biblical exegesis.

75. Melissa Gregg and Gregory J. Seigworth, "An Inventory of Shimmers," in *The Affect Theory Reader,* ed. Gregg and Seigworth (Durham: Duke University Press, 2010), 2.

76. Ibid., 1.

77. Rebecca Schneider discusses the "affected effects and after-effects" of reenactment and specifically mentions "the mutually disruptive energy of moments that are not yet past and yet are not entirely present either." She describes that energy as "an energy of affect's transmission." *Performing Remains: Art and War in Times of Theatrical Reenactment* (London: Routledge, 2001), 2, 15. I will discuss a related idea of energetic exchange in Chapter Two.

78. Gregg and Seigworth, "Inventory of Shimmers," 1.

79. Ruth Leys, "The Turn to Affect: A Critique," *Critical Inquiry* 37 (2011): 434, 443. She notes that many affect theorists, especially those using evidence from the neurosciences, share "a commitment to the idea that there is a disjunction or gap between the subject's affective processes and his or her cognition or knowledge of the objects that caused them. The result is that the body not only 'senses' and performs a kind of 'thinking' below the threshold of conscious recognition and meaning but . . . because

of the *speed* with which the autonomic, affective processes are said to occur, it does all this before the mind has time to intervene" (original emphasis). Leys, "Turn to Affect," 450.

80. Ibid., 458.

81. Sianne Ngai, *Ugly Feelings* (Cambridge: Harvard University Press, 2005), 27.

82. Ibid., 27–28.

83. Anna Gibbs, "After Affect: Sympathy, Synchrony, and Mimetic Communication," in *The Affect Theory Reader*, ed. Gregg and Seigworth (Durham: Duke University Press, 2010), 196.

84. Ibid.

85. McNamer, *Affective Meditation,* 13. The texts McNamer examines span from the mid-eleventh century through the mid-sixteenth century.

86. Ibid., 19.

87. Ibid., 30. About this same text, McNamer writes, "Rhapsodic momentum is clearly calculated to stir its performer's blood, quickening her pulse, generating a breathless intensity through its increasingly rapid exclamations as the events of the Passion approach their terrible climax" (30).

88. Ibid., 40.

89. Ibid. "Those who have not legitimately earned the title will be rejected at the moment of truth; those who have earned the title will be taken by the right hand, by Christ, and accepted as his bride." Ibid., 42.

90. Ibid., 52.

91. Ibid., 75.

92. Ibid., 53.

93. Frykholm, *Rapture Culture,* 146.

94. For a discussion of medieval consecration rites, see McNamer, *Affective Meditation,* 37–40.

95. Frykholm, *Rapture Culture,* 146.

96. LaHaye and Jenkins, *Left Behind,* 195–97.

97. Frykholm, *Rapture Culture,* 146–47.

98. Ibid., 147.

99. Andy Lavender, "Mise En Scène, Hypermediacy, and the Sensorium," in *Intermediality in Theatre and Performance,* ed. Freda Chapple and Chiel Kattenbelt (Amsterdam: Rodopi, 2006), 64.

100. Christian Smith, *American Evangelicalism: Embattled and Thriving* (Chicago: University of Chicago Press, 1998), 110.

101. Ibid., 116–17.

102. Ibid., 116.

103. As Smith explains, "Embedded in most versions of evangelical faith are the ideas that each individual must ultimately decide for themselves to follow God or not; that truly meaningful moral actions cannot be forced, but must come voluntarily from the heart; and that Christians ultimately can't make people who do not want to be Christians to act as if they were. . . . Furthermore, American individualism—which most evangelicals, we have seen, endorse—prescribes that individuals should not be coerced by social institutions, especially by the government, and particularly not on personal matters." *American Evangelicalism,* 211.

104. Ibid., 103.

105. Christian Smith explains how a group of young, mostly moderate Christian fundamentalist scholars and pastors, among them Billy Graham, "began to formulate a critique of their own fundamentalist subculture and a vision for its transformation." An important element of this "neo-evangelical" movement was engaged orthodoxy,

the conviction that believers could be "fully committed to maintaining and promoting confidently traditional, orthodox Protestant theology and belief, *while at the same time* becoming confidently and proactively engaged in the intellectual, cultural, social, and political life of the nation." *American Evangelicalism,* 9, 10, original emphasis.

106. Phillip Zarrilli, *Psychophysical Acting: An Intercultural Approach after Stanislavski* (London: Routledge, 2009), 49.

Chapter 2

1. Phillip Zarrilli, *Psychophysical Acting: An Intercultural Approach after Stanislavski* (London: Routledge, 2009).

2. Holy Land Experience, "About the Experience," http://www.holylandexperience.com/about/about.html.

3. ITEC Entertainment Corporation, "The ITEC Solution: The Holy Land Experience Project," http://www.itec.com/Portals/20/Skins/itec/pdf/solutions/2008_Holy_Land.pdf.

4. Ibid.

5. Zion's Hope, "The Ministry," http://www.zionshope.org/ZH_ministry.aspx.

6. Brad Flora, "The Holy Land Experience: Who Shall Inherit the Kingdom?" *News 21: A Journalism Initiative of the Carnegie and Knight Foundations,* 23 August 2007, http://newsinitiative.org/story/2007/08/23/the_holy_land_experience_who.

7. Flora, "Holy Land Experience." Powell resigned from HLE on 21 August 2007, just months after the merger and weeks after he was named CEO of the park. Consequently, "the resignation of Powell, who had been the only board member not directly related to Paul Crouch Sr., the network's founder and current president, consolidates full control of the park in TBN hands." Brad Flora, "Holy Land Experience Chief Resigns 10 Weeks into TBN Takeover," *News 21: A Journalism Initiative of the Carnegie and Knight Foundations,* 28 August 2007, http://newsinitiative.org/story/2007/08/28/holy_land_experience_chief_resigns.

8. Trinity Broadcasting Network, "Trinity Broadcasting Network Acquisition of 'Holy Land Experience' Theme Park Seeks to Change More Lives," Press Release, 9 June 2007, http://www.tbn.org/announcements/trinity-broadcasting-network-acquisition-of-holy-land-experience-theme-park-seeks-to-change-more-lives.

9. Joan Branham, "The Crucifixion and Ice Cream," *Newsweek,* 23 May 2008, http://www.newsweek.com/2008/05/22/the-crucifixion-and-ice-cream.html#.

10. Branham, "Crucifixion and Ice Cream."

11. This was the Mission Statement as of April 2012. Holy Land Experience, "Mission," http://www.holylandexperience.com/about/mission.html.

12. In addition, Branham explains that the park holds a large collection of Torah scrolls and that when it first opened certain segments of ancient Hebrew Torah scrolls were attached directly to walls around the park and sprayed with acrylic. TBN has since removed those scrolls. Branham, "The Temple that Won't Quit: Constructing Sacred Space in Orlando's Holy Land Experience Theme Park," *Crosscurrents* 59, no. 3 (2009): 373.

13. Holy Land Experience, "About the Experience," http://www.holylandexperience.com/about/about.html.

14. Ronald Lukens-Bull and Mark Fafard, "(Re)Creating Israel in Christian Zionism," *Journal of Religion and Society* 9 (2007): 11, http://moses.creighton.edu/JRS/2007/2007–16.pdf. This journal is published by the Kripke Center, an organization "dedicated to facilitating scholarly activity in the areas of religion and society. Special attention is given to promoting understanding between and among faith communities,

including especially Judaism, Christianity, and Islam. The Kripke Center's primary audience is the academic community, but its scholarship and services are available to all who seek them." Kripke Center, "Homepage," http://moses.creighton.edu/kripke/.

15. Timothy Beal, *Roadside Religion: In Search of the Sacred, the Strange, and the Substance of Faith* (Boston: Beacon Press, 2005), 67.

16. I discuss Holy Land recreations in greater detail in Chapter Four.

17. Stephen Di Benedetto, "Guiding Somatic Responses within Performative Structures: Contemporary Live Art and Sensorial Perception," in *The Senses in Performance*, ed. Sally Banes and André Lepecki (New York: Routledge, 2007), 133–34. Similarly, Rebecca Schneider suggests that observers at reenactments are, in a sense, participants and thus also engaged in the "temporal tangle" of these events. Rebecca Schneider, *Performing Remains: Art and War in Times of Theatrical Reenactment* (London: Routledge, 2011), 9–10.

18. Beal, *Roadside Religion*, 51.

19. I contacted Holy Land Experience directly to obtain demographic information about their guests, but they replied that they do not collect such information. I found the racial mix particularly interesting because all of the actors who portrayed Jesus in the many different shows that I saw at HLE (including film versions) were Caucasians. One even had long blond hair. This may reflect evangelical dramaturgy's use of popular culture imagery, in this case, certain recognizable Jesus tropes. For work on popular images of Jesus in U.S. Protestant culture, see David Morgan, *Visual Piety* (Berkeley: University of California Press, 1998).

20. Randall Balmer, *Encyclopedia of Evangelicalism* (Waco, TX: Baylor University Press, 2004), 533.

21. Ibid., 533–34. See also *Pentecostal Currents in American Protestantism*, ed. Edith L. Blumhofer, Russell P. Spittler, and Grant A. Wacker (Urbana: University of Illinois Press, 1999). The Institute for the Study of American Evangelicals also includes a page on Pentecostalism on its website. Institute for the Study of American Evangelicals, "Pentecostalism & the Charismatic Movement," http://isae.wheaton.edu/defining-evangelicalism/pentacostalism-and-the-charismatic-movement/.

22. Holy Land Experience, "Testimonials," http://www.holylandexperience.com/tickets/testimonials.html.

23. TripAdvisor.com, "Holy Land Experience," http://www.tripadvisor.com/Attraction_Review-g34515-d318444-Reviews-Holy_Land_Experience-Orlando_Florida.html. These numbers were recorded on 16 April 2012. All of the reviews I cite are transcribed exactly as they appear on the website, without corrections to grammar. They can be found on the TripAdvisor website listed by date.

24. This comment is from a review dated 12 January 2012. Of the 220 reviews, 20 rated it as "poor" and 39 as "terrible." In another negative review, this one dated 9 May 2011, the author complains, "the park is there to glorify TBN and its owners and not to give us a feel of the Holy Land as the title of the Park would suggest." Another review dated 19 February 2011 notes, "For me it bordered on disrespect," while another posted on 29 April 2011 argues, "If you want to worship a fake wall, the [*sic*, then] go. God wants us to worship him and only him." Another major complaint is poor customer service; however, this too is usually framed as an insult to Christian witnessing, as this review from 31 December 2010 argues: "The staff are at best indifferent and at worst obnoxious and unprofessional. If this is someone's initial exposure to Christianity and Christians they would be turned off. Very poor witnesses of the grace, love, and patience of Jesus! As A Christian I am embarrassed by this park." TripAdvisor.com, "Holy Land Experience," http://www.tripadvisor.com/Attraction_Review-g34515-d318444-Reviews-Holy_Land_Experience-Orlando_Florida.html#REVIEWS.

25. Schneider, *Performing Remains,* 104.

26. Ibid., 101.

27. Although the reenactments Schneider describes may not be officially or principally designed to cultivate the kind of re-experience I identify within evangelical dramaturgy, I do believe that Schneider's language allows for the possibility that some reenactors may have a more metaphysical sense of presence: "In affective engagement, many of them find reenactment to be, if not the thing itself (the past), somehow also *not not* the thing (the past), as it passes across their bodies in again-time." Schneider, *Performing Remains,* 8.

28. Zarrilli, *Psychophysical Acting,* 19–20.

29. Ibid., 29, 57.

30. I visited HLE on Friday, 28 May, and Saturday, 29 May, in 2010, which was Memorial Day weekend. The park was open from 10:00 a.m. to 6:00 p.m. on both days.

31. Bruce Holsinger, "Liturgy," in *Oxford Twenty-First Century Approaches to Literature: Middle English,* ed. Paul Strohm (Oxford: Oxford University Press, 2007), 298.

32. Donnalee Dox, "The Willing Sustenance of Belief: Religiosity and Mode of Performance," *Journal of Religion and Theatre* 8, no. 1 (2009): 41, http://www.athe.org/associations/12588/files/Dox.pdf.

33. Phillip Zarrilli, "An Enactive Approach to Understanding Acting," *Theatre Journal* 59, no. 4 (2007): 647.

34. Ibid., 636. This energetic exchange is related to what Erika Fischer-Lichte calls the "stream of magic." Fischer-Lichte, *The Transformative Power of Performance: A New Aesthetics,* trans. Saskya Iris Jain (2004; London: Routledge, 2008), 96–97. Fischer-Lichte also describes Eugenio Barba's observations about Eastern acting traditions, which are similar to Zarrilli's: "The 'stream of magic' communicated itself to Barba with a particular intensity at performances of Indian and far Eastern theatre forms, which he studied closely. In his discussions about performers he came to the conclusion that their techniques and practices served the purpose of generating energy in the performer, which then transferred to the spectator." *Transformative Power,* 97.

35. Zarrilli, "Enactive Approach," 645.

36. Alva Noë, *Action in Perception* (Cambridge: MIT Press, 2004), 135.

37. Zarrilli, "Enactive Approach," 645.

38. Ibid., 641.

39. Zarrilli, *Psychophysical Acting,* 21.

40. Ibid., 40.

41. Lukens-Bull and Fafard, "(Re)Creating Israel in Christian Zionism," 2.

42. Ibid., 6.

43. Although I could not find employment information with the same specificity on the current HLE website, Joan Branham notes that in 2008 the website's employment page read, "We are currently looking for qualified associates that demonstrate Christian characteristics to subordinates, peers, and management staff." Quoted in Branham, "Temple that Won't Quit," 381 n. 13. Although he does not provide evidence for this, John D. Spalding also writes, "Everyone who works at Holy Land Experience is a born-again Christian." Spalding, "Authentic Replica: My Holy Land Experience," *Christian Century* 119, no. 14 (2002), accessed through Academic OneFile, http://slb.mmm.edu:2138/ps/i.do?id=GALE%7CA89580851&v=2.1&u=nysl_me_mmcl&it=r&p=AONE&sw=w.

44. Lukens-Bull and Fafard, "(Re)Creating Israel," 6.

45. Quoted in Lukens-Bull and Fafard, "(Re)Creating Israel," 7.

46. As Robert P. Crease and John Lutterbie explain, "what technique provides is not an obstacle to the expression of presence, but the controlled release of energy that gives

the illusion of presence, the closest that we can get to the pure energy of being." Crease and Lutterbie, "Technique," in *Staging Philosophy: Intersections of Theater, Performance, and Philosophy,* ed. David Krasner and David Z. Saltz (Ann Arbor: University of Michigan Press, 2006), 174.

47. Zarrilli describes "acting as enquiry" and writes, "Enquiry is a process of exploration born out of intellectual and aesthetic curiosity." Although he is primarily speaking about acting as the actor's enquiry, given his larger theory I would extend this to include the audience as well. *Psychophysical Acting,* 5–6.

48. Anna Gibbs, "After Affect: Sympathy, Synchrony, and Mimetic Communication," in *The Affect Theory Reader,* ed. Melissa Gregg and Gregory J. Seigworth (Durham: Duke University Press, 2010), 194.

49. Fischer-Lichte, *Transformative Power,* 62.

50. Ibid., 63.

51. Jennifer Fisher writes, "A haptic aesthetic engages knowledge emergent in proximity, undeferred presence, and the in-between spaces of becoming." Fisher, "Tangible Acts: Touch Performances," in *The Senses in Performance,* ed. Sally Banes and André Lepecki (New York: Routledge, 2007), 176.

52. Ibid., 174.

53. Ibid.

54. Lukens-Bull and Fafard pull this quote from the "Testimonials" page on the HLE website. See Lukens-Bull and Fafard, "(Re)Creating Israel," 2.

55. Although Pentecostals refer to many Bible verses for evidence of the gifts of the Spirit, see especially the Book of Acts 1:8 and Chapters 2, 8, and 10, as well as Chapters 12–14 of Paul's first Letter to the Corinthians.

56. Balmer, *Encyclopedia of Evangelicalism,* 533. Glossolalia, or speaking in tongues, is one mark of this Second baptism, and some say it is the "initial physical evidence" that a person has been baptized in the Holy Spirit. As one Assemblies of God minister explains, "We do not encourage people to seek tongues. We encourage them to seek God and to seek the power of the Holy Spirit for witnessing. Tongues is just a byproduct of that." As quoted in Tim Townsend, "Pentecostals Split over 'Tongues,'" *St. Louis Post-Dispatch,* 1 November 2009.

57. Zarrilli, *Psychophysical Acting,* 84.

58. Bruce McConachie, "Doing Things with Image Schemas: The Cognitive Turn in Theatre Studies and the Problem of Experience for Historians," *Theatre Journal* 53, no. 4 (2001): 583.

59. Lukens-Bull and Fafard, "(Re)Creating Israel," 12.

60. Zarrilli discusses how culture shapes our body and, thus, our beliefs and values. Zarrilli, *Psychophysical Acting,* 23.

61. Di Benedetto, "Guiding Somatic Responses," 128.

62. Zarrilli, *Psychophysical Acting,* 42.

Chapter 3

1. Claire Sponsler, *Ritual Imports: Performing Medieval Drama in America* (Ithaca: Cornell University Press, 2004), 138.

2. Ibid., 147.

3. Marcus Bull writes that medievalism involves "running different parts of the past together and getting things mixed up." *Thinking Medieval* (New York: Palgrave, 2005), 9. Also relevant here is Umberto Eco's suggestion that "the Middle Ages have never been reconstructed from scratch: We have always mended or patched them up,

as something in which we still live." *Travels in Hyperreality: Essays* (San Diego: Harcourt Brace Jovanovich, 1986), 67–68.

4. Sponsler, *Ritual Imports*, 149.

5. Ibid.

6. Ibid., 150.

7. Ibid.

8. Ibid., 155.

9. *Via Dolorosa* translates to "Way of Grief," but the term is also used to refer to the "Way of the Cross," the path that Jesus walked when carrying his cross to his crucifixion on Golgotha.

10. I will reference various YouTube clips of "Behold the Lamb" near the end of this chapter. For now, I simply wish to note that in all of these videos the physical relationship between audience and actors looks very similar to what I have described here.

11. Timothy Beal, *Roadside Religion: In Search of the Sacred, the Strange, and the Substance of Faith* (Boston: Beacon Press, 2005), 58.

12. I discuss Praise Music at length in Chapter Six.

13. Anna Gibbs, "After Affect: Sympathy, Synchrony, and Mimetic Communication," in *The Affect Theory Reader*, ed. Melissa Gregg and Gregory J. Seigworth (Durham: Duke University Press, 2010), 193, 194.

14. Ibid., 196–98.

15. Giacomo Rizzolatti, Laila Craighero, and Luciano Fadiga, "The Mirror System in Humans," in *Mirror Neurons and the Evolution of Brain and Language*, ed. Maxim I. Stamenov and Vittorio Gallese (Amsterdam: John Benjamins, 2002), 37–59. As a result, a number of articles challenged the notion of action understanding through the MNS in humans, while other authors questioned the existence of an MNS in humans entirely. See Gregory Hickok, "Eight Problems for the Mirror Neuron Theory of Action Understanding in Monkeys and Humans," *Journal of Cognitive Neuroscience* 21, no. 7 (2008): 1229–43, and Angelika Lingnaua, Benno Gesiericha, and Alfonso Caramazzaa, "Asymmetric fMRI Adaptation Reveals No Evidence for Mirror Neurons in Humans," *Proceedings of the National Academy of Sciences* 106, no. 24 (2009): 9925–30. Subsequent publications challenged these positions: Christian Keysers, "Mirror Neurons," *Current Biology* 19, no. 21 (2009): R971–R973.

16. Christian Keysers and Valeria Gazzola, "Social Neuroscience: Mirror Neurons Recorded in Humans," *Current Biology* 20, no. 8 (2010): R354. The specific study they cite is Roy Mukamel, Arne D. Ekstrom, Jonas Kaplan, Marco Iacoboni, and Itzhak Fried, "Single-neuron Responses in Humans during Execution and Observation of Actions," *Current Biology* 20, no. 8 (2010): 750–56.

17. Many articles throughout the 2010 and 2011 issues of *Current Biology* relate to advances in mirror neuron research.

18. Vittorio Gallese, "Embodied Simulation: From Neurons to Phenomenal Experience," *Phenomenology and the Cognitive Sciences* 4, no. 1 (2005): 35. Not all of the neurons that fire when we execute an action also fire when we perceive that action; only a percentage of our brain cells function as mirror neurons.

19. Vittorio Gallese and George Lakoff, "The Brain's Concepts: The Role of Sensory-Motor System in Conceptual Knowledge," *Cognitive Neuropsychology* 22, no. 3–4 (2005): 463. Gallese argues that experiencing an emotion like disgust and "witnessing disgust expressed by the facial mimicry of someone else both activate the same neural structure." Gallese, "Embodied Simulation," 39. More recently, see Leonardo Fogassi, "The Mirror Neuron System: How Cognitive Functions Emerge from Motor Organization," *Journal of Economic Behavior & Organization* 77, no. 1 (2011): 66–75,

and Istvan Molnar-Szakacs, "From Actions to Empathy and Morality: A Neural Perspective," *Journal of Economic Behavior & Organization* 77, no. 1 (2011): 76–85.

20. Jean Decety, "To What Extent Is the Experience of Empathy Mediated by Shared Neural Circuits?" *Emotion Review* 2, no. 3 (2010): 205. However, it is important to recognize that some scholars remain unconvinced by the action-understanding hypothesis. See Gregory Hickok and Marc Hauser, "(Mis)understanding Mirror Neurons," *Current Biology* 20, no. 14 (2010): R593–R594.

21. Gibbs, "After Affect," 193.

22. Patrik N. Juslin, "From Mimesis to Catharsis: Expression, Perception, and Induction of Emotion in Music," in *Musical Communication*, ed. Dorothy Miell, Raymond MacDonald, and David J. Hargreaves (Oxford: Oxford University Press, 2005), 88.

23. Ibid.

24. Ibid., 92.

25. Ibid., 100. For a discussion of evidence from neuroscience that reveals music as "biologically powerful, meaning that it can have lasting effects on nonmusical abilities (such as language or attention) during the lifetime of individual humans," see Aniruddh Patel, "Music, Biological Evolution, and the Brain," in *Emerging Disciplines: Shaping New Fields of Scholarly Inquiry In and Beyond the Humanities*, ed. Melissa Bailar (Houston: Rice University Press, 2010), 91–144.

26. Michael H. Thaut, "Rhythm, Human Temporality, and Brain Function," in *Musical Communication*, ed. Dorothy Miell, Raymond MacDonald, and David J. Hargreaves (Oxford: Oxford University Press, 2005), 176. I am employing the traditional definition of entrainment from physics that Thaut uses—when the "frequency of one moving system becomes locked to the frequency of another 'driver' system" (176).

27. R. Keith Sawyer, "Music and Communication," in *Musical Communication*, ed. Dorothy Miell, Raymond MacDonald, and David J. Hargreaves (Oxford: Oxford University Press, 2005), 52. Sawyer is citing W. S. Condon and W. D. Ogston, "Sound Film Analysis of Normal and Pathological Behavior Patterns," *Journal of Nervous and Mental Diseases* 143 (1966): 338–47.

28. Sawyer, "Music and Communication," 52.

29. Peter Boenisch, "Aesthetic Art to Aisthetic Act: Theatre, Media, Intermedial Performance," in *Intermediality in Theatre and Performance*, ed. Freda Chapple and Chiel Kattenbelt (Amsterdam: Rodopi, 2006), 104. Following Walter Benjamin, Boenisch argues that "media translate and infuse historical circumstances into our senses and thus into our bodies," thereby generating realities that impact our perception of the world (105).

30. Ibid., 112.

31. Ibid., 114.

32. As Boenisch notes, "For the creation of a reality that is happening in real time theatre is a hard medium to beat; for it makes worlds that are in a very tangible way real for the observers and they experience that world in actual time." "Aesthetic Art to Aisthetic Act," 110.

33. Ibid., 114–15.

34. Ibid., 115. I introduced Fischer-Lichte's concept of "perceptual multistability" and its relationship to evangelical dramaturgy in Chapter One.

35. Timothy Beal discusses this in "They Know Not What They Watch," in *Mel Gibson's Bible: Religion, Popular Culture, and* The Passion of the Christ, ed. Timothy K. Beal and Tod Linafelt (Chicago: University of Chicago Press, 2006), 199–204.

36. A. O. Scott, "'The Passion of the Christ': Good and Evil Locked in Violent Showdown," *New York Times*, 25 February 2004, http://query.nytimes.com/gst/fullpage.html?res=9A07EFD6143CF936A15751C0A9629C8B63.

37. William G. Little, "Jesus's Extreme Makeover," in *Mel Gibson's Bible: Religion, Popular Culture, and* The Passion of the Christ, ed. Timothy K. Beal and Tod Linafelt (Chicago: University of Chicago Press, 2006), 174.

38. Beal, "They Know Not What They Watch," 203.

39. Jill Stevenson, "The Material Bodies of Medieval Religious Performance in England," *Material Religion: The Journal of Objects, Art, and Belief* 2, no. 2 (2006): 204–32.

40. Thomas J. J. Altizer, "The Passion and the Death of God," in *Mel Gibson's Bible: Religion, Popular Culture, and* The Passion of the Christ, ed. Timothy K. Beal and Tod Linafelt (Chicago: University of Chicago Press, 2006), 156.

41. Beal, "They Know Not What They Watch," 202.

42. Vincent Miller, "Contexts: Theology, Devotion, and Culture," in *Mel Gibson's Bible: Religion, Popular Culture, and* The Passion of the Christ, ed. Timothy K. Beal and Tod Linafelt (Chicago: University of Chicago Press, 2006), 47.

43. George Smiga, "The Good News of Mel Gibson's *Passion,*" in *Mel Gibson's Bible: Religion, Popular Culture, and* The Passion of the Christ, ed. Timothy K. Beal and Tod Linafelt (Chicago: University of Chicago Press, 2006), 27.

44. Beal, "They Know Not What They Watch," 200.

45. Timothy K. Beal and Tod Linafelt discuss this audience preparedness in "Introduction," in *Mel Gibson's Bible: Religion, Popular Culture, and* The Passion of the Christ, ed. Beal and Linafelt (Chicago: University of Chicago Press, 2006), 3.

46. In the Introduction I discussed the emotionally charged public discourse that preceded and surrounded the release of *The Passion of The Christ.*

47. Christian Smith, *American Evangelicalism: Embattled and Thriving* (Chicago: University of Chicago Press, 1998), 89.

48. "The Passion of the Christ," The Numbers, http://www.the-numbers.com/movies/2004/PASON.php.

49. A year after its theatrical premier, Gibson released a less violent version of the film, *The Passion Recut,* on 11 March, in time for Lent. Interestingly, HLE screened this version of the film on Friday and Saturday evenings during April 2012 for the three weekends following Easter. Visitors interested in seeing the film could enter the park free after 5:00 p.m. Holy Land Experience, "Special Event," http://www.holylandexperience.com/calendar/home_special_event.html.

50. For example, Gibson hosted a number of preview screenings for pastors and religious organizations, many of them oriented toward evangelical denominations. See Staff Writer, "5,000 Pastors Cheer Mel Gibson's *Passion,*" *Washington Times,* 21 January 2004, http://www.washingtontimes.com/news/2004/jan/21/20040121-113810-3164r/; Peter Chattaway, "Mel Gibson's Jesus Film Inspires Impassioned Discussion among Pastors, Ministry Leaders," *Canadian Christianity,* undated, http://canadianchristianity.com/cgi-bin/na.cgi?nationalupdates/040122gibson.

51. Beal, *Roadside Religion,* 57.

52. Ronald Lukens-Bull and Mark Fafard, "(Re)Creating Israel in Christian Zionism," *Journal of Religion and Society* 9 (2007): 10, http://moses.creighton.edu/JRS/2007/2007-16.pdf.

53. "Resurrection," by John Debney, on *The Passion of The Christ (Original Motion Picture Soundtrack),* released February 2004 by Sony BMG Music Entertainment. I have watched a number of YouTube videos of "Behold the Lamb" and, while there are a number of differences among them, for instance, the Centurion monologue appears to be a relatively new addition, in every video I have viewed from the last few years this song is heard during the resurrection scene. For examples, see the following YouTube clips: "Holyland Experience," http://www.youtube.com/watch?v=vpMohsJzD4E, posted 26 May 2011 (music begins at 12:45); "Death and Resurrection of Jesus Part Three,"

http://www.youtube.com/watch?v=yUf8JIOo-AE&NR=1&feature=fvwp, posted 19 December 2009 (music begins at 8:00); "He is Risen!" http://www.youtube.com/watch?v=HyeJyFPEDfo&NR=1&feature=fvwp, posted on 24 December 2008 (music begins at 4:45); "'The Holy Land Experience' in Orlando Florida," http://www.youtube.com/watch?v=5IdUn6uzkwI&feature=related, posted 23 June 2011 (music begins at 5:40).

54. Bruce Barton, "Paradox as Process: Intermedial Anxiety and the Betrayals of Intimacy," *Theatre Journal* 61, no. 4 (2009): 575.

55. Ibid., 577.

56. Peter Cockett, "*Bigger than Jesus:* Mediating the Larger than Live Story," *Canadian Theatre Review* 127 (2006): 7.

Chapter 4

1. Program for *The Great Passion Play* (Eureka Springs: Elna M. Smith Foundation, 2010), 1. For a compelling history of Oberammergau's Passion Play, see James Shapiro, *Oberammergau: The Troubling Story of the World's Most Famous Passion Play* (New York: Vintage, 2000).

2. Program for *The Great Passion Play,* 1. See also, The Great Passion Play, "Seating," http://www.greatpassionplay.com/seating.asp.

3. Glen Jeansonne, *Gerald L. K. Smith: Minister of Hate* (New Haven: Yale University Press, 1988), 5.

4. Ibid., 192. Throughout his book, Jeansonne offers a rich history of Smith's political and religious work.

5. Ibid., 193. Calvin Trillin writes that as early as January 1965, "Smith mentioned, in a private letter . . . the hope that the statue would lead to a Passion play 'which might make Eureka Springs the Oberammergau of America.'" Trillin, "U.S. Journal: Eureka Springs, ARK. The Sacred Projects," *New Yorker* 45 (26 July 1969): 75.

6. Gerald L. K. Smith, "The Passion Play: An Open Letter by Gerald L. K. Smith," *Eureka Springs Times-Echo,* 1 February 1968.

7. Jeansonne, *Gerald L. K. Smith,* 193–94.

8. Timothy Kovalcik, *Images of America: The Great Passion Play* (Charleston: Arcadia, 2008), 29.

9. Ibid., 78.

10. Ibid., 47.

11. Although I will not analyze it here, as in "Behold the Lamb," a diabolical black-cloaked figure appeared in the 2010 "Great Passion Play" production. And, as in HLE's production, this figure seemed to exert a kind of cosmic force over characters—displayed here through very large, over-dramatic gestures—in order to manipulate them into "sinful" actions. For instance, a kind of tug-of-war over Judas's soul was staged as he vacillated over whether or not to betray Jesus to the Jewish High Council. This figure also appeared to lead Judas to his suicide. The character's costuming alone would certainly remind spectators of the related character in *The Passion of The Christ,* and, in fact, the character in the Eureka Springs production looked even more like Gibson's character than did the figure in HLE's play. As in Gibson's film, the actor in the "Great Passion Play" was fully hooded and sexually ambiguous; neither was the case in "Behold the Lamb." Interestingly, this character is a new addition to the production. While I was in Eureka Springs I purchased a DVD of the "Great Passion Play" with a 2001 copyright, and this version was different from the live production I saw in many significant ways (*Great Passion Play,* 2001; transferred to DVD by Grace Enterprises, 2004). Most interesting to me was the absence of this cloaked figure in the 2001 play. The figure in the 2010 production was so reminiscent of Gibson's film that I find it

difficult to believe the producers are not pointedly referencing the film. Other changes between the 2001 and 2010 plays might indicate that, by reviving conversation about the anti-Semitic legacy of Passion plays, Gibson's film may have helped the producers in Eureka Springs recognize certain problematic elements in their own play, prompting them to change these. This is a very different response from the one I proposed with respect to "Behold the Lamb"; however, given Smith's controversial anti-Semitic legacy, such erasures may seem especially relevant to this production. (Notably, Smith is not mentioned in most of the play's publicity and marketing materials.) For example, the staging of the Last Supper in the 2010 production is reminiscent of a Passover Seder, while on the 2001 DVD this scene looks like a Christian communion ritual, with Jesus raising a metal chalice as a minister typically does when consecrating the elements. On the DVD, Pilate seems more frustrated by the Jewish High Priests than he was in the 2010 play and, in the earlier play, it is by a unanimous vote that the Sanhedrin finds Jesus guilty; in the 2010 production, the vote was divided. Moreover, in the 2001 version the Jewish High Priests wake the people of Jerusalem and have them follow the soldiers when they arrest Jesus in Gethsemane. The people appear as an angry rabble, and Judas even remarks, "There is blood in their eyes"; this did not occur in the 2010 production. (Judas speaks these words at minute 41 on the DVD.) I would situate these recent changes within a longer tradition of script revision with respect to anti-Semitic elements in the "Great Passion Play." Apparently, the original production that debuted in July 1968 included a host of anti-Semitic elements. Trillin writes, "A few months before [the debut], the National Council of Catholic Bishops had listed a half-dozen or so ways in which a Passion play might be subverted into an exercise in anti-Semitism—portraying Pilate as a more or less innocent bystander, for instance, or presenting the enemies of Christ as caricatures, or highlighting 'those texts of the gospel narrative that are amenable to misinterpretation by uninformed audiences, such as: "His Blood be upon us and upon our children"'—and Hyde's version contained just about all of them." Trillin, "U.S. Journal: Eureka Springs," 76.

12. Kovalcik, *Images of America: The Great Passion Play,* 111.

13. Ibid., 56.

14. Erika Fischer-Lichte, *The Transformative Power of Performance: A New Aesthetics,* trans. Saskya Iris Jain (2004; London: Routledge, 2008), 106.

15. Likewise, Fischer-Lichte notes that increased mediatization in a live show can sometimes stimulate "the audience's desire for the bodily presence of the actors, bestowing a special aura on their 'real' bodies." *Transformative Power of Performance,* 73.

16. Dorothy Chansky, "North American Passion Plays: 'The Greatest Story Ever Told' in the New Millennium," *TDR* 50, no. 4 (2006): 125.

17. Fischer-Lichte, *Transformative Power of Performance,* 125.

18. Steven Feld, "Places Sensed, Senses Placed: Toward a Sensuous Epistemology of Environments," in *Empire of the Senses: The Sensual Culture Reader,* ed. David Howes (Oxford: Berg, 2005; originally published, 1996), 179.

19. Ibid., 185.

20. Ibid.

21. David Morgan, *Sacred Gaze: Religious Visual Culture in Theory and Practice* (Berkeley and Los Angeles: University of California Press, 2005), 243, 242. The chapter in which this appears is quite relevant to my arguments about the Great Passion Play. See "National Icons: Bibles, Flags, and Jesus in American Civil Religion," in *Sacred Gaze,* 220–55.

22. Ibid., 242–43. About nationalism, Morgan also writes, "Othering is crucial to this enterprise, and the corporate veneration of national icons casts love of nation in religious terms: those who do not worship the national deity are infidels" (243). Such

"othering" relates to the issue of embattlement that I will take up at the end of this chapter.

23. Jeansonne, *Gerald L. K. Smith,* 194.

24. Smith, "Passion Play: An Open Letter."

25. I discuss Sponsler's analysis of the Black Hills play at the beginning of Chapter Three.

26. Jeansonne, *Gerald L. K. Smith,* 193.

27. Smith, "Passion Play: An Open Letter."

28. Linda Kintz, *Between Jesus and the Market: The Emotions that Matter in Right-Wing America* (Durham: Duke University Press, 1997), 28.

29. Ibid. For socio-linguistic work on myths and stigmas associated with "non-standard" American accents and dialect, especially those associated with Southern and Appalachian regions, see especially Rosina Lippi-Green, *English with an Accent: Language, Ideology and Discrimination in the United States* (London: Routledge, 1997); Nancy A. Niedzielski and Dennis Preston, *Folk Linguistics* (Berlin: Mouton de Gruyter, 2000); and Natalie Schilling-Estes and Walt Wolfram, *American English: Dialects and Variation,* 2nd ed. (Cambridge: Basil Blackwell, 2006).

30. Although not about Southerners specifically, consider the wording of, and impassioned debate surrounding, this comment by President Barack Obama at a campaign fundraising event in San Francisco in April 2008: "You go into some of these small towns in Pennsylvania, and like a lot of small towns in the Midwest, the jobs have been gone now for 25 years and nothing's replaced them. . . . And they fell through the Clinton Administration, and the Bush Administration, and each successive administration has said that somehow these communities are gonna regenerate and they have not. And it's not surprising then they get bitter, they cling to guns or religion or antipathy toward people who aren't like them or anti-immigrant sentiment or anti-trade sentiment as a way to explain their frustrations." Quoted in Mayhill Fowler, "Obama: No Surprise that Hard-Pressed Pennsylvanians Turn Bitter," *Huffington Post,* 11 April 2008, http://www.huffingtonpost.com/mayhill-fowler/obama-no-surprise-that-ha_b_96188.html.

31. Originally, and perhaps still today, the accents may also reinforce associations with Oberammergau, since they evoke the local, amateur, village production motif.

32. Timothy K. Beal, "They Know Not What They Watch," in *Mel Gibson's Bible: Religion, Popular Culture, and* The Passion of the Christ, ed. Timothy K. Beal and Tod Linafelt (Chicago: University of Chicago Press, 2006), 201.

33. Ibid.

34. Kintz notes that U.S. culture typically depicts "normal" people as "hip and urban, and if they do not come from the Northeast or Hollywood, their intellectual formation does." *Between Jesus and the Market,* 28.

35. The Great Passion Play, "Tickets: Value Package," https://tickets.greatpassionplay.com/scripts/172.16.217.16-7000/maxweb.exe?ACTION=ORDER&MAXWEB_172.16.217.16_7213=.

36. I discuss this venue briefly in Chapter Five.

37. Program for *The Great Passion Play,* 18.

38. Ibid., 22.

39. Tzachi Zamir, "Watching Actors," *Theatre Journal* 62, no. 2 (2010): 229.

40. Ibid., 232. Zamir argues that such existential amplification may help to explain why people are drawn to act and to watch live theater (227).

41. Ibid., 234–35.

42. This is also true in other venues. For instance, at the Sacred Arts Museum

guides asked guests about their personal salvation and belief in Jesus Christ as part of the museum tour.

43. Rebecca Schneider, *Performing Remains: Art and War in Times of Theatrical Reenactment* (London: Routledge, 2011), 30.

44. According to the website, "The Great Passion Play is a 501C-3 non-profit organization with an independent Board of Directors. . . . A non-denominational ministry founded in 1967, the Great Passion Play is dedicated to providing opportunities for people to deepen their knowledge of the heritage, teachings and inspirations of Jesus Christ and the Christian faith. As a spiritual center for Christians world-wide, we are continually sponsoring new educational programs and interactive on-site attractions designed to encourage brotherhood, compassion and understanding among all who visit our complex." The Great Passion Play, "Donations," http://www.greatpassionplay.com/contact.asp.

45. Gilles Fauconnier and Mark Turner, *The Way We Think: Conceptual Blending and the Mind's Hidden Complexities* (New York: Basic Books, 2002), 103.

46. Ibid., 102–4.

47. Ibid., 104.

48. Ibid., 18, 30.

49. Ibid., 205, 206.

50. Ibid., 83.

51. Fauconnier and Turner assert, "In the case of sensation and perception, our conscious experience comes entirely from the blend—we 'live in the blend,' so to speak. In other activities, conscious apprehension has more leeway to go back and forth, to 'live in the full integration network.'" *Way We Think,* 83.

52. Ibid., 266.

53. Ibid., 266–67.

54. Bruce McConachie, "Falsifiable Theories for Theatre and Performance Studies," *Theatre Journal* 59, no. 4 (2007): 566–67.

55. Fauconnier and Turner, *Way We Think,* 267.

56. I discuss how conceptual blending functioned in the late medieval York Corpus Christi cycle in Stevenson, *Performance, Cognitive Theory, and Devotional Culture: Sensual Piety in Late Medieval York* (New York: Palgrave, 2010), 92–104, 130–32, 145–49.

57. Fischer-Lichte, *Transformative Power of Performance,* 115.

58. Ibid.

59. Ibid., 116.

60. Lynn Dierking and John Falk note that "neuroscience research has revealed that 'spatial learning' is not just a spatialized and isolated type of learning but is integrated with all types of learning; all learning is influenced by the awareness of place." Dierking and Falk, *Museum Experience* (Washington, DC: Whalesback Books, 1992), 62.

61. All of these descriptions are from Holy Land Experience, "Exhibits," http://www.holylandexperience.com/exhibits/exhibits.html.

62. Much of the scholarship and press surrounding Holy Land Experience registers an obsession with the park's attempts at verisimilitude and authenticity—largely failed attempts, according to most authors. For example, in his piece in *Christian Century,* John Spalding writes, "Battling with the authentic Holy Land feel are a few incongruities"; the very title of Spalding's article, "Authentic replica," suggests that the park is unable to attain true verisimilitude. Spalding, "Authentic replica," *Christian Century* 119, no. 14 (2002), accessed through Academic OneFile, http://slb.mmm.edu:2138/ps/i.do?id=GALE%7CA89580851&v=2.1&u=nysl_me_mmcl&it=r&p=AONE&sw=w.

Even Timothy Beal expresses frustration in this regard, with an attachment to authenticity that I find striking: "I think that what repelled me the most about the Holy Land Experience was its lack of authenticity. I mean that in two different ways. First, it is inauthentic in that it is not forthright about its larger agendas, especially its mission to proselytize Jews into its own peculiar form of Christianity. . . . Second, it was inauthentic in that the actual physical place lacked personality and soul. It was a production rather than a creation." As Beal later suggests, for him, Holy Land Experience's ideology prevented the religious experience it offered from becoming religiously real. *Roadside Religion,* 68, 69. Although I understand Beal's conclusion—at moments I, too, felt an absence of those human traces that give spaces and events "personality and soul"—as I have noted, I saw many visitors who appeared to become a part of, and lose themselves in, the performances I witnessed. As I noted in Chapter One, Beal argues that during a religiously real experience "one feels as though one has become a part of it. As though one has lost oneself in it." Beal, *Roadside Religion,* 41.

63. Burke O. Long, *Imagining the Holy Land: Maps, Models, and Fantasy Travels* (Bloomington: Indiana University Press, 2003), 1.

64. Holy Land Experience, "Exhibits," http://www.holylandexperience.com/exhibits/exhibits.html.

65. Long, *Imagining the Holy Land,* 6.

66. Ibid., 5.

67. I discuss HLE as an ideal pilgrimage in Chapter Two.

68. As Timothy Beal notes, "Beneath the explicit aim of giving guests a glimpse of life during biblical times is a far more zealous ideological interest in promoting a very specific biblical theology of the end times, one in which knowledge of Israelite ritual practices, especially those associated with the Jerusalem Temple, is foundational." He also writes, "Populated by live biblical characters who act in Broadway-style musicals, the Holy Land Experience has been created as a popular, relatively accessible entry point into Rev. Rosenthal's ideological-theological movement, Zion's Hope." Beal, *Roadside Religion,* 63, 69. On the role of Judaism and Jewish tradition in apocalyptic theology, see Paul Boyer, *When Time Shall Be No More: Prophecy Belief in Modern American Culture* (Cambridge: Harvard University Press, 1992). Also instructive is the documentary film *Waiting for Armageddon,* DVD, directed by Kate Davis, David Heilbroner, and Franco Sacchi (Dallas, TX: Eureka Film Productions, 2009).

69. Joan R. Branham, "The Temple that Won't Quit: Constructing Sacred Space in Orlando's Holy Land Experience Theme Park," *Crosscurrents* 59, no. 3 (2009): 378–79.

70. Holy Land Experience, "The Scriptorium," http://www.holylandexperience.com/exhibits/the_scriptorium.html.

71. Beal, *Roadside Religion,* 59.

72. Holy Land Experience, "The Wilderness Tabernacle," http://www.holylandexperience.com/exhibits/the_wilderness_tabernacle.html.

73. Here again I use Andy Lavender's term from "Mise En Scène, Hypermediacy, and the Sensorium," in *Intermediality in Theatre and Performance,* ed. Freda Chapple and Chiel Kattenbelt (Amsterdam: Rodopi, 2006), 64.

74. Branham, "The Temple that Won't Quit," 372.

75. Smith, "Passion Play: An Open Letter."

76. Quoted in Stephanie Simon, "Acting on Faith in Arkansas," *Los Angeles Times,* 22 September 2005. Kovalcik writes, "*The Great Passion Play* is a large production. But the employees of the foundation are a family. This idea was fostered from the beginning." *Images of America: The Great Passion Play,* 111.

77. Long, *Imagining the Holy Land,* 71.

78. Christine Ballengee Morris and James H. Sanders III, "Culture, Identity, Repre-

sentation: The Economic Policies of Heritage Tourism," *International Journal of Education through Art* 5, nos. 2–3 (2009): 130.

79. Quoted in Simon, "Acting on Faith in Arkansas."

80. Quoted in ibid.

81. Quoted in ibid.

82. Trillin writes, "If there were such a thing as a Victorian hill town, it would look like Eureka Springs." "U.S. Journal: Eureka Springs," 69.

83. Simon, "Acting on Faith in Arkansas."

84. There are a number of nearby hotels that are not in downtown Eureka Springs and, indeed, it appeared that most spectators at the play did not stay in lodging downtown. Traveling to the downtown area from the Passion Play grounds requires drivers to take a sharp right turn out of the parking lot and to navigate a narrow, sharply twisting, and poorly lit one-lane road in the dark of night. Considering the number of spectators, I was certain that it would take ages to get back to my downtown hotel after the play. But, in fact, I didn't see a single car take that right turn, and not a single pair of headlights appeared behind my car during the slow drive down the hill toward the city center. Most cars leaving the parking lot kept driving straight, apparently heading to hotels that were not located downtown. Of course, these are most likely also less expensive accommodations, so the political and social dynamic are not the only factors at work.

85. Christian Smith, *American Evangelicalism: Embattled and Thriving* (Chicago: University of Chicago Press, 1998), 110, 116.

86. The Great Passion Play, "Tickets: Value Package," https://tickets.greatpassionplay.com/scripts/172.16.217.16-7000/maxweb.exe?ACTION=ORDER&MAXWEB_172.16.217.16_7213=.

87. Like the audience at the "Great Passion Play" performance, the vast majority of spectators at the dinner theater were Caucasian, although there were a few African Americans in the crowd as well.

88. Bethany Moreton discusses how "histories of the 'kitchen-table activists' behind the rise of the New Christian Right show the centrality of white women to the new political dispensation." *To Serve God and Wal-Mart: The Making of Christian Free Enterprise* (Cambridge: Harvard University Press, 2009), 3.

89. Fischer-Lichte, *Transformative Power of Performance*, 115.

90. Thanks to Kelly Matika for bringing this detail to my attention.

91. Here I am referring once again to Bruce Holsinger's definition of liturgy that I introduce in Chapter Two. Holsinger, "Liturgy," in *Oxford Twenty-First Century Approaches to Literature: Middle English*, ed. Paul Strohm (Oxford: Oxford University Press, 2007), 298.

92. Sarah McNamer, *Affective Meditation and the Invention of Medieval Compassion* (Philadelphia: University of Pennsylvania Press, 2010), 4.

Chapter 5

This chapter is a somewhat expanded version of my article "Embodying Sacred History: Performing Creationism for Believers," *TDR* 56, no. 1 (2012): 93–113. This material began as a brief section in the Coda of my book *Performance, Cognitive Theory, and Devotional Culture: Sensual Piety in Late Medieval York* (New York: Palgrave, 2010), 156–60.

1. One example is Ben McGrath's 2010 *New Yorker* article on the Tea Party movement. Don Seely, one of the people profiled in the piece, takes McGrath to the Creation Museum where his wife also works. McGrath writes, "The first exhibit showed two

paleontologists, a Darwinist and a Biblical literalist, examining a fossil. 'Depending on what your world view is, and what you believe and what you've been taught, you can look at the same thing and come to a different conclusion,' Seely explained. The exhibit, called 'Starting Points,' was intended to demonstrate the plausible divergence in theories about man's relation to dinosaurs, but it could just as easily have spoken for the assumptions we make about Barack Obama's past associations with figures like Bill Ayers and Bernardine Dohrn." McGrath, "The Movement: The Rise of Tea Party Activism," *New Yorker,* 1 February 2010, 85.

2. For example, Melanie B. Smith, "Great Divide Separates Creationists, Evolutionists," *Decatur Daily,* 19 February 2010; Dennis O'Connor, "Science and Faith: Three Years On Creation Museum Is Evolving," *Houston Chronicle,* 10 September 2010; A. A. Gill, "Roll Over, Charles Darwin!" *Vanity Fair* (February 2010): 72–75.

3. John Fletcher, "Tasteless as Hell: Community Performance, Distinction, and Countertaste in Hell House," *Theatre Survey* 48, no. 2 (2007): 325. Fletcher makes this claim with respect to Hell Houses, describing this performance genre as "a form of activist, community-based performance" that responds to what evangelical Christians see as a morally bankrupt culture (316). In a paper delivered at the 2009 Association for Theatre in Higher Education conference, entitled "'Of Course, the Dinosaurs on Noah's Ark Were Very Small': Staging the Facts of Faith at the Creation Museum," Fletcher also linked the Creation Museum to the "activist, community-based performance tradition" and suggested ways in which the space constructs a "worldview apologetic." At that same 2009 conference, I delivered a shorter version of this chapter. Although Fletcher and I use different theoretical approaches and have different goals, we interpret certain elements of the museum in similar ways, and I see our work as complementary. For Fletcher's analysis of the Creation Museum, see his forthcoming book *Preaching to Convert* (Ann Arbor: University of Michigan Press, forthcoming). I am very grateful to John for sharing his work with me.

4. Kenneth Chang, "Paleontology and Creationism Meet but Don't Mesh," *New York Times,* 30 June 2009, final edition.

5. Stephen Asma, "Dinosaurs on the Ark: The Creation Museum," *Chronicle of Higher Education* 53, no. 37 (2007), accessed through EbscoHost.

6. The website also lists four international venues in Holland, the United Kingdom, Hong Kong, and Canada. These figures were current as of August 2012.

7. Pew Forum, "Science in America: Religious Belief and Public Attitudes," 18 December 2007, http://pewforum.org/docs/?DocID=275. The percentage of people who directly reject evolution may be increasing. In Pew's more recent U.S. Religious Landscape Study, released in 2008, 45 percent of respondents directly rejected "the notion that evolution best explains the origins of human life." Pew Forum, "U.S. Religious Landscape Survey," 23 June 2008, page 95, http://religions.pewforum.org/pdf/report2religious-landscape-study-chapter-2.pdf.

8. Pew Forum, "U.S. Religious Landscape Survey," 23 June 2008, page 95, http://religions.pewforum.org/pdf/report2religious-landscape-study-chapter-2.pdf.

9. I was particularly struck by the many Mennonite families who were visiting the Creation Museum on the days I was there. I contacted the Creation Museum directly for statistics on their visitor demographics. A representative did respond and indicated that she would try to collect this data. However, despite my follow-up efforts I never received these figures.

10. Creation Evidence Museum, "Homepage," http://www.creationevidence.org/.

11. For a discussion of the increasing number of high-tech museums and theme parks with evangelical themes, see Annalee Ward, "Faith-Based Theme Parks and Museums: Multidimensional Media," in *Understanding Evangelical Media: The Changing*

Face of Christian Communication, ed. Quentin J. Schultze and Robert H. Woods Jr. (Downers Grove, IL: InterVarsity Press, 2008), 161–72.

12. According to the *Pensacola News Journal*, Hovind "is serving 10 years in federal prison as a result of a tax-fraud conviction for failing to pay more than $470,000 in employee taxes in a long-running dispute with the Internal Revenue Service." As of early August 2009, "the nine properties that make up Dinosaur Adventure Land, and two bank accounts associated with the park will be used to satisfy $430,400 in restitution owed to the federal government." Kris Wernowsky, "Feds Can Seize Dinosaur Adventure Land," *Pensacola News Journal*, 31 July 2009, http://www.pnj.com/article/20090731/NEWS01/90731016/1006.

13. Abby Goodnough, "Darwin-Free Fun for Creationists," *New York Times*, 1 May 2004, final edition.

14. Ibid.

15. Museum of Earth History, "Home," http://www.moeh.org.

16. The mission statements for both of these organizations are available online. See Christ for the Nations, "Mission Statement," http://www.cfn.org/mission/; Creation Truth Foundation, "Mission Statement," http://www.creationtruth.com/index.php?option=com_content&view=article&id=72&Itemid=129.

17. Museum of Earth History, "The Project," http://www.museumofearthhistory.com/. This website was active until fall 2011 but has since been replaced by the much abbreviated website www.moeh.org.

18. Another tactic involves amending the content of public school textbooks. See James McKinley Jr., "In Texas, a Line in the Curriculum Revives Evolution Debate," *New York Times*, 21 January 2009, final edition; McKinley, "Texas Conservatives Win Curriculum Change," *New York Times*, 12 March 2010, final edition; Russell Shorto, "Founding Father?" *New York Times Magazine*, 14 February 2010, http://www.nytimes.com/2010/02/14/magazine/14texbooks-t.html?scp=5&sq=Founding%20Father&st=cse.

19. Elizabeth Crooke, *Museums and Community: Ideas, Issues and Challenges* (London: Routledge, 2007), 110. Comments by Ken Ham, the Creation Museum's founder and director, suggest that he would agree with this trajectory and what the Creation Museum represents with respect to it. In an interview with *Christianity Today*, Ham said of the Creation Museum, "Twenty-five years ago, we didn't have all the arguments fine-tuned. . . . This is part of the maturing of the biblical creationist movement." Quoted in Rob Moll, "Creation Display," *Christianity Today* 51, no. 7 (2007): 13.

20. Crooke, *Museums and Community*, 130.

21. American Association of Museums, "AAM Press Release: Americans Identify Museums as a Source of Information They Can Really Trust," 2001, www.aam-us.org/pressreleases.cfm?mode=list&id=21.

22. José-Marie Griffiths and Donald W. King, "InterConnections: The Institute for Museum and Library Services (IMLS) National Survey on the Use of Libraries, Museums, and the Internet: Museum Survey Results" (January 2008), table on page 41, http://interconnectionsreport.org/reports/IMLSMusRpt20080312kjm.pdf. Interestingly, the average rises when visitors do not have to pay an entrance fee (4.66) and is slightly lower when they do (4.59). See table on page 78. Thanks to the American Association of Museums for supplying me with a distillation of this report, which indicates that, by comparison, government websites received an average score of 3.00, commercial websites 2.54, and private individual websites 2.14.

23. Crooke asserts, "The freedom to speak for oneself, in a place where one will be heard, is one of the core strands of achieving a sense of empowerment." *Museums and Community*, 134. With respect to the Creation Museum particularly, Jandos Rothstein

argues that creationists visit the museum for a confirmation of their beliefs and "the masses are part of the appeal: They represent an affirmation for the visitors that they are not alone." Rothstein, "Graphic Displays of Faith," *Print* 62, no. 1 (2008): 97.

24. Quoted in Goodnough, "Darwin-Free Fun for Creationists."

25. Answers in Genesis, "Statement of Faith," http://www.answersingenesis.org/about/faith.

26. Ibid.

27. Many of the megachurches that I visited as part of my research sold AiG materials in their bookstores. Interestingly, during the sermon at the service I attended at Immanuel Bible Church in Virginia, the pastor encouraged the congregation to register for an upcoming class offered by AiG and Ken Ham. The theme of the sermon was "Boldness," and the pastor said this class would prepare believers to be like the disciple Peter by giving them the courage to speak the gospel message publicly. On a related note, the Crystal Cathedral, one of the oldest megachurches in the nation, staged a creationist play in 2005, although not one based in young earth creationism and therefore not a play that AiG endorsed. See Kevin J. Wetmore Jr., "Intelligent Design (after Julie Taymor): Opposing Darwinism in The Crystal Cathedral's *Creation: Once Upon All Time*," *Journal of Religion and Theatre* 6, no. 2 (Fall 2007): 124–39, http://www.athe.org/associations/12588/files/wetmore2.pdf.

28. Answers in Genesis, *Creation Museum Souvenir Guidebook* (undated), 36.

29. Ibid., 3.

30. This fact is repeated in various articles and in museum materials, including in the *Creation Museum Souvenir Guidebook*.

31. Creation Museum, "What's Here," http://creationmuseum.org/whats-here/. A promotional blurb on the website reads, "Our Special Effects Theater, complete with rumbling seats and rising mists, takes visitors on a fantastic quest to find the real purpose and meaning of life." Creation Museum, "About," http://creationmuseum.org/about/.

32. Creation Museum, "Homepage," http://creationmuseum.org/.

33. For example, the inside front cover of the official *Creation Museum Souvenir Guidebook* explains that "The Creation Museum presents a 'walk through history'" that was "designed by a former Universal Studios exhibit director."

34. The main attraction in the petting zoo when I visited was the "Zonkey," the offspring of a donkey and zebra coupling. This animal served as evidence that it does not take millions of years for new species to develop.

35. Vincent Crapanzano, *Serving the Word: Literalism in America from the Pulpit to the Bench* (New York: New Press, 2000), 184.

36. Answers in Genesis, *Museum Guide: A Bible-Based Handbook to Natural History Museums* (China: Answers in Genesis, 2007), 14.

37. Ibid., 14–15.

38. AiG is one of several organizations involved in building Ark Encounter, "a one-of-a-kind historically themed attraction" that will include "a number of historical events centered on a full-size, all-wood Ark." Similar to the Creation Museum, this project is being marketed as providing visitors with an "entertaining, educational, and immersive" experience. The Ark Encounter website notes, "A private Limited Liability Company (LLC) will own the Ark Encounter. A non-profit subsidiary of Answers in Genesis will be one of the members of the LLC and will also be the managing member responsible for day-to-day operations." Ark Encounter, "FAQ," http://arkencounter.com/faq/. As of April 2012, the timeline on this FAQ page had construction beginning in 2012 with "a grand opening for the full-size Ark (the first of nine attractions and the centerpiece of the entire attraction) in 2014." There are links to AiG and the Creation Museum websites on the Ark Encounter homepage.

39. Apparently there used to be a dinosaur model at the end of the walk that visitors could sit on, providing yet another dinosaur-themed photo opportunity. That model was no longer part of the museum's exhibit when I visited.

40. Quoted in Leah Arroyo, "Science on Faith at the Creation Museum," *Museum News* (November–December 2007), http://www.aam-us.org/pubs/mn/scienceonfaith.cfm.

41. Crooke, *Museums and Community,* 130.

42. A. Larry Ross Communications, "The Creation Museum," http://www.alrc-newskitchen.com/creationmuseum/index.htm. AiG also produces material designed to help creationists navigate traditional natural history museums, such as the *Museum Guide: A Bible-Based Handbook to Natural History Museums.* The first section of this guide, entitled "Before You Go," begins, "Museums are found the world over—from one-room exhibits filled with local fossils to grandiose halls loaded with specimens from every part of the globe. . . . Although each is unique in presentation, every museum (with few exceptions) is united around a common goal: to tell the history of the universe from a naturalistic point of view. This view, by definition, excludes any type of supernatural intervention or revelation, and attempts to explain how things made themselves. 'Evolution' and 'millions of years' stories abound throughout their presentations. Is it possible for a Bible-believing Christian to visit such a place and yet leave with his faith intact? As we'll see, the answer is a resounding 'yes!' Yes, we *can* learn about the natural world, and we *can* do it from a biblical perspective. Before you go, you'll want to learn how to tell what is true from what is fiction by learning to be discerning, as the Bible exhorts us to be. . . . We can do this by understanding the nature of science and biblical history." Answers in Genesis, *Museum Guide: A Bible-Based Handbook,* 7.

43. Quoted in Kenneth Chang, "Paleontology and Creationism Meet but Don't Mesh," *New York Times,* 30 June 2009, final edition.

44. Answers in Genesis, *Creation Museum Souvenir Guidebook,* 8.

45. Heather Hendershot, *Shaking the World for Jesus: Media and Conservative Evangelical Culture* (Chicago: University of Chicago Press, 2004), 147.

46. Ibid., 158.

47. Ibid., 174.

48. Interestingly, the museum takes the same position with respect to natural selection and has a large room along the Museum Experience Walk devoted to natural selection. The museum's Guidebook explains, "Natural selection, as shown in post-flood geology, is supported biblically and scientifically. Viewed as a God-ordained process, it allows organisms to survive in a sin-cursed, post-fall world. Natural selection allows limited variation within populations, preserves their viability, and is, in fact, a great confirmation of the Bible's history." Answers in Genesis, *Creation Museum Souvenir Guidebook,* 21.

49. Similarly, the Museum of Earth History's previous website included explanations of recent scientific discoveries, all of which appeared at the bottom of the homepage under the heading "What They Didn't Teach You At School." For example, the fourth example read: "Spontaneous generation is the idea that non-living chemicals just 'sprang' to life. Science says that life can only come from life. Spontaneous generation has never been observed, yet it continues to be the explanation for the origin of life in a creator-less world. *Explanations for the origin of life that don't follow the rules of science must not go unchallenged*" (original emphasis). Museum of Earth History, "Homepage," http://www.museumofearthhistory.com/.

50. Jason Byassee, "Dinosaurs in the Garden," *Christian Century* 125, no. 3 (2008): 23.

51. In AiG's Statement of Faith, point thirteen under "Theology" reads, "It is the duty of Christians to attend a local Bible believing church, as portrayed in the New Testament." Answers in Genesis, "Statement of Faith," http://www.answersingenesis.org/about/faith.

52. Answers in Genesis, *Museum Guide: A Bible-Based Handbook,* 9.

53. Thanks to Kelly Matika for pointing this out to me.

54. This phrase appears on a sign in the museum's Dinosaur Dig exhibit.

55. As Crapanzano explains, creationists view evolutionists as denying "any moral dimension to time and history. . . . They deny any divine plan, aim, or intervention and, in the creationists' eyes, promote a terrifying, meaningless version of history that is subject only to chance and mechanical causality—a causality that serves but poorly (because humanly conceived) to assuage the terror inherent in their godless vision." *Serving the Word,* 184.

56. Anna Gibbs, "After Affect: Sympathy, Synchrony, and Mimetic Communication," in *The Affect Theory Reader,* ed. Melissa Gregg and Gregory J. Seigworth (Durham: Duke University Press, 2010), 192.

57. Ibid.

58. Ibid.

59. Crooke, *Museums and Community,* 134.

60. Peter W. Williams, "Creation Museum," *Material Religion: The Journal of Objects, Art and Belief* 4, no. 3 (2008): 373.

61. Quoted in Arroyo, "Science on Faith."

62. One of the angel-narrators in *Men in White* proclaims, "God loves science!"

63. Tony Bennett, *The Birth of the Museum: History, Theory, Politics* (London: Routledge, 1995), 179, 183.

64. Tracy C. Davis, "Performing and the Real Thing in the Postmodern Museum," *TDR* 39, no. 3 (1995): 16.

65. Ibid., 35–36.

66. Tony Bennett, *Pasts Beyond Memory: Evolution, Museums, Colonialism* (London: Routledge, 2004), 161–62.

67. Answers in Genesis, *Creation Museum Souvenir Guidebook,* "Helpful Hints page."

68. Austin Dacey, "Science and the Public: Is Science Making Us More Ignorant?" *Skeptical Inquirer* 28, no. 6 (2004), http://www.csicop.org/si/show/is_science_making_us_more_ignorant. As an example, Dacey cites the ways in which neuroscientific evidence has challenged many cultural understandings of the self. Dacey is the former director of Science and the Public, a program of the Center for Inquiry and State University of New York at Buffalo, and currently a representative to the United Nations for the International Humanist and Ethical Union.

69. Giovanni Frazzetto, "Who's Afraid of Darwin?" *European Molecular Biology Organization Reports* 5, no. 7 (2004): 665. Here, Frazzetto builds upon the work of Umberto Galimberti.

70. Quoted in Frazzetto, "Who's Afraid of Darwin?", 665. AiG issues press releases and articles in response to scientific discoveries that are perceived as anti-creationist, and these regularly reinforce the idea that evolutionary science is unstable with a constantly changing narrative. A recent example was AiG's response to the 9 April 2010 article in the journal *Science* regarding fossil remains of a female adult and a juvenile male discovered in South Africa (Lee R. Berger, Darryl J. de Ruiter, Steven E. Churchill, Peter Schmid, Kristian J. Carlson, Paul H. G. M. Dirks, and Job M. Kibii, "*Australopithecus sediba:* A New Species of *Homo*-Like Australopith from South Africa," *Science* 328, no. 5975 (2010): 195–204). Scientists dated the fossils (*Australopithecus sediba*) as

between 1.8 and 2 million years old, and various popular news sources suggested they were evidence of a "new hominid species" (see Jonathan Amos, "South African fossils could be new hominid species," *BBC News,* 8 April 2010, http://news.bbc.co.uk/2/hi/science/nature/8609192.stm). AiG responded immediately with articles and press releases. In Mark Looy's 9 April 2010 article posted on AiG's website, he explains the find and then writes, "Interestingly, some media outlets are reporting that the story of human evolution now has to be redrawn. That observation begs the question: why has so much been so wrong in the evolutionists' recounting of their story of human evolution, and now it has to be redrawn? Will some science textbooks be seen as obsolete and have to be tossed?" He concludes by asserting, "As creationists, we can be confident of one thing: the Creator God created humans distinct from all animals, and we were made in His image and not from an ape-like creature (Genesis 1)." Looy, "Rewriting Human Evolution—Again?", 9 April 2010, http://www.answersingenesis.org/articles/2010/04/09/rewriting-human-evolution-again.

71. Asma, "Dinosaurs on the Ark."

72. Asma discusses Stephen Jay Gould's "cold bath" theory in "Dinosaurs on the Ark."

73. Ibid.

74. Ibid.

75. Bruce McConachie, "Falsifiable Theories for Theatre and Performance Studies," *Theatre Journal* 59, no. 4 (2007): 122.

76. I am referring once again to Erika Fischer-Lichte's discussion of atmosphere that I introduced in Chapter Four. See Fischer-Lichte, *The Transformative Power of Performance: A New Aesthetics,* trans. Saskya Iris Jain (2004; London: Routledge, 2008), 115.

77. One sign in "Corruption Valley" reads: "Before Adam's Sin No Death. According to the Bible, animals and humans have 'life' (Hebrew *nephesh*), but plants do not. So humans and animals were created to eat plants, and in the original world before sin, humans and animals would never die."

78. Ham recounts: "I got a testimonial yesterday in an e-mail from a man whose son told him, 'Dad, I don't like that place,' referring to the museum's dark Cave of Sorrows after Adam and Eve are cast out of Eden. 'Can we go back to the Garden?'" Quoted in Asma, "Dinosaurs on the Ark."

79. Fischer-Lichte, *The Transformative Power of Performance,* 116.

80. Hendershot, *Shaking the World for Jesus,* 174–75.

81. Ibid., 175.

82. Byassee, "Dinosaurs in the Garden," 25.

83. Quoted in Fischer-Lichte, *The Transformative Power of Performance,* 187. From Martin Seel, "Inszenieren als Erscheinenlassen. Thesen ueber die Reichweite eines Begriffs," in *Aesthetik der Inszenierung,* ed. J. Fruechtl and J. Zimmermann (Frankfurt: Suhrkamp, 2001), 48–62. Fischer-Lichte quotes from pages 53 and 50.

84. Fischer-Lichte, *The Transformative Power of Performance,* 187.

85. Ibid., 190.

86. Asma, "Dinosaurs on the Ark."

87. John H. Dierking and Lynn D. Falk, *Museum Experience* (Washington, DC: Whalesback Books, 1992), 93.

88. Asma, "Dinosaurs on the Ark."

89. Edward Rothstein, "Adam and Eve in the Land of Dinosaurs," *New York Times,* 24 May 2007, final edition.

90. Quoted in Chang, "Paleontology and Creationism Meet."

91. McConachie, "Falsifiable Theories," 559.

92. Crapanzano, *Serving the Word,* 166.

93. Davis, "Performing and the Real Thing," 35.

94. Timothy Beal, *Roadside Religion: In Search of the Sacred, the Strange, and the Substance of Faith* (Boston: Beacon Press, 2005), 41.

95. Rothstein, "Graphic Displays of Faith," 101.

96. Naomi Rokotnitz, "'It is required/You do awake your faith': Learning to Trust the Body through Performing *The Winter's Tale,*" in *Performance and Cognition: Theatre Studies and the Cognitive Turn,* ed. Bruce McConachie and F. Elizabeth Hart (New York: Routledge, 2006), 138.

97. Dierking and Falk cite consistent evidence demonstrating that "visitors perceive their museum experience as a gestalt" and cannot analyze distinct aspects of it. *Museum Experience,* 93.

98. Christian Smith, *American Evangelicalism: Embattled and Thriving* (Chicago: University of Chicago Press, 1998), 103. I introduced this point in Chapter One.

99. Hasia Diner, the Paul S. and Sylvia Steinberg Professor of American Jewish History at New York University, is quoted in "Episode Four: 'A New Light'" of the PBS documentary miniseries *God in America,* directed by Sarah Colt and Thomas Jennings. From *God in America: How Religious Liberty Shaped America,* DVD, series directed by David Belton (Boston: American Experience and Frontline, 2010). Transcript available at *God In America,* "Transcript: Episode Four: 'A New Light,'" http://www.pbs.org/godinamerica/transcripts/hour-four.html.

100. Ideas about the innate Christian character of the United States are still a part of evangelical dialogues today, especially when they concern political action. For example, various political organizations around the country currently sponsor two-day "Pastors' Policy" meetings aimed specifically at evangelical pastors that are designed to help these leaders "promote 'biblically informed' political advocacy" among their congregants. At a March 2011 "Pastors' Policy" meeting held in Iowa, former Arkansas governor Mike Huckabee declared, "We face a spiritual war in this country. Let this weekend be a time when you say, 'We will not fail, and America will not fail.'" An article describing the Iowa meeting also notes that during his presentation, Newt Gingrich "described the 'Rediscovering God in America' films he has made with his wife, Callista, and said America is exceptional because its founding documents enshrine rights 'endowed by our creator.' He told the church that it was their Christian duty to fight for the 'truth,' exposing threats like overreaching by the Environmental Protection Agency." From Erik Eckholm, "An Iowa Stop in a Broad Effort to Revitalize the Religious Right," *New York Times,* 2 April 2011.

101. These are some of the goals that Scott Magelssen associates with living history museums. See Magelssen, "Making History in the Second Person: Post-tourist Considerations for Living Historical Interpretation," *Theatre Journal* 58, no. 2 (2006): 291–312. Annalee Ward notes that Holy Land Experience theme park "describes itself as a living history museum." "Faith-Based Theme Parks and Museums," 162.

102. Here I am borrowing Stanton Garner Jr.'s phrase. Garner proposes that "theatrical space is 'bodied' in the sense of being comprised of bodies positioned within a perceptual field, but it is also 'bodied' in the more fundamental sense of being 'bodied forth,' oriented in terms of a body that exists not just as the object of perception, but as its originating site." *Bodied Spaces: Phenomenology and Performance in Contemporary Drama* (Ithaca: Cornell University Press, 1994), 4.

103. Magelssen, "Making History in the Second Person," 291–93.

104. Creation Museum, "About the Museum," http://creationmuseum.org/about/.

105. It is perhaps noteworthy that the actor playing Kim, the evolutionist, appears to be of Asian descent, while the narrator is Caucasian. Here, again, the museum might be reinforcing certain nationalistic conceptualizations held by some visitors.

106. Evan Thompson, *Mind In Life: Biology, Phenomenology, and the Sciences of the Mind* (Cambridge: Harvard University Press, 2007), 393.

107. Thompson, *Mind In Life,* 386. See also Shaun Gallagher and Dan Zahavi, *The Phenomenological Mind: An Introduction to Philosophy of Mind and Cognitive Science* (London: Routledge, 2008), 183.

108. Thompson explains, "One of the most important reasons that human mentality cannot be reduced simply to what goes on inside the brain of an individual is that human mental activity is fundamentally social and cultural. Culture is no mere external addition or support to cognition; it is woven into the very fabric of each human mind from the beginning." *Mind In Life,* 403.

109. John H. Dierking and Lynn D. Falk, *Learning From Museums: Visitor Experiences and the Making of Meaning* (Walnut Creek, CA: AltaMira, 2000), 128.

110. David Morgan, *Visual Piety: A History and Theory of Popular Religious Images* (Berkeley: University of California Press, 1998), 152–80.

111. Alice Rayner, "Presenting Objects, Presenting Things," in *Staging Philosophy: Intersections of Theater, Performance, and Philosophy,* ed. David Krasner and David Z. Saltz (Ann Arbor: University of Michigan Press, 2006), 196. Rayner analyzes stage props specifically and uses this phrase with respect to the work of Tadeusz Kantor.

112. Ibid., 192.

113. Jennifer Williams, "Acquire the Fire: Affect, Ideology, and Contagion in Evangelical Performance," *Journal of Religion and Theatre* 7, no. 1 (2008): 33, http://www.athe.org/associations/12588/files/Williams.pdf.

114. Ibid.

115. Ibid., 21, 22.

Chapter 6

1. Pascal Boyer, *Religion Explained: The Evolutionary Origins of Religious Thought* (New York: Basic Books, 2001), 274.

2. Ibid., 276.

3. Ibid., 278.

4. Ibid.

5. Ibid., 277.

6. Ibid.

7. Harry Stout, *The Divine Dramatist: George Whitefield and the Rise of Modern Evangelicalism* (Grand Rapids, MI: William Eerdmans, 1991), xx.

8. I have already referred to William E. Connolly's *Capitalism and Christianity, American Style* (Durham: Duke University Press, 2008) in my Introduction. Other examples include Wade Clark Roof, *Spiritual Marketplace: Baby Boomers and the Remaking of American Religion* (Princeton: Princeton University Press, 1999); Kimon Howard Sargeant, *Seeker Churches: Promoting Traditional Religion in a Nontraditional Way* (New Brunswick: Rutgers University Press, 2000); Stephen M. Hoover, "The Cross at Willow Creek: Seeker Religion and the Contemporary Marketplace," in *Religion and Popular Culture in America,* ed. Bruce David Forbes and Jeffrey H. Mahan (Berkeley: University of California Press, 2000), 145–59; Roger Finke and Rodney Stark, *The Churching of America, 1776–2005: Winners and Losers in Our Religious Economy* (New Brunswick: Rutgers University Press, 2005); Shayne Lee and Phillip Luke Sinitiere, *Holy Mavericks: Evangelical Innovators and the Spiritual Marketplace* (New York: New York University Press, 2009).

9. Lee and Sinitiere, *Holy Mavericks,* 3. Lee and Sinitiere's book includes a cogent overview of this body of work entitled "Bibliographic Essay: Theory of Religious Economy," 159–76.

10. Lee and Sinitiere, *Holy Mavericks,* 3.

11. Boyer, *Religion Explained,* 277.

12. Leadership Network, "Resources," http://leadnet.org/resources.

13. Leadership Network, "Mission," http://leadnet.org/index.php/about/page/mission.

14. Saddleback Church, "Our Pastor," http://saddleback.com/aboutsaddleback/ourpastor/.

15. In his book *Megachurch and the Mainline,* Stephen Ellingson discusses how the resources developed by ministers like Warren and groups like the Willow Creek Association, as well as the "Seeker" megachurch model that I will discuss in the next section of this chapter, have impacted the strategies and missions of some mainline Protestant churches. He writes, "The proliferation of nondenominational congregations (including many of the new megachurches) and the growing importance of church growth consultants may be weakening the historic traditions of mainline Protestantism. Nondenominational churches self-consciously eschew many hallmarks of these traditions such as hymns, routinized liturgies, theological idioms and symbols, and recognizable church architecture. Nondenominationalism, especially the Seeker church model created by prominent megachurches, is both sold by church growth consultants as the panacea for all that ails declining mainline Protestant churches and identified as the path to success by many leaders within mainline Protestant denominations who then push their congregations to emulate nondenominational churches. At the same time, many megachurches aggressively market their worship, educational, and leadership resources, and several have established quasi-denominational associations that expand the influence of the nondenominational evangelical tradition. Some commentators suggest that we are seeing a shift from a diverse array of Protestant traditions to a more unified Protestant tradition that is grounded in nondenominational evangelicalism." Ellingson, *Megachurch and the Mainline: Remaking Religious Tradition in the Twenty-First Century* (Chicago: University of Chicago Press, 2007), 7. Moreover, a 2010 article in the *Houston Chronicle* describes how certain Catholic churches have begun to utilize worship strategies that Protestant megachurches commonly employ. These Catholic congregations are often associated with the charismatic revival, which began to gain traction in both the Catholic and Protestant traditions during the 1970s. For example, at some of these churches the services include high-tech enhancements, loud Praise Music led by a band, and "conversational, humorous sermons." See Kate Shellnutt, "Adore Ministries Blends Contemporary Worship with Ancient Tradition," *Houston Chronicle,* 12 March 2010, http://www.chron.com/life/houston-belief/article/Adore-Ministry-blends-contemporary-worship-with-1601561.php.

16. Faith Church, "Our History," http://www.faithchurchct.com/main/about/history.html.

17. Frances FitzGerald, "Come One, Come All," *New Yorker,* 3 December 2007, 53.

18. The A-Group, "About Us," http://www.agroup.com/about.html.

19. Ibid.

20. Quoted in FitzGerald, "Come One, Come All," 53.

21. Ibid., 54.

22. Scott Thumma and Dave Travis, *Beyond Megachurch Myths: What We Can Learn from America's Largest Churches* (San Francisco: Jossey-Bass, 2007), xviii. Thumma and Travis, like other scholars, use "attendance" rather than "membership" as the standard for measuring size, since "membership means different things in different traditions" and attendance is a better "barometer of participation" (xix–xx). As Thumma and Travis note, the 2,000 size determination has been the standard used in most work on megachurches, although some surveys use 1,800.

23. See John Vaughn, *Megachurches and America's Cities: How Churches Grow* (Grand Rapids, MI: Baker Books, 1993); Lyle E. Schaller, *The Very Large Church* (Nashville: Abingdon Press, 2000); Anne C. Loveland and Otis B. Wheeler, *From Meetinghouse to Megachurch: A Material and Cultural History* (Columbia: University of Missouri Press, 2003); Mark Chaves, *Congregations in America* (Cambridge: Harvard University Press, 2004); George Barna, *The State of the Church* (Ventura, CA: Barna Group, 2006). Just a few examples of articles in popular press venues include Charles Trueheart, "Welcome to the New Church," *Atlantic Monthly* (August 1996): 37–58; Jonathan Mahler, "The Soul of the New Exurb," *New York Times Magazine,* 27 March 2005, http://www.nytimes.com/2005/03/27/magazine/327MEGACHURCH.html?scp=1&sq=The%20Soul%20of%20the%20New%20Exurb&st=cse; William C. Symonds, "Earthly Empires: How Evangelical Churches are Borrowing from the Business Playbook," *Business Weekly,* 23 May 2005, 78–93; Jesse Bogan, "America's Biggest Megachurches," *Forbes,* 26 June 2009, http://www.forbes.com/2009/06/26/americas-biggest-megachurches-business-megachurches.html; David Van Biema, "Can Megachurches Bridge the Racial Divide," *Time,* 11 January 2010, http://www.time.com/time/magazine/article/0,9171,1950943-1,00.html; David Brooks, "The Gospel of Wealth," *New York Times,* 6 September 2010; John Leland, "The Evangelical Squad," *New York Times,* 22 April 2011.

24. Michael S. Hamilton, "The Triumph of the Praise Songs: How Guitars Beat Out the Organ in the Worship Wars," *Christianity Today: A Magazine of Evangelical Conviction,* 12 July 1999, http://www.christianitytoday.com/ct/1999/july12/9t8028.html. When this article was published, Hamilton was coordinator of the Pew Scholars Programs and concurrent assistant professor of history, University of Notre Dame.

25. Loveland and Wheeler, *From Meetinghouse to Megachurch,* 2.

26. See particularly the sources I cite above in note 23.

27. Thumma and Travis, *Beyond Megachurch Myths,* xvii.

28. Immanuel has an average weekly attendance of 2,000 members and is nondenominational (Immanuel Bible Church, "Homepage," http://www.immanuelbible.net/); Lakewood is nondenominational, has an average attendance of 43,500, and is led by the influential evangelical minister Joel Osteen (Lakewood Church, "Homepage," http://www.lakewood.cc/pages/home.aspx); McLean Bible Church is nondenominational and has an average attendance of 11,512 including all campuses (McLean Bible Church, "Homepage," http://www.mcleanbible.org/); Willow Creek Community Church is nondenominational and has a weekly attendance of 23,400 including all campuses (Willow Creek Community Church, "Homepage," http://www.willowcreek.org/home1.aspx); The Potter's House is a nondenominational church with an average weekly attendance of 17,000 and is led by the well-known evangelical pastor Bishop T. D. Jakes (The Potter's House, "Homepage," http://www.thepottershouse.org/). I used the following database to acquire denominational and weekly attendance data: Hartford Institute for Religion Research, "Database of Megachurches in the U.S.," http://hirr.hartsem.edu/megachurch/database.html.

29. Thumma and Travis supply a detailed overview of these studies in *Beyond Megachurch Myths* on pages 193–97. You can find the detailed data and summary reports for the Megachurches Today surveys at Hartford Institute of Religious Research, "Megachurch Research," http://hirr.hartsem.edu/megachurch/research.html.

30. Detailed data and summary reports for these two surveys are available at Hartford Institute of Religious Research, "Megachurch Research," http://hirr.hartsem.edu/megachurch/research.html.

31. Hartford Institute of Religious Research, "Profiles of Total U.S. Megachurches," http://hirr.hartsem.edu/megachurch/megastoday_profile.html. In the United States,

there are approximately 1,361 congregations of any denomination or affiliation with an average attendance of 1,800.

32. Thumma and Travis, *Beyond Megachurch Myths*, 5.

33. Ibid.

34. Ibid., 6.

35. Hartford Institute of Religious Research, "Megachurches Today Summary Report 2008. Changes in American Megachurches: Tracing Eight Years of Growth and Innovation in the Nation's Largest-attendance Congregations," http://hirr.hartsem.edu/megachurch/megastoday2008_summaryreport.html. The mean dropped to 3,585 in 2005. However, this dip may be due to an increase in the number of newer megachurches; the total number of megachurches nearly doubled between 2000 and 2005. This increase may have skewed overall growth statistics given that the report from 2005 indicates that those churches included in both the 2000 and 2005 surveys actually experienced notable growth: "The megachurches in our survey reported a 2005 average regular weekly attendance of 3,585 persons. These same churches claimed that 5 years earlier they had an average attendance of 2,279—an average increase in attendance of 57%." Hartford Institute of Religious Research, "Megachurches Today Summary Report 2005," http://hirr.hartsem.edu/megachurch/megastoday2005_summaryreport.html. In addition, the Hartford Institute's "Profile of U.S. Megachurches" web page includes a statistical breakdown of megachurches by geographic region, affiliation, size, and other criteria. See Hartford Institute of Religious Research, "Profiles of Total U.S. Megachurches," http://hirr.hartsem.edu/megachurch/megastoday_profile.html.

36. Thumma and Bird's "Megachurches Today Summary Report" is entitled "Changes in American Megachurches: Tracing Eight Years of Growth and Innovation in the Nation's Largest-attendance Congregations," http://hirr.hartsem.edu/megachurch/megastoday2008_summaryreport.html.

37. Respondents were asked to "describe the political outlook of the majority of the church's regularly participating adults" and were given five categories from which to choose: "Predominantly conservative," "Somewhat on the conservative side," "Right in the middle," "Somewhat on the liberal side," and "Predominantly liberal." In 2005 the study showed 51 percent in the "Predominantly conservative" category and 33 percent in "Somewhat on the conservative side." The 2008 survey reported 33 percent "Predominantly conservative" and 44 percent "Somewhat on the conservative side." Hartford Institute of Religious Research, "Megachurches Today Summary Report 2008. Changes in American Megachurches: Tracing Eight Years of Growth and Innovation in the Nation's Largest-attendance Congregations," http://hirr.hartsem.edu/megachurch/megastoday2008_summaryreport.html.

38. Ibid.

39. Thumma and Travis, *Beyond Megachurch Myths*, xxiv. Travis is currently Managing Director of Leadership Network, while Thumma is a professor at Hartford Seminary in Connecticut who has published in a variety of venues and worked on many of the megachurch surveys.

40. Thumma and Travis, *Beyond Megachurch Myths*, 30.

41. Ibid., 31.

42. Ibid., 30–41. These pages also include a useful comparative table (Table 2.3 on pages 32–35).

43. Ibid., 36. This stream is covered on pages 31 and 36–37.

44. Jane Lampman, "Pentecostalism at 100: A Major Religious Force," *Christian Science Monitor*, 24 April 2006, http://www.csmonitor.com/2006/0424/p01s01-lire.html.

45. Thumma and Travis, *Beyond Megachurch Myths*, 37–38. As I explained in Chap-

ter Two, Pentecostalism is a form of evangelicalism that contends that Christians must have a Second baptism in the Holy Spirit, a doctrine principally based upon passages in the New Testament book of Acts. For a definition of Pentecostal see Randall Balmer, *Encyclopedia of Evangelicalism* (Waco, TX: Baylor University Press, 2004), 533–34.

46. Lee and Sinitiere devote a chapter to Osteen in *Holy Mavericks*, 25–51.

47. The company Endless Games even adapted Osteen's 2004 best-selling book *Your Best Life Now* into a board game.

48. Thumma and Travis, *Beyond Megachurch Myths*, 38.

49. Lakewood Church, "Victoria Osteen," http://www.lakewood.cc/pages/new-here/victoria-osteen.aspx.

50. Thumma and Travis, *Beyond Megachurch Myths*, 38.

51. Warren is somewhat of an exception as a result of his book *The Purpose Driven Life* (Zondervan, 2007) and its various spin-off books, DVDs, journals, and other devotional material. See *The Purpose Driven Life*, "Homepage," http://www.purposedrivenlife.com/en-US/Home/home.htm. However, I would argue that because Warren devotes a great deal of time to helping other church leaders develop their institutions, his identity is intimately connected to Saddleback Church itself and to how he has helped establish the contemporary megachurch institution, rather than to his gifts as a dynamic preacher or his personal charisma. His biography on *The Purpose Drive Life* website identifies him as a pastor and a global strategist. *The Purpose Driven Life*, "About: Rick Warren," http://www.purposedrivenlife.com/en-US/AboutUs/AboutTheAuthor/AboutTheAuthor.htm.

52. Thumma and Travis, *Beyond Megachurch Myths*, 40.

53. Ibid., 39.

54. Ibid.

55. Ibid.

56. Ibid., 40. As Thumma and Travis explain, if the church's "vision or purpose is evangelism, they will have a pastor specifically charged with evangelism duties. If they highly value small group ministry, they will have a pastor who oversees the small group ministry." Ibid., 40.

57. FitzGerald, "Come One, Come All," 55.

58. William C. Symonds, "Marketing God's Word," *Stanford Business Alumni Magazine* (February 2009): 18, http://www.gsb.stanford.edu/news/bmag/packages/2009/february/MarketingGodsWord.pdf.

59. FitzGerald, "Come One, Come All," 56. This study is also discussed at length in Symonds, "Marketing God's Word."

60. FitzGerald, "Come One, Come All," 56.

61. Symonds, "Marketing God's Word," 16.

62. As described on the Willow Creek Association website, "REVEAL is a research-based view of how the spiritual journey unfolds, validated to date through survey input from over 157,000 congregants in more than 500 churches. The distinction of REVEAL is its ability to 'measure the unseen,' using a research approach that assesses how people's spiritual attitudes, needs and motivations align with spiritual behaviors." Willow Creek Association, "Products: Follow Me," http://www.willowcreek.com/wca_prod.asp?invtid=PR31455.

63. Thumma and Travis, *Beyond Megachurch Myths*, 41.

64. Ibid.

65. Ibid.

66. Frank Newport, "Americans' Church Attendance Inches Up in 2010," *Gallup*, 25 June 2010, http://www.gallup.com/poll/141044/americans-church-attendance-inches-2010.aspx.

67. The Pew Forum on Religion and Public Life, "U.S. Landscape Survey: Frequency of Attendance at Religious Services," http://religions.pewforum.org/comparisons#11.

68. Hamilton, "The Triumph of the Praise Song," http://www.christianitytoday.com/ct/1999/july12/9t8028.html.

69. Thumma and Travis note, "Megachurches have proven to be excellent at developing new forms and methods to adapt to current realities that will continue to serve them into the future." *Beyond Megachurch Myths,* 183.

70. As Immanuel's website explains, "The oversight of this church is vested in a body of elders who operate in concert with the deacons and the congregation. . . . The elders are responsible to guard the purity of church doctrine, to shepherd the flock, and to oversee church matters. The elders will ensure that the truths of the Bible are accurately taught and applied. The elders will minister to the needs of individuals and families through personal visitation, counseling, leading by example, teaching, discipline and restoration, and the general oversight of all church ministries. The elders will oversee all church matters." Immanuel Bible Church, "Leadership," http://www.immanuelbible.net/index.php/discover/leadership.html.

71. Gateway Bible Church, "History," http://gatewaybiblechurch.net/pages/page.asp?page_id=24890.

72. Thumma and Travis, *Beyond Megachurch Myths,* 65, Figure 4.1. The detailed reports are available at Hartford Institute of Religious Research, "Megachurches Today 2000," http://hirr.hartsem.edu/megachurch/faith_megachurches_FACTsummary.html and Faith Communities Today, "FACT 2000," http://faithcommunitiestoday.org/faith-communities-today-2000-study.

73. Acts 3:1–4:31 describes the disciples Peter and John preaching the Gospel message and their subsequent imprisonment for doing so. The seven "Confidence Builders" in Hartman's sermon were: Depend on the authority of Jesus; Be prepared to share the gospel; Expect victory over death; Be powered/filled with the Holy Spirit; Know Jesus as the Only Way; Share your personal experience; and Trust that God is in control.

74. Mahler, "Soul of the New Exurb."

75. Ibid. It is important to note that this article was published in 2005 and that Radiant's culture and aesthetic may have changed since then.

76. After taking over as pastor, Santora changed the name of his church from Bright Clouds Christian Church to Faith Church. As one pastor at Faith Church explained to FitzGerald, "to evangelicals, 'Christian' has a denominational ring to it." Quoted in FitzGerald, "Come One, Come All," 52.

77. Mahler, "Soul of the New Exurb."

78. Thumma and Travis, *Beyond Megachurch Myths,* 173.

79. McLean Bible Church, "Vision and Core Values," http://www.mbctysons.org/pages/page.asp?page_id=83701.

80. McLean Bible Church, "The Edge," http://www.mbctysons.org/pages/page.asp?page_id=85450.

81. McLean Bible Church, "About Frontline," http://www.frontlinedc.com/pages/page.asp?page_id=93309.

82. Thumma and Travis, *Beyond Megachurch Myths,* 173.

83. Ibid., 174.

84. Ibid., 41.

85. McLean Bible Church, "Apologetics Ministry Team," http://www.mbctysons.org/pages/page.asp?page_id=84210.

86. Loveland and Wheeler, *From Meetinghouse to Megachurch,* 1, 226.

87. Thumma and Travis, *Beyond Megachurch Myths,* 24.

88. Ibid.

89. Of course, this is not always the case, particularly with young adults who might attend services like those that McLean's Frontline ministry offers. But I would maintain that Sunday services are the entry point for most adult visitors to megachurches, and they are therefore designed to introduce new visitors to the church's culture and worship style.

90. Here, again, it is important to underscore the fact that I only visited a few churches and services. For example, none of the services I attended included the ritual of the Last Supper/Holy Communion. Yet, according to the 2008 megachurches survey, 48 percent of churches claim their services always or often include Holy Communion, Lord's Supper, or the Eucharist. This figure represented an increase of 8 percentage points from the 2005 survey. This may be due to an increase in fourth stream churches, which typically incorporate more traditional elements and rituals into their services. Hartford Institute of Religious Research, "Megachurches Today Summary Report 2008," http://hirr.hartsem.edu/megachurch/megastoday2008_summaryreport.html.

91. As the Service Builder website explains, "The products Dramas, Music, Messages and Video are literal transcriptions of the service elements as performed by the Willow Creek Community Church artists at services, conferences and ministry events." Willow Creek Association, "Service Builder: FAQs," http://www.willowcreek.com/servicebuilder/faq.asp#arrange.

92. Willow Creek Association, "Service Builder: Weekend Seeker Services," http://www.willowcreek.com/servicebuilder/servicepages/seekerindex.asp. According to the website, GenNeXt is defined as "single and married people in the postmodern generation (18- to 20-something)." Willow Creek Association, "Service Builder: FAQs," http://www.willowcreek.com/servicebuilder/faq.asp#Mtypes.

93. Willow Creek Association, "Service Builder: Washed Clean Seeker Service," http://www.willowcreek.com/service.asp?servid=2129.

94. Houston is the Creative Director of the Australian megachurch Hillsong Church, leader of the well-known Christian band Hillsong United, and is now copastor at Hillsong NYC. Hillsong Collected, "Joel Houston," http://hillsongcollected.com/contributor/joel-houston.

95. Willow Creek Association, "Service Builder: Washed Clean Seeker Service," http://www.willowcreek.com/service.asp?servid=2129.

96. For instance, a Seeker service entitled "Leadership Matters" dated 5 June 2010 is described on the website as emphasizing "the importance of leaders in all arenas leading with diligence. Leaders must have the ability to cast vision that's more compelling and more powerful than people's fears. They must be willing and able to develop support teams. And they shouldn't hesitate to invest in themselves in order to advance their leadership skills. When leadership fails to lead well within the church, the church falters and the kingdom is lost to people who need to see God's goodness through the actions of Christ-followers. And for those whose lives are impacted by leaders in the church and elsewhere, it's important to acknowledge them and their influence." This service includes an opening video, six songs, four scriptural readings (all four from the book of Psalms and three of them accompanied by songs), offering and announcements, a "comments" element described as "Communion Set-Up. Based on Psalm 139:23–34," Communion, and the sermon message from Hybels. Willow Creek Association, "Service Builder: Leadership Matters Seeker Service," http://www.willowcreek.com/service.asp?servid=2181.

97. Most of the GenNeXt service pages do not contain outlines of the services. Those that do are shorter but follow a structure similar to the one I have described. The Student Services are sold as packages, and their outlines are not available online.

98. Lee and Sinitiere, *Holy Mavericks,* 37. In 2004, the church signed a sixty-year lease for the facility with the city of Houston. Bogan, "America's Biggest Megachurches."

99. Interestingly, on our second visit we hoped for the same treatment and tried to look noticeably "confused" as we entered. However, nobody offered us an escort this time. Our first experience may have been part of an effort to fill seats near the front, since Osteen was absent that week.

100. Loveland and Wheeler, *From Meetinghouse to Megachurch,* 232–33.

101. There are a number of YouTube videos of Willow Creek events available online. One apparently shows clips from the Willow Creek Arts Conference in June 2009 and it gives viewers a good sense of the space, as well as the musical energy that often fills the space during worship services. YouTube, "Mighty to Save—Willow Creek Worship Team / CPNV at Willow Creek Arts Conference June 2009," http://www.youtube.com/watch?v=A9TB-aarDUI. Another video, apparently uploaded in September 2009 by someone who attended a service at Willow, shows the use of a center screen. YouTube, "Worship Session at Willow Creek Community Church," http://www.youtube.com/watch?v=RmplOc6nu0s&feature=related. These videos also highlight the different kinds of scenic design elements that the church incorporates around the stage space.

102. Hamilton, "The Triumph of the Praise Song," http://www.christianitytoday.com/ct/1999/july12/9t8028.html.

103. Hamilton argues that "democratic sensibilities" prompted church leaders to revise hymns to meet the baby boomer generation. Hamilton, "The Triumph of the Praise Song," http://www.christianitytoday.com/ct/1999/july12/9t8028.html. I will discuss praise and worship music in the next section.

104. Bo Emerson, "Wired for Worship," *Atlanta Journal-Constitution,* 26 January 2002. In LexisNexis Academic's online database.

105. Marvin Carlson, *Performance: A Critical Introduction,* 2nd ed. (London: Routledge, 2003), 22.

106. Andy Lavender, "Mise En Scène, Hypermediacy, and the Sensorium," in *Intermediality in Theatre and Performance,* ed. Freda Chapple and Chiel Kattenbelt (Amsterdam: Rodopi, 2006), 56.

107. Ibid.

108. Ibid.

109. Ibid., 62–63.

110. Anna Gibbs, "Contagious Feelings: Pauline Hanson and the Epidemiology of Affect," *Australian Humanities Review* (December 2001–February 2002), http://www.australianhumanitiesreview.org/archive/Issue-December-2001/gibbs.html.

111. Sergei Eisenstein, "Montage of Attractions: For *Enough Stupidity in Every Wiseman,*" *TDR* 18, no. 1 (1974): 78.

112. Ibid.

113. Jennifer Williams, "Acquire the Fire: Affect, Ideology, and Contagion in Evangelical Performance," *Journal of Religion and Theatre* 7, no. 1 (2008): 26, http://www.athe.org/associations/12588/files/Williams.pdf.

114. Lavender, "Mise En Scène," 56.

115. Microphones hang over the congregation at Lakewood, making it even clearer that attendees are considered an important visual and vocal element of the worship event.

116. Lakewood Church, "Watch Online," http://www.lakewood.cc/pages/watchonline.aspx.

117. Lakewood Church, "Watch Online: July 31, 2011," http://www.lakewood.cc/pages/watchonline.aspx#videoContainer.

118. See particularly Hamilton, "The Triumph of the Praise Song," http://www.christianitytoday.com/ct/1999/july12/9t8028.html; Greg Scheer, "A Musical Ichthus: Praise & Worship and Evangelical Identity," *International Journal of Community Music* 2, no. 1 (2009): 91–97; the collection *The Message in the Music: Studying Contemporary Praise and Worship,* ed. Robert Woods and Brian Walrath (Nashville: Abingdon Press, 2007), which contains essays that analyze the lyrical content, musical content, and styles of some of the most popular Christian Worship Music songs; see especially Bert Polman's essay in this collection, "Praise the Name of Jesus: Are All Praise and Worship Songs for Congregations?" 127–37. There is also a great deal of scholarship on gospel music, worship music in the specifically African American tradition, and Praise Music outside the United States.

119. Robert Woods and Brian Walrath, "Introduction," in *The Message in the Music: Studying Contemporary Praise and Worship,* ed. Woods and Walrath (Nashville: Abingdon Press, 2007), 14. An op-ed piece in the *New York Times* discussed how politics impacted the role of religious music in U.S. popular culture: David Stowe, "Jesus Christ Rock Star," *New York Times,* 23 April 2011, http://www.nytimes.com/2011/04/24/opinion/24Stowe.html?_r=1&scp=1&sq=jesus%20christ%20rock%20star&st=cse.

120. Polman, "Praise the Name of Jesus," 127.

121. Hamilton, "The Triumph of the Praise Song," http://www.christianitytoday.com/ct/1999/july12/9t8028.html.

122. Ibid.

123. Greg Scheer notes, "Evangelicals have a history of being utilitarian in their approach to the arts. In the late nineteenth century, and later evangelistic outreaches, it was a matter of using popular music to draw people in to hear the Gospel message, but now it has become more a matter of understanding one's market. If your church wants to reach a particular demographic, you use that demographic's music just as any advertiser would." "A Musical Ichthus," 94.

124. Hamilton, "The Triumph of the Praise Song," http://www.christianitytoday.com/ct/1999/july12/9t8028.html.

125. Polman, "Praise the Name of Jesus," 132.

126. I discuss musical entrainment in Chapter Three.

127. Polman, "Praise the Name of Jesus," 134.

128. Hamilton, "The Triumph of the Praise Song," http://www.christianitytoday.com/ct/1999/july12/9t8028.html. Hamilton also notes, "Over 100,000 churches in the United States (nearly one-third of all churches) participate in the reporting program of Christian Copyright Licensing Inc., which distributes royalties to publishers based on how many overhead projector transparencies churches make of each song. Most of their songs are in the praise and worship genre, the most popular of all being Rick Founds's 'Lord, I Lift Your Name on High.'"

129. For information on Maranatha! visit Maranatha! Music, "Homepage," http://www.maranathamusic.com/.

130. Thanks to David Baumann for this comment and for his help in articulating the specific sound of these songs.

131. Scheer, "A Musical Ichthus," 93, 95.

132. Hamilton argues that Praise Music "focuses on intensifying the individual's experience of God." Hamilton, "The Triumph of the Praise Song," http://www.christianitytoday.com/ct/1999/july12/9t8028.html.

133. Woods and Walrath, "Introduction," 16.

134. Hamilton, "The Triumph of the Praise Song," http://www.christianitytoday.com/ct/1999/july12/9t8028.html.

135. Another example is the first verse and chorus of "Blessed Be Your Name": "Blessed Be Your Name, / In the land that is plentiful, / Where Your streams of abundance flow. / Blessed be Your name. / Blessed Be Your name, / When I'm found in the desert place, / Though I walk through the wilderness, / Blessed Be Your name. / Every blessing You pour out, / I'll turn back to praise, / When the darkness closes in, Lord, / Still I will say. / Blessed be the name of the Lord, / Blessed be Your name, / Blessed be the name of the Lord, / Blessed be Your glorious name."

136. Hamilton, "The Triumph of the Praise Song," http://www.christianitytoday.com/ct/1999/july12/9t8028.html.

137. Ibid.

138. Scheer, "A Musical Ichthus," 95.

139. Notably, in every case the congregation was less than half full at the beginning of the service but steadily filled during this opening segment; I suspect that some regulars may skip the lengthy musical preludes. But this also contributed to the opening section's dramatic arc and momentum. As the music progressed, the bodies, voices, and energy seemed to multiply.

140. Brian Massumi, "Everywhere You Want To Be: Introduction to Fear," in *The Politics of Everyday Fear,* ed. Massumi (Minneapolis: University of Minnesota Press, 1993), page 30 of electronic version available at http://www.brianmassumi.com/textes/EVERYWHERE%20YOU%20WANT%20TO%20BE.pdf.

141. A common remark about Christian rock is that if you took a standard rock song and replaced words like "girl" and "baby" with "God" and "Jesus" you would have a popular Praise Song. The South Park episode "Christian Rock Hard" (Season 7, Episode 9; original air date 29 October 2003) is a wonderful riff on this idea. Available on the special edition *South Park: The Passion of the Jew,* DVD, dir. Trey Parker (Paramount Pictures, 2004).

142. This same passage appears on the website. McLean Bible Church, "Small Groups: General Information," http://www.mbctysons.org/pages/page.asp?page_id=83118.

143. Willow Creek Community Church, "New to Willow," http://www.willowcreek.org/newtowillow.

144. Willow Creek Community Church, "I Want to Connect," http://www.willowcreek.org/story.aspx?storyid=64.

145. I discuss Stephen di Benedetto's ideas in Chapter Two.

146. Thumma and Travis, *Beyond Megachurch Myths,* 94.

147. During the prayer partner section, the praise singers often speak these kinds of affirmations between verses. This particular statement was made by a singer at the service I attended in June.

148. For example, the lyrics of a song like "Free to Worship" help focus congregants on the personal, intimate relationship they can have with God: "Now I'm Free / To worship You, Lord / With all of my soul / And everything within me / I'm free to worship You, here / Casting out fear / Your love draws me near / to worship You / Draw me close, Draw me close."

149. Jennifer Williams asserts, "Contact is as essential to the ritual of ideological contagion on the scale of communal experience as it is on the scale of private intimacy." "Acquire the Fire," 28.

150. FitzGerald, "Come One, Come All," 55.

151. Bogan, "America's Biggest Megachurches."

152. Thumma and Travis, *Beyond Megachurch Myths,* 98. The sermon may, in fact,

be quite different in tone and substance from the other ministries of the church. For example, FitzGerald explains that "Faith Church today teaches Pentecostal theology in advanced Bible-study courses and holds special healing services once a month, but Santora rarely preaches on Pentecostal doctrine or speaks of Armageddon at the Sunday-morning services. 'Sundays are about real life, inspiration, and hope,' he told me. 'What good is it to have somebody know the ins and outs of eschatology if their marriage is falling apart, their kids are in all sorts of trouble, and they can't find a job?' Instead . . . Santora preaches thinking positively about God's purposes for one's life." "Come One, Come All," 52.

153. Thumma and Travis, *Beyond Megachurch Myths,* 100.

154. Ibid., 65.

155. Ephesians 6:4: "And, fathers, do not provoke your children to anger, but bring them up in the discipline and instruction of the Lord"; Hebrews 12:9: "Moreover, we had human parents to discipline us, and we respected them. Should we not be even more willing to be subject to the Father of spirits and live?"; 1 Thessalonians 2:11: "As you know, we dealt with each one of you like a father with his children."

156. 1 John 1:5–10 and 2:1–2: "This is the message we have heard from him and proclaim to you, that God is light, and in him there is no darkness at all. If we say we have fellowship with him while we walk in darkness, we lie and do not do what is true; but if we walk in the light as he himself is in the light, we have fellowship with one another, and the blood of Jesus his Son cleanses us from all sin. If we say we have no sin, we deceive ourselves, and the truth is not in us. If we confess our sins, he who is faithful and just will forgive us our sins and to cleanse us from all unrighteousness. If we say that we have not sinned, we make him a liar, and his word is not in us." 1 John 3:1: "See what love the Father has given us, that we should be called children of God; and that is what we are. The reason the world does not know us is that it did not know him."

157. Vincent Crapanzano, *Serving the Word: Literalism in America from the Pulpit to the Bench* (New York: New Press, 2000), 66.

158. As Balmer explains, an altar call in the evangelical tradition "is generally an invitation by the preacher to step toward the pulpit for conversion, baptism, or church membership." Because most evangelical churches do not have an actual physical altar, it is best understood as "an invitation to a spiritual rather than a physical location." Balmer, *Encyclopedia of Evangelicalism,* 14.

159. Lakewood Church, "Frequently Asked Questions," http://english.lakewood.cc/pages/contact/frequently-asked-questions.aspx.

160. I have copied this creed as it appears on Lakewood's website and have been careful to retain that version's punctuation and capitalization. Lakewood Church, "Frequently Asked Questions," http://english.lakewood.cc/pages/contact/frequently-asked-questions.aspx.

161. Quoted in Bogan, "America's Biggest Megachurches."

162. Crapanzano, *Serving the Word,* 56. Crapanzano is speaking here about Fundamentalist literalism as expressed in sermons, but I see a similar rhetorical shift happening in the Lakewood creed ritual.

163. Sometimes during his sermons, usually near the end, Osteen appears overcome with emotion. For example, during the 31 July 2011 service that I watched online, close to the end of his sermon Osteen suddenly stopped, pressed his hands to his eyes, and appeared to hold back tears. This pause lasted about twenty-five seconds before he recovered and began speaking again. Lakewood Church, "Watch Online: July 31, 2011," http://www.lakewood.cc/pages/watchonline.aspx#videoContainer. This occurs at 1:36 on the video.

164. Jane Goodall, *Stage Presence* (London: Routledge, 2008), 46.
165. Ibid., 43.
166. Ibid., 46.
167. Based upon the many services I have watched, these lines and others that I will quote seem to vary only slightly, if at all, from service to service. The quotes I use in the next few paragraphs are taken directly from the 31 July 2011 service currently available on Lakewood's website: Lakewood Church, "Watch Online: July 31, 2011," http://www.lakewood.cc/pages/watchonline.aspx#videoContainer.
168. Osteen also uses relatively vague language that likely resonates with most congregants. For instance, during his 31 July 2011 sermon he told congregants that although "your mind may try to talk you out of it happening . . . down deep you'll feel a fire, a burning, a restlessness, a stirring. That's the promise that God put in you." This passage also reinforces my claims about the personal, "felt" nature of the theology that evangelical dramaturgy is used to communicate. Lakewood Church, "Watch Online: July 31, 2011," http://www.lakewood.cc/pages/watchonline.aspx#videoContainer.
169. Sarah McNamer, *Affective Meditation and the Invention of Medieval Compassion* (Philadelphia: University of Pennsylvania Press, 2010), 53.
170. Erika Fischer-Lichte, *The Transformative Power of Performance: A New Aesthetics*, trans. Saskya Iris Jain (2004; London: Routledge, 2008), 199–200.
171. Thumma and Travis, *Beyond Megachurch Myths*, 149.
172. Fischer-Lichte, *The Transformative Power of Performance*, 179.
173. Lavender, "Mise En Scène," 64.
174. Quoted in Lavender, "Mise En Scène," 65.
175. FitzGerald, "Come One, Come All," 56.
176. Gilles Fauconnier and Mark Turner, *The Way We Think: Conceptual Blending and the Mind's Hidden Complexities* (New York: Basic Books, 2002), 131.
177. Ibid., 136.
178. Willow Creek Community Church, "Visiting Willow," http://www.willowcreek.org/visitingwillow.
179. Willow Creek Community Church, "Harvest/Dr. Bs," http://www.willowcreek.org/harvest.
180. Willow Creek Community Church, "Visiting Willow," http://www.willowcreek.org/visitingwillow.
181. As quoted in Mahler, "Soul of the New Exurb."
182. Loveland and Wheeler, *From Meetinghouse to Megachurch*, 257.
183. Mahler, "Soul of the New Exurb."
184. Lavender, "Mise En Scène," 63.
185. See, for example, Willow Creek's mission as outlined on its website: "Raising the level of risk when it comes to reaching out to those who are far from God, coaching Christ-followers as they pursue full devotion to God, unleashing unprecedented levels of compassion into our broken world." Willow Creek Community Church, "New to Willow," http://www.willowcreek.org/newtowillow.
186. I discuss parish churches at length throughout *Performance, Cognitive Theory, and Devotional Culture: Sensual Piety in Late Medieval York* (New York: Palgrave, 2010). In the Coda of that book I also briefly compare the medieval parish church to the megachurch. See *Performance, Cognitive Theory, and Devotional Culture*, 160–63.
187. I argue this point in *Performance, Cognitive Theory, and Devotional Culture*, 71.
188. Katherine French, *The People of the Parish: Community Life in a Late Medieval English Diocese* (Philadelphia: University of Pennsylvania Press, 2001), 20. Eamon Duffy lists various objects for which parishioners were responsible in *The Stripping*

of the Altars: Traditional Religion in England, 1400–1580 (New Haven: Yale University Press, 1992), 132–34. A few other sources on the medieval parish church include *Mass and Parish in Late Medieval England: The Use of York*, ed. Barnwell, Cross, and Ann Rycraft (Reading: Spire Books, 2005); Paul Binski, "The English Parish Church and Its Art in the Later Middle Ages: A Review of the Problem," *Studies in Iconography* 20 (1999): 1–25; Clive Burgess, "For the Increase of Divine Service: Chantries in the Parish in Late Medieval Bristol," *Journal of Ecclesiastical History* 36 (1985): 46–65; *Parish, Church and People: Local Studies in Lay Religion, 1350–1750*, ed. Susan Wright (London: Hutchinson, 1988).

189. As FitzGerald notes, "a third of all megachurch pastors do not have seminary degrees; and in younger churches the less formal religious training a pastor has, the higher the growth rate of his church is likely to be. [Scott] Thumma thinks there are two reasons for this. First, pastors without seminary training are less removed from secular life, and less liable to speak 'churchese.' Second, and just as important, religious training has nothing to do with the entrepreneurial and managerial talents required to build and run a very large church." "Come One, Come All," 54.

190. Thumma and Travis, *Beyond Megachurch Myths*, 24.

Coda

1. Timothy Beal, *Roadside Religion: In Search of the Sacred, the Strange, and the Substance of Faith* (Boston: Beacon Press, 2005), 12.
2. Jill Lepore, *The Whites of Their Eyes: The Tea Party's Revolution and the Battle Over American History* (Princeton: Princeton University Press, 2010).
3. Ibid., 4.
4. Ibid., 7.
5. Ibid., 15.
6. Ibid., 15–16.
7. Ibid., 47.
8. Ibid., 68.
9. Ibid., 96.
10. Ibid., 69.
11. Ibid., 15, 97.
12. Ibid., 15.
13. Ibid., 16.
14. Vincent Crapanzano, *Serving the Word: Literalism in America from the Pulpit to the Bench* (New York: New Press, 2000), 183. Crapanzano's project examines the relationship between Christian Fundamentalist literalism and "legal thinking that gives priority to 'plain meaning,' 'original meaning,' or 'original intent'" (xviii). The overlap between the two may be a direct result of—and innate to—U.S. secularism. In the Introduction to their collection *Secularisms*, Janet Jakobsen and Ann Pellegrini argue that "in its dominant, market-based incarnation," secularism "constitutes a specifically Protestant form of secularism." More specifically, they maintain that the "universality and reasonableness" that this secularism offers "are actually particular (to European History) and religious (Protestant) in form." Jakobsen and Pellegrini, ed., *Secularisms* (Durham: Duke University Press, 2008), 3.
15. Crapanzano, *Serving the Word*, 181–82.
16. I discuss the concept of "spheres of presence" in Chapter Four.
17. Frank Rich, "The Billionaires Bankrolling the Tea Party," *New York Times*, 28 August 2010.

18. Jane Mayer, "Covert Operations," *New Yorker,* 30 August 2010, http://www.newyorker.com/reporting/2010/08/30/100830fa_fact_mayer.

19. Ibid.

20. In an op-ed piece in which they discuss the August 2011 *New York Times*/CBS News survey of opinions related to the Tea Party, David E. Campbell and Robert Putnam explain, "Next to being a Republican, the strongest predictor of being a Tea Party supporter today was a desire, back in 2006, to see religion play a prominent role in politics. And Tea Partiers continue to hold these views: they seek 'deeply religious' elected officials, approve of religious leaders' engaging in politics and want religion brought into political debates. The Tea Party's generals may say their overriding concern is a smaller government, but not their rank and file, who are more concerned about putting God in government. This inclination among the Tea Party faithful to mix religion and politics explains their support for Representative Michele Bachmann of Minnesota and Gov. Rick Perry of Texas. Their appeal to Tea Partiers lies less in what they say about the budget or taxes, and more in their overt use of religious language and imagery, including Mrs. Bachmann's lengthy prayers at campaign stops and Mr. Perry's prayer rally in Houston." Campbell and Putnam, "Crashing the Tea Party," *New York Times,* 17 August 2011, http://www.nytimes.com/2011/08/17/opinion/crashing-the-tea-party.html?_r=1&scp=1&sq=crashing%20the%20tea%20party&st=cse.

21. Ann Pellegrini, "Feeling Secular," *Women and Performance: A Journal of Feminist Theory* 19, no. 2 (2009): 207. Pellegrini is here paraphrasing conclusions from Jakobsen and Pellegrini, "World Secularisms at the Millennium: Introduction," *Social Text* 64 (2000): 1–27.

22. Pellegrini, "Feeling Secular," 211–12.

23. Jeremy Peters, "Appealing to Evangelicals, Hopefuls Pack Religion into Ads," *New York Times,* 27 December 2011.

24. Ross Douthat, "American Theocracy Revisited," *New York Times,* 28 August 2011. As a conservative practicing Catholic who writes for major mainstream media outlets, Douthat is likely especially alert to (and, perhaps, also invested in revealing) instances of religious illiteracy, particularly among those in the press corps.

25. William E. Connolly, *Capitalism and Christianity, American Style* (Durham: Duke University Press, 2008), 7.

26. Ibid.

27. Ibid., 34.

28. Bethany Moreton, *To Serve God and Wal-Mart: The Making of Christian Free Enterprise* (Cambridge: Harvard University Press, 2009), 16. As Mark Gimein, writing in *Fortune,* notes, the "paradox" of Wal-Mart is that it "stands for both Main Street values and the efficiencies of the huge corporation, aw-shucks hokeyness and terabytes of minute-by-minute sales data, fried-chicken luncheons at the Waltons' Arkansas home and the demands of Wall Street." Mark Gimein, "Sam Walton Made Us a Promise," *Fortune,* 18 March 2002, http://money.cnn.com/magazines/fortune/fortune_archive/2002/03/18/319920/index.htm. Quoted in Moreton, *To Serve God and Wal-Mart,* 6.

29. Moreton, *To Serve God and Wal-Mart,* 89.

30. Ibid., 89, 122. In 1995, Ralph Reed, then head of the Christian Coalition, remarked, "If you want to reach the Christian population on Sunday, you do it from the church pulpit. If you want to reach them on Saturday, you do it in Wal-Mart." Quoted in Moreton, *To Serve God and Wal-Mart,* 1.

31. Connolly, *Capitalism and Christianity,* 66. I discuss Linda Kintz's work on resonance in Chapter One. Kintz, *Between Jesus and the Market: The Emotions that Matter in Right-Wing America* (Durham: Duke University Press, 1997), 6–7.

32. Moreton, *To Serve God and Wal-Mart,* 89.
33. Ibid., 88.
34. Pellegrini, "Feeling Secular," 215.
35. Crapanzano notes the "longing for belief" of "the Bible-believing Christian." *Serving the Word,* 31.
36. Barack Obama's 2008 presidential campaign may represent a notable exception, one that is quite relevant to evangelical dramaturgy. Arguably, this campaign's grass-roots, entrepreneurial nature and its intensive use of social media forms offered many voters meaningful, intimate, affective encounters in response to pervasive cultural longing for political change. Immediately after the campaign, Claire Cain Miller reported that "by using interactive Web 2.0 tools, Mr. Obama's campaign changed the way politicians organize supporters, advertise to voters, defend against attacks and communicate with constituents." Internet tools gave voters a strong sense of agency and choice during the campaign. For example, Obama's campaign took advantage of free advertising on YouTube and, as one political consultant explained, 'those videos were more effective than television ads because viewers chose to watch them or received them from a friend instead of having their television shows interrupted." The use of Facebook for the first time by a presidential nominee also added degrees of intimacy and immediacy to the voter's campaign experience. Moreover, internet tools offered plenty of opportunities for self-directed, one-on-one virtual interactions with the candidate's views. For better or worse, YouTube gave voters a sense of unmediated access to the candidate's "genuine" beliefs; as Joe Trippi, a political consultant, noted, "this medium demands authenticity, and television for the most part demanded fake. Authenticity is something politicians haven't been used to" (see Claire Cain Miller, "How Obama's Internet Campaign Changed Politics," *New York Times,* 7 November 2008). The Obama campaign also generated affective scripts through other means that correspond to the tactics of evangelical dramaturgy. For example, the phrase *Yes We Can* gave voters a literal script in direct response to their longing, as did the campaign's embrace of the term *Hope,* notably one of the four secular feelings that Pellegrini identifies. Furthermore, this message was packaged into an iconic commodity through Shepard Fairey's incredibly popular and ubiquitous Obama poster, which usually contained the word *Hope,* but in other iterations promoted *Progress, Change,* or *Vote.* The fact that Fairey was a street artist further supported the personal, entrepreneurial ethos of the campaign. As a result of these various tactics, for many voters, most of whom probably never attended a live event, Obama's campaign constituted a truly energetic encounter. And, yet, this example also reveals the constant struggle over affect in U.S. political discourse today. In the weeks and months after his inauguration, much of the campaign's energy dissipated as voters had to wait and see what "Change" would actually occur and how it would impact their lives. Beyond casting a vote, the "Yes We Can" script did not supply any meaningful answers or concrete actions for the long term. It is not entirely surprising, then, that almost immediately after Obama's election the Tea Party began to use various performative means—some of them strategies borrowed from Obama's campaign—in order to produce alternative scripts that could fill the affective void in U.S. politics.
37. Rebecca Schneider, *Performing Remains: Art and War in Times of Theatrical Reenactment* (London: Routledge, 2011), 174, 173.
38. Ibid., 172, 174.
39. Ibid., 180.
40. Ibid., 3, 22.
41. Ibid., 182–83.
42. Ibid., 23.

43. Ibid., 25.

44. I believe there is a genuine and widespread desire for this kind of exploration, evidenced by films such as *Hell House* (2001; dir. Ratliff), *Jesus Camp* (2006; dir. Ewing and Grady), *Friends of God: A Road Trip with Alexandra Pelosi* (2007; dir. Pelosi), and *Waiting for Armageddon* (2009; dir. Davis, Heilbroner, and Sacchi), as well as books like Daniel Radosh, *Rapture Ready! Adventures in the Parallel Universe of Christian Pop Culture* (New York: Scribner, 2008), Gina Welch, *In the Land of Believers: An Outsider's Extraordinary Journey into the Heart of the Evangelical Church* (New York: Metropolitan Books, 2010), and Tanya M. Luhrmann, *When God Talks Back: Understanding the American Evangelical Relationship with God* (New York: Knopf, 2012). This desire is also reflected in the many recent books that aim to understand how conservatives—particularly evangelicals—"think," among them Drew Westen, *The Political Brain: The Role of Emotion in Deciding the Fate of the Nation* (New York: PublicAffairs, 2007); William Saletan, *Bearing Right: How Conservatives Won the Abortion War* (Berkeley: University of California Press, 2004); George Lakoff, *The Political Mind: A Cognitive Scientist's Guide to Your Brain and Its Politics* (New York: Penguin, 2009); Lakoff, *The Political Mind: Why You Can't Understand 21st-Century American Politics with an 18th-Century Brain* (New York: Viking, 2008); Lakoff, *Moral Politics: How Liberals and Conservatives Think* (Chicago: University of Chicago Press, 1996; 2nd ed., 2002); and Jonathan Haidt, *The Righteous Mind: Why Good People Are Divided by Politics and Religion* (New York: Pantheon, 2012).

45. Notably, none of my professional colleagues who were raised in evangelical or Fundamentalist traditions, or who themselves study evangelical Christianity, expressed similar sentiments.

46. Crapanzano, *Serving the Word*, 349. He also notes that "despite their real and professed ignorance, many of them launched into diatribes against the Fundamentalists—diatribes they would have condemned as prejudice and bigotry if somebody else were addressing another religion in the same terms" (348). Such responses were rare among my colleagues.

47. Pellegrini, "Feeling Secular," 215.

Bibliography

Published Primary and Secondary Sources

Allen, Tom, et al., eds. *A Guide to The Passion of The Christ: 100 Questions about* The Passion of The Christ. Encinitas, CA: Catholic Exchange Press, 2004.

Altizer, Thomas J. J. "The Passion and the Death of God." In *Mel Gibson's Bible: Religion, Popular Culture, and* The Passion of the Christ, edited by Timothy Beal and Tod Linafelt, 155–58. Chicago: University of Chicago Press, 2006.

American Association of Museums. "AAM Press Release: Americans Identify Museums as a Source of Information They Can Really Trust." 2001, www.aam-us.org/pressreleases.cfm?mode=list&id=21.

Amos, Jonathan. "South African Fossils Could Be New Hominid Species." *BBC News*, 8 April 2010, http://news.bbc.co.uk/2/hi/science/nature/8609192.stm.

Amsler, Mark. "Affective Literacy: Gestures of Reading in the Later Middle Ages." *Essays in Medieval Studies* 18 (2001): 83–110.

Answers in Genesis. *Museum Guide: A Bible-Based Handbook to Natural History Museums*. China: Answers in Genesis, 2007.

Arroyo, Leah. "Science on Faith at the Creation Museum." *Museum News* (November–December 2007), http://www.aam-us.org/pubs/mn/scienceonfaith.cfm.

Asma, Stephen. "Dinosaurs on the Ark: The Creation Museum." *Chronicle of Higher Education* 53, no. 37 (2007), accessed through Academic Search Premier.

Ballengee Morris, Christine, and James H. Sanders III. "Culture, Identity, Representation: The Economic Policies of Heritage Tourism." *International Journal of Education through Art* 5, nos. 2–3 (2009): 129–42.

Balmer, Randall. *Encyclopedia of Evangelicalism*. Waco, TX: Baylor University Press, 2004.

Balmer, Randall. *Mine Eyes Have Seen the Glory: A Journey into the Evangelical Subculture in America*. Oxford: Oxford University Press, 1989; 4th ed., 2006.

Balmer, Randall. *The Making of Evangelicalism*. Waco, TX: Baylor University Press, 2010.

Barna, George. *The State of the Church*. Ventura, CA: Barna Group, 2006.

Barnwell, Cross, and Ann Rycraft, eds. *Mass and Parish in Late Medieval England: The Use of York*. Reading: Spire Books, 2005.

Barry, Dan. "A Passion Play Endures as a Seasonal Miracle." *New York Times*, 20 April 2011.

Barton, Bruce. "Paradox as Process: Intermedial Anxiety and the Betrayals of Intimacy." *Theatre Journal* 61, no. 4 (2009): 575–601.

Beal, Timothy. *Roadside Religion: In Search of the Sacred, the Strange, and the Substance of Faith*. Boston: Beacon Press, 2005.

Beal, Timothy. "They Know Not What They Watch." In *Mel Gibson's Bible: Religion, Popular Culture, and* The Passion of the Christ, edited by Beal and Tod Linafelt, 199–204. Chicago: University of Chicago Press, 2006.

Beal, Timothy K., and Tod Linafelt, eds. *Mel Gibson's Bible: Religion, Popular Culture, and* The Passion of the Christ. Chicago: University of Chicago Press, 2006.

Beckwith, Sarah. *Christ's Body: Identity, Culture and Society in Late Medieval Writings*. London: Routledge, 1993.

Beckwith, Sarah. *Signifying God: Social Relation and Symbolic Act in the York Corpus Christi Plays*. Chicago: University of Chicago Press, 2001.

Belting, Hans. *The Image and Its Public in the Middle Ages: Form and Function of Early Paintings of the Passion*. Translated by M. Bartusis and R. Meyer. New Rochelle, NY: Caratzas, 1990.

Bennett, Tony. *The Birth of the Museum: History, Theory, Politics*. London: Routledge, 1995.

Bennett, Tony. *Pasts Beyond Memory: Evolution, Museums, Colonialism*. London: Routledge, 2004.

Berger, Lee R., Darryl J. de Ruiter, Steven E. Churchill, Peter Schmid, Kristian J. Carlson, Paul H. G. M. Dirks, and Job M. Kibii. "*Australopithecus sediba:* A New Species of *Homo*-Like Australopith from South Africa." *Science* 328, no. 5975 (2010): 195–204.

Biernoff, Suzannah. *Sight and Embodiment in the Middle Ages*. New York: Palgrave, 2002.

Biernoff, Suzannah. "Carnal Relations: Embodied Sight in Merleau-Ponty, Roger Bacon and St Francis." *Journal of Visual Culture* 4, no. 1 (2005): 39–52.

Binski, Paul. "The English Parish Church and Its Art in the Later Middle Ages: A Review of the Problem." *Studies in Iconography* 20 (1999): 1–25.

Binski, Paul. *Becket's Crown: Art and Imagination in Gothic England, 1170–1350*. New Haven: Yale University Press, 2004.

Blumhofer, Edith L., Russell P. Spittler, and Grant A. Wacker, eds. *Pentecostal Currents in American Protestantism*. Urbana: University of Illinois Press, 1999.

Boenisch, Peter. "Aesthetic Art to Aisthetic Act: Theatre, Media, Intermedial Performance." In *Intermediality in Theatre and Performance*, edited by Freda Chapple and Chiel Kattenbelt, 103–16. Amsterdam: Rodopi, 2006.

Bogan, Jesse. "America's Biggest Megachurches." *Forbes*, 26 June 2009, http://www.forbes.com/2009/06/26/americas-biggest-megachurches-business-megachurches.html.

Boyer, Pascal. *Religion Explained: The Evolutionary Origins of Religious Thought*. New York: Basic Books, 2001.

Boyer, Paul. *When Time Shall Be No More: Prophecy Belief in Modern American Culture*. Cambridge: Harvard University Press, 1992.

Boyer, Peter J. "The Jesus War." *New Yorker*, 15 September 2003, 58–71.

Branham, Joan. "The Crucifixion and Ice Cream." *Newsweek*, 23 May 2008, http://www.newsweek.com/2008/05/22/the-crucifixion-and-ice-cream.html#.

Branham, Joan. "The Temple that Won't Quit: Constructing Sacred Space in Orlando's Holy Land Experience Theme Park." *Crosscurrents* 59, no. 3 (2009): 358–82.

Brantley, Jessica. *Reading in the Wilderness: Private Devotion and Public Performance in Late Medieval England*. Chicago: University of Chicago Press, 2007.

Brooks, David. "The Gospel of Wealth." *New York Times*, 6 September 2010.

Bull, Marcus. *Thinking Medieval*. New York: Palgrave, 2005.

Burgess, Clive. "For the Increase of Divine Service: Chantries in the Parish in Late Medieval Bristol." *Journal of Ecclesiastical History* 36 (1985): 46–65.

Byassee, Jason. "Dinosaurs in the Garden." *Christian Century* 125, no. 3 (2008): 22–26.

Camille, Michael. "Before the Gaze: The Internal Senses and Late Medieval Practices of Seeing." In *Visuality Before and Beyond the Renaissance*, edited by Robert S. Nelson, 197–223. Cambridge: Cambridge University Press, 2000.

Campbell, David E., and Robert Putnam. "Crashing the Tea Party." *New York Times*, 17 August 2011, http://www.nytimes.com/2011/08/17/opinion/crashing-the-tea-party.html?_r=1&scp=1&sq=crashing%20the%20tea%20party&st=cse.

Carlson, Marvin. *Performance: A Critical Introduction*. 2nd ed. London: Routledge, 2003.

Cashion, Debra Taylor. "The Man of Sorrows and Mel Gibson." In *Tributes in Honor of James H. Marrow: Studies in Painting and Manuscript Illumination of the Late Middle Ages and Northern Renaissance*, edited by Jeffrey Hamburger and Anne Korteweg, 139–45. Turnhout: Brepols, 2006.

Chang, Kenneth. "Paleontology and Creationism Meet but Don't Mesh." *New York Times*, 30 June 2009, final edition.

Chansky, Dorothy. "North American Passion Plays: 'The Greatest Story Ever Told' in the New Millennium." *TDR* 50, no. 4 (2006): 120–45.

Chattaway, Peter. "Mel Gibson's Jesus Film Inspires Impassioned Discussion Among Pastors, Ministry Leaders." *Canadian Christianity*, undated, http://canadianchristianity.com/cgi-bin/na.cgi?nationalupdates/040122gibson.

Chaves, Mark. *Congregations in America*. Cambridge: Harvard University Press, 2004.

Clark, Anne. "Why All the Fuss about the Mind? A Medievalist's Perspective on Cognitive Theory." In *History in the Comic Mode: Medieval Communities and the Matter of Person*, edited by Rachel Fulton and Bruce Holsinger, 170–81. New York: Columbia University Press, 2007.

Cockett, Peter. "*Bigger than Jesus:* Mediating the Larger than Live Story." *Canadian Theatre Review* 127 (2006): 7–10.

Condon, W. S., and W. D. Ogston. "Sound Film Analysis of Normal and Pathological Behavior Patterns." *Journal of Nervous and Mental Diseases* 143 (1966): 338–47.

Connolly, William E. *Capitalism and Christianity, American Style*. Durham: Duke University Press, 2008.

Corliss, Richard. "Holy Hypocrisies." *Time*, 27 February 2004, http://www.time.com/time/columnist/corliss/article/0,9565,596038,00.html.

Corliss, Richard. "Movies: The Goriest Story Ever Told." *Time*, 1 March 2004, http://www.time.com/time/magazine/article/0,9171,993485,00.html.

Crapanzano, Vincent. *Serving the Word: Literalism in America from the Pulpit to the Bench*. New York: The New Press, 2000.

Crease, Robert P., and John Lutterbie. "Technique." In *Staging Philosophy: Intersections of Theater, Performance, and Philosophy*, edited by David Krasner and David Z. Saltz, 160–79. Ann Arbor: University of Michigan Press, 2006.

Crooke, Elizabeth. *Museums and Community: Ideas, Issues and Challenges*. London: Routledge, 2007.

Dacey, Austin. "Science and the Public: Is Science Making Us More Ignorant?" *Skeptical Inquirer* 28, no. 6 (2004), http://www.csicop.org/si/show/is_science_making_us_more_ignorant.

Davis, Tracy C. "Performing and the Real Thing in the Postmodern Museum." *TDR* 39, no. 3 (1995): 15–40.

Decety, Jean. "To What Extent Is the Experience of Empathy Mediated by Shared Neural Circuits?" *Emotion Review* 2, no. 3 (2010): 204–7.

Di Benedetto, Stephen. "Guiding Somatic Responses Within Performative Structures: Contemporary Live Art and Sensorial Perception." In *The Senses in Performance*, edited by Sally Banes and André Lepecki, 124–34. New York: Routledge, 2007.

Dierking, Lynn, and John D. Falk. *Museum Experience*. Washington, DC: Whalesback Books, 1992.

Dierking, Lynn, and John D. Falk. *Learning from Museums: Visitor Experiences and the Making of Meaning*. Walnut Creek, CA: AltaMira, 2000.

Dinshaw, Carolyn. *Getting Medieval: Sexualities and Communities, Pre- and Postmodern*. Durham: Duke University Press, 1999.

Douthat, Ross. "American Theocracy Revisited." *New York Times*, 28 August 2011.

Dowd, Maureen. "Stations of the Crass." *New York Times*, 26 February 2004.

Dox, Donnalee. "The Willing Sustenance of Belief: Religiosity and Mode of Performance." *Journal of Religion and Theatre* 8, no. 1 (2009): 20–47, http://www.athe.org/associations/12588/files/Dox.pdf.

Dox, Donnalee. "Ceremonial Embodiment: The Problem of 'Liturgical Drama.'" *Ecumenica* 3, no. 2 (2010): 31–41.

Duffy, Eamon. *The Stripping of the Altars: Traditional Religion in England, 1400–1580*. New Haven: Yale University Press, 1992.

Duffy, Eamon. "Late Medieval Religion." In *Gothic Art for England, 1400–1547*, edited by Richard Marks and Paul Williamson, 56–67. London: V&A Publications, 2003.

Duffy, Eamon. *Marking the Hours: English People and Their Prayers, 1240–1570*. New Haven: Yale University Press, 2006.

Eckholm, Erik. "An Iowa Stop in a Broad Effort to Revitalize the Religious Right." *New York Times*, 2 April 2011.

Eco, Umberto. *Travels in Hyperreality: Essays*. San Diego: Harcourt Brace Jovanovich, 1986.

Eisenstein, Sergei. "Montage of Attractions: For *Enough Stupidity in Every Wiseman*." *TDR* 18, no. 1 (1974): 77–85.

Eldred, Jody. *Changed Lives: Miracles of the Passion*. Eugene, OR: Harvest House, 2004.

Ellingson, Stephen. *Megachurch and the Mainline: Remaking Religious Tradition in the Twenty-First Century*. Chicago: University of Chicago Press, 2007.

Emerson, Bo. "Wired for Worship." *Atlanta Journal-Constitution*, 26 January 2002. Accessed through LexisNexis database.

Essig, Laurie. "No Rapture, but the End Days Are Upon Us." *Chronicle of Higher Education*, 23 May 2011, http://chronicle.com/blogs/brainstorm/no-rapture-but-the-end-days-are-upon-us/35598.

Feld, Steven. "Places Sensed, Senses Placed: Toward a Sensuous Epistemology of Environments." In *Empire of the Senses: The Sensual Culture Reader*, edited by David Howes, 179–91. Oxford: Berg, 2005.

Finke, Roger, and Rodney Stark. *The Churching of America, 1776–2005: Winners and Losers in Our Religious Economy*. New Brunswick: Rutgers University Press, 2005.

Fischer-Lichte, Erika. *The Transformative Power of Performance: A New Aesthetics*. Translated by Saskya Iris Jain. London: Routledge, 2008. Originally published as *Ästhetik des Performativen*. Frankfurt: Suhrkamp, 2004.

Fisher, Jennifer. "Tangible Acts: Touch Performances." In *The Senses in Performance*, edited by Sally Banes and André Lepecki, 166–78. New York: Routledge, 2007.

FitzGerald, Frances. "Come One, Come All." *New Yorker*, 3 December 2007, 46–56.

Fletcher, John. "Tasteless as Hell: Community Performance, Distinction, and Countertaste in Hell House." *Theatre Survey* 48, no. 2 (2007): 313–30.

Fletcher, John. *Preaching to Convert: Evangelical Outreach and Performance Activism in a Secular Age*. Ann Arbor: University of Michigan Press, forthcoming.

Flora, Brad. "The Holy Land Experience: Who Shall Inherit the Kingdom?" *News 21: A Journalism Initiative of the Carnegie and Knight Foundations*, 23 August 2007, http://newsinitiative.org/story/2007/08/23/the_holy_land_experience_who.

Flora, Brad. "Holy Land Experience Chief Resigns 10 weeks into TBN Takeover." *News 21: A Journalism Initiative of the Carnegie and Knight Foundations*, 28 August 2007, http://newsinitiative.org/story/2007/08/28/holy_land_experience_chief_resigns.

Fogassi, Leonardo. "The Mirror Neuron System: How Cognitive Functions Emerge from Motor Organization." *Journal of Economic Behavior & Organization* 77, no. 1 (2011): 66–75.

Foister, Susan. "Paintings in Sixteenth-Century English Inventories." *Burlington Magazine* 123, no. 938 (May 1981): 273–82.

Forbes, Bruce David, and Jeffrey H. Mahan, eds. *Religion and Popular Culture in America*. Berkeley: University of California Press, 2000.

Fowler, Mayhill. "Obama: No Surprise that Hard-Pressed Pennsylvanians Turn Bitter." *Huffington Post*, 11 April 2008, http://www.huffingtonpost.com/mayhill-fowler/obama-no-surprise-that-ha_b_96188.html.

Franklin, Robert M. "*The Passion* in Black and White." In *Mel Gibson's Bible: Religion, Popular Culture, and* The Passion of the Christ, edited by Timothy Beal and Tod Linafelt, 195–97. Chicago: University of Chicago Press, 2006.

Frazzetto, Giovanni. "Who's Afraid of Darwin?" *European Molecular Biology Organization Reports* 5, no. 7 (2004): 662–65.

Frederickson, Paula, ed. *On "The Passion of the Christ": Exploring the Issues Raised by the Controversial Movie*. Berkeley and Los Angeles: University of California Press, 2006.

French, Katherine. *The People of the Parish: Community Life in a Late Medieval English Diocese*. Philadelphia: University of Pennsylvania Press, 2001.

Frykholm, Amy Johnson. *Rapture Culture:* Left Behind *in Evangelical America*. Oxford: Oxford University Press, 2004.

Fulton, Rachel. *From Judgment to Passion: Devotion to Christ and the Virgin Mary, 800–1200*. New York: Columbia University Press, 2002.

Fulton, Rachel. "Praying with Anselm at Admont: A Meditation on Practice." *Speculum* 81, no. 3 (2006): 700–733.

Gallagher, Shaun, and Dan Zahavi. *The Phenomenological Mind: An Introduction to Philosophy of Mind and Cognitive Science*. London: Routledge, 2008.

Gallese, Vittorio. "Embodied Simulation: From Neurons to Phenomenal Experience." *Phenomenology and the Cognitive Sciences* 4, no. 1 (2005): 23–48.

Gallese, Vittorio, and George Lakoff. "The Brain's Concepts: The Role of Sensory-Motor System in Conceptual Knowledge." *Cognitive Neuropsychology* 22, no. 3–4 (2005): 455–79.

Garber, Zev, ed. *Mel Gibson's* Passion: *The Film, the Controversy, and Its Implications*. West Lafayette: Purdue University Press, 2006.

Garner, Stanton B., Jr. *Bodied Spaces: Phenomenology and Performance in Contemporary Drama*. Ithaca: Cornell University Press, 1994.

Garrison, Jennifer. "Mediated Piety: Eucharistic Theology and Lay Devotion in Robert Mannyng's *Handlyng Synne*." *Speculum* 85, no. 4 (2010): 894–922.

Gates, David. "Jesus Christ Movie Star." *Newsweek*, 8 March 2004, http://www.newsweek.com/2004/03/07/jesus-christ-movie-star.html.

Gibbs, Anna. "Contagious Feelings: Pauline Hanson and the Epidemiology of Affect." *Australian Humanities Review* (December 2001–February 2002), http://www.australianhumanitiesreview.org/archive/Issue-December-2001/gibbs.html.

Gibbs, Anna. "After Affect: Sympathy, Synchrony, and Mimetic Communication." In *The Affect Theory Reader,* edited by Melissa Gregg and Gregory J. Seigworth, 186–205. Durham: Duke University Press, 2010.

Gibson, Gail McMurray. *The Theater of Devotion: East Anglian Drama and Society in the Late Middle Ages.* Chicago: University of Chicago Press, 1989.

Gill, A. A. "Roll Over, Charles Darwin!" *Vanity Fair* (February 2010): 72–75.

Gimein, Mark. "Sam Walton Made Us a Promise." *Fortune,* 18 March 2002, http://money.cnn.com/magazines/fortune/fortune_archive/2002/03/18/319920/index.htm.

Goodall, Jane. *Stage Presence.* London: Routledge, 2008.

Goodnough, Abby. "Darwin-Free Fun for Creationists." *New York Times,* 1 May 2004, final edition.

Green, John Clifford, James L. Guth, Corwin E. Smidt, and Lyman A. Kellstedt. *Religion and the Culture Wars: Dispatches from the Front.* Lanham, NY: Rowman and Littlefield, 1991.

Gregg, Melissa, and Gregory J. Seigworth. "An Inventory of Shimmers." In *The Affect Theory Reader,* edited by Gregg and Seigworth, 1–25. Durham: Duke University Press, 2010.

Grossberg, Lawrence. *We Gotta Get Out of This Place: Popular Conservatism and Postmodern Culture.* New York: Routledge, 1992.

Haidt, Jonathan. *The Righteous Mind: Why Good People Are Divided by Politics and Religion.* New York: Pantheon, 2012.

Hamburger, Jeffrey F. *The Visual and the Visionary: Art and Female Spirituality in Late Medieval Germany.* New York: Zone, 1998.

Hamilton, Michael S. "The Triumph of the Praise Songs: How Guitars Beat Out the Organ in the Worship Wars." *Christianity Today: A Magazine of Evangelical Conviction,* 12 July 1999, http://www.christianitytoday.com/ct/1999/july12/9t8028.html.

Harding, Susan. "The Gospel of Giving: The Narrative Structure of a Sacrificial Economy." In *Vocabularies of Public Life: Empirical Essays in Symbolic Structure,* edited by R. Wuthnow, 39–56. London: Routledge, 1992.

Hart, D. G. *That Old-Time Religion in Modern America: Evangelical Protestantism in the Twentieth Century.* Chicago: Ivan R. Dee, 2002.

Hatch, Nathan. *The Democratization of American Christianity.* New Haven: Yale University Press, 1989.

Hendershot, Heather. *Shaking the World for Jesus: Media and Conservative Evangelical Culture.* Chicago: University of Chicago Press, 2004.

Hickok, Gregory. "Eight Problems for the Mirror Neuron Theory of Action Understanding in Monkeys and Humans." *Journal of Cognitive Neuroscience* 21, no. 7 (2008): 1229–43.

Hickok, Gregory, and Marc Hauser. "(Mis)understanding Mirror Neurons." *Current Biology* 20, no. 14 (2010): R593–R594.

Holsinger, Bruce. "Liturgy." In *Oxford Twenty-First Century Approaches to Literature: Middle English,* edited by Paul Strohm, 295–314. Oxford: Oxford University Press, 2007.

Hoover, Stephen M. "The Cross at Willow Creek: Seeker Religion and the Contemporary Marketplace." In *Religion and Popular Culture in America,* edited by Bruce David Forbes and Jeffrey H. Mahan, 145–59. Berkeley: University of California Press, 2000.

Horwitz, Paul. "How to Respond to Rick Perry and 'The Response.'" *New York Times,* 5 August 2011, http://www.nytimes.com/2011/08/06/opinion/how-to-respond-to-rick-perrys-response.html?_r=1&scp=1&sq=paul%20horwitz&st=cse.

Hunter, James Davidson. *Culture Wars.* New York: Basic Books, 1991.

Jakobsen, Janet R., and Ann Pellegrini. "World Secularisms at the Millennium: Introduction." *Social Text* 64 (2000): 1–27.

Jakobsen, Janet R., and Ann Pellegrini, eds. *Secularisms.* Durham: Duke University Press, 2008.

Jauss, Hans Robert. *Toward an Aesthetic of Reception.* Minneapolis: Minnesota University Press, 1982.

Jeansonne, Glen. *Gerald L. K. Smith: Minister of Hate.* New Haven: Yale University Press, 1988.

Johnson, Mark. *The Body in the Mind.* Chicago: University of Chicago Press, 1987.

Johnson, Mark. *The Meaning of the Body: Aesthetics of Human Understanding.* Chicago: University of Chicago Press, 2008.

Juslin, Patrik N. "From Mimesis to Catharsis: Expression, Perception, and Induction of Emotion in Music." In *Musical Communication,* edited by Dorothy Miell, Raymond MacDonald, and David J. Hargreaves, 85–115. Oxford: Oxford University Press, 2005.

Kamerick, Kathleen. *Popular Piety and Art in the Late Middle Ages: Image Worship and Idolatry in England, 1350–1500.* New York: Palgrave, 2002.

Kessler, Herbert L. *Seeing Medieval Art.* Ontario: Broadview Press, 2004.

Keysers, Christian. "Mirror Neurons." *Current Biology* 19, no. 21 (2009): R971–R973.

Keysers, Christian, and Valeria Gazzola. "Social Neuroscience: Mirror Neurons Recorded in Humans." *Current Biology* 20, no. 8 (2010): R353–R354.

King, Pamela. *The York Mystery Cycle and the Worship of the City.* Cambridge: D. S. Brewer, 2006.

Kintz, Linda. *Between Jesus and the Market: The Emotions that Matter in Right-Wing America.* Durham: Duke University Press, 1997.

Kintz, Linda, and Julia Lesage, eds. *Media, Culture, and the Religious Right.* Minneapolis: University of Minnesota Press, 1998.

Klan, Nicole. "Margery Kempe and Pentecostalism." *Religion and Literature* 42, no. 1–2 (2010): 163–84.

Kovalcik, Timothy. *Images of America: The Great Passion Play.* Charleston: Arcadia, 2008.

Kupfer, Marcia, ed. *The Passion Story: From Visual Representation to Social Drama.* University Park: Pennsylvania State University Press, 2008.

LaHaye, Tim, and Jerry B. Jenkins. *Left Behind: A Novel of the Earth's Last Days.* Carol Stream, IL: Tyndale House, 1995.

Lakoff, George. *Moral Politics: How Liberals and Conservatives Think.* Chicago: University of Chicago Press, 1996; 2nd ed., 2002.

Lakoff, George. *The Political Mind: Why You Can't Understand 21st-Century American Politics with an 18th-Century Brain.* New York: Viking, 2008.

Lakoff, George. *The Political Mind: A Cognitive Scientist's Guide to Your Brain and Its Politics.* New York: Penguin, 2009.

Lampman, Jane. "Pentecostalism at 100: A Major Religious Force." *Christian Science Monitor,* 24 April 2006, http://www.csmonitor.com/2006/0424/p01s01-lire.html.

Lavender, Andy. "Mise En Scène, Hypermediacy, and the Sensorium." In *Intermediality in Theatre and Performance,* edited by Freda Chapple and Chiel Kattenbelt, 55–67. Amsterdam: Rodopi, 2006.

Lee, Shayne, and Phillip Luke Sinitiere. *Holy Mavericks: Evangelical Innovators and the Spiritual Marketplace.* New York: New York University Press, 2009.

Leland, John. "The Evangelical Squad." *New York Times,* 22 April 2011.

Lepore, Jill. *The Whites of Their Eyes: The Tea Party's Revolution and the Battle Over American History.* Princeton: Princeton University Press, 2010.

Lerer, Seth. "'Representyd now in yower syght': The Culture of Spectatorship in Late-Fifteenth-Century England." In *Bodies and Disciplines: Intersections of Literature and History in Fifteenth-Century England*, edited by Barbara Hanawalt and David Wallace, 29–62. Minneapolis: University of Minnesota Press, 1996.

Leys, Ruth. "The Turn to Affect: A Critique." *Critical Inquiry* 37 (2011): 434–72.

Lingnaua, Angelika, Benno Gesiericha, and Alfonso Caramazzaa. "Asymmetric fMRI Adaptation Reveals No Evidence for Mirror Neurons in Humans." *Proceedings of the National Academy of Sciences* 106, no. 24 (2009): 9925–30.

Lippi-Green, Rosina. *English with an Accent: Language, Ideology and Discrimination in the United States*. London: Routledge, 1997.

Little, William G. "Jesus's Extreme Makeover." In *Mel Gibson's Bible: Religion, Popular Culture, and* The Passion of the Christ, edited by Timothy Beal and Tod Linafelt, 169–76. Chicago: University of Chicago Press, 2006.

Long, Burke O. *Imagining the Holy Land: Maps, Models, and Fantasy Travels*. Bloomington: Indiana University Press, 2003.

Looy, Mark. "Re-writing Human Evolution—Again?" 9 April 2010, http://www.answersingenesis.org/articles/2010/04/09/rewriting-human-evolution-again.

Loveland, Anne C., and Otis B. Wheeler. *From Meetinghouse to Megachurch: A Material and Cultural History*. Columbia: University of Missouri Press, 2003.

Luhrmann, Tanya M. *When God Talks Back: Understanding the American Evangelical Relationship with God*. New York: Knopf, 2012.

Lukens-Bull, Ronald, and Mark Fafard. "(Re)Creating Israel in Christian Zionism." *Journal of Religion and Society* 9 (2007): 1–20, http://moses.creighton.edu/JRS/2007/2007-16.pdf.

MacDonald, Alasdair, Bernhard Ridderbos, and R. M. Schlusemann, eds. *The Broken Body: Passion Devotion in Late Medieval Culture*. Groningen: Egbert Forsten, 1998.

Magelssen, Scott. "Making History in the Second Person: Post-tourist Considerations for Living Historical Interpretation." *Theatre Journal* 58, no. 2 (2006): 291–312.

Mahler, Jonathan. "The Soul of the New Exurb." *New York Times Magazine*, 27 March 2005, http://www.nytimes.com/2005/03/27/magazine/327MEGACHURCH.html?scp=1&sq=The%20Soul%20of%20the%20New%20Exurb&st=cse.

Marks, Richard. "An Age of Consumption: Art for England c. 1400–1547." In *Gothic Art for England, 1400–1547*, edited by Richard Marks and Paul Williamson, 12–25. London: V&A Publications, 2003.

Massumi, Brian. *The Politics of Everyday Fear*. Minneapolis: University of Minnesota Press, 1993.

May, Max. *Isaac Mayer Wise The Founder Of American Judaism: A Biography*. New York: Knickerbocker Press, 1916.

Mayer, Jane. "Covert Operations." *New Yorker*, 30 August 2010, http://www.newyorker.com/reporting/2010/08/30/100830fa_fact_mayer.

McConachie, Bruce. "Doing Things with Image Schemas: The Cognitive Turn in Theatre Studies and the Problem of Experience for Historians." *Theatre Journal* 53, no. 4 (2001): 569–94.

McConachie, Bruce. "Falsifiable Theories for Theatre and Performance Studies." *Theatre Journal* 59, no. 4 (2007): 553–77.

McConachie, Bruce. *Engaging Audiences: A Cognitive Approach to Spectating in the Theatre*. New York: Palgrave, 2008.

McDannell, Colleen. *Material Christianity: Religion and Popular Culture in America*. New Haven: Yale University Press, 1998.

McGrath, Ben. "The Movement: The Rise of Tea Party Activism." *New Yorker*, 1 February 2010, http://www.newyorker.com/reporting/2010/02/01/100201fa_fact_mcgrath.

McKinley, James, Jr. "In Texas, a Line in the Curriculum Revives Evolution Debate." *New York Times,* 21 January 2009, final edition.

McKinley, James, Jr. "Texas Conservatives Win Curriculum Change." *New York Times,* 12 March 2010, final edition.

McNamer, Sarah. *Affective Meditation and the Invention of Medieval Compassion.* Philadelphia: University of Pennsylvania Press, 2010.

Meacham, Jon. "Who Killed Jesus?" *Newsweek,* 16 February 2004, http://www.newsweek.com/2004/02/15/who-killed-jesus.html#.

Miles, Margaret. *Seeing and Believing: Religion and Values in the Movies.* Boston: Beacon Press, 1996.

Miles, Margaret. "The Passion for Social Justice and *The Passion of the Christ.*" In *Mel Gibson's Bible: Religion, Popular Culture, and* The Passion of the Christ, edited by Timothy Beal and Tod Linafelt, 121–27. Chicago: University of Chicago Press, 2006.

Miller, Claire Cain. "How Obama's Internet Campaign Changed Politics." *New York Times,* 7 November 2008.

Miller, Vincent. "Contexts: Theology, Devotion, and Culture." In *Mel Gibson's Bible: Religion, Popular Culture, and* The Passion of the Christ, edited by Timothy Beal and Tod Linafelt, 39–49. Chicago: University of Chicago Press, 2006.

Moll, Rob. "Creation Display." *Christianity Today* 51, no. 7 (2007): 13.

Molnar-Szakacs, Istvan. "From Actions to Empathy and Morality: A Neural Perspective." *Journal of Economic Behavior & Organization* 77, no. 1 (2011): 76–85.

Moreton, Bethany. *To Serve God and Wal-Mart: The Making of Christian Free Enterprise.* Cambridge: Harvard University Press, 2009.

Morgan, David. *Visual Piety: A History and Theory of Popular Religious Images.* Berkeley: University of California Press, 1998.

Morgan, David. "Catholic Visual Piety and *The Passion of the Christ.*" In *Re-Viewing The Passion: Mel Gibson's Film and Its Critics,* edited by S. Brent Plate, 85–96. New York: Palgrave Macmillan, 2004.

Morgan, David. *Sacred Gaze: Religious Visual Culture in Theory and Practice.* Berkeley and Los Angeles: University of California Press, 2005.

Morgan, David. *The Lure of Images: A History of Religion and Visual Media in America.* London: Routledge, 2007.

Mukamel, Roy, Arne D. Ekstrom, Jonas Kaplan, Marco Iacoboni, and Itzhak Fried. "Single-neuron Responses in Humans during Execution and Observation of Actions." *Current Biology* 20, no. 8 (2010): 750–56.

Nellhaus, Tobin. "Performance Strategies, Image Schemas, and Communication Frameworks." In *Performance and Cognition: Theatre Studies and the Cognitive Turn,* edited by Bruce McConachie and F. Elizabeth Hart, 76–94. New York: Routledge, 2006.

Nelson, Robert E. *Economics As Religion: From Samuelson to the Chicago School and Beyond.* University Park: Pennsylvania State University Press, 2001.

Newport, Frank. "Americans' Church Attendance Inches Up in 2010." *Gallup,* 25 June 2010, http://www.gallup.com/poll/141044/americans-church-attendance-inches-2010.aspx.

Ngai, Sianne. *Ugly Feelings.* Cambridge: Harvard University Press, 2005.

Niedzielski, Nancy A., and Dennis Preston. *Folk Linguistics.* Berlin: Mouton de Gruyter, 2000.

Noë, Alva. *Action in Perception.* Cambridge: MIT Press, 2004.

Nord, David Paul. "The Evangelical Origins of Mass Media in America, 1815–1835." *Journalism Monographs* 88 (May 1984): 1–30.

Nord, David Paul. *Faith in Reading: Religious Publishing and the Birth of Mass Media in America.* New York: Oxford University Press, 2004.

O'Connor, Dennis. "Science and Faith: Three Years On Creation Museum Is Evolving." *Houston Chronicle,* 10 September 2010, http://www.chron.com/life/houston-belief/article/Three-years-on-Creation-Museum-is-evolving-1705245.php.

Orsi, Robert. *Between Heaven and Earth: The Religious Worlds People Make and the Scholars Who Study Them.* Princeton: Princeton University Press, 2005.

Parker, Ashley. "Make My Bed? But You Say the World's Ending." *New York Times,* 20 May 2011.

Patel, Aniruddh. "Music, Biological Evolution, and the Brain." In *Emerging Disciplines: Shaping New Fields of Scholarly Inquiry In and Beyond the Humanities,* edited by Melissa Bailar, 91–144. Houston: Rice University Press, 2010.

Pellegrini, Ann. "'Signaling Through the Flames': Hell House Performance and Structures of Religious Feeling." *American Quarterly* 59, no. 3 (2007): 911–35.

Pellegrini, Ann. "Feeling Secular." *Women and Performance: A Journal of Feminist Theory* 19, no. 2 (2009): 205–18.

Peters, Jeremy. "Appealing to Evangelicals, Hopefuls Pack Religion into Ads." *New York Times,* 27 December 2011.

Petersen, Nils Holger. "Devotion and Dramaticity in the *Bordesholmer Marienklage* (1476)." In *Dies est leticie: Essays on Chant in Honour of Janka Szendrei,* edited by David Hiley, 413–27. Ottawa: Institute of Medieval Music, 2008.

Plate, S. Brent, ed. *Re-Viewing the Passion: Mel Gibson's Film and Its Critics.* New York: Palgrave Macmillan, 2004.

Polman, Bert. "Praise the Name of Jesus: Are All Praise and Worship Songs for Congregations?" In *The Message in the Music: Studying Contemporary Praise and Worship,* edited by Robert Woods and Brian Walrath, 127–37. Nashville: Abingdon Press, 2007.

Radosh, Daniel. *Rapture Ready! Adventures in the Parallel Universe of Christian Pop Culture.* New York: Scribner, 2008.

Rayner, Alice. "Presenting Objects, Presenting Things." In *Staging Philosophy: Intersections of Theater, Performance, and Philosophy,* edited by David Krasner and David Z. Saltz, 180–99. Ann Arbor: University of Michigan Press, 2006.

Rees Jones, Sarah, and Felicity Riddy. "The Bolton Hours of York: Female Domesticity, Piety and the Public Sphere." In *Household, Women and Christianities in Late Antiquity and the Middle Ages,* edited by Anneke B. Mulder-Bakke and Jocelyn Wogan-Browne, 215–60. Turnhout: Brepols, 2006.

Rich, Frank. "Mel Gibson's Martyrdom Complex." *International Herald Tribune,* 3 August 2003.

Rich, Frank. "The Billionaires Bankrolling the Tea Party." *New York Times,* 28 August 2010.

Rizzolatti, Giacomo, Laila Craighero, and Luciano Fadiga. "The Mirror System in Humans." In *Mirror Neurons and the Evolution of Brain and Language,* edited by Maxim I. Stamenov and Vittorio Gallese, 37–59. Amsterdam: John Benjamins, 2002.

Rokotnitz, Naomi. "'It is required/You do awake your faith': Learning To Trust the Body Through Performing *The Winter's Tale.*" In *Performance and Cognition: Theatre Studies and the Cognitive Turn,* edited by Bruce McConachie and F. Elizabeth Hart, 122–46. New York: Routledge, 2006.

Roof, Wade Clark. *A Generation of Seekers: The Religion of the Baby Boom Generation.* San Francisco: HarperCollins, 1993.

Roof, Wade Clark. *Spiritual Marketplace: Baby Boomers and the Remaking of American Religion*. Princeton: Princeton University Press, 1999.
Rothstein, Edward. "Adam and Eve in the Land of Dinosaurs." *New York Times*, 24 May 2007, final edition.
Rothstein, Jandos. "Graphic Displays of Faith." *Print* 62, no. 1 (2008): 96–101.
Saletan, William. *Bearing Right: How Conservatives Won the Abortion War.* Berkeley: University of California Press, 2004.
Sargeant, Kimon Howard. *Seeker Churches: Promoting Traditional Religion in a Nontraditional Way.* New Brunswick: Rutgers University Press, 2000.
Sarna, Jonathan. *American Judaism: A History.* New Haven: Yale University Press, 2004.
Sawyer, R. Keith. "Music and Communication." In *Musical Communication*, edited by Dorothy Miell, Raymond MacDonald, and David J. Hargreaves, 45–60. Oxford: Oxford University Press, 2005.
Schaller, Lyle E. *The Very Large Church*. Nashville, TN: Abingdon Press, 2000.
Scheer, Greg. "A Musical Ichthus: Praise & Worship and Evangelical Identity." *International Journal of Community Music* 2, no. 1 (2009): 91–97.
Scherb, Victor I. *Staging Faith: East Anglian Drama in the Later Middle Ages*. Madison: Fairleigh Dickinson University Press, 2001.
Schilling-Estes, Natalie, and Walt Wolfram. *American English: Dialects and Variation*. 2nd ed. Cambridge: Basil Blackwell, 2006.
Schleif, Corine. "Hands That Appoint, Anoint and Ally: Late Medieval Donor Strategies for Appropriating Approbation Through Painting." *Art History* 16, no. 1 (March 1993): 1–32.
Schneider, Rebecca. *Performing Remains: Art and War in Times of Theatrical Reenactment*. London: Routledge, 2011.
Schultze, Quentin, and Robert Woods Jr., eds. *Understanding Evangelical Media: The Changing Face of Christian Communication*. Downers Grove, IL: InterVarsity Press, 2008.
Scott, A. O. "'The Passion of the Christ': Good and Evil Locked in Violent Showdown." *New York Times*, 25 February 2004.
Scribner, Robert. "Popular Piety and Modes of Visual Perception in Late Medieval and Reformation Germany." *Journal of Religious History* 15 (1989): 448–69.
Seel, Martin. "Inszenieren als Erscheinenlassen. Thesen ueber die Reichweite eines Begriffs." In *Aesthetik der Inszenierung*, edited by J. Fruechtl and J. Zimmermann, 48–62. Frankfurt: Suhrkamp, 2001.
Shapiro, James. *Oberammergau: The Troubling Story of the World's Most Famous Passion Play.* New York: Vintage, 2000.
Shelley, Bruce L., and Marshall Shelley. *The Consumer Church: Can Evangelicals Win the World Without Losing Their Souls?* Downers Grove, IL: InterVarsity Press, 1992.
Shellnutt, Kate. "Adore Ministries Blends Contemporary Worship with Ancient Tradition." *Houston Chronicle*, 12 March 2010, http://www.chron.com/life/houston-belief/article/Adore-Ministry-blends-contemporary-worship-with-1601561.php.
Shepherd, Simon. *Theatre, Body and Pleasure*. London: Routledge, 2006.
Shorto, Russell. "Founding Father?" *New York Times Magazine*, 14 February 2010, 32–39; 46–47, http://www.nytimes.com/2010/02/14/magazine/14texbooks-t.html?scp=5&sq=Founding%20Father&st=cse.
Simon, Stephanie. "Acting on Faith in Arkansas." *Los Angeles Times*, 22 September 2005, http://articles.latimes.com/2005/sep/22/nation/na-passion22.
Sklar, Deidre. "Unearthing Kinesthesia: Groping Among Cross-cultural Models of the Senses in Performance." In *The Senses in Performance*, edited by Sally Banes and André Lepecki, 38–46. New York: Routledge, 2007.

Smiga, George. "The Good News of Mel Gibson's *Passion*." In *Mel Gibson's Bible: Religion, Popular Culture, and* The Passion of the Christ, edited by Timothy Beal and Tod Linafelt, 21–28. Chicago: University of Chicago Press, 2006.

Smith, Christian. *American Evangelicalism: Embattled and Thriving*. Chicago: University of Chicago Press, 1998.

Smith, Gerald L. K. "The Passion Play: An Open Letter by Gerald L. K. Smith." *Eureka Springs Times-Echo,* 1 February 1968.

Smith, Melanie B. "Great Divide Separates Creationists, Evolutionists." *Decatur Daily,* 19 February 2010, http://www.decaturdaily.com/stories/Great-divide-separates-creationists-evolutionists,53891.

Soukup, Paul. "Considering a Catholic View of Evangelical Media." In *Understanding Evangelical Media: The Changing Face of Christian Communication,* edited by Quentin Schultze and Robert Woods Jr., 263–73. Downers Grove, IL: InterVarsity Press, 2008.

Spalding, John D. "Authentic Replica: My Holy Land Experience." *Christian Century* 119, no. 14 (2002), Accessed through Academic OneFile.

Spencer, Brian. *Pilgrim Souvenirs and Secular Badges*. London: Stationery Office, 1998.

Sponsler, Claire. *Drama and Resistance: Bodies, Goods, and Theatricality in Late Medieval England*. Minneapolis: University of Minnesota Press, 1997.

Sponsler, Claire. *Ritual Imports: Performing Medieval Drama in America*. Ithaca: Cornell University Press, 2004.

Staff Writer. "5,000 Pastors Cheer Mel Gibson's *Passion*." *Washington Times,* 21 January 2004, http://www.washingtontimes.com/news/2004/jan/21/20040121-113810-3164r/.

Stanbury, Sarah. *The Visual Object of Desire in Late Medieval England*. Philadelphia: University of Pennsylvania Press, 2008.

Stevenson, Jill. "The Material Bodies of Medieval Religious Performance in England." *Material Religion: The Journal of Objects, Art, and Belief* 2, no. 2 (2006): 204–32.

Stevenson, Jill. *Performance, Cognitive Theory, and Devotional Culture: Sensual Piety in Late Medieval York*. New York: Palgrave, 2010.

Stevenson, Jill. "Embodying Sacred History: Performing Creationism for Believers." *TDR* 56, no. 1 (2012): 91–111.

Stout, Harry. *The Divine Dramatist: George Whitefield and the Rise of Modern Evangelicalism*. Grand Rapids, MI: William Eerdmans, 1991.

Stowe, David. "Jesus Christ Rock Star." *New York Times,* 23 April 2011, http://www.nytimes.com/2011/04/24/opinion/24Stowe.html?_r=1&scp=1&sq=jesus%20christ%20rock%20star&st=cse.

Stowe, David. *No Sympathy for the Devil: Christian Pop Music and the Transformation of American Evangelicalism*. Chapel Hill: University of North Carolina Press, 2011.

Symonds, William C. "Earthy Empires: How Evangelical Churches Are Borrowing from the Business Playbook." *Business Weekly,* 23 May 2005, 78–93.

Symonds, William C. "Marketing God's Word." *Stanford Business Alumni Magazine* (February 2009): 16–19, http://www.gsb.stanford.edu/news/bmag/packages/2009/february/MarketingGodsWord.pdf.

Taylor, Mark C. "The Offense of Flesh." In *Mel Gibson's Bible: Religion, Popular Culture, and* The Passion of the Christ, edited by Timothy Beal and Tod Linafelt, 139–52. Chicago: University of Chicago Press, 2006.

Temkin, Sefton. *Isaac Mayer Wise, Shaping American Judaism: Shaping American Judaism*. Oxford: Oxford University Press, 1991.

Thaut, Michael H. "Rhythm, Human Temporality, and Brain Function." In *Musical Communication,* edited by Dorothy Miell, Raymond MacDonald, and David J. Hargreaves, 171–91. Oxford: Oxford University Press, 2005.

Thompson, Evan. *Mind In Life: Biology, Phenomenology, and the Sciences of the Mind.* Cambridge: Harvard University Press, 2007.

Thumma, Scott, and Dave Travis. *Beyond Megachurch Myths: What We Can Learn from America's Largest Churches.* San Francisco: Jossey-Bass, 2007.

Townsend, Tim. "Pentecostals Split over 'Tongues.'" *St. Louis Post-Dispatch,* 1 November 2009.

Trillin, Calvin. "U.S. Journal: Eureka Springs, ARK. The Sacred Projects." *New Yorker* 45 (26 July 1969): 69–79.

Trueheart, Charles. "Welcome to the New Church." *Atlantic Monthly,* August 1996, 37–58.

Turan, Kenneth. "A Narrow Vision and Staggering Violence." *Los Angeles Times,* 24 February 2004, http://www.latimes.com/et-passion24-2004feb24,0,6930255.story.

Turner, Cathy, and Synne K. Behrndt. *Dramaturgy and Performance.* New York: Palgrave Macmillan, 2008.

Van Biema, David. "Can Megachurches Bridge the Racial Divide." *Time,* 11 January 2010, http://www.time.com/time/magazine/article/0,9171,1950943-1,00.html.

Van Os, Henk. *The Art of Devotion in the Late Middle Ages in Europe, 1300–1500.* Translated by Michael Hoyle. Princeton: Princeton University Press, 1995.

Varela, Francisco J. "Neurophenomenology: A Methodological Remedy for the Hard Problem." *Journal of Consciousness Studies* 3 (1996): 330–50.

Vaughn, John. *Megachurches and America's Cities: How Churches Grow.* Grand Rapids, MI: Baker Books, 1993.

Ward, Annalee. "Faith-Based Theme Parks and Museums: Multidimensional Media." In *Understanding Evangelical Media: The Changing Face of Christian Communication,* edited by Quentin J. Schultze and Robert H. Woods Jr., 161–72. Downers Grove, IL: InterVarsity Press, 2008.

Welch, Gina. *In the Land of Believers: An Outsider's Extraordinary Journey into the Heart of the Evangelical Church.* New York: Metropolitan Books, 2010.

Wernowsky, Kris. "Feds Can Seize Dinosaur Adventure Land." *Pensacola News Journal,* 31 July 2009, http://www.pnj.com/article/20090731/NEWS01/90731016/1006.

Westen, Drew. *The Political Brain: The Role of Emotion in Deciding the Fate of the Nation.* New York: PublicAffairs, 2007.

Wetmore, Kevin J., Jr. "Intelligent Design (after Julie Taymor): Opposing Darwinism in The Crystal Cathedral's *Creation: Once Upon All Time.*" *Journal of Religion and Theatre* 6, no. 2 (2007): 124–39, http://www.athe.org/associations/12588/files/wetmore2.pdf.

Wetmore, Kevin J., Jr. "The Devil Is an Ass: Radical Evil Redefined as Ridiculous Evil from the English Renaissance to Contemporary Hollywood." *Journal of Religion and Theatre* 9, no. 1 (2010): 28–40, http://www.athe.org/associations/12588/files/Wetmore.pdf.

Williams, Jennifer. "Acquire the Fire: Affect, Ideology, and Contagion in Evangelical Performance." *Journal of Religion and Theatre* 7, no. 1 (2008): 20–34, http://www.athe.org/associations/12588/files/Williams.pdf.

Williams, Peter W. "Creation Museum." *Material Religion: The Journal of Objects, Art and Belief* 4, no. 3 (2008): 373–75.

Woods, Robert, and Brian Walrath, eds. *The Message in the Music: Studying Contemporary Praise and Worship.* Nashville: Abingdon Press, 2007.

Wright, Susan, ed. *Parish, Church and People: Local Studies in Lay Religion, 1350–1750.* London: Hutchinson, 1988.

Zamir, Tzachi. "Watching Actors." *Theatre Journal* 62, no. 2 (2010): 227–43.

Zarrilli, Phillip. "An Enactive Approach to Understanding Acting." *Theatre Journal* 59, no. 4 (2007): 635–47.

Zarrilli, Phillip. *Psychophysical Acting: An Intercultural Approach after Stanislavski*. London: Routledge, 2009.

Websites, Online Reports, and Multimedia Sources

The A-Group. "Homepage." http://www.agroup.com.
A. Larry Ross Communications. "The Creation Museum." http://www.alrcnewskitchen.com/creationmuseum/index.htm.
Answers in Genesis. "Homepage." http://www.answersingenesis.org/.
Ark Encounter. "FAQ." http://arkencounter.com/faq/.
Christ for the Nations. "Homepage." http://www.cfn.org.
Cloud Ten Pictures. "Plans for Big Budget Left Behind Remake." 13 October 2010, http://www.cloudtenpictures.com/site2/news_article.php?id=42.
Cloud Ten Pictures: Left Behind The Next Film. "Homepage." http://leftbehind4.com/.
Colt, Sarah, and Thomas Jennings, dirs. "Episode Four: 'A New Light.'" *God in America: How Religious Liberty Shaped America*. DVD. Series Directed by David Belton. Boston: American Experience and Frontline, 2010.
Colt, Sarah, and Thomas Jennings, dirs. "Transcript: Episode Four: 'A New Light.'" *God in America: How Religious Liberty Shaped America*. Series Directed by David Belton. http://www.pbs.org/godinamerica/transcripts/hour-four.html.
Creation Museum. "Homepage." http://creationmuseum.org.
Creation Truth Foundation. "Homepage." http://www.creationtruth.com.
Creationism.org. "Homepage." http://www.creationism.org/.
Davis, Kate, David Heilbroner, and Franco Sacchi, dirs. *Waiting for Armageddon*. DVD. Dallas, TX: Eureka Film Productions, 2009.
Debney, John. "Resurrection." On *The Passion of The Christ (Original Motion Picture Soundtrack)*. Sony BMG Music Entertainment. Released 2004.
Faith Church. "Homepage." http://www.faithchurchct.com.
Faith Communities Today. "FACT 2000." http://faithcommunitiestoday.org/faith-communities-today-2000-study.
Friends of God: A Road Trip with Alexandra Pelosi. Directed by Alexandra Pelosi. HBO, 2007.
Gateway Bible Church. "Homepage." http://gatewaybiblechurch.net.
GodTube. "Homepage." http://www.godtube.com/.
Great Passion Play. 2001. Transferred to DVD by Grace Enterprises, 2004.
The Great Passion Play. "Homepage." http://www.greatpassionplay.org/.
Griffiths, José-Marie, and Donald W. King. "InterConnections: The Institute for Museum and Library Services (IMLS) National Survey on the Use of Libraries, Museums, and the Internet: Museum Survey Results." January 2008, http://interconnectionsreport.org/reports/IMLSMusRpt20080312kjm.pdf.
Hartford Institute for Religion Research. "Homepage." http://hirr.hartsem.edu/.
Hell House. DVD. Directed by George Ratliff. Cantina Pictures Inc., 2001.
Hillsong Collected. "Homepage." http://hillsongcollected.com.
Holy Land Experience. "Homepage." http://www.holylandexperience.com.
Immanuel Bible Church. "Homepage." http://www.immanuelbible.net/.
Institute for the Study of American Evangelicals. "Homepage." http://isae.wheaton.edu.
ITEC Entertainment Corporation. "The ITEC Solution: The Holy Land Experience Project." http://www.itec.com/Portals/20/Skins/itec/pdf/solutions/2008_Holy_Land.pdf.
Jesus Camp. DVD. Directed by Heidi Ewing and Rachel Grady. A&E Indie Films, 2006.
Lakewood Church. "Homepage." http://www.lakewood.cc/pages/home.aspx.
Leadership Network. "Homepage." http://leadnet.org.

Left Behind. "Homepage." http://www.leftbehind.com.
Maranatha! Music. "Homepage." http://www.maranathamusic.com/.
McLean Bible Church. "Homepage." http://www.mcleanbible.org/.
Museum of Earth History. "The Project." http://www.museumofearthhistory.com/.
National Association of Evangelicals. "Homepage." http://www.nae.net.
The Numbers. "The Passion of the Christ." http://www.the-numbers.com/movies/2004/PASON.php.
Parker, Trey, dir. *South Park: The Passion of the Jew.* DVD. Paramount Pictures, 2004.
The Pew Forum on Religion and Public Life. "Homepage." http://religions.pewforum.org.
The Pew Forum on Religion and Public Life. "U.S. Religious Landscape Survey." 23 June 2008, http://religions.pewforum.org/pdf/report2religious-landscape-study-chapter-2.pdf.
The Potter's House. "Homepage." http://www.thepottershouse.org/.
The Purpose Driven Life. "Homepage." http://www.purposedrivenlife.com/en-US/Home/home.htm.
Regent University. "About Us." http://www.regent.edu/about_us/.
Saddleback Church. "Homepage." http://saddleback.com.
The Text This Week. "'The Passion of the Christ' Mel Gibson Movie—Articles, Study Guides, & Opinions." http://www.textweek.com/response/passion_movie.htm.
Trinity Broadcasting Network. "Trinity Broadcasting Network Acquisition of 'Holy Land Experience' Theme Park Seeks to Change More Lives." Press Release, 9 June 2007, http://www.tbn.org/announcements/trinity-broadcasting-network-acquisition-of-holy-land-experience-theme-park-seeks-to-change-more-lives.
TripAdvisor.com. "Holy Land Experience." http://www.tripadvisor.com/Attraction_Review-g34515-d318444-Reviews-Holy_Land_Experience-Orlando_Florida.html.
Tyndale House Publishers. "Tyndale Repackages 'Left Behind' Titles for New Generation of Readers." 7 March 2011, http://mediacenter.tyndale.com/downloads/press_kits/LBRepackagePR.pdf.
Waiting for Armageddon. DVD. Directed by Kate Davis, David Heilbroner, and Franco Sacchi. Eureka Film Productions, 2009.
Willow Creek Community Church. "Homepage." http://www.willowcreek.org/home1.aspx.
Zion's Hope. "The Ministry." http://www.zionshope.org/ZH_ministry.aspx.

Unpublished Sources

Answers in Genesis. *Creation Museum Souvenir Guidebook.* Undated.
Program for *The Great Passion Play.* Eureka Springs: The Elna M. Smith Foundation, 2010.

Index